LIVING

SOCIOLOGY

A Critical Introduction

DEENA WEINSTEIN
De Paul University

MICHAEL A. WEINSTEIN
Purdue University

David McKay Company, Inc.
New York

To Liberation through Criticism

INTRODUCTION

An introduction has, as one possibility, the purpose of explaining and, perhaps, justifying, the form and content of a book. Our first task is, therefore, to explain what kind of text we have written, to compare our idea of a text to other possible notions, and to emphasize why we think our approach is particularly applicable to a book on sociology.

ONE BOOK AMONG MANY

The most prevalent type of text in sociology (though not the kind that we have written) is the "comprehensive introduction" to the field. The purpose of this kind of book is to communicate to the reader the conclusions sociologists have reached at a particular period in time about the structures of human relationships and organizations. In this approach, groups, organizations, and societies are viewed as objects of study similar to the cells, tissues, and organisms of the biologist, or the planets, solar systems, and galaxies of the astronomer. The student is expected to learn about the characteristics of some object in which he does not directly participate, and the uses to which he puts the knowledge are not an explicit concern of the writers. The "comprehensive introduction" does not ordinarily introduce the student to the methods by which sociologists gain knowledge, nor does it organize information around a perspective about the nature of history and the goals human beings pursue. However, most important from our viewpoint is that the "comprehensive introduction" does not view the student as an active participant in the subject, and we feel that this is a fatal flaw in the study of sociology. In learning about the chemical composition of an asteroid, the student does not gain knowledge on which he can directly act, unless he becomes a professional astronomer. In contrast, when learning about the structure of the family, the student gains an interpretation of a set of human relations on which he can act immediately. He can attempt to change the relations in his own family, ignore the new information, or attempt to preserve the relations more intelligently. In any case, he will have made a commitment about his own social life based upon what he has learned. We have not written a "comprehensive introduction" because we believe that we should explicitly recognize the active implications of sociology for the individual person's life.

A second kind of sociology text is the "introduction to the discipline." Here the authors attempt to explain the methods by which sociologists gain knowledge about human relations and organizations. In the "introduction to the discipline," conclusions about the way societies work are subordinated to the description of sets of techniques used by a group of specialists in their work. The writers do not expect the student to apply these techniques to his own social relations, but instead to appreciate how it is possible for experts to study the human condition scientifically. Again the student is viewed as a learner or, at best, a potential expert rather than as an actor; only here what he learns is a body of specialized techniques and definitions rather than a set of factual conclusions and generalizations. The "introduction to the discipline" puts sociological methods on a par with natural-science methods. Observing a small group through a one-way mirror is viewed as no different from observing a cell through a microscope or a planet through a telescope. No attention is given to the possibility that methods of studying human beings are also ways of relating to them as human beings. For example, observing people through a one-way mirror means that the researcher believes that at least in some cases it is morally justified to conceal from people the full meaning of the situation in which they are involved. Similar problems are not encountered in the study of an asteroid, because an asteroid does not have the capacity to respond to the people who study it. Thus, we have not written an "introduction to the discipline" because we believe that methods imply moralities.

A third type of sociology text is the "focused introduction." Here the authors organize certain conclusions about social relations and organizations around a perspective on the meaning of human history and the values that are—or should be—sought in social life. While the "comprehensive introduction" frequently presents a set of unrelated conclusions, the "focused introduction" selects key themes to illuminate facts and generalizations. For example, a "focused introduction" might be based on the problem of social inequality and then trace the ways in which inequality appears in business organizations, political parties, families, and churches. The "focused introduction" does not apply the natural-science model to the study of human events, since it begins with an interpretation of significant human problems and then attempts to show the student that he confronts these problems in his daily life and is often part of them. In some ways our book is a "focused introduction" because it selects, out of all possible human concerns, the problem of gaining freedom and understanding within large-scale, impersonal organizations. Facts and generalizations are gathered to illuminate this problem and to show the reader how he might confront it and be involved in it. However, our book differs from most "focused introductions" because we do not claim that our theme of freedom and reason is the most significant one for all people, or that it is the one key for unlocking the secrets of contemporary social organization. We are aware that there are other perspectives and we discuss them. We are not out to convert people to our definition of the situation and we encourage readers to challenge our interpretation with their own. We are not engaged in brainwashing or ideology-formation, but in creating one possible way in which current human relations and organizations can be plausibly understood in their totality.

Our recognition that information about society can lead directly to action, our belief that methods imply moralities, and our conviction that there is no absolutely true perspective lead us to write a sociology text which is meant to encourage the active, morally sensitive, and critical use of sociology by our readers. This fourth kind of text is a "practical introduction" aimed at showing people the ways in which sociology can help them inquire into their actual relations with others and thereby act more freely and intelligently in them. The outline of the book reveals this purpose. The first chapter discusses the ways in which people can come to understand their social relations and their images of society. The second chapter reviews some of the different perspectives on the nature of social relations, and invites the reader to determine which tradition is closest to his own viewpoint. The third chapter analyzes the ways in which social science can be conceived, while the fourth chapter reviews the methods by which social situations can be studied. The fifth chapter discusses the very nature of human experience, and raises the question of how experience may be defined. Having introduced in the first five chapters a way of applying sociology to one's own life, we then in the sixth and seventh chapters present an image of contemporary society. This image of mass society, which is based on the obstacles people encounter in attaining freedom and reason, is compared to other perspectives, and defended. At this point in the book the reader should be careful not to slip into assuming that we are expounding the absolutely true interpretation of contemporary society. We often appear to say "this is the way things are," but that is because it would be awkward and redundant to keep repeating "this is the way we see things, based upon the evidence we have reviewed, but there are certainly other ways of interpreting social life which are also backed up by impressive evidence." We trust the reader not to adopt our view as a creed, but to consider it as a live possibility. Chapters 8 through 15 apply the image of mass society to particular social processes and institutions. The eighth and ninth chapters discuss economic activity, the tenth and eleventh chapters discuss political activity, the twelfth and thirteenth chapters discuss family, community and religion (appreciative activity), and the fourteenth and fifteenth chapters discuss education, knowledge and communication (inquiry). Throughout these applications of the mass society image our aim is to show readers how they can better understand the context of their everyday lives and, particularly, how they can inquire into their social relations.

The purposes of a "practical introduction" to sociology can best be served if the readers attempt to relate their own experiences to the text, and then to imagine new ways of conceiving their experience. In order to help this process along we have included exercises throughout the book. These exercises are of two types. First, there are exercises meant to help the reader clarify his own interpretation of social relations and his own social life. For example, in the discussion of mass media there is an exercise in which the reader is invited to draw up an inventory of the media he consumes and of the time he spends consuming them. The purpose of this media profile is to sensitize the person to his sources of information and their bias. A second kind of exercise is meant to help the reader create alternative possibilities for understanding social relations. For example, in the section on crime we present a way of classifying criminal activity. In this section the reader is invited to draw up a different classification of criminal activity and to defend it. The purpose of this exercise is to show the person that he can create alternative perspectives and need not accept a single interpretation of a phenomenon. If readers attempt to do both kinds of exercises, we believe they will expand their awareness of their present and possible social relations, and will also be immunized against blind faith in any particular image of human events, including the one in this book.

The spirit in which we write this book may be grasped by considering what we have done so far in this introduction. We have discussed various kinds of sociology texts, have shown their purposes, and have explained why we have chosen to write a particular kind of text. We have not argued that we have written the best possible text for all purposes, nor have we argued that if people follow our discussion they will have access to absolute truth. We have, instead, revealed our idea of a text in contrast to other notions, so that readers can be clear about what they can expect to derive from our work. This process of critical comparison (we call it the process of self-understanding in the book) is what we would like people to apply to their ideas about social relations and organizations.

THE INTELLECTUAL CONTEXT

Carrying the process of critical comparison one step farther, our second task is to identify the intellectual context in which this book appears. This book appears at a time in which sociologists are becoming increasingly aware of the connections of their ideas to the social organization in which they work. This awareness is symbolized by the increasing use of such terms as the sociology of knowledge, the sociology of sociology, and the philosophy of social science to identify the study of how thought about social relations and organizations is relative to those very relations and organizations. We are in the tradition of such sociologists as Auguste Comte, Karl Marx, Pitirim Sorokin, Georges Gurvitch, Karl Mannheim, and C. Wright Mills, who attempt to trace the relations between the ideas people have about their society and the particular social groups to which they belong and the interests of these groups. However, we depart from the sociology of knowledge tradition in one important respect. In the past, sociologists have claimed that in one way or another they have been able to rise above partial and interest-bound interpretations of society, and to give an accurate statement of social reality in terms of the major social groups, their relations and their principles of organization. We believe that the problem of contemporary sociology is not to cut through the web of competing interpretations of human existence until we reach the solid core of social fact, but to describe a way in which people can move through the competing interpretations, understand and appreciate each of them, and create a perspective that will aid them in preserving or transforming their social relations according to values they have chosen to realize. This is another way of saying that we do not have access to any absolute truth—religious, political, sociological or psychological. However, it is also something more. We believe that, while there is neither a bedrock of social fact nor a mountain top for objective contemplation, there is a process for improving one's grasp of social relations by discovering the various groups with which one might identify, of understanding their projects and interests, of seeing how these groups relate to other groups, and of making commitments to act on the basis of widened understanding. This means that we cannot tell people what side they should be on in social conflicts or what side will necessarily win in the struggles of our time. We can only present the best analysis we can devise through our own process of critical comparison, and then make it clear which side we are on and why. This is how we understand the meaning of the "sociology of knowledge" tradition in contemporary social science.

We are hampered in realizing our purposes by the very structure of the language, by the things people expect to derive from a book, and indeed by the very structure of a book. The English language hinders us because there are viewpoints we would like to express that are not easily communicated in the language. For example, the words "he" and "his" appear throughout the text when we are referring to the singular-third-person subject (the abstract human being). This general usage of the masculine third person for the human third person has an obvious bias. It may lead people to believe that only men are significant in social life and that only men, not women, should reflect upon their social relations. This is contrary to our belief that both men and women can share equally in a human process of growth and inquiry. Yet we adopted ordinary usage of the language because any other strategy (for example, alternating "his" and "her," or using "the human being") would have made the presentation stilted, awkward, and might have distracted the reader from other insights. We avoided the use of "man" to refer to human being, and "mankind" to refer to humanity, but the language prohibited us from being as human as we desired. Perhaps in the future the language will develop gender-neutral terms, but for us to coin such terms (*shis* for his/hers) would be distracting, to say the least.

What people expect to derive from a book also hampered us. It probably does not matter how much we insist upon the relativity of our position; there will be many people who will embrace it as a creed or react against it as a faith. People expect a book either to tell them the truth about something or to confirm their prejudices. Our book does neither, yet it may appear to do both. For example, supporters of black power, gay liberation, Chicano liberation, or any other social movement may be angered because we have not written a chapter or section exclusively on their group. This does not mean that we oppose these movements or that we believe that they are insignificant. Instead, we believe that each of these particular interests is part of a wider rebellion against inequality and domination which should be appreciated before considering the problems of any particular group. However, this, again, is only one perspective or opinion. The best that we can say is that we have attempted to make our values explicit and that we do not have a corner on the truth. We encourage people to rearrange our evidence and gather new evidence to create alternative perspectives, whether they are based on the conflict of races, the cooperation of religious believers, or any other image of groups in relation.

Finally, we have been limited by the structure of a book itself. The print medium is best suited to describing a particular point of view, and where only one-way communication is possible. Conversations are bilateral or multilateral, in the sense that a number of people speaking with each other can simultaneously work out several perspectives. Books, however, are unilateral—the authors present their ideas and the readers have no opportunity to respond immediately and present different possibilities. We could, perhaps, have begun to present as many images of contemporary society as we could think of, but then we would have had to multiply the length of the book by the number of images we used. Both writing and reading such a work would be a project extending over several human lifetimes. Thus, we return again to the theme that we encourage the reader to take an active responsibility for her image of society: to try to clarify her beliefs, to compare them to our perspective, and to choose the ways she will commit herself to preserving or transforming social relations. We ask her not to respond passively to our viewpoint, and to test it in her own life. (And this applies to him as well as to her!)

Introductions ordinarily end with acknowledgments. There have, of course, been many people, living and dead, who have helped us formulate our ideas constructively. The people who have made the greatest positive contributions need not be mentioned by name, because their primary interest is to clarify ideas, not to take credit for them. We thus acknowledge those who have aided us through conversation and through their writings and say no more. We do not want to identify with a school of thought or with an academic clique, nor do we want to create such a school or clique. We do, however, wish to acknowledge explicitly those who have helped us negatively. We have been moved to write this book partly because of the barbarous acts of contemporary leaders. In studying these acts we have gained many of our insights and have found the reason to write a book about the prospects for freedom in a society with irresponsible and arbitrary leadership. Thus, we must pay our respects to United States leaders who ordered the bombing of Vietnam, to contemporary mayors who unleashed the police on peace demonstrators, to officials who unleashed police dogs on black demonstrators, to communist bosses who ordered the tanks into Czechoslovakia, to those who sent troops into Cambodia, and to numerous other politicians, public relations men, university administrators and department heads, businessmen, labor union bureaucrats, military leaders, contract researchers, and other managers and manipulators who seem to make a virtue out of dominating others through force, bribery, fraud, and the mobilization of guilt, envy, and self-esteem. These are the people who act so that others will obey rather than learn, and who wish their names to be known by all. We acknowledge their presence—how can we help it?—and tell them (if they are willing to listen) that we have learned from their example to oppose them.

Tippecanoe and
Cook Counties, 1974

CONTENTS

PART I
THE STRUCTURE OF
SOCIAL INQUIRY

1

THE HUMAN CONDITION

The twentieth century is an age of contrasts, a time of beginnings and endings. At the very time when some people speak hopefully about the possibilities of a world without war and poverty, others warn of impending disaster through nuclear warfare or famine. The spread of the scientific method into new areas of human experience is extolled in some quarters, while elsewhere growing numbers of people experiment with witchcraft and astrology. Suburban homes are replete with electrical appliances, while the shacks of the rural poor may not even have indoor plumbing. Millions of human beings spend their working lives in vast organizations whose operations cannot be understood by any single individual, but return after work to the nuclear family, the smallest social unit yet devised. Depending upon the slice of experience being presented at the moment, the human condition is one of promise or peril. Bertrand Russell has expressed this twentieth-century mentality: "I see, in my mind's eye, a world of glory and joy, a world where minds expand, where hope remains undimmed, and what is noble is no longer condemned as treachery to this or that paltry

3

aim. All this can happen if we will let it happen. It rests with our generation to decide between this vision and an end decreed by folly."[1]

It is by no means certain that the present generation will determine whether humanity progresses to a new expansion of freedom or commits collective suicide. More than one generation in the twentieth century has already found itself torn between promise and peril, and has left the issue unresolved. This uncertainty may continue for many decades into the future. What is important, however, is that many people in the twentieth century have felt that they were at the crossroads between despair and hope. Nietzsche likened human existence to a rope over an abyss. Experiencing the tensions of twentieth-century life, many people have felt like tightrope walkers over a bottomless pit. To either side of them was Nothingness. Ahead of them was a vision of creative freedom and the development of human potentials. Often they were seized by vertigo and became unable to rivet their attention on the vision of hope. They fell into that bottomless pit, committing barbarous acts of torture and self-destruction on that descent. Nausea, the physical symptom of those possessed by Nothingness, continues to haunt the contemporary human condition. William Ernest Hocking has vividly described the terror of those torn apart by the conflicts and paradoxes of the twentieth century: "What we see is the moment-to-moment boundary of our being, the nothingness that completes itself in death, our own and that of the race: in such a world, riddled the while with horrorfilled actualities, how can a being aspiring and infinite be other than condemned to frustration?"[2]

Not everyone in the twentieth century, of course, has seen the situation as a tension between promise and peril. The perspective that guides this book has been held by many social thinkers, but not the majority. Its exponents have tended to be those sociologists and social philosophers who were concerned with the greater attainment of human freedom, the patterns of coercion and domination which restrict freedom in contemporary society, and the development of methods for studying social relations which take account of feeling, choice and mental image of the world, as well as behavior. Sociologists such as Erving Goffman, Georges Gurvitch, Pitirim Sorokin, Morris Ginsberg, C. Wright Mills, Radhakamal Mukerjee, E. T. Hiller, and Peter Berger, among others, fall into this tradition. Other perspectives have interpreted the twentieth century as a time of increasing progress towards a society in which people will be judged by their achievement of tasks rather than by their family, racial, and national origins, while other views have stressed the possibility or inevitability of a revolution which would abolish distinctions between social classes. These perspectives are optimistic about the future. Still other views have projected a decline of civilization and a relapse into barbarism. Both this pessimistic attitude and the optimistic viewpoints do not find ambivalence, paradox and uncertainty in the human condition, but identify clear trends. Often the way people think about society will be strongly influenced by such basic judgments of hope and despair.[3]

Among the most striking contrasts presented by the twentieth century is that between propaganda and science. The past several decades have seen the growing perfection of means to deceive people through the conscious manipulation of language and other media of communication. At the same time there has been an expansion of the use of scientific methods in the study of human action. Frequently the methods of science have been joined to the purpose of deceit, as when expert advisers to commercial and political elites determine just what distortions of the truth will best serve the interests of their employers.[4] The use of precise knowledge about human activity to deceive human beings has been, in part, responsible for the widespread feeling that human existence is bounded by Nothingness.[5] One of the factors that allows people to act in pursuit of their visions of hope is the presence of trust in human relations. When people begin to feel that they can no longer trust in the honesty of the messages communicated to them by their leaders, they lose confidence in the accuracy of their judgments about political and economic affairs. They believe that they cannot make intelligent decisions about public affairs, and withdraw to the restricted circle of private life where they can at least check their judgments by engaging in face-to-face relations.[6] Public life becomes a question mark to them, and it is a short step from a bare question mark to Nothingness. Responses to the "credibility gap" that marks contemporary life regardless of changes in leadership include impotent rage, cynicism, acceptance of the situation, apathy, continued faith that good men in power will set everything right, and serious attempts to understand the current human condition and the possibilities for its transformation.[7] This book is an attempt to contribute to understanding of the human condition in a world filled with propaganda, distortion, lies, and self-deception. The first step toward such understanding is a method of studying human existence.

THE METHOD OF SELF-UNDERSTANDING

How does an individual go about understanding the human condition? A satisfactory answer to this question can best be gained by trying to respond to another query, How does an individual go about understanding anything? Let us say that a person wanted to know how his automobile worked. It would be reasonable to direct someone with such a desire to a book about auto mechanics, a course on auto repair, or a person who knew how to fix cars and was willing to share his knowledge. After the person had learned the necessary background information, it would be wise to let him attempt to repair some automobiles himself. Through knowledge about automobiles gained through books, courses, or conversations, and knowledge by acquaintance with automobiles gained through fixing them, the individual would attain a fair understanding of how his automobile worked. Similarly, it appears that people go about understanding things by finding out what other people know about these things and directly acquainting themselves with them. Thus, understanding involves drawing upon previously acquired knowledge and testing this knowledge in particular cases. Through the test a person may meet unexpected situations, gain new knowledge and thereby add to the common stock of information about the thing.

Understanding the human condition is of course far more tricky than learning about how an automobile works. Understanding the human condition involves understanding people, and since the individual attempting to find out about human existence is a person himself, understanding the human condition includes self-understanding. Understanding the human condition is thus more complex: the individual who wants to learn about an automobile goes to others for the basic information that he needs, but the person who wants to understand the human condition must examine himself. In learning about automobiles there are good reasons for the individual to acquire knowledge about them before he gains knowledge by acquaintance with them. In understanding the human condition, the person is acquainted with it before he knows anything about it.[8] Thus, the method for understanding the human condition must be adapted to the task of self-understanding.

Figure 1.1. THE PROCESS OF SELF-UNDERSTANDING

Clarification: Awareness of general beliefs about human existence

Generalization: Identification of the intellectual tradition and social groups with which you share beliefs

Relativization: Comparison of your beliefs with other traditions and groups

Commitment Decision to attempt to realize a vision of human existence

---

The process of self-understanding involves four general phases—clarification, generalization, relativization, and commitment. In the phase of *clarification* the individual becomes aware of the general beliefs he holds about what is significant in human existence, and what is good and bad about it. In the phase of *generalization* the person discovers that he shares his beliefs with the members of certain present social groupings and is part of an historical tradition. In the phase of *relativization* the individual finds that other groupings and traditions hold some beliefs different from his own about the basic facts and central values of human existence. In the phase of *commitment* the person chooses a certain view of human existence as the basis for his action and makes it a living experiment. The following discussion will describe these phases in some detail.

CLARIFICATION

Consider the following question carefully. When you are not involved in any particular activity, when you are not attempting to satisfy any specific desire—when, in short, you are letting your mind roam free in thought—what do you think about? Many people experience great diffiiculty in answering a question like this. Frequently they say that they never let their thoughts roam free, and if they do, they never remember what passes through their minds. Other people experience no difficulty at all in responding. Some individuals say that they think about religion, and whether or not God exists. Others say that they think about how certain social changes might be accomplished. Still others say that they think about their future careers and what they might be able to accomplish in them. Still others relate fantasies that they conjure up in their minds.

The thoughts a person has when he lets his mind roam free are good indicators of what that individual considers important in the human condition. They are the basis from which the process of self-understanding begins. Bringing these thoughts clearly into awareness will provide the person with insight into his own vision of the human condition. For example, if a person says that when his mind roams free he thinks about how he can make large sums of money, it is likely that money is a central fact and value in his vision of the human condition. If he is asked why he thinks about money, he may answer with the cliché, "Money can't buy everything, but it sure helps." On further inspection it may turn out that this person believes that the good life consists in material luxury and independence from the commands of others. More careful examination may disclose that this individual believes that people are basically greedy and that they are in an endless rat race to acquire ever greater sums of money. At this point it can be said that the person has a fairly well developed vision of his view of the human condition. His central belief about human existence is that people are motivated to seek as much wealth as they can lay their hands on. His key values are luxury and independence.

Not everyone believes that money is the most important factor in human existence, although this belief is relatively popular in the United States.[9] There are many visions of the human condition, some of which conflict with one another. Some place freedom at the center of existence, some make one or another supposed instinct central, others focus attention on a particular activity like work, others believe that a relationship, like love, is most important, and still others orient existence around an idea of God. The phase of clarification involves bringing such beliefs into awareness so that the person can understand his general orientation to the human condition.

Once it has been described, the phase of clarification does not seem difficult to undertake. It appears to be far easier than attempting to understand how an automobile works. Yet many people stubbornly resist clarifying their beliefs about the human condition. This resistance need not be conscious, but may simply stem from a lack of exposure to multiple views. The reasons for this resistance help one to grasp the obstacles in the way of understanding the human condition.

Barriers to Clarification   One of the most important reasons why people do not want to clarify their beliefs about the human condition is that they think that these beliefs may be stupid. Particularly among many people in the United States, there is fear of being judged ridiculous.[10] The twentieth century has been an age in which scientific knowledge has grown at a rapid rate. More and more areas of human experience have been turned over to specialists, and there has even been an effort to turn the mind over to experts. In addition to clergymen, who have always claimed to be specialists in the soul, there has been the growth of such professions as journalism, psychiatry, psychology, social work, advertising, public relations, and the various social sciences. The members of each of these professions view themselves, and are often viewed by others, as experts in the mind and its beliefs. Those who are intimidated by the experts in the mind are often afraid to examine their own beliefs. In order to understand the human condition, it is necessary to conquer this fear and to realize that one's mind is worthy of respect. Groups that hold economic and political power are quite satisfied to have people fear that they are stupid;[11] as long as such fear is widespread these groups have a better chance of getting their own way.

Related to the fear of being judged stupid is the fear that one will be judged insane. In some circles it is fashionable to brand as mentally ill people with whom one does not agree. People who take such insults to heart, or fear such insults will follow a declaration of beliefs, are likely to bury their beliefs about the human condition and forget about them. It is clear that the idea that one's beliefs about the human condition will indicate that one is mentally ill leads people to distrust their own judgments and makes it easier for elite groups to impose their definitions of experience on others.[12] This does not mean that the elite are responsible for the fears of being judged as stupid or mentally ill. Rather, such fears lessen the probability that critical self-examination will take place and thus leave the field open to imposed visions of the human condition. The best way to conquer the fear of being judged mentally ill is to carry through the entire process of self-understanding.

A third reason why people do not want to clarify their beliefs about the human condition is that they often think that beliefs are unimportant. One very frequently used cliché in the United States is that "talk is cheap." If talk is cheap, thoughts and beliefs are even cheaper. For many Americans, some vague notion of "action," "getting things done," or "doing something," is far more important than thinking.[13] A political system based on compromise between interest groups leads many people to hold that the reasons for acting are unimportant so long as decisions are made and the groups that scream the loudest get a larger piece of the pie.[14] Most advertising is based on the idea that as long as people buy the given product, and continue to buy it, the reasons for the purchases are unimportant.[15] The centrality of "selling" in American life has led people to the extreme notions that teachers are engaged in "selling" their subjects to students and that psychologists are engaged in "selling" interpretations of human existence to their patients.[16] The idea that beliefs are unimportant is itself a very important, and also a false, belief. It is important because it prevents people from examining their visions of the human condition. It is false because it makes a sharp separation between thought and action, when in fact thought and action are two inseparable phases of the same human process.[17]

The idea that beliefs are unimportant is based on the partial truth that much propaganda and advertising use ideas as a smokescreen to hide the pursuit of narrow interest. This partial truth ignores the wider truth that propaganda and advertising are themselves based on beliefs about the human condition. Some of these beliefs are that people are basically little children who crave pleasure, who attempt to avoid confronting unpleasant facts, who seek to blame their troubles on others, and who have a very short attention span.[18] Paradoxically, these beliefs appear to be true when large numbers of people act on the belief that ideas are unimportant. This discussion should show that there is no way of cutting off beliefs from action. The choice is not between whether one is a "thinker" or a "doer," but between whether one acts on beliefs that have been critically examined or on beliefs that are taken for granted without inspection.

There is another side to the idea that beliefs are unimportant. Many people use their beliefs about the human condition to "sell" themselves. The most pathetic way in which people make themselves into consumer goods is by adopting whatever beliefs about the human condition are current in the groups in which they want to gain acceptance. In this case, expressing certain beliefs is very important, but the truth of the beliefs is of little or no consideration. Those who use beliefs merely to gain acceptance are usually not interested in submitting their ideas about the human condition to critical self-examination. This is because they are ready to change their ideas as soon as it becomes fashionable to do so. Beneath, this chameleonlike existence, however, is a particular vision of the human condition, in which the most important factor in human life is making a favorable impression on people and being accepted as an insider.[19] For the person who uses beliefs to gain acceptance, existence is not so much a rat race in which people compete for wealth as a popularity contest without end. Perhaps the ultimate paradox in using beliefs to win popularity is the person who expresses the idea that one should strive for independent judgment in order to be accepted into a group of people who claim to cherish nonconformity.

There is an apparent contradiction in using beliefs merely to gain acceptance. If everyone acted merely to win popularity, each person would be trying to discover the widely held beliefs. However, there would be no source of beliefs about the human condition. Thus, people who use beliefs to gain acceptance depend for their ideas on people who are motivated by other considerations. In the United States, many of the beliefs adopted by those in the popularity rat race spring from business advertising and political propaganda, which are motivated by profit and power rather than by social acceptance. This means that the acceptance seekers are abdicating their judgment to the image makers of complex organizations.[20] They are content to trade their minds for a smile.

Using beliefs to gain acceptance is only a special case of using them for any number of ulterior purposes. Sometimes people who become aware of the techniques of advertising and propaganda reach the conclusion that, if so many of those highly placed in organizations resort to deception and distortion, they ought to get in on the action too. Everyone is familiar with the salesman who is willing to adopt racist attitudes when he believes that they will influence a purchase, but will become a staunch defender of human equality when this posture will help along a sale. Underlings will adopt the views of supervisers to speed their promotions, and politicians are notorious for changing their views of human nature in response to the polled opinions of the various groups in their constituencies. In many cases politicians conduct their own polls when running for office so that they can make their appeals effective. Those who simply manipulate beliefs for profit or power normally resist examining their visions of the human condition. Underlying their cynical use of ideas is the firm conviction that human life is a frantic scramble after power and privilege, and that only those willing to face up to the necessity of using force, fraud and bribery emerge the victors. It is apparent, however, that this view has a serious defect. If everybody was out to gain power and privilege, then nobody could be manipulated through an appeal to beliefs. Everyone would know that talk is cheap, and in that situation it would become so cheap as to be completely ineffective. This means that the success of people who manipulate beliefs for power and profit depends upon the existence of people who take ideas seriously and care about whether or not they are true. Hence, the manipulators invent a category of "suckers" who are mentally defective in the sense that they do not believe that the human condition is an endless rat race. Suckers are defined as subhumans who are soft-headed and woolly-minded enough to care whether or not their beliefs are true and their princi-

ples of action are right. While this is not the explicit view of all advertisers and propagandists, it has been the belief of many of them—for
example, the promoter P. T. Barnum and the Nazi Joseph Goebbels.

One way of responding to advertising and propaganda is to make
oneself into a manipulator of ideas. Many intelligent people reach the
conclusion that truth is of little value in the contemporary world, and
decide that if they are not going to be victims they will have to victimize
others. A second way of responding to manipulation is the one which
guides this book. This mode of response assumes that many current
visions of the human condition, particularly those communicated by
large organizations, are not offered in good faith. Given this situation,
a person who believes everything that he reads and hears is a sucker.
If an individual does not want to become an exploiter and also does
not want to be a sucker, he must develop a way of understanding the
human condition that will allow him to see through the various forms
of propaganda and self-deception present in the contemporary world.
The first step toward such understanding is clarification of one's own
vision of the human condition.

Another reason why people do not want to clarify their beliefs
about the human condition is that they think that beliefs are private
matters. Taking this attitude into account, public opinion pollsters
usually assure that their respondents will remain anonymous. In the
United States a popular response when an individual's ideas are being
questioned is, "I have a right to my own opinions." It is frequently
difficult to determine just what this statement means. In most conversations where ideas are brought into question, there is no attempt by
the critic to throw the other person into jail, do brain surgery on him,
deprive him of a job, or ridicule him. Thus, the critic is not usually out
to punish the other person for his ideas. He is not even trying to stop
the other person from holding his ideas by any means other than
discussion. Why, then, does the other individual assert a right to his
own opinions?

The person being questioned appears to be saying that people
have a right to their own opinions whether or not they are false or
contradictory. This is presumably not a legal right to be enforced by
the police and the courts. There are many reasons why it is desirable
not to make the holding of false and contradictory beliefs illegal,
including the tremendous expense that would be involved in enforcing
such laws. Further, efficient mind-reading devices have not yet been
invented; and finally it is frequently difficult to determine that a belief
is false. Thus, when a person claims that he has a right to his own
beliefs, he seems to be asserting a moral right. This often is seen

essentially as a right not to engage in self-examination. Can such a right be defended?

The basis for the claim that one has a right not to engage in self-examination is that beliefs are a form of private property. Just as a person has a right to decorate his room with banana peels rather than paintings, regardless of canons of good taste, so, it is claimed, he also has a right to decorate his mind with any ideas that appeal to him, regardless of their truth or consistency. This might be a plausible claim if ideas were merely decorative property. However, if thought and action are closely linked together, and if basic ideas about the human condition are orientation points of the entire structure of a person's action, then basic beliefs about the human condition affect others besides the individual people who hold them.[21] These other people may have a legitimate interest in seeing that the individual's beliefs about the human condition do not result in harm to them. Further, it is difficult to determine in just what sense beliefs are private. Beliefs about the human condition can be put into words and communicated to others. Thus, they are not impenetrable "secrets" of the "mind." Beliefs about the human condition can be tested for their truth or falsity. Such beliefs are never the result of pure invention by the individual. How, then, are they private? The most that can be said is that beliefs about the human condition can be kept secret. Whether or not one has an absolute right to refrain from examining them is another question. The previous discussion shows that such a right is not self-evident.

The idea that beliefs are private matters and, therefore, need not be submitted to examination, is usually related to the fears of being judged stupid or insane and the use of beliefs to further ulterior purposes. This fear frequently goes beyond an unwillingness to clarify one's intimate personal concerns to a resistance to examining beliefs about public matters. It is a stock trick of propagandists to tell people that they can trust their own unexamined judgments, and that they do not have to take criticisms of their life-styles seriously. This trick is played when the propagandist has good reason to believe that widespread prejudices and attitudes are favorable to increasing the power and profit of his employers. When prejudices run against the interests of elite groups, propagandists will talk about the need for "leading public opinion," educating the public, and courageous leadership in the long-term interest in the face of short-sighted criticism. Hence, propagandists believe that people have a right to their opinions so long as those opinions support the interests of influential groups. One of the guiding themes of this book is that nobody has a right to his own opinions about the human condition if he is unwilling to undertake self-examination. This does not mean that we would like to send the police after those who do not examine themselves, or that we would like people to submit their beliefs about the human condition to a panel of sociologists for scrutiny and approval. Rather, we hold that because thought and action are so intimately related, nobody has the right to abdicate this judgment about human affairs and to make himself the unwitting tool of one or another pressure group. While this statement may appear to be harsh, we would rather be candid about our values than disguise them. It is partly for our own benefit that we urge you to examine your beliefs about the human condition. We would be far happier in a world where more people had respect for their minds. The fastest way to respect your mind is to get to know it. Also, it is important to remember that if you have any misgivings, nobody else has to know that you are questioning yourself.

The Comfort of Unquestioning Faith   Finally, people do not want to clarify their beliefs about the human condition because they believe that the opinions they hold are correct and are in no need of further definition. Many people think that, since their beliefs have served them fairly well for a number of years, there is no sense in taking the trouble to examine them and see what they really are. Others are convinced that they have some sort of "intuition" that allows them to make correct snap judgments about the situations they confront. For example, the promotion of myths about women's intuition may encourage females to renounce careful examination of their ideas. Still other people are content to follow some authority, such as a church, political party, or prestigious relative. They hold that this authority is far more likely to interpret the human condition correctly than they are. Other people have adopted a dogma, or a set of articles of faith, through which they interpret the human condition. They repeat the formulas of this dogma, whether it is based in a religious creed, a political program, an economic doctrine, or a theory of human nature, without understanding what they mean. Holding such a creed makes them appear to know what they are talking about, and they seem to have an answer to every question. However, when they are asked to define the meanings of their central terms and to account for inconsistencies in what they say, it becomes obvious that they usually are hopelessly confused. Their pat formulas have been concealing ill-formed and unclarified visions of the human condition. They have been using their dogmas as an excuse for avoiding self-examination—and even for avoiding any thinking at all.

Many people say, "I would really be happy if I could only have a faith and believe that all of my opinions were correct." There is no way of responding to this statement but to ask oneself whether one really would be happy in such a situation. There are some benefits to believing that all of one's ideas about the human condition are correct. First, there is a freedom from nagging doubts about what it is possible to expect from oneself and others. Once a person has settled on a particular vision of the human condition, his moral universe is structured, in the sense that he has figured out a way of apportioning rights and duties among people. He knows which actions are right and which ones are wrong, what things are good for human beings and what things are bad, when people are to be held responsible for their behavior and when they are not to be held accountable, and even, perhaps, in what the destiny of the human species consists. Freedom from doubt leads into the second benefit of certainty—i.e., confidence in action. People who have unquestioned faith in the correctness of a particular vision of the human condition often find it easier to take decisive action than do others.[22] When they are confronted with disputes they will unwaveringly support those who share their faith, even to the extent of making such statements as, "My country right or wrong." When they are confronted with problems, they will straightforwardly point out that these problems were caused by people who did not share their creed. They have a program for the future and are not faced with agonizing decisions about what actions will be most productive nor with wrenching second thoughts about whether they have accomplished anything.

The advantages of unexamined faith should be weighed against one central disadvantage. Once a person believes that the opinions he holds about the human condition are correct and are in no need of further definition, personal growth becomes very difficult for him.[23] Such a person has frozen himself at a particular place and time in history, and as events proceed he becomes more and more to look like an antique.[24] He becomes incapable of assimilating fresh experience and appreciating it for what it is. Everything new is twisted to look like a tired example of the old. Adaptation to significant changes is impeded and, even more important, it becomes difficult for the person to make a creative contribution to the continual task of reorganizing the human condition. The person who locks himself into a narrow set of beliefs which he refuses to examine, or even bring clearly into awareness, sacrifices his chances to appreciate the complexities and fresh experiences of the human condition.[25] He is the same today as he was yesterday, and he can look forward to a similar tomorrow. In cutting himself off from large chunks of experience, the person has gained a superficial and, ultimately, a false security. Since he will not understand others who do not share his beliefs, some of them will be able to take advantage of him. If his beliefs are inappropriate to changing circumstances he may bring himself to personal ruin. However, even if a set of rigid beliefs did not involve the risk of ruin, is the vision of being the same tomorrow as you are today and were yesterday really that appealing? Essentially, it is your answer to this question which will decide whether or not you will undertake the task of self-examination. If you conceive of the self as a process, continually encountering and organizing new experiences, you will welcome self-examination. If you conceive of the self as property, which can be stolen by greedy brain pickers and which must be protected by a veil of secrecy, you will shun self-examination. It is apparent that we are writing this book because we believe that the self is process, not property.[26] The idea that the self is property is behind most of the obstacles to clarifying one's orientation towards the human condition. It shows a profound disrespect for the creative capacities of the mind.

Figure 1.2. BARRIERS TO CLARIFICATION

People tend to avoid clarifying their images of human existence when:
1. They believe that their ideas may betray stupidity.
2. They believe that others may judge them to be mentally ill.
3. They use ideas merely to gain social acceptance.
4. They use ideas merely to gain such ulterior ends as power or profit.
5. They believe that ideas about human existence are private matters.
6. They believe that ideas are private property to be used as the "owner" sees fit.
7. They believe that their ideas are absolutely correct.

Do you confront any of these barriers? If so, are you willing to overcome them?

GENERALIZATION

Clarification was discussed at such great length because it is the single most important step in the process of self-examination. Once people have enough interest in their thoughts about the human condition to subject them to scrutiny, the obstacles in the way of completing the process are relatively minor. Yet even though clarification of one's basic beliefs about the human condition is the most decisive step that one takes on the road to self-understanding, it is merely a beginning. The next step, generalization, takes the person outside of himself.

Once a person has clarified what he considers to be significant and valuable in the human condition, he is prepared to begin the search for the tradition of which he is a representative. Finding the tradition of thought that one's ideas about the human condition represent is the essential feature of the phase of generalization. There are two aspects of the search, both of which are integral to self-examination. First, there is an attempt to identify the present social groupings whose ideas are closest to one's own. Second, there is an effort to trace the historical development of one's beliefs. The key to the process of generalization is that the person situates himself in a social and cultural field, rather than conceiving of himself as a detached and isolated individual.

The process of generalization is based on a particular way of looking at human existence which follows from the idea that the self is a process. According to some people, human beings are born into the world with a fixed nature from which they cannot deviate.[27] Such people view the self as a thing with certain properties: a kind of machine. Once there is knowledge about how the machine works, it is possible to use the machine for one's own purposes. For example, if one is sure that human beings are "naturally" greedy, one will attempt to play upon greed to gain one's purposes. Other motivations, such as curiosity and desire for love, will be ignored. As another example, suppose that a person believes that human beings will do what brings them rewards and shun what brings them punishments. In order to gain his purposes, such a person will attempt to manipulate rewards and punishments rather than appeal to the independent judgment of human beings.

Pitfalls of Depersonification There are several criticisms of viewing the self as a thing. First, once a person has adopted a fixed view of human nature, he is forced to explain away all evidence to the contrary. For example, the person who believes that human beings are naturally greedy must explain away acts that are apparently motivated by such impulses as curiosity or love. There are two ways in which this is normally done. First, the person argues that the curiosity or love merely hides conscious or unconscious greed. Once the greed has been made unconscious it becomes virtually useless as a way of understanding human activity. Second, the person argues that curiosity and love are merely forms of greed, because people enjoy satisfying their curiosity and engaging in relations of love. If it is pointed out that many lovers undergo pain to aid their loved ones, the person responds that they still "like love better," or else they would never have suffered the pain. This kind of argument convinces many people that human beings really are motivated by greed. However, a close look at it reveals that it proves almost nothing. To say that people are greedy because they do what they prefer to do is to define greed as acting on one's preferences, regardless of what they are. There is no law against defining greed in this way, but it deprives the term of almost all its ordinary meaning and force. Also, there is a problem in the idea of preferences. How does one find out about someone's preferences? It seems that this discovery can only be made by seeing what the person does. Thus, there are no preferences apart from actions. This means that all actions are being defined as greedy simply because they are actions. Again, there is no law against using the word greed as a synonym for the word action. It is appropriate, though, to ask whether this is really what the defender of the greed theory originally intended to say.

The second defect in viewing the self as a thing is that it tears the human condition out of history. For those who believe in a fixed human nature, the human condition always remains essentially the same. For example, those who believe that human nature is greedy often hold that politics has always been and always will be a form of highway robbery.[28] For them, it does not matter who controls the state; the rulers will always be trying their hardest to extort the last pound of flesh out of the ruled. Cases of political corruption, crime, and espionage (for example, the Watergate affair) tend to give support for this view. Frequently, they draw the lesson from this argument that concerted and collective action to promote social change is foolhardy, and that the only sensible strategies for the individual are to get a piece of the action or to withdraw from the battle into private consumption, drugs, or a "home in the heart of the country." Paradoxically, the ruling elite thrive on such cynicism as long as they do not have to mobilize the population for great sacrifices. Cynicism, bred by fixed theories of human nature, at least keeps people out of the opposition.

Tearing the human condition out of history deprives people of clear knowledge of their concrete historical possibilities. Every situation in which people find themselves provides some opportunities and closes off others. For example, most university classrooms, built with fixed seats all pointing in the same direction, make lecturing by the professor easy and open discussion difficult. Rigid views of human nature are entirely irrelevant to analyzing such concrete opportunities. Simply stating that human beings are greedy will not account for why university classrooms are arranged with lecturing rather than discussion in mind. Such a statement also will not provide any help in understanding how it might be possible to provide spaces for learning and inquiry which would encourage discussion. Similarly, the five-subject undergraduate schedule provides opportunities for information about a variety of experiences, but little chance for in-depth study of any experience. Fixed theories of human nature will be of no help in analyzing this situation either. The general ideas that do help in understanding such situations are those clustering around the view of the self as a process with multiple possibilities for development at each historical juncture.

The phase of generalization, or searching for the social groupings and historical traditions that one represents, is only possible because the self is a process organizing meanings and relations. Human beings act on visions of the future (projects), which involve human creations (cultural objects) and other people (relations).[29] If each human being was a completely unique and self-contained individual, there would be no possibility for generalization. It is only because the person learns about possible meanings of the human condition *from* others and can communicate them *to* others that visions of the human condition come to be shared by people over time. Thus, the idea that human beings are naturally greedy is historically specific. It was created by particular human beings at a particular time, has been held more by some groups than by others, and has served a variety of specific purposes. It is an idea most widely held where private business is important, because many business methods play upon the motivation of greed. Where business methods are not very important the idea is not likely to become dominant.[30]

The phase of generalization can be defined best through an example. There are a number of people in the United States who believe that the social group, rather than the individual, is the most important source of creative ideas, that the ultimate need of human beings is belongingness and group membership, and that there are systematic methods available through which people can be engineered into belongingness.[31] Taken together, these beliefs form a powerful and sometimes compelling vision of the human condition. The vision is compelling because many innovations and new developments appear to emerge anonymously out of vast organizations, composed of endless agencies and committees, and because many human beings seem to be lost and in search of belongingness.[32] The vision is powerful because large organizations frequently try to control the kinds of human relations that occur within them, and the kinds of personalities that develop out of these relations.

Suppose that, after clarifying his vision of the human condition, a person discovered that he held the beliefs listed above. If he wanted to proceed to the phase of generalization he would ask, "Who else

holds these ideas and where did they come from?" He would find out
that these ideas are current among many people who work in the
middle levels of large organizations and who are given little opportunity for independent initiatives. He would also find out that these
ideas began to become widespread after World War I, when the image
of the self-made man was tarnished by contact with the realities of vast
organizations. These organizations required people who would cooperate with their co-workers rather than compete with them, and in
order to help meet this requirement a literature developed on ways of
engineering consent. William H. Whyte, Jr., in *The Organization Man*
did an extensive study of this vision of the human condition and
summarized its claims: "Man exists as a unit of society. Of himself, he
is isolated, meaningless; only as he collaborates with others does he
become worthwhile, for by sublimating himself in the group, he helps
produce a whole that is greater than the sum of its parts."[33] Whyte also
identified the groups of middle managers who hold these beliefs and
showed how they grew out of tendencies in American philosophy
which emphasize the importance of human relations over human creations and personal choices. Through his work, Whyte was able to
generalize the central beliefs about the human condition held by many
Americans.

It is important to note that a person willing to exercise his imagination and listen closely to what is said around him could go quite
deeply into the phase of generalization without reading books such as
Whyte's. A person holding the middle manager's creed could try to
remember where he picked it up and try to figure out whose purposes
it might serve. Once he had made some judgments about these matters
he could seek out books that would tell him the history of these ideas
and how they had developed over time. Through generalization the
person would be able to situate himself historically. He would find out
which groupings shared his ideas about the human condition and what
kind of world these groupings were trying to create. Generalization,
then, makes the process of self-examination social rather than individual. The person is no longer locked up inside of himself with private
and arbitrary judgments and feelings. He shares his problems, interpretations, and programs with others. He has, in the terms of C.
Wright Mills, made his private problems public.[34]

Obstacles to Generalization   Just as there were obstacles to clarifying
one's basic ideas about the human condition, so there are obstacles to
undertaking the phase of generalization. The most important barrier
to generalization is the desire that one's beliefs be unique. Many peo-

ple in the United States believe that it is a virtue to be unique, and become upset whenever they realize that they have a great deal in common with others.[35] They refuse to look for social groupings expressing ideas similar to their own, because they feel that they are less human if they are representatives of a tradition.[36] This attitude demands careful examination.

The most obvious defect in the attitude is that, whether or not one wants to admit it, most of his beliefs have a long past and are widespread among one or more present social groupings. Thus, when a person refuses to generalize his beliefs on the grounds that he is unique, he is not stating a fact, but merely burying his head in the sand. Further, it is appropriate to ask whether or not beliefs about the human condition serve any purpose if they are unique. A central belief about the human condition is a statement that claims to be true about the human condition in general. If such a statement is unique to an individual and that individual claims it is true, it means that he also claims that others are living in falsehood. He then must ask himself whether he values his uniqueness more than he values others believing the truth. He may also ask himself how it happened that he alone has been able to perceive the truth about the human condition.

The preceding discussion was intended to open the possibility that beliefs about the human condition are not the kinds of things that one would want to make a mark of one's uniqueness. Every human being is at least unique in the sense that no two human beings have been through exactly the same experiences, and no two human beings share exactly the same position in space-time. Individuality and uniqueness can be emphasized through differences in taste and the organization of life-style. Such differences lead to the expansion of human appreciation. However, seeking uniqueness through beliefs seems to be a misplaced use of beliefs, which are claims that certain judgments are true. If a person argues that his ideas about the human condition are true for him, but not for others, he is either saying that his judgments are based on a limited slice of experience (a sensible statement) or that everybody is completely different (a questionable judgment). The wish that one's beliefs be unique is an outcome of the idea that the self is private property and that beliefs are a part of that property. It is similar to the desire of many women not to wear the same outfit to a party as someone else.

The desire for unique beliefs has two social consequences. First, it prevents people from recognizing their allies in social struggles and thereby furthers the spread of dispersed masses of floating individuals.[37] Second, it is useful to ruling elite groups because it prevents the

formation of oppositions. It is merely another way in which people are
tricked out of using their minds.

Related to the desire for unique beliefs is the desire for originality.
The worship of originality is only a specialized form of the worship of
uniqueness. Often when people clarify their beliefs about the human
condition they experience a joy in self-understanding and, since they
have never seen themselves so clearly before, think that they have far
surpassed what others have been able to learn. Sometimes they experience a letdown when they find that many people in the past have
shared their beliefs about the human condition and have expressed
these beliefs with great precision. Sometimes those who desire originality more than understanding will attempt to prove that their ideas
really are completely new and bear only superficial resemblance to the
beliefs of the past and present. Perhaps what is saddest is that some
people who have overcome the fear of being labeled stupid, and have
clarified their beliefs, come to think of themselves as stupid when they
learn that their ideas are not original. This misplaced judgment shows
that many people are at least as embarrassed and misinformed about
their minds as they are about their sexual relations and their capabili-
ties for violence.

Placing originality above understanding has the same consequences as placing uniqueness above truth. The most important
consequence is to impede the growth of solidarity among human beings. There are some great benefits to solidarity. First, generalization
allows one to learn about one's own thoughts from people who have
spent time and effort trying to work out their implications. Someone
who believes that the emphasis on group creativity of the middle
managers works against human dignity can learn a great deal from
Whyte's attacks on the ethic of belongingness. Second, generalization
helps a person find out who his allies are in current social struggles.
If thought and action are related, generalization adds a new significance and importance to one's action. Third, and most important,
generalization provides what can best be called intellectual friendships. The person finds out that he is not a lonely thinker, crying in
a wilderness. There are others who have shared important parts of his
vision, even if it is possible that nobody else's vision has been exactly
the same.[38] Originality and uniqueness may have some snob appeal
and romantic glamour, but in the long run they leave a person alienated and alone. This does not mean that people should seek "belongingness" for its own sake. Rather, it means that people should not
avoid finding out just how far their beliefs about the human condition
extend in time and space. At this point, we cannot resist firing a parting

shot at those who resist generalization. How many people get upset when they realize that their belief that the earth is round is not unique to them? How many people are uncomfortable that their discovery that two plus two equals four is not original? Why, then, do some people care whether or not their visions of the human condition are unique and original? We believe that it has something to do with the widespread idea that a person's life is his private property.

Figure 1.3 BARRIERS TO GENERALIZATION

People tend to avoid generalizing their images of human existence when:
  1. They would like to believe that their beliefs are unique.
  2. They would like their beliefs to be original.
Do you value uniqueness over truth and originality over understanding?

RELATIVIZATION

The person who generalizes learns that there are people who share his central beliefs about the human condition. However, at the very moment that one becomes conscious of his intellectual friends, one is also made aware of those who disagree with him, and of their ideas. Recognition—and, hopefully, appreciation—of intellectual opponents goes along with acquiring intellectual friends.

The next step after the phase of generalization in the process of self-examination is the phase that has come to be known by the cumbersome word *relativization.* Through relativizing his beliefs about the human condition, the person becomes conscious that his view of human existence is merely one among many visions, and that sincere and intelligent people have fundamental differences with him. He also learns about the structure and content of some of these other beliefs and comes to appreciate why others would hold them. He discovers that different beliefs about the human condition are associated with different social groupings and represent long historical traditions.[39]

Aspirations of Different Groups   The phase of relativization can be understood through an illustration of how it might occur in a specific case. Suppose a person discovers that he holds the middle manager's vision of human existence, and that he believes that the fundamental motivation of human beings is to seek "belongingness." This person has clarified and generalized his beliefs. However, in the process of clarifying and generalizing he has found out about other visions of the human condition. He has discovered that, for certain specialists and higher managers in organizations, the fundamental drive of human beings is for interesting work to which they can make a personal and creative contribution. For these people, belongingness is far less valued than autonomy and individual initiative. Further, he comes to realize that most of the clerical and production force in the organization is interested primarily neither in belongingness nor creative initiative, but in security. These people view the human condition primarily in terms of the social life-cycle of birth, marriage, child rearing, and/or breadwinning, leisure, and death. They believe that human beings are motivated to acquire the "good things in life," among which are security of income, a happy family life, a decent neighborhood to live in, and some of the comforts and diversions provided by consumer goods. Finally, he becomes acutely aware of the poor and of the members of minority groups who consider themselves dispossessed by the other social groupings, and who believe that human existence is a power struggle between dominant and subordinate groups. For them, the fundamental human drive is for self-determination, in the sense of economic independence, political freedom, control over the content of education and determination over the style of living that will characterize their communities. Through relativization, the person who arrives at an understanding of these diverse groups has performed a revolution perhaps greater in its impact than the one performed by Copernicus when he argued that the earth was not at the center of the universe. The person who relativizes is no longer at the center of the social universe. He merely represents one stream of thought and one mode of action among many.

As the person becomes aware of the different images of the human condition held by the members of different social groupings, he grasps how closely related these visions are to the activities that people perform.[40] The middle manager and technician must work in a group setting. They do not make policies, but are given directives from above. Thus, their main problem is to cooperate efficiently to fulfill plans programmed by others. A vision of group creativity, a drive to belongingness and the systematic adjustment of human efforts fits very well with this kind of work. The upper-professional higher manager, however, does make policy, and is continually confronted with new challenges from the competition of other organizations and the demands of more specialized groups at lower echelons. For him, a vision of human existence stressing creative initiative is more appropriate than one emphasizing belongingness. Similarly, belongingness is not a primary factor in the work of most clerical and production personnel, because their tasks center around operating machines or engaging in standardized interpersonal relations (e.g., checking groceries in a supermarket), rather than in coordinating group efforts toward programmed goals. Their satisfactions lie mainly outside of their jobs and, therefore, their visions of the human condition stress family and leisure life. Finally, while the dispossessed emphasize group solidarity, they are not chiefly concerned with belongingness. They are on the outside of the major organizations, and are demanding greater rights and a greater share of the social product. They have the least secure and most menial work, and relatively high proportions of their members are unemployed. Thus, the vision of human existence as a power struggle fits their situation well. Rather than belongingness, they want respect, and the rights that go along with it.

Relativization gives a person a more accurate understanding of the human condition and of his place in it, a firmer grounding for his action with respect to others and a deeper appreciation for different kinds of people. Understanding is furthered by recognition of the partiality of one's own vision and the cogency of other visions. Action is more intelligent because one knows better what to expect from members of other groups and how one's communications will be received by members of these groups. Appreciation is aided by imaginatively living through the visions of other people. While the phase of relativization provides all these benefits, there are obstacles that people confront in undertaking it. As with the other phases, the barriers to relativization are tied up with the image of the self as property.

Barriers to Relativization The most important obstacle to relativization is the fear that seriously considering other beliefs about the human condition will disclose that one's own ideas are trivial. There are two varieties of this fear. First, there is anxiety that one will find that he has been a dupe and a fool for most of his life. While this hardly ever proves to be the case, because most widespread visions of the human condition have compelling features, there is serious question about whether a person really wants to keep himself in the dark about other ideas simply to preserve a false sense of certainty. Refusing to relativize one's beliefs is one of the greatest inhibitors to personal growth. Second, there is the anxiety that relativization leads to making all beliefs about the human condition trivial. There is an idea that just because honest and intelligent people hold different, and frequently clashing, visions of the human condition, all such visions are equally true or equally false. This means that beliefs about the human condition become merely matters of arbitrary personal preference.[41]

It should be clear that this kind of corrosive attitude does not necessarily follow from the process of relativization. First, the idea that all central beliefs about the human condition are equally true or equally false often stems from confusing honesty and intelligence with truth. Just because a person is sincere and bright does not mean that he is correct. The truth of a proposition is determined by testing it against experience, not by the sincerity with which it is held. Second, many differences between visions of the human condition are based on the slices of experience to which the people who hold them have access. The differences between the beliefs of the middle manager and the dispossessed person are in great part a result of the different experiences they have undergone. The middle manager does not confront discrimination and prejudice every day. The dispossessed person does not spend much of his life coordinating complex activities in accordance with organizational plans. The ideas about the human condition current in the various groupings are not so much falsehoods as distortions of the whole stemming from partial experience of the whole and manipulations of ideas by elite groups. Basic ideas about the human condition arise out of people taking the most central experiences of their own lives and projecting them onto the whole of human existence.[42] This process of distortion is speeded along by packaged interpretations of the human condition communicated to specific groups by advertisers and propagandists. The only way to prevent one's partial truths from becoming monstrous falsehoods is through undertaking the process of relativization.

A second obstacle to relativization is the comfort that some people feel with their beliefs and their unwillingngess to suffer the pains of questioning them. It is pleasant to feel that the world is in order, that one is at the center of the social universe, and that one's own tradition is the only one worth understanding. However, the same objections apply both to the person who is unwilling to relativize his beliefs because he is comfortable with them and to the person who is unwilling to clarify his beliefs because he thinks he has a "right" to them. It is appropriate to select a bed with an eye to whether it will be comfortable, but since beliefs and activities are so closely linked, comfort may not be the proper criterion for determining whether or not beliefs should be held. Placing comfort ahead of truth is very closely linked with the idea that the self is private property. People often hold on to consumer goods or get rid of them on the basis of the pleasure or pain that they derive from them. The goods are their property to dispose of as they wish. When the idea of property dominates the self, even beliefs are made into consumer goods.

Distortions Brought about by the Communication-Gap Theory A third
obstacle to relativization is the idea that all differences in basic beliefs
about the human condition stem from communication gaps. The person possessed by this idea believes that there is only one "reasonable"
way of viewing the human condition (his own), and that every sincere
and "normal" person shares his vision.[43] He is convinced there are no
fundamental disagreements among honest human beings, and apparent conflict is a result of misunderstandings rather than clashing interests or contradictory premises. Since there is only one "reasonable"
way of viewing the human condition, there is no reason to relativize
one's beliefs. All that needs to be done is to translate what others are
saying into one's own frame of reference.

The idea that all disagreements over human destiny stem from
communication gaps is simply false. However, it is very widespread in
the United States today, particularly in large organizations. Accepting
his organization's propaganda as the only normal way of looking at the
world, the middle manager will tell the workers that management is
trying to look out for the workers' interests, and will tell the dispossessed that they really crave belongingness rather than self-determination.[44] The idea that all disagreements result from communication
gaps is extremely useful to the elite. It allows them to twist the demands of dispossessed groups for power into demands for equal opportunity within the system. It allows them to say that "violence will
accomplish nothing; come let us reason together." Of course, those
who already have power can afford to spend their time "reasoning" for
as long as it takes to wear down the opposition. Further, the communications media can be blamed for creating passions and divisions, and
the responsibility of leadership can be avoided. Finally, the communication-gap theory allows elite groups to play on "good intentions"
rather than performance. They can try to convince people that they are
"trying as hard as humanly possible" to right all the wrongs. This
seems to mean that as long as they are "trying" it does not matter a
bit what they accomplish.

The communication-gap theory lulls a great many people into
complacency. It allows them to say such things as: "We're all basically
the same, aren't we? Why can't we start talking about some of the good
things about the country, rather than trying to tear it down all the time?
After all, the minorities just want a little more of the pie. If people only
used a little common sense they'd see that we have a good country and
that we're trying hard to give everyone a fair shake. It's just that you
can't change everything overnight." Such people would be quite disturbed if they became acutely aware that there are blacks in the United

States who want to bake their own pie and who do not see themselves
as basically the same as whites.[45] Thus, the communication-gap theory
is another way in which people bury their heads in the sand (or in the
pie). It is simply the most sophisticated of the myths that keep people
from self-examination, and is to be avoided like the plague by anyone
out to seek truth. The communication-gap theory also has another
disagreeable feature. It is quite conceited to believe that one's own
view of the human condition is the only "reasonable" one and that no
"normal" person would hold any other. This is making disagreement
a form of mental illness.[46] It is quite useful for the elite to spread the
rumor that the opposition is mentally ill. Relativization increases understanding, effectiveness in action, and appreciation. Its only draw-
back is that it decreases conceit.

Figure 1.4. BARRIERS TO RELATIVIZATION

People tend to avoid relativizing their images of human existence when:
1. They are afraid that confrontation with new beliefs will show them that
   they have been fools and dupes.
2. They are afraid that they will find all beliefs to be trivial.
3. They feel comfortable with their present beliefs.
4. They believe that all differences of opinion about human existence are
   a result of communications gaps.

Do you avoid discussions about politics and religion? If so, why?

COMMITMENT

The final phase of the process of self-examination is commitment,
or the development of a conscious view of the human condition and
a plan of action based upon it. In clarification, one becomes aware of
one's vision of the human condition and principles of action. In generalization, one discovers the roots of that vision in space and time. In
relativization, one comes to understand and appreciate other basic
beliefs about the human condition. In commitment, one uses the
knowledge and appreciation one has gained about the human condition to devise a more adequate vision and to act in terms of it. This
does not mean that increased understanding will always lead to altered
action. There are barriers to commitment. However, if one has clarified, generalized, and relativized, he will at least be aware of whether
he is acting on his explicit vision or on some implicit one—or, worst
of all, on one forced upon him.

The phase of commitment is based on the insight that one is
always acting in terms of some view of the human condition, whether

or not one is fully aware of that vision. In the light of this, human freedom resides in becoming aware of alternative perspectives, and consciously choosing to act on one of them or to create a new vision out of the given material and whatever fresh insights are available. It is important to note that the phase of commitment does not necessarily come to a definite end, and that it contains all of the other phases within it. Each new situation presents a human being with fresh experience and new opportunities for extending awareness. In order to continue the process of self-examination, this experience must be clarified, generalized, relativized, and then judged with respect to its bearing on action. The phase of commitment means that human existence is a continual living experiment in which visions of the human condition are tested for their factual accuracy, logical consistency, comprehensiveness, felt quality, and fruitfulness for future action. These visions are tested not in some laboratory set apart from social life, but in the concrete human relations that take place from day to day. Each day that people try to solve their problems by assuming that human beings crave belongingness and that all disagreements stem from communication gaps, these assumptions are being tested. Each day that people go to work assuming that human nature is greedy and that good sense means getting in on the action, these assumptions are being tested. Of course, the tests are always incomplete, because it never happens that everybody is testing the same assumptions. This means that the results are never completely decisive, and that it is almost impossible to dislodge completely any widespread vision of the human condition. Further, the tests are self-certifying, because, for example, if everybody acted on the assumption that human nature is greedy, everybody would be greedy.[47] Theories of human nature are realized when people act on them. This is why the phase of commitment is so important. By acting on a vision of the human condition, one helps make that vision come true.

The incompleteness and self-certifying character of basic beliefs about the human condition are keys to why we consider the process of self-examination to be so important. If people merely take their visions of the human condition for granted they are actively creating a world which they do not even understand. Usually their unexamined beliefs help serve the interests of one or another elite group. Sometimes these beliefs, if fully carried out, would result in consequences that the holder of the beliefs would deplore. Imagine a world in which everybody was greedy, or a world in which everybody was passionately seeking belongingness. Most important, without conscious commitment undertaken after the other phases of self-examination, a person cannot have respect for his mind. Lacking such respect, an individual easily becomes the pawn of others, who most likely do not have his interests at heart. We, at least, find it very difficult to respect people who are unwilling to undertake self-examination, because we know that such people refuse to take responsibility for their lives. While this again may appear to be a harsh judgment, we make it because at one time we avoided self-inspection, and can remember what we were like at that time. We are aware of the obstacles to self-examination, not because we have engaged in laboratory experiments with human guinea pigs, but because we encountered these obstacles ourselves. Particularly difficult are some of the barriers standing in the way of passing from relativization to commitment.

Problems in Attaining Commitment   The first obstacle to entering the phase of commitment is the idea that all central beliefs about the human condition are trivial. This idea, which has been discussed under the topic of relativization, appears in a slightly different context here. Sometimes the idea that visions of the human condition are trivial turns into the belief that the human condition itself is trivial or absurd.[48] This is not a difficult transition to make, especially in the light of the fact that visions are an integral component of human existence.

Frequently the person who believes that the human condition is trivial holds that life is merely a game, or that it does not matter what he does. Sometimes this is a convenient way of avoiding responsibility for one's actions. When questioned about some harmful action, an individual can say, "What does it matter since life is absurd anyway?" At other times the belief is a cry of regret for an absolute authority and a certainty which has been lost forever. At still other times it is a cry of despair from people who have been pushed into a corner and only have the narrowest of choices. There are times when an individual has a choice between doing something utterly repulsive or committing suicide. In such situations existence does seem absurd.

The idea that human existence is trivial or absurd is itself a vision of the human condition that can be judged against other visions. If a person acts in terms of it, she has made a commitment. As she lives out her experiment, she can judge whether or not she really finds life trivial. Perhaps there are some experiences that she particularly values over others. Perhaps she seeks these experiences and plans the rest of her life around them. For example, she may find happiness when she is alone in the woods or when she is making love or when she is eating a good meal. She may forget about the triviality of life when having these experiences. If she recognizes that she is taking something seriously, she is beyond the framework of triviality. She may still hold the belief that there is no ultimate meaning to human existence that can be determined by human beings, and she may feel pangs of regret about this, and even get periodically dizzy from looking into the abyss. However, she will also live for those experiences that seem valuable in themselves. If, on the other hand, she continues to find existence trivial, she will be stuck with that judgment and the actions that go along with it. In either case, she will have made a commitment and performed a living experiment.

A second obstacle to commitment is the fear of closing one's options. Many people who have gone as far as relativization view existence as a set of pure possibilities. They do not want to experiment with any particular possibility because this will prevent them from having other experiences. Thus, they remain in limbo, afraid of living out a particular life.[49] It is clear, however, that remaining in limbo is itself a particular kind of life with its own specific experiences of suspense, vacancy and always being on the edge of things but never fully participating. The person who fears closing his options has effectively closed them anyway.

There is no way of having one's cake and eating it too. Each person is always in a particular situation doing specific things.[50] There is, however, a way of preventing narrowness in one's life. This is by continually going through the process of self-examination, particularly the phase of relativization, and incorporating into one's commitment the valuable experiences that one discovers. For example, by observing the social protests of blacks and trying to understand the experience of dispossessed peoples, many whites added a new experience of militant social action to their lives. Such opportunities for incorporating new experience and acting on it are readily available in the complex world of today.

The final obstacle to commitment is the fear that one's actions will reveal one to be a fool. Here we return to the very beginning of the discussion, and to the major themes that we have emphasized. Too many people in the contemporary world lack confidence in their own minds. They are told that they should turn their thinking over to experts, that they cannot make their own decisions, that the world is too complex for them to understand. They are afraid to examine their own beliefs because they think that these beliefs are probably worthless anyway. They are afraid to commit themselves to living experiments because there are experts who supposedly know much more about human existence than they do. The purpose of this book is to combat these attitudes by showing that it is possible to increase your awareness of the human condition, and to provide you with a method for continually reconstructing your beliefs about human existence. It is our purpose to show you that you are not a fool, but that you are instead a representative of a long historical tradition with capacities for altering that tradition. With this end in mind, the next chapter will summarize the history of social thought. In reading that chapter try to separate your intellectual friends from your intellectual opponents. Through that process you will be generalizing and relativizing, and on your way to making a conscious commitment.

Figure 1.5. BARRIERS TO COMMITMENT

People tend to avoid making commitments when:
1. They think that all beliefs are trivial.
2. They believe that the human condition is absurd.
3. They would like to keep their options perpetually open.
4. They think that they may appear foolish to others.

Do you like to exist above life?

2

A BRIEF GUIDE
TO SOCIAL THOUGHT

How does a person begin to understand the human condition and his projects within it? If an individual simply went to the library and began paging through books in the sociology section with the intent of clarifying and generalizing his ideas about human relations, he would probably meet with frustration. He would be confronted by a bewildering array of books and articles, directed to a wide variety of questions and containing different and often clashing answers to these questions. It would be possible for him to spend several years reading some of these books and articles at random. Through this experience he would slowly create an overall framework in which the various kinds of social thought made sense. He would have a map which would enable him to locate the various types of social thought as he encountered them, and to see how they related to his ideas about the human condition. It is the purpose of this chapter to try to save an individual concerned with understanding the human condition some time in identifying where he stands with respect to the history of social thought. This chapter, then, presents the broad outlines of a map of social thought. As you read through this chapter try to figure out which kinds of social thought you most agree with and then, if you have the time, read some of the authors with whom this type of thought is identified. This will allow you to clarify and generalize your image of the human condition. If you do not agree with any of the ideas discussed in the following pages, pick out the ideas that you disagree with most, read the authors who have expressed them and try to figure out why you disagree with them. This procedure will be just as useful in the process of self-understanding as the one stressing your agreement with a type of social thought.

There are many maps of social thought.[1] Some of them divide thought about the human condition according to place or time. Thus, there are books on German sociology, American social thought, Oriental social philosophy, and so on. Similarly, there are books on nineteenth-century sociology, twentieth-century sociology, and so on. Other maps divide social thought according to different answers to a central question. This is the approach taken here. The central question which will guide the following discussion is, What fundamental assumptions about the human condition have characterized social thought? Philip S. Haring has called such assumptions "grand conceptions by which I make sense of reality."[2] He argues that, whether or not a person realizes it, he is using such a grand conception to interpret the human condition. The task of the social thinker is to bring these conceptions clearly into awareness so that human beings can make conscious choices among the various frameworks through which human existence can be interpreted.

THE TYPES OF SOCIAL THOUGHT

There are four general ways in which the human condition can be interpreted, each one of which has many adherents in the contemporary world. The first grand conception is the *natural-law model*. This type of thinking, which appeared in the ancient civilizations of Greece, the Middle East, India and China, and was carried through in the Middle Ages, views the human being as an integral part of an orderly universe. According to this view, human beings are regulated by a moral law which they can grasp through divine revelation or reason, but which they are not free to change. Therefore, natural-law thinkers believe that there is a proper order to human existence, and that even if human beings do not always conform to that order, they are still ethically bound by it. The aim of natural-law thinkers has traditionally been to criticize the social life around them when it has not measured up to the moral standards they hold, and to describe the kinds of human relations that would measure up to these standards. If this discussion seems to be difficult to grasp, it is well to remember that most religious people hold some conception of natural law. For example, many Christians believe that the commandment to love thy neighbor as thyself is a natural law which people may break in many cases, but which they cannot change because it has been instituted by God.

The second general way in which the human condition can be interpreted is in some type of *monistic* or *one-factor model.* Those who hold the monistic model believe that the human condition should be interpreted in terms of a single organizing factor. According to this view, the activities of human beings can be understood in terms of the working of certain key forces that operate under one overriding concept. For example, some people believe that human beings have a primary drive to seek power over others. Whatever events occur in human relations, these people attempt to relate them to the power drive. Besides clear relations of domination, in which power is obviously involved, such relations as love are interpreted as concealed attempts to impose one's will on the other.[3] There are almost as many monistic theories of the human condition as there are human motivations and activities. Some monists hold that economic factors are primary (Marxism), others stress relations between the sexes (Freudianism), others racial factors (Lothrop Stoddard), and still others climate (Montesquieu). A person is likely to be a monist if he can give a precise answer to the question, What is human nature? Such a person frequently reduces human activity to some factor like greed, lust for power, desire for love, desire for approval, or the urge to survive biologically. Whatever factor is picked out, it is likely that there is a past or present thinker who has interpreted the human condition in its terms.

The third grand conception of the human condition is the *pluralistic model.* Those who hold some type of pluralistic model believe that there are a multiplicity of factors involved in the human condition, and that it is necessary to take account of all of these for a complete understanding of human existence. Pluralists tend to believe that each individual or each group is a unique combination of factors that will never be repeated again. Frequently they believe that the human condition is divided up into sectors such as the economic, political, social and cultural, each of which is relatively separate from the others, and each of which is studied by a special science (economics, political science, sociology, and anthropology). Both pluralism and monism are responses to the decline of natural law. Natural-law theorists are primarily concerned with discovering and applying the moral laws that people should follow if they are to lead the good or righteous life. Monists and pluralists, who frequently believe that there are no such discoverable laws, are far more interested in discovering and applying the factors they think determine human behavior.

The fourth grand conception of the human condition is the *process model*. This is the model held by the authors of this book. Those who hold the process model believe that events in the human condition can be best understood by organizing them around a single human process in which people continuously create and re-create the conditions under which they live. The image of the human condition associated with the process model is one in which human beings have multiple possibilities for future action, yet face present conditions that tend to limit these possibilities. Thus, the central idea in the process model is that of human freedom.

The process model differs from the natural-law model because it does not picture a universe in which there are moral laws that exist regardless of human choice. It differs from the monist and pluralist models because it does not aim at the discovery of the factors that cause people to behave as they do. It holds that there are degrees of causation in human affairs and corresponding degrees of freedom. Natural law, monism, pluralism, and process represent distinctive ways of interpreting the human condition. In the following discussion each one of them will be considered from the viewpoint of one who seeks to clarify his vision of the human condition.

NATURAL LAW

The central idea of natural law is that there is a moral order in the universe which binds human choice. Once a person has come to know this order through the use of reason, he also understands the pattern of human relations that is consistent with natural law. John Courtney Murray, a Catholic social thinker, has described the general features of natural law. First, natural law asserts that the nature of man is "a unitary and constant concept beneath all individual differences."[4] This means that, however much human beings appear to differ from one another, their ultimate fulfillment would be found in the realization of a purpose open to discovery by them. A consequence of this is that "for man, a rational being, the order of nature is not an order of necessity, to be fulfilled blindly, but an order of reason and therefore of freedom."[5]

Murray describes concretely what it means to take the natural-law viewpoint in everyday life. He considers the case of a man who is protesting against injustice where his own interests are not directly involved and where the injustice does not violate any civil law. An example would be someone protesting the denial of voting rights to eighteen-year-olds before the law was passed allowing them to vote. Murray argues that such a protestor is claiming that there is an idea of justice which exists apart from the will of any legislator and is rooted in the "nature of things." Further, Murray states that the protestor implies that he really knows this idea of justice, that it is not created by him but is instead an external standard for judging his action, that the idea should be realized in law and action, that its violation is unreasonable and "that this unreason is an offense not only against his own intelligence but against God, Who commands justice and forbids injustice."[6] Murray concludes that the protestor, who may know very little about social philosophy, "is thinking in the categories of natural law and in the sequence of ideas that the natural-law mentality (which is the human mentality) follows."[7]

Difficulties of The Natural-Law Viewpoint A first major difficulty with natural law is that it is possible to question whether or not the person engaged in political protest necessarily implies all the points listed by Murray. There is no doubt that the protestor makes his judgment that injustice has been done on the basis of a general standard of justice that he holds. This standard is often closely related to his vision of a good human condition. It is not clear, however, that the protestor necessarily claims that there is an idea of justice which exists apart from any particular human will and which is somehow rooted in the "nature of things." Instead, he may simply be claiming that he prefers to see a world in which the idea of justice that he holds is realized over a world in which this idea is not put into effect. This preference may be based on the judgment that he would feel better if his idea of justice was realized or that this idea of justice is part of a vision of the good life that he holds. If the protestor does not necessarily claim that his idea of justice is valid apart from any particular human will, he also does not imply that it is an external standard and that its violation is an offense against God. In fact, even if a person accepts natural law, he is not logically bound to accept the notion that God exists.

There is a second important difficulty in the natural-law position. While almost everybody may agree with such general maxims as "justice should be done," "equals should be treated equally," and "good should be sought and evil avoided," people may have serious disagreements about what is just, in what respects people should be deemed equal, and what is good. For example, some may hold that it is just to allow eighteen-year-olds to vote, while others may hold that such a privilege would create injustice. There seems to be nothing about the "nature of things" that would help in solving this dispute or in determining which camp was on the side of natural justice. This vagueness in natural law has made it a useful tool for groups seeking to defend or expand their rights and privileges. Defenders of the status quo have insisted that the current social order approximates the dictates of natural law, while those in favor of change have argued that the present order does not measure up to the standards of natural law. Sidney Hook has summed up this difficulty of the natural-law position: "Our own time has spawned a whole series of moral problems in which the right to security conflicts with the right to liberty and which challenges us to fruitful and creative devices that aim at giving us as much as possible of both but must on occasion risk our security or curb our freedom. The theory of natural law does not take us an inch forward in negotiating such conflicts."[8]

The natural-law position appears in a wide variety of forms in current social thought. Every person who claims that there are certain basic human needs which should be met, certain basic human rights which should be respected, or certain fixed standards of the social good or social justice which should guide action shares the natural-law position. Careful consideration of the preceding list will reveal that natural law remains the most widespread type of social thought in the contemporary world. Many people believe that there is a fixed "human nature" characterized by particular needs. Some people believe that these "needs" center around physical survival, and mainly include food, clothing, and shelter. Others hold that "man does not live by bread alone" and has "needs" for love or respect. Still others claim that human beings "need" to develop their potentialities to the fullest extent. Often the idea that human beings have certain inalienable rights goes along with the notion of human needs. Thus, some claim that there is a right to freedom from want, some assert a right to be treated with respect (or even to be loved), and some claim a right to full development. Frequently, such notions of needs and rights are turned into fixed standards of social good or social justice.

The Concept of Human Need It is worthwhile to spend some time on the idea of human need because it is at the root of most visions of the human condition. The central problem in notions of human need is that the supposed needs are not always met and there are people who seem not to want them to be met. For example, the most elementary need seems to be that for the means to continue physical existence. Most people agree that human beings "need" food, clothing, and shelter. However, while there is no dispute that these things are necessary for the continuation of physical existence, there is great disagreement about whether physical existence should be continued in all cases. There are people who say that they would rather be "dead than Red." Many others commit suicide for various reasons. Some governments spend more money on armaments than they do on encouraging the provision of food, clothing, and shelter. People go on hunger strikes to protest social conditions and even court death to further a cause. Others sacrifice their own lives in acts of heroism to save friends, relatives, or even total strangers. In each of these cases, of course, there is the assumption that some human beings will continue physical existence. However, there are people who believe that the universe would be better off without any human beings in it, and that the most noble human act would be to extinguish human life.

What does the person who holds the idea that human beings need food, clothing, and shelter say to the person who believes that human life should be destroyed? Frequently he says that this person is mentally ill, weird, perverted, deviant, abnormal, sinful, misguided, or some other term that makes the pessimist into less than a "real" human being. The assumption here is that anyone who does not fulfill the requirements set by a particular idea of human nature has thereby lost his standing as a human being. The usual follow-up to this judgment is either an attempt to make the deviant "see the light" or an effort to eradicate the deviant. These kinds of responses show how slippery the idea of human need can become. What begins as a call to universal good becomes an effort to liquidate the opposition, spiritually or physically.

Most natural-law thinkers draw consequences for social relations and group life from their descriptions of human nature. For example, Erich Fromm, who believes that the existence of human needs can be demonstrated scientifically, holds that women have a need to bear children: "Women have the power to bear children and to nurse them; if this power remains unused, if a woman does not become a mother, if she can not spend her power to bear and love a child, she experiences a frustration which can be remedied only by increased realization of her powers in other realms of her life."[9] How does one account for the childless woman who claims that she is not frustrated and who does not seem to be driven to achieve in other human activities?

A more serious application of natural law to social relations has been given by Mary Elizabeth Walsh and Paul Hanly Furfey. According to them, one learns how society ought to function by "examining its nature, that is, by studying what the thing essentially is."[10] They state that such an examination discloses that the common good implies the preservation of public order and the furtherance of economic and cultural welfare. Any deviation from these standards constitutes a social problem, and the denial of the natural law is itself "the root cause of modern social problems."[11] In the Catholic tradition of natural law that Walsh and Furfey represent, public order and economic and cultural welfare require monogamous marriage, the state, and the church. Where these institutions do not appear, human beings will not be able to attain the good life and will be living unnaturally and, therefore, unjustly. In the light of the earlier discussion it is appropriate to ask whether the necessity of particular institutions can be derived from such vague commandments as "preserve public order" and "further economic and cultural welfare."

The Western tradition of social thought has grown out of a natural-law basis. The Greek philosophers Plato and Aristotle both held conceptions of natural law that stressed that human reason could discover the principles of harmonious social relations. For Plato, justice meant each member of the community making the contribution for which he was best suited. Aristotle had a similar idea, but emphasized distribution of the social product to those who most deserved it and the participation of equals in making social decisions. In the Middle Ages natural law was tied to Christianity, and biblical revelation was viewed as a supplement to the principles of Plato and Aristotle. In modern times, natural law has become tied more and more to ideas of human need and mental health. Some thinkers like Branislaw Malinowski, Talcott Parsons, and Marion Levy have attempted to determine the "needs" that must be met if societies are to continue in existence. Others such as Erich Fromm, Sigmund Freud, Abraham Maslow, and Harry Stack Sullivan have attempted to determine the "needs" that must be met for the attainment of a "healthy personality." These examples show the persistence of natural law in contemporary social thought, although many of the thinkers would not so label their ideas.

Monism

Natural law thrives as an explicit social philosophy where people are relatively unaware of any other ways of life that might compete with their own. Where there is no immediate clash between alternative ways of organizing human relations and performing human activities, it is understandable that people might come to believe that their ways were just as natural as day succeeding night and apples falling from trees. Deviations from ordinary patterns of activity would be infrequent, and would likely be viewed as unnatural exceptions to the natural order. Such people would believe that their ways of organizing human life were part of the "nature of things."

When diverse peoples are thrown into contact with each other it becomes difficult to maintain a natural-law position unchallenged. Each of the different peoples is likely to hold that its way of life is part of the nature of things. In such a situation it becomes necessary to explain why those who follow different ways seem to violate "human nature" or the "natural law." Just such a situation happened at the end of the Middle Ages when, through the crusades and the age of exploration, Europeans were brought into extensive and intensive contact with the peoples of other continents. Over several centuries, two different approaches developed to account for the differences among ways of life. The first approach was monistic, in the sense that it explained the differences through a single factor or cause operating in variable conditions. The second approach was pluralistic, because it explained the differences through a multiplicity of conditions mutually determining a given result. Both monism and pluralism are responses of human beings in the modern age to the encounter of different ways of life and the growing complexity and specialization of human relations. The present section will treat monism and some of its particular varieties.

The hallmark of monism, and modern thought in general, is that it substitutes the problem of causation for the problem of the social ideal. According to natural law, "the social ideal springs from the very nature of human society itself."[12] When there is a clash of life-ways it becomes difficult to determine the "very nature" of human society. One can no longer look at his own community and see in it an image of the ideal. Confronted with this problem, some people do not abandon the search for the social ideal. They carry forward the natural-law tradition and frequently attempt to make it more universal. However, other people become concerned with a new problem: Why do people behave in such diverse ways? In his attempts to answer this question, the monist looks for an underlying cause or factor that will make sense out of all of the diversity.

Categories of Monism   There are as many possible types of monism as there are different kinds of human activities, different human characteristics and different factors in the human environment. For example, some monists find economic, political, educational, or religious factors unifying the human condition. Others unify the human condition through such characteristics as race or sex. Still others believe that differences are accounted for by environmental "forces" such as geographical location or climate. In each case one part of human existence is separated out from all of the others and made the determinant of them.

Marxism The structure of monistic thought can best be illustrated by an example. Perhaps the most influential and compelling variety of monistic thought has been Marxism. Many social thinkers in the twentieth century owe an enormous debt to Marx for his detailed criticism of modern life. Numerous social thinkers since Marx can be usefully regarded as either revisionists of his thought or as critics reacting against it and substituting other interpretations. With the success of communist revolutions in many parts of the world, Marxism has become the official philosophy of regimes governing hundreds of millions of people. This fact alone makes Marxism the most significant variety of monism in the contemporary world.

The most accessible basic document of Marxism is the *Communist Manifesto,* drawn up as the platform of the Communist League, a workers' association, in 1848, shortly before the revolutions that took place in Europe during that year. The *Communist Manifesto* presents a monistic interpretation of the human condition based on the operation of economic factors in determining historical events.

The *Manifesto* begins with the assertion that the "history of all hitherto existing society is the history of class struggles."[13] For Karl Marx and Friedrich Engels, who wrote the *Manifesto,* class meant a group of people sharing a common relation to tools, or the means of producing goods and services. Whether or not one belongs to a certain class in the Marxist scheme of things depends upon one's relation to the ownership of the means of production and the types of tools that exist. In all historical societies there has been a continuous struggle between those who own and control the means of production and those who must depend on the owners for their survival. According to Marxists, the owners tend to exploit the rest of the population up to the point that such exploitation would threaten their very domination: "Hitherto, every form of society has been based . . . on the antagonism of oppressing and oppressed classes. But in order to oppress a class, certain conditions must be assured to it under which it can, at least, continue its slavish existence."[14] At bottom, exploitation means that the classes composed of owners attempt to appropriate for themselves all of what has been produced by the other classes beyond what is necessary to continue the existence of these other classes as efficient producing units. Insofar as they are capable, the other classes attempt to fight against this exploitation.

Historical change comes about, in the Marxist model, through the rise of classes owning and controlling new and more efficient means of production. For example, the transition from the medieval to the modern era was accomplished by the bourgeoisie which controlled the means to international commerce and eventually the means to industrial manufacturing. The bourgeoisie, through a long series of struggles, was able to displace the hereditary land-owning nobility from its position as the dominant class. Ultimately, it gained its success because its members owned and controlled a form of productive property (the factory) which was a far more efficient means of production than the property (arable land) owned by the nobility.

Along with each dominant means of production goes an entire system of classes. In the Middle Ages, there was a multiplicity of classes. The nobility was the ruling class, gaining its importance from the ownership and control of land. Under the nobility were the vassals and serfs who, to a greater or lesser degree, were contractually bound to provide rents and services to their lord in return for the use of his land. In some cases, the serfs were attached to the land in the sense that they and their children were legally bound to work it unless released by their lord. Alongside the manor system were the towns, populated by merchants and skilled laborers who provided goods and services not available on the manor. It was from these merchants and laborers that the bourgeoisie grew.

After the triumph of the bourgeoisie through various legal and revolutionary conflicts, a new class system began to appear. According to Marx, this system would eventually develop to contain only two classes—the bourgeoisie and the proletariat. The bourgeoisie would centralize in their hands the ownership and control of all the means of production, and the proletariat, or working class, would have nothing to sell but their labor. Under these conditions, Marx thought, the bourgeoisie would no longer perform the function of organizing production and would become mere parasites on the rest of the population. Thus, there would be a sharp breach between those who owned the means of production and did no work and those who did all of the work, but did not own any tools. Under these conditions, Marx thought, there would be another series of revolutions in which the proletariat would displace the bourgeoisie and organize the means of production in its own interest. The interest of the proletariat, however, would be the interest of all, because there would no longer be any split between exploiters and workers. Humanity would be one, because people would no longer identify themselves first as members of a class and second as individuals.

The chief importance of Marxism as a monistic theory lies in the way that it organizes the whole of human activity around the idea of class, which in turn is based on economic differences. Such classes as the bourgeoisie and the proletariat are not simply groups based on ownership. They are also political groups, groups of thought, and groups with distinctive styles of life. This point is made strikingly in the *Manifesto* in a denunciation of the bourgeoisie: "Your very ideas are but the outgrowth of the conditions of your bourgeois production and bourgeois property, just as your jurisprudence is but the will of your class made into a law for all, a will whose essential character and direction are determined by the economic conditions of existence of your class."[15] Thus, for Marxists the diversity of human existence becomes understandable when it is organized by economic factors.

Monism's Attractions   Like natural law, monistic social thought has many attractions. First, well-thought-out doctrines like Marxism are able to make a great deal of sense out of apparently disconnected events by fitting them into a single pattern. Monistic thinkers often provide new and fresh perspectives on everyday life. For example, many people in sympathy with the women's liberation movement have been impressed by Marx' observation: "The bourgeois sees in his wife a mere instrument of production."[16] These insights, though often partial, are helpful in fashioning a coherent vision of the human condition. Second, monistic thinkers provide a direction for human action. If economic relations pattern all of the other human relations, then social changes will come through the alteration of economic relations. This kind of reasoning has given social movements based on monistic doctrines a clarity of program lacking in other movements. Third, monistic theories are attractive because of their seeming realism. Marx called himself a "scientific" socialist who had discovered the causes of historical change rather than a "utopian" socialist who would dream about ideal communities, but never think seriously about what would be necessary to put them into effect.

Monism's Difficulties   There are two major problems in monistic theories. The first stems from the effort to organize all of human existence around a single activity. Even with respect to such a compelling view as Marxism, does it make sense to claim that such a factor as economic conditions underlies the whole of human affairs? For example, take the observation that the bourgeois sees in his wife a mere instrument of production. While there may be some people in the ownership classes who view their wives merely as machines for producing children, objects for giving them physical pleasure, and trophies of their success in the rat race, these kinds of relations do not exhaust the possibilities within marriage in the industrial age. There are many other attitudes and viewpoints embodied in bourgeois marriages, such as cooperative sharing of experience, mutual support, and development of common interests. This does not mean that the typical modern view of the woman is as a full person. With great frequency women are treated as mere instruments of production and consumption, and this conception is enshrined in religion, literature, and political thought.[17] However, it is inaccurate to reduce the condition of women to economic relations, and this inaccuracy frequently results in actual blocks to the realization of personal freedom.

Suppose that someone points out that he does not treat his wife as a mere instrument of production, and that his wife agrees with this judgment. Suppose, further, that an impartial outside observer also agrees with the judgment. Confronted with this evidence, a dogmatic Marxist might try to search for any evidence of exploitation in the relationship. If he found evidence of exploitation he might say that this meant that the entire relationship was oppressive. If he found no evidence of oppression he might still say that exploitation was "really" there whether or not it was obvious or even discoverable after long investigation. This conclusion would mean that nothing could convince the dogmatic Marxist that a bourgeois marriage could be founded on anything but exploitation. Such a conclusion, if accepted by the people involved, would block their realization of personal freedom because it would destroy their confidence in their own powers of critical judgment. Thus, through attempting to account for all human activity through the operation of a single factor, extreme monism leads to factual inaccuracy and blocks to freedom.

The second difficulty with monism is related to the first. It concerns the notion that a person's very ideas are the outgrowth of the so-called driving factor in human existence. While there are profound connections between work and thought, and while becoming aware of these connections increases the range of freedom, thought cannot necessarily be reduced to some non-conscious factor. Stating that thought is caused by economic relations frequently leads to the denial of reasoned conversation. For example, two people may claim that their marriage is based on the development of common interests. A dogmatic Marxist may respond, "You are only saying that because you are members of the bourgeoisie, and your class position determines your ideas." This kind of response is equivalent to the idea that a person is mentally ill or evil if he does not hold someone's idea of natural law. It makes people lose respect for their minds.

Monism is very important in contemporary life. It takes many other forms than economic determinism, but is always characterized by the belief that a single factor unites the diverse aspects of the human condition. The coherence gained by concentrating on a single theme, however, frequently involves the sacrifice of factual accuracy and the expansion of freedom.

PLURALISM

Pluralism arose as a response to some of the problems in monistic thought described in the preceding section. Some social thinkers were struck by the fact that the single-factor interpretations of monism often stretched the imagination by distorting events to fit the preconceived mold. Others were disturbed by the tendency of monists to claim that their pet factors were responsible for causing events when no such connection appeared to be discoverable. Still others were concerned with the ways in which monistic theories seemed to limit freedom by claims that certain future events, such as the displacement of the bourgeoisie by the proletariat, were inevitable regardless of human choice. All monistic theories seemed to lead to a paradox. The social movements based on them made frantic efforts to recruit followers while at the same time proclaiming the inevitability of their success. Explanations that such recruiting was done to make the inevitable happen sooner were not entirely satisfactory. Together, these criticisms formed the basis of pluralist thought.

The most basic assumption of pluralism is that a large number of factors determines human events, rather than a single dominant theme. However, if this claim was all there was to pluralism it could not be considered a serious type of social thought. There is a kind of crude pluralism that appears in everyday life and in political propaganda that criticizes Marxism and other monistic theories by stating simply that "reality is far more complex than the Marxists would have it." From these kinds of remarks one is supposed to draw the conclusion that all efforts at major social change are misguided. Crude pluralists tend to believe that out of the competition between social groups grows a balance of interests and a progressive solution to social problems. Crude pluralism is the doctrine contained in most American propaganda and, therefore, should not be confused with pluralism as a major type of social thought. It sidesteps any serious encounter with monistic theories through a vague idea of "complexity," while serious pluralism reworks the root assumptions of monism.

Once certain social thinkers adopted the idea of multifactor causation of human events, they were faced with the serious problem of how to compare these factors to one another. There was wide agreement that economic factors, as well as political, religious, familial, educational, and other factors played a part in determining the character of the human condition. However, comparing these factors to one another seemed like comparing apples and oranges. In order to make any sense out of the multitude of factors (something that crude pluralists do not care to do) the serious pluralists set out to discover a basis for comparison, or what the various factors had in common.

The results of this search were a series of concepts that have become the basis of contemporary sociology. What the search revealed appears to be quite simple, but was in fact revolutionary in the changes it accomplished in social thought. The pluralists discovered that all of the major factors suggested in the monistic theories were forms of human activity. The economic factor was the activity of producing and distributing goods and services. The political factor was the activity of making decisions and trying to see that they were carried out. The educational factor was the activity of transmitting information from one person to another. These factors and many others were responsible for the pattern of human events, but they were all activities.[18]

The discovery that human activity underlies all the particular factors suggested by monistic theories was an impressive advance in thought because it removed social thought from what is immediately visible in the commonsense world. A moment's thought will show that one never encounters human activity in general in everyday life. One always encounters a particular type of human activity, whether it be economic, political, religious, educational, or some other. Thus, for pluralists activity itself is the *form* of social life, while each particular activity is distinguished by a particular *content* (production, communication, or some other). The distinctions between form and content are not, of course, absolute. For example, the particular activity of production is never encountered in everyday life. One always finds people producing something specific. Thus, the activity of production is in this case the *form* of economic activity, while the *content* of economic activity varies according to what is being produced (automobiles, color-television sets, machine guns, or some other objects).

The reasoning behind pluralist thought discloses its major departure from monist thought. Monistic perspectives attempt to unify the diverse aspects of the human condition around a single factor or content. Pluralistic perspectives attempt to unify the various aspects of the human condition around the forms common to all contents. This difference can be illustrated by considering briefly how Marxism is revised by pluralist thought.

The Pluralist's View of Marxism   The central idea of Marxism is that the history of all hitherto existing society is the history of class struggles. The pluralist thinker would change this sentence to read, "The history of all hitherto existing society is the history of group relations." According to the pluralist all human activity takes place within the context of groups. Among these groups are classes, as defined by Marx. However, the classes may not be the most important groups in every situation. Sometimes family groups, religious sects, or schools of thought are more important than economic classes in determining the character of human existence. Further, the pluralist would argue that struggle is only one form of human relationship. In addition to struggle and conflict, there are also such relationships as cooperation, competition, exchange, and love. There is no guarantee that struggle will be the most important human relation in all cases. The pluralist holds that the only way of finding out which group or which relation is the most important in a particular situation is to go out and investigate that situation. Thus, pluralistic thought attempts to make no assumptions about the dominant factors in the human condition in advance of investigation.

Most of the discussion that follows will be based on the contributions of pluralistic thinkers, because they have dominated twentieth-century sociology. Sociologists such as Max Weber, Emile Durkheim, George Herbert Mead, Vilfredo Pareto, Gaetano Mosca, Georg Simmel, Arthur F. Bentley, and Talcott Parsons identified different aspects of human activity that overarch the particular factors contained in monistic social thought. Their works contain images of the contemporary human condition that put into order many of the problems that people confront today. These images will not be considered at this point because they will be revealed throughout the following discussion.

Pluralism's Problems   Like the other types of social thought, pluralism has difficulties. They center around the idea that the task of social thought is to find the conditions that determine human events. Some pluralists tend to believe that it is possible to look at the human condition from the outside, like a geologist inspects a rock, and find out what factors gave it the character it displays. Thus, they often forget that they themselves are actors in the human condition, and that their very social thought is a guide to social action. Like every other type of social thought, pluralism is both a description of the human condition and a way of orienting activity within that condition. In natural law and monism, it is clear how social thought performs this double function. Natural-law thinkers claim to describe a series of human needs and a set of social relations for meeting these needs. Thus, natural law serves as a guide to action by orienting people to creating or perfecting the relations required for satisfying human needs. Similarly, monistic thinkers claim to describe a single force around which all social relations can be organized. Thus, monistic thought serves as a guide to action by showing people what factors they should take account of in their efforts to gain certain social changes. For example, as a guide to action, Marxism directs one to work upon economic conditions, rather than the religious life or some other factor, to effect desired changes.

It is more difficult to show how pluralism is a guide to action, because most pluralists believe that they are simply describing and explaining human events, rather than orienting action toward those events. However, pluralist thinking does give rise to a distinctive type of action. According to the pluralist, there can be no conclusive judgments made in advance of observation and experimentation about the factor that is most important in determining a given human situation. This means that the adoption of pluralism prevents one from subscribing to any particular variety of monistic thought. Further, the pluralist finds human activity to be the basic factor unifying the human condition, and cannot adopt any particular natural-law interpretation of social relations. For him, there is no hidden set of needs lurking behind activity and experience.

How, then, does pluralism serve as a guide to action? Since pluralists can neither assume that any particular factor is of decisive importance in determining the human condition nor claim that a fixed set of needs characterizes human nature, they must adopt an experimental attitude toward human existence. They must treat every natural law and monistic perspective as a possible social experiment. For example, Marxism could be treated as an experiment in transforming social relations through collective action on economic conditions. The human condition itself would be the laboratory for social experimentation. Further, pluralists must treat their own pluralism as an experiment in taking an experimental attitude. Thus, pluralism demands that all types of social thought be viewed as possible guides to action. This recognition that each vision of the human condition is a guide to action as well as a description demands an assumption that human beings are free to choose among competing visions. Through their choices, human beings help determine which interpretation of the human condition will come true. It is this fact that makes it difficult for pluralists to claim that they are merely outside observers seeking the causes of human events. The idea that pluralism is a guide to action, counseling experimentalism rather than dogmatism, and that it is one guide to action among many, leads directly to the process pattern of social thought.

PROCESS

Process thought arises in response to conditions in the contemporary world that are equal in their impact to the encounter of diverse ways of life that led to the development of monistic and pluralistic perspectives. Talcott Parsons has noted that the primary question that modern (monistic and pluralistic) thinkers sought to answer was the problem of order: How is society possible?[19] Impressed by the conflicts brought about by European exploration and exploitation of the rest of the world, and by progressive specialization and industrialization, modern thinkers were concerned to discover how human beings avoided a chaotic war of all against all. Three general answers were developed to this question. One group of thinkers held that the stability of human relations was secured by superior might and wealth. Marx was one representative of this position. A second group held that the order present in human relations was sustained by agreement on the rules of social living. Many pluralists have held this position. In its most popular form it asserts that, through rewards for conforming to the rules and punishments for breaking them, human beings learn to obey the standards prevailing in social groups. In this process of learning, so its advocates argue, people come to believe that the prevailing standards are right and that they have an obligation to obey them. The ideas that stability results from exploitation and that order is maintained by agreement on rules of conduct are not in necessary conflict with each other, unless either one is defined as the only answer to the problem of order. Thus, a third group of social thinkers, the most numerous, has argued that both might and agreement are factors in the maintenance of social order.

In the twentieth century, there has been an increasing challenge to the idea that the central question in social thought is the problem of order. Part of the reason for this challenge is contained in the fact that in recent decades for many people order has not appeared to be the greatest problem in social life. The twentieth century has witnessed the growth of enormous organizations, or conglomerates, performing a multitude of functions, in which decisions affecting the lives of millions of people are made on a daily basis. For some of those who are workers within the conglomerates such as the state, the large university, or the multinational corporation, and for those who feel the consequences of their decisions, there is no problem of order—the lives of these people are structured by an order that is beyond their ability to control. Further, as time goes on more reports appear of drugs that can be used to control moods and behaviors, of improved propaganda and brainwashing methods, and of the accumulation by conglomerates of information on peoples' lives. In the face of these conditions it is understandable that a number of people have no difficulty in believing how order is possible.

The new question that has arisen to challenge the problem of order can be called the problem of liberation. Rather than asking how society is possible in a world of diversity and conflicting individual and group interests, the process thinkers are concerned with how freedom is possible in a world increasingly dominated by mammoth organizations. The emergence of patterns of social thought based on answers to the problem of freedom shows how closely social thought is tied to events and characteristics in other sectors of the human condition. Throughout the world, people have become aware of the problem of liberation. People throughout Asia, Africa, and Latin America are demanding liberation from order imposed by the nations of Europe and Anglo-America. Minority, sex, and age groups within Europe and Anglo-America are demanding liberation from order imposed by dominant groups on these continents. Rebels within the Soviet bloc are demanding liberation from controls on freedom of expression and freedom of political participation. Individuals throughout the world are demanding liberation from the constraints on their thought and action imposed by the conglomerates. This worldwide movement for liberation has impressed many twentieth-century social thinkers in much the same way that the encounter with diversity and complexity impressed social thinkers of past centuries.

Process thought is based upon the central premise that the human condition is unified by a single process of action. This process of action is defined by the fact that human beings can reject their present conditions in favor of a vision of the future. Herbert Marcuse has called this fact "the power of negative thinking" because it discloses the ability of human beings to deny that their present conditions are necessary and must inevitably continue.[20] Bound up with this notion is the idea that the human process has four dimensions.

Four Dimensions Inherent in the Human Process   The first dimension is *lived experience.* Lived experience means that human beings are directly aware of their feelings and of the constant transformation they undergo. Human beings are aware of time through felt organic change. Their original experience is of feelings. The second dimension is *social experience.* This means that the human process involves social relations such as competition, cooperation, conflict, and love. Through such relations people become aware that they are different from their environment and from other human beings. The third dimension is *cultural experience.* This is the aspect of meaning in the human process. Out of experience, human beings create and carve objects they can use over and over again to produce similar results. The set of these objects is culture, and the complexes of culture provide people with opportunities to store and stabilize experience. Finally, the fourth dimension is *creative experience.* While cultural experience is the appreciation of objects created in the past, creative experience is the generation and use of new meaningful objects.

In sum, the human process involves people experiencing in common, acting in relation to one another, using meaningful objects and continually creating anew the conditions for their existence. It is this idea of the human process that underlies the present book.

The preceding description of the human process reveals a great deal about the interpretation of the problem of freedom in the twentieth century. For the existentialists, the pragmatists, and the humanists who disclosed the various dimensions of this process, freedom is something positive.[21] In one way or another each thinker who has attempted to respond to the problem of freedom has challenged the idea of vacant freedom which has been so popular in the modern era.[22] Vacant freedom is the notion that freedom is merely the absence of all restraints. It is the cry of all those who seek freedom *from* domination. However, vacant freedom by itself contains little satisfaction for human beings. It is the freedom that appears when a person has nothing left to do. If they clarify their images of the human condition, most people discover that behind their struggle to gain freedom from domination is a quest after freedom *for* something. The process thinkers have attempted to describe the aspects of "freedom for" and to show the possibilities for such freedom in the present human condition.

Some Details of Human Freedom   One aspect of "freedom for" is *clarification* of one's vision of the human condition. Without such clarification one's consciousness remains merely a bundle of desires and myths without any rhyme or reason. A second aspect of positive freedom is *generalization of the vision*, which allows one to identify the group that is composed of one's allies. The third aspect of freedom for is *relativization*, which allows one to identify competing groups and visions. Finally, the fourth aspect of positive freedom is *commitment*, or the decision to act upon an image of a future human condition after the consideration of one's own ideas and the ideas of others. For the thinkers who have attempted to deal seriously with the problem of freedom, any worthwhile vision of the human condition will include the project to continue, deepen and extend the process of self-examination. They find it is this very process that is discouraged by the massive conglomerates of the contemporary world, whose propaganda systematically distorts the human condition and aims at lulling human beings into complacency and obedience. In the nineteenth century Marx could declare: "Workers of the world unite, you have nothing to lose but your chains." Today in the face of propaganda, advertising, and other forms of mental manipulation the process thinkers tell us: "Examine yourselves and your society, you have your minds to gain." Thus, in the end, *freedom for* means well founded respect for one's mind.

Process thought does not reject the contributions of natural law, monism and pluralism, but reinterprets them. It makes the needs of the natural-law thinker into possibilities for human action. It makes the causes of the monists and the pluralists into aspects of the human condition that must be taken account of in any attempts at intelligent action. It also asserts that human beings have some control over whether or not they will make such factors as economic conditions central in their lives. In sum, it finds in the fact that all types of social thought are both guides for action and descriptions of action evidence for the existence of a process of self-examination; it is this that opens the door to positive freedom.

Figure 2.1. THE TYPES OF SOCIAL THOUGHT

Natural Law:	Defines a set of human needs and devises a social ideal in which these needs would be met
Monism:	Defines a single factor in human existence which supposedly accounts for social relations and organization
Pluralism:	Explains social relations and organization through a multiplicity of factors
Process:	Organizes social relations and organization around a single human process of freedom

SOCIAL THOUGHT IN REVIEW

There are many possible maps of social thought. The one presented above is especially adapted to aiding the process of self-examination. It identifies four general types of social thought, each based on a different image of the human condition. While there may be other types of social thought than the ones identified and, therefore, other visions of the human condition, these four have appeared most frequently in the history of civilizations, both East and West. In order to simplify the process of self-examination, one should attempt to discover whether his own thought fits roughly into any one of these four patterns and then read more deeply the works of a writer who develops that pattern. Although the idea of process guides this book, there is no reason why one has to adopt this pattern. We would be acting in bad faith if we did not attempt to defend the type of thought which we think is most sound. However, many intelligent and thoughtful people disagree with us on fundamental issues, and it is worth your while to find out what serious natural-law thinkers, monists, and pluralists have to say. You may very well adhere to one of these three patterns, particularly natural law or monism, and you may end up sticking to your position. It is up to you to find out.

To sum up, natural-law thinkers attempt to answer the question, "What is the good life?" Their answer is usually that the good life is the fulfillment of some basic human "needs" that they have identified. In one form or another, natural law was the dominant form of social thought up until modern times. It is still probably the most widespread perspective, since most people believe that there is some such thing as "mental health" or "moral goodness," that can be defined with precision. Pluralism and monism arose in the modern era, primarily as a response to the breakdown of the older traditions and the growing diversity in the human condition. Monistic theorists searched for a single cause or factor that would account for the observed differences in human life and would explain why stability in human relations was maintained in the face of fierce conflicts. Pluralistic theorists claimed that a multitude of factors determined the precise character of the human condition, and unified thought about human relations around the idea of human activity. Growing out of monism and pluralism, process thought has analyzed the idea of human activity and has found that it is based on a notion of human process which involves positive freedom. The possibilities for such freedom have become particularly important for many people in the twentieth century who are less interested in how order can be maintained than they are concerned with how to win liberation from powerful organizations.

As one studies social thought with a view to its effects on one's own thought and action, it is important to know the standards by which it can be evaluated. The discussion of such standards is the aim of the next chapter.

A SAMPLER OF THEORISTS

The following list of theorists is a small sampling of representatives of the four perspectives discussed in this chapter: natural law, monism, pluralism, and process. It may be used as a beginning in the attempt to clarify one's own vision of social structure and human relations. Select the perspective which seems closest to your own, choose a theorist from the list, and as you read the work identify the points at which you agree and disagree with the presentation. If you follow this process through you should be able to clarify your own assumptions about society and then be ready to appreciate other perspectives.

Natural Law   Scientific sociology was, in part, a rebellion against natural-law theories of society. There are therefore, few representatives of this perspective in contemporary sociology. Older religious visions of natural law still survive, however, and to them have been added theories of the "normal" or healthy self derived from personality theory.

RELIGIOUS INTERPRETATIONS

FURFEY, PAUL HANLY. *Three Theories of Society.* New York: Macmillan, 1937. Furfey criticizes the model of society promoted by scientific sociology and attempts to show how sociological theories imply moralities. He then introduces a traditional interpretation of natural law as an alternative sociological theory and morality.

MARITAIN, JACQUES. *Scholasticism and Politics.* Garden City, N.Y.: Image Books, 1960. Maritain attempts to apply traditional natural law to contemporary social problems, tracing these problems to an erosion of public morality.

PSYCHOLOGICAL INTERPRETATIONS

FREUD, SIGMUND. *Civilization and Its Discontents.* New York: W. W. Norton, 1961. Freud traces contemporary social conflicts to repressed instincts and drives.

FROMM, ERICH. *The Revolution of Hope: Toward a Humanized Technology.* New York: Harper & Row, 1968. Fromm presents a critique of contemporary institutions based on a view of the healthy personality.

Monism   Monism was the characteristic perspective of nineteenth-century sociology. While pluralistic and process theories have displaced it in the mainstream of contemporary American sociology, there are still many monists, particularly Marxists, who are actively theorizing. Monisms may be divided according to the key factors which they stress in their interpretations of social life.

ECONOMIC MONISMS

MARCUSE, HERBERT. *Negations.* Boston: Beacon Press, 1968. Marcuse adapts a basically Marxist view to contemporary organizational society.

MARX, KARL, and ENGELS, FRIEDRICH. *The Communist Manifesto.* New York: Appleton-Century-Crofts, 1955. This is still the most accessible and best introduction to economic monism.

TECHNOLOGICAL MONISMS

CHILDE, V. GORDON. *Man Makes Himself.* New York: New American Library, 1951. Childe presents an interpretation of civilization based on successive technological innovations.

VEBLEN, THORSTEIN. *The Theory of the Leisure Class.* New York: New American Library, 1953. Veblen's classic is a critique of the predatory nature of modern society.

GEOPHYSICAL MONISMS

HUNTINGTON, ELLSWORTH. *Mainsprings of Civilization.* New York: New American Library, 1959. Huntington analyzes the role of biological inheritance and physical environment in influencing the course of history.

WITTFOGEL, KARL A. *Oriental Despotism.* New Haven: Yale University Press, 1957. Wittfogel links the appearance of absolutist bureaucratic regimes to the need to coordinate agricultural production.

BIORACIAL MONISMS

CHAMBERLAIN, HOUSTON STEWART. *Foundations of the Nineteenth Century.* New York: Dodd, Mead, 1912. Chamberlain's defense of the Germanic or Aryan "race" was a source of much Nazi propaganda.

STORR, ANTHONY. *Human Aggression.* New York: Atheneum, 1968. Storr draws conclusions from ethology (the study of animal behavior) about the nature of human social organization.

POSITIVISTIC MONISMS

DEGRANGE, MACQUILKIN. *The Nature and Elements of Sociology.* New Haven: Yale University Press, 1953. DeGrange attempts to bring Auguste Comte's positivism and his theory of the stages of human society and understanding up to date.

WHITE, LESLIE A. *The Science of Culture.* New York: Farrar, Straus & Young, 1949. White presents a positivistic theory of historical evolution heavily laced with technological monism.

Pluralism Pluralism is the dominant perspective in twentieth-century sociology. Like natural law and monism, it is not a homogeneous perspective, but is characterized by a number of different emphases. Some pluralists are interested primarily in the conflict among diverse groups, others are concerned with the ways in which some groups dominate others, others are concerned with how different social activities are integrated together, others are interested in patterns of organizational coordination, and others are concerned with the formation of the human self out of social relations.

CONFLICT APPROACH

DAHRENDORF, RALF. *Class and Class Conflict in Industrial Society.* Stanford: Stanford University Press, 1959. Dahrendorf "pluralizes" Marx by pointing to a number of conflicts in contemporary society.

SIMMEL, GEORG. *Conflict and the Web of Group Affiliation.* New York: Free Press, 1955. Simmel describes the various forms which conflict takes in social life.

ELITE AND DOMINATION APPROACH

MANNHEIM, KARL. *Man and Society in an Age of Reconstruction.* New York: Harcourt, Brace, 1940. Mannheim presents an argument for elite planning in a multi-group society.

PARETO, VILFREDO. *Sociological Writings.* New York: Frederick A. Praeger, 1966. Pareto "pluralizes" Marx by analyzing elitism and domination as general social phenomena.

FUNCTIONALIST OR INTEGRATIVE APPROACH

DURKHEIM, EMILE. *The Division of Labor in Society.* New York: Free Press, 1947. Durkheim "pluralizes" Marx by outlining the general forms of "solidarity," or the way diverse activities in society are coordinated.

PARSONS, TALCOTT. *The Social System.* New York: Free Press, 1951. Parsons presents a general theory of social control, emphasizing the way social roles are integrated into systems of coordinated action through the coordination of sanctions.

ORGANIZATIONAL APPROACH

GERTH, H. H., and MILLS, C. WRIGHT. *From Max Weber.* New York: Oxford University Press, 1958. Weber "pluralizes" Marx by outlining a general pattern of hierarchical organization characteristic of modern societies—the bureaucracy.

BLAU, PETER M., and SCOTT, W. RICHARD. *Formal Organizations.* San Francisco: Chandler, 1962. Blau and Scott "pluralize" Weber by pointing out structural dilemmas within organizations as well as the dynamics of "informal organizations" which grow up around formal structures.

SOCIAL PSYCHOLOGICAL APPROACH

MEAD, GEORGE H. *Mind, Self, and Society.* Chicago: University of Chicago Press, 1934. Mead describes how the self is formed through interaction with other human beings and how people are "socialized" to obey the rules of the "game."

GOFFMAN, ERVING. *The Presentation of Self in Everyday Life.* Garden City: N.Y.: Doubleday, 1959. Goffman shows how people engage in "impression management" to regulate their relations with others.

Process   Process theory, the most recent general perspective in sociological analysis, has, like the other frameworks, several distinct foci of concern. Some thinkers are primarily concerned with the types of human activity, others are interested in analyzing the images and perspectives through which people view their social life, others are concerned with the principles of contemporary social structure and others are interested in the possible patterns of relations ("dialectics") which can characterize intergroup and interpersonal activity.

ACTIVITY FOCUS

BENTLEY, ARTHUR F. *Relativity in Man and Society.* New York: G. P. Putnam's Sons, 1926. Bentley describes human society as an interlacing of cross sections of activity and presents a method of "socioanalysis" similar to the process of self-understanding described in this book.

ZNANIECKI, FLORIAN. *The Cultural Sciences.* Urbana: University of Illinois Press, 1952. Building the idea of creative activity into his analysis, Znaniecki presents a general theory of culture and society.

EPISTEMOLOGICAL (PERSPECTIVAL) FOCUS

NORTHROP, F. S. C. *The Meeting of East and West.* New York: Collier Books, 1966. Northrop shows how different cultures express different theories of knowledge and experience.

SOROKIN, PITIRIM. *Sociological Theories of Today.* New York: Harper & Row, 1966. Sorokin presents a review of contemporary sociological theories from a perspective similar to Northrop's.

SOCIAL-ORGANIZATION FOCUS

JORDAN, ELIJAH. *Business Be Damned.* New York: Henry Schuman, 1952. Jordan offers a scathing critique of contemporary social institutions from the viewpoint of a philosophy of creative freedom.

HILLER, E. T. *The Nature and Basis of Social Order.* New Haven: College and University Press, 1966. Following from Jordan's critique of the privatization of contemporary society, Hiller applies the notion of human process to a theory of social organization.

DIALECTICAL FOCUS

GURVITCH, GEORGES. *Dialectique et Sociologie.* Paris: Flammarion, 1962. Gurvitch shows how dialectical analysis of social relations is consistent with a process of creative freedom. See also, Philip Bosserman's commentary on Gurvitch's sociology, published in English.

MUKERJEE, RADHAKAMAL. *The Philosophy of Social Science.* London: Macmillan, 1960. Like Gurvitch, Mukerjee develops a multifaceted dialectic and coordinates it with a theory of social structure and a philosophy of freedom.

3
SOCIOLOGY AND SCIENCE

The first two chapters of this book contain an introduction to thinking about the human condition. The first chapter shows that to understand oneself fully it is necessary to understand the social situation in which one is acting. The way to attain such understanding is to clarify one's vision of the human condition, generalize it and relativize it with respect to the images held by others, and then commit oneself to the resulting vision and start the process all over again. The second chapter describes various images of the human condition that have been held in the past and that have adherents at the present time, with the aim of making the process of self-understanding more easy to undertake.

Throughout these first two chapters an important question has been left unanswered, even unasked: Are there any standards for choosing among competing visions of the human condition? We believe that the answer is yes. If we thought that the answer was no, or even maybe, we would probably not have written this book, because we would have despaired that the process of self-examination led

60

nowhere but to a bottomless pit. Our affirmative answer to the question is based on a judgment that the investigation of human affairs can be scientific. Thus, the standards for choosing among competing visions of the human condition are rooted in science, and to grasp those standards it is necessary to understand what is meant by a human science.[1]

SCIENCE

Science (and, somehow, particularly, the term social science) is terminology that frightens and mystifies many people. It is, of course, one of the major aims of this chapter to dispel this fear and worship because we would like everyone to become a sociologist, at least in the sense that we would like everyone continually to reexamine the human condition in a critical way. This means that we believe that everyone who is reading this book is capable of understanding the scientific method and applying it to his own existence.

The fear and awe that the term science awakens is due to a narrow and distorted interpretation of scientific activity. According to this distorted interpretation, scientists carve up human experience into distinct and highly specialized fields, invent terms to describe events that only they can understand, and then provide information to engineers who invent machines that nobody can control.[2] It is no wonder that those who have such a view of science stand in awe of it. Yet this interpretation of science only describes a very small part of scientific inquiry. At the heart of science is a series of standards for evaluating thought, and these standards have little to do with specialized fields, mysterious languages, and complicated machines. The scientific method and scientific standards are available to all for use in their daily lives, not just to a new caste of academic priests. This should be kept in mind whenever anyone tries to browbeat you into doing something that you do not understand on the grounds that it is in some way "scientific."

The best way of understanding the scientific method as it applies to the study of human affairs is to view it as an answer to the question, By what standards does one evaluate an image of the human condition? There are four general standards for evaluating a vision of the human condition—accuracy, consistency, adequacy, and fruitfulness. These standards will each be discussed in turn.

ACCURACY

Probably the first response that most people would give to the question of evaluating images of the human condition is that they would apply a standard of truth. Usually what is meant by "truth" is factual accuracy. Do the word pictures that make up the vision describe what is really going on? For example, is Marx correct that there is a connection between class position and what people think about human relations? This kind of question, which at first appears easy to answer, hides a great many difficulties. Awareness of these difficulties allows a person to apply better the standard of factual accuracy to his image of the human condition.

Many people in the United States have a love affair with facts. This attitude is strikingly illustrated by Sergeant Friday, hero of the old television police drama, "Dragnet." Friday would spend his time tracking down criminals by interviewing witnesses and other leads. Whenever the individual who he was questioning would wander off the subject and start talking about personal opinions, feelings or theories, Friday would sharply say, "Just the facts!" There are many Sergeant Fridays in the United States, in all walks of life. They believe that the world rests on a solid bedrock of fact and become very impatient when they believe that their associates are ignoring this bedrock in favor of cloudlike "pleasing illusions." Yet Sergeant Friday should have known that the "facts" cannot be easily separated from opinions, feelings, or theories.

A good police detective knows that the facts are rarely obvious. Suppose a murder has been committed in front of a crowd of people. Perhaps the most that everyone in the crowd will agree with is that someone is dead. When the police are summoned, some people in the crowd will tell them that the killing was surely done in self-defense. Others will say that it was certainly the case that cold-blooded murder was committed. Some will say that the killer was tall and thin, while others will state that he was short and fat. Others will not be sure whether it was a man or a woman who did the killing. "Positive identification" of the killer will prove to be very difficult, as will even the description of the killing itself. As time goes on, memories of the event will become vague in the minds of onlookers or, worse, some of them will begin to believe that they are certain about things that at the time of the killing they were in doubt about. When it comes time to question "leads," so-called facts will often count for far less than "theories." There will be an attempt to determine motivation for the killing. Thus, part of the investigation will focus on the opinions that people have about the suspects, their ideas about possible motivations and even their feelings. (The amazingly different interpretations and recollections on the Watergate-related events are another vivid example of this phenomenon.)

The situation becomes far more complex when a suspect is arrested and tried for the crime. The defense may attempt to argue that there was not any crime committed, and that the killing was in self-defense. Or, it may argue that while the defendant did the killing he was insane at the time. Of course, it may argue that the defendant is not the killer, and try to "prove" its case by questioning the testimony of prosecution witnesses, bringing in witnesses of its own, questioning the motives brought up by the prosecution and calling upon "expert" witnesses to demonstrate that it was "impossible" for the defendant to have committed the murder. The prosecution will call upon its own set of "facts" which will often be completely at odds with those brought up by the defense. Some of the so-called facts relied upon by each side will be considered "evidence" and, thus, will be allowed to count towards a verdict. Others will not be allowed into evidence and will not be allowed to count towards a verdict, because they will not measure up to a legally valid fact. It is the presence of rules of evidence that points up more than anything else in the administration of law the difficulty of determining the "facts" in complex human situations.[3]

Another indication that fact is not always obvious is the care with which juries are often selected. Each side tries to get people on the jury who are predisposed toward its case. They do this not because they believe that human beings are cynical creatures who invariably let the interest in truth be obscured by passion, but because they know that prejudices and predispositions color one's interpretations of the "facts" and lead to selectivity in which facts will be deemed important. When a verdict is reached in a complex case, then, it is not at all certain that the relevant facts were brought out, or considered in reaching the verdict.

Why spend so much time on an example from legal administration when the aim is describing the role of fact in science? The answer is that fact is no more obvious in science than it is in law. Before it is possible to get the facts, it is necessary to know what one is looking for. This means that the facts normally *succeed* rather than *precede* images of the human condition.[4] Since this idea runs against what most people consider "common sense" it is necessary to inspect it more closely.

Problems in Acquiring Facts   When Sergeant Friday asked for "just the facts" he got both more and less than he bargained for. He got more than he bargained for because the people who responded to his questions gave him their interpretations of the event along with the "facts" about it. He got less than he bargained for because he conducted the investigation with a certain view of what was relevant. Thus, his questions were determined by a notion of what it is important to find out when one is conducting a criminal investigation. This means that he was likely to miss out on some facts that did not fit into the framework of his questions. The scientist studying human affairs is in no different position from Sergeant Friday. If he is in search of the "pure facts" he also gets more and less than he bargains for.[5] He gets more than he bargains for because, like Sergeant Friday, he is normally considering the interpretations that people give to events as well as the events themselves. This makes him differ somewhat from the natural scientist who, if he is studying squirrels, does not have to take account of the squirrel's beliefs about his own behavior. He gets less than he bargains for because he is always approaching his study with a certain framework of questions in mind. It is this aspect of a framework that is most important in the judgment that facts succeed rather than precede images of the human condition.[6]

In the second chapter we showed that in the twentieth century some social thinkers have shifted from concern with the problem of order to an interest in the problem of freedom. This shift will illustrate how facts tend to follow frameworks or images. Those social thinkers who are most concerned with the problem of order tend to look for facts that will support proposed solutions to this problem. For example, those who believe that order is maintained through exploitation will look for the instances in which human beings are controlled by such means as force, fraud, and bribery.[7] On the other hand, those who believe that order is maintained through adherence to common standards will look for the instances in which people appear to obey rules on their own volition.[8] They will weave their responses to their questions around the facts that they have gathered in the net of their initial concepts. Similarly, those interested in the problem of freedom will look for facts that will support solutions to this problem. Rather than focusing attention on how people come to behave in predictable patterns, they are concerned with how people surmount obstacles to self-determination.[9] This conceptual searchlight casts a beam over a different set of facts than the set revealed by the problem of order. For example, rather than force, fraud, bribery, or rote learning, those concerned with the problem of freedom tend to look at the dynamics of criticism; how people can burst through the structures of myth in which they are often enveloped.[10] For those seeking solutions to the problem of order, the process of criticism, or self-examination, might not even appear to be a fact. Some of these thinkers seem to be unaware that such a process occurs. On the other hand, those seeking solutions to the problem of freedom may tend to minimize or even ignore the role of such factors as bribery (subtle and overt) or of praise and blame in determining behavior. They will just not "see" these processes taking place, and may reduce the human drama to an interplay between force and freedom.[11]

Processes of Assimilating Facts The preceding discussion should make it clear that human beings are not born with the capability of knowing the facts. Although none of us knows what it is like to be a newborn infant, it is probable that experience is originally a humming and buzzing confusion.[12] The infant does not distinguish himself from the world and others until adult human beings initiate a process of learning.[13] As the child grows up he learns how to carve up his experience into slices and to tag those slices with names supplied by language. Names, or words, can be detached from particular experiences and carried over to new ones that are similar in certain respects. When it appears that a set of names is appropriate to a given experience, the person who makes that judgment claims that he has observed or discovered a fact. This interpretation can be disputed by someone else, who applies a different set of names to what he calls the same experience. For example, two witnesses to a murder may differ on the description of the killer. One may say the killer is a light-skinned, blue-eyed individual, and the other may say the killer is a swarthy, brown-eyed person. Neither of the witnesses, however, could have observed the "fact" had they not learned how to carve up the flux of experience into slices through the use of language.

The realization that facts do not appear in human experience apart from language should not lead to extreme skepticism and despair about one's ability to interpret experience. Rather, it should put one on guard against too ready acceptance of the "facts" in any particular case. The first reason that it is wise to be on guard is that without the aid of intelligence, the human senses are quite unreliable. They are mainly unreliable because of prejudices and predispositions that people carry with them into situations. A prejudice against dark-skinned individuals might lead someone to see a killer as someone with a dark skin even if the killer was light-skinned.[14] The second reason why it is wise to maintain a healthy skepticism is that particular sets of names are intertwined with each judgment of fact. The Marxist tends to see conflict everywhere in social life, while the pluralist tends to see competition and basic agreement. When somebody states the "facts" about a particular social situation, such as a strike or a family quarrel, it is wise to check out his vision of the human condition, if this is possible, and see if this influences his judgment.

One of the most common devices of propaganda and advertising is to play on the naive belief in "just the facts." The propagandist or mass manipulator who can convince his audience that there are pure facts apart from concepts, frameworks, theories, prejudices, predispositions, opinions, and visions has won much more than half his battle. The reason why he tends to cultivate the belief in pure facts should be clear by now. If people believe that there are facts apart from interpretations, then it becomes possible to play on prejudices that they are not always aware of. The cards can be stacked by building such assumptions into the propaganda as "the underdog is always right," "whites should feel guilty about the past slavery of blacks," "women are primarily creatures of emotion," and many other "principles" that may appear absurd when examined systematically. These assumptions are never stated outright, but lurk right beneath the surface of so-called factual reports. Also, if one believes that there are pure facts, there is no need to examine the vision of the human condition held by the propagandist. For example, a propagandist concerned with damaging the reputation of a government that has come to power through revolution may sketch a portrait of the revolution in which the execution of the members of the old ruling class, the disruption of everyday life and the dictatorial methods of the new governers are stressed. The image of the human condition underlying this portrait may be that revolutions are always greater evils than whatever preceded them, and that forms of government should only be changed peacefully.[15] Thus, the propagandist selects "facts" to fit his underlying image of the human condition without ever informing his audience about that image. Of course, he leaves out those "facts" that would tend to cast doubt on the accuracy of his image, such as reports of the abuses of the old regime, the low standard of living and extreme inequalities of wealth that were present in the past, and the failure of the old ruling class to respond to peaceful movements for improvement. The propagandist hopes that his audience will accept his portrait of the horrors of the revolution as the relatively complete description of the "facts of the case" and that they will not look any farther for other facts or for his underlying image of the human condition.

Separating Facts from Opinion   Holding the belief that it is possible
to get "just the facts" without an overlay of interpretation makes one
an easy mark for propaganda and shows that one has little respect for
his thought processes. The scientific attitude toward studying the human condition goes in the very opposite direction from asking immediately for the facts. The first step in scientific investigation is to make
sure of the question that one is asking. Suppose that one is asking the
question: Should the federal government support day-care centers for
the children of working mothers?[16] Before this question can be answered yes or no, it must be analyzed and clarified. First, it is necessary
to understand what is meant by the term "should." Usually, it refers
to urging adoption of those actions that are required to realize a vision
of the good society held by the person who is using the term. So, the
first step that must be taken is not to get any facts, but to see whether
or not day-care centers are part of one's vision of the good society. If
it turns out that they are, the next question is whether or not the
federal government is the proper agency to support day-care centers.
The word "proper" here usually means: Will federal funding be an
efficient means to the end of day-care centers without blocking the
realization of other aspects of the good society? Alternative answers
to this question will be debated fiercely by opposing sides. Those in
favor of day-care centers will point to the successes of the federal
government as an agent in supporting programs, while those opposed
to them will point to failures. Both sides will be drawing upon "facts"
to support their cases. In order to interpret these "facts" it is necessary
to have a standard of what makes for success and failure. This is not
a factual judgment either. Those opposed to day-care centers will try
to show that every deviation from some ideal of a perfect government
program is a dismal failure, while those in favor of them will try to show
that slight improvements over past conditions are glowing successes.
One must decide what he means by success. Only after this is done is
it time to look at the "facts" and, perhaps, for them. In this case, the
facts will be examples of similar programs that have been attempted
in the past and a determination of their results. All of those results will
not be investigated; only those consequences that bear on the definition of success and failure that has been chosen. Thus, the "facts"
follow the framework supplied by the questions. Out of the enormous
complexity of human events, the questions that one asks illuminate
slices of activity and identify them as facts.[17]

Once a person has a good idea of the facts that he is seeking, the
accuracy of these facts becomes extremely important. This is why in
the natural sciences and in some parts of sociology the development

of means of accurate measurement is considered a central aspect of investigation. The significance of accuracy can be illustrated by following the example of day-care centers further. Suppose that one has decided to find out whether or not federally supported programs similar to a possible program of day-care centers have been successful. The major task now is to identify the results of these programs. These results will be framed by such questions as whether or not the federal monies got spent on the people who were supposed to benefit from them, whether the projected benefits actually accrued, and whether there were unintended consequences, favorable and not, of the federal support. There are many ways of attempting to gain answers to such questions, some of which will be discussed in the next chapter. However, what is important at this point is to note that, in the absence of factual accuracy, one will not be able to make an intelligent decision about the desirability of federal funding for day-care centers. Accuracy will be judged according to certain standards set up within the methods of determining "facts." Each method will have its own standards for determining what kinds of observations are fit to enter the realm of fact. Some methods will consider as fact what appears in official documents, firsthand reports, travelogues, newspaper and magazine articles, and other such sources. Other methods will consider as fact what is personally observed by the investigator after he has familiarized himself directly with the human activity he is studying. Still other methods will state that facts are what appear in census reports, while others will claim that facts are found in responses to questionnaires. Finally, some methods will admit as full scientific facts only those activities observed under experimentally controlled conditions. Whatever the standards, of course, the sociologist will attempt to be as accurate as possible according to those standards.

Scientific Inquiry and Fact Finding   The interest of scientists in factual accuracy is another way that they are distinguished from propagandists and advertisers. The scientist is often more concerned with the ways in which the facts were arrived at (their grounds) than with their content. If the "facts" merely represent wishful thinking on someone's part they are worthless from the scientist's viewpoint, unless he happens to be studying wishful thinking. On the other hand, the propagandist will use any facts that he can get hold of that appear to support his case. If he becomes concerned with accuracy it will not be because he is interested in furthering inquiry into the object of study, but because he is afraid if he becomes too inaccurate his opponents will expose him and he will lose effectiveness. Thus, the very propagandist who claims to offer "just the facts" is often engaging in as much distortion and outright fraud as he can get away with. At the same time, the scientist who is doubtful about ever reaching a point where he knows "just the facts" is engaged in a quest for accuracy.

This seeming paradox reveals something very important about scientific inquiry and the entire process of self-examination. Science begins with doubt rather than certainty, questions rather than answers, problems rather than solutions.[18] It does not rest with quick answers based upon wishful thinking, but it also does not remain in a mass of confusion and extreme skepticism. Rather, it attempts to disclose the principles of clear thinking and then apply them to the investigation of experience. When one applies these principles to the study of human activity, one is a sociologist. A statement of fact is an answer to the question, What happened? The scientist knows the obstacles in the way of answering that question and attempts to perfect methods for surmounting these obstacles. The propagandist merely attempts to cook up an answer which will serve his purposes and gain the belief of people who think that there are facts without interpretations.

EXERCISE

Listen to an advertisement on TV for a product you have used. Then determine which facts were used in the advertisement and attempt to discover the underlying image of the product the commercial seeks to convey. What facts about the product could you organize to give a different image from the one in the advertisement?

EXERCISE

Listen to or read about a debate on some political issue (for example, the Arab-Israeli conflict). Determine which facts are considered important by each side and then reconstruct the image each side has of the conflict. Which "facts" do the two images have in common? Which "facts" are included by one side and not the other?

PRECISION

Closely related to factual accuracy is precision. Precision has to do with the way in which ideas relate to observations. Suppose that someone says that "India and Pakistan have fought a war." This is a factual statement. However, before we know whether to judge this statement true or false, we must determine the meaning of the term "war." Does this term allow us to distinguish precisely between one kind of event and others? Perhaps the person who made the statement meant that war is "what happens when two groups or individuals do not like each other." This would be an imprecise or vague definition, because it is quite difficult to determine when two nations do not like each other. When does indifference end and disliking begin? What about mixed emotions? Do groups have feelings in the first place and, if they do, how are these feelings expressed? These are the kinds of questions that appear when social thinking is founded on vague ideas, rather than on precise relations between ideas and observations. Due to a healthy skepticism about facts, scientists attempt to maximize precision in their observations. They attempt to approach a situation in which any human being who understood the definition that they were using would reach the same decision about identifying a particular case as anyone else using that definition.[19] With this in mind, one sociologist has defined war as "armed extensive conflict between organized bodies of people, regarding themselves as politically sovereign and ethically entitled to assert by force their rights, which they claim to be blocked or invaded by their armed opponents."[20] This definition makes it far easier to determine whether or not there is a "war" going on than the definition of war as "what happens when two groups or individuals do not like each other."

Does the preceding discussion mean that one definition of war is "better" than the other? Is the definition given by the sociologist the "real" definition of war? What if one does not like this sociologist's definition of war because it does not include such events as "wars" between teenage gangs and bands of organized criminals? These questions lead to the conclusion that, until other information is provided, the sociologist's definition of war is better than the other only in the sense that it is more precise. One could define "war" as the number of clams in Mrs. Murphy's chowder. This would be a precise definition, but it might not be altogether adequate.

The Importance of Definitions A definition identifies a slice of experience and attaches a name to it. This means that no definition is more "real" than any other. If someone defines "war" as the number of clams in Mrs. Murphy's chowder it is not enough to answer that he has not "really" defined war. What could the word "really" mean in this case? It could only mean that experience comes to human beings as a set of pigeon holes that put everything in place and leave a place for everything. This would mean that education is a process of learning to pigeonhole everything in its proper place. Once a person had mastered the great filing system of the mind, he could sit back with a contented smile on his face with the knowledge that nothing in the world could ever disturb him again, because he would know where to file every future experience. For someone who adopts this view of experience, the present book is useless. The present book is based upon the idea that experience is a continually shifting and dynamic process with many facets. According to this perspective, there are no "real" definitions because language is like a net cast over experience with the purpose of catching certain slices or phases of this experience and holding them for future reference. "In the beginning was the word" because, without the word, experience would be merely a formless and chaotic flux.[21]

Although there are no "real" definitions, some definitions are better than others, in the sense that they are well adapted to the solution of particular problems or to the attainment of particular goals. If the goal is understanding what happened between India and Pakistan, defining war as the number of clams in Mrs. Murphy's chowder is not as useful as defining war in some more traditional way. It is only after the purpose of inquiry has been defined that the standard of precision can be applied meaningfully to definitions. Thus, if the purpose is to describe what happens between teen-age gangs when they come into conflict, it may be quite useful to define the term "war" to include these events.

Propaganda and Precision When it comes to precision, propagandists work in the very opposite way from scientists. They are usually imprecise and they also attempt to make people believe that there are "real" definitions of happenings. One staple of propaganda is to stretch the ordinary meaning of words to include new events. The aim is to have the audience associate the event with the emotion that normally accompanies the word. For example, when people raise their voices during a demonstration, administrators say that their words are "violent." This stretches the ordinary meaning of violence to include loud voices, and has the aim of turning opinion against the demonstrators. Another staple of propaganda is to narrow the ordinary meaning of words to exclude new events. For example, when administrators call in police to break up demonstrations and the police begin clubbing the demonstrators, the administrators may state that clubbing is not "violence" but "self-defense."[22] This narrows the ordinary meaning of violence to exclude the use of force by police, and has the aim of turning opinion in favor of the police and the administrators. In such cases, the underlying definition of violence seems to be "any activity the administrators do not like." This is quite an imprecise definition and does not allow people to hold particular slices of experience for future reference.

Propagandists also attempt to convince people that certain definitions are more "real" than others. Such attempts are usually made when the propagandist is trying to use words that have highly favorable emotional associations attached to them. For example, suppose a group of Christians such as the Campus Crusade for Christ or the Jesus People is attempting to convert radical students to their creed. They will claim that Christianity is truly "revolutionary" whereas demonstrations are not "really" revolutionary. On the other hand, such radical groups as the SDS will claim that they are the authentic revolutionaries while the Jesus People are "really" reactionaries. Both groups believe that the people they are trying to convert have favorable emotional associations with the term "revolution." Thus, instead of trying to convince people to join them by telling them what kind of experiences they can expect if they enter the given movement, they try to induce people to join them by throwing around words with favorable emotional associations. Perhaps this means that they believe that people would never join up if they knew what they were in for.[23]

Some people have been so disturbed by such propaganda tactics that they have suggested that only the precise use of ordinary language will prevent the domination of the mind by power groups.[24] This position is understandable in the light of the abuses noted above, but in the long run it is unsound. If experience is dynamic, then shifting and multidimensional ordinary language must change along with it if it is to express the new possibilities seen by free human beings. Such change demands experimentation and a relatively large measure of imprecision.

EXERCISE

Listen to or read a political speech or an advertisement. Were there any terms used so imprecisely that you could interpret the statement in more than one way? If so, determine what purposes the imprecision might serve.

CONSISTENCY AND COHERENCE

In the discussion of precision we noted the tendency of propagandists to expand and narrow the definitions of terms to suit their particular purposes. What would be called violence if done by the opposition would be called peaceful advocacy if done by the propagandist's allies. What would be called self-defense if done by the propagandist's allies would be called violence if done by the opposition. In the first case the definition of violence is expanded to include shouting. In the second case it is contracted to exclude the use of force by one's allies. This shifting of definitions should not be confused with inconsistency. When definitions are shifted, the same word is used to mean more than one thing. When definitions are inconsistent or contradictory, they both affirm and deny the same thing.

A contradictory claim is a claim that a statement and its negation are both true. An example of a contradictory definition is, "War is what happens when two groups dislike one another and not what happens when two groups dislike one another." An example of a contradictory claim is, "India and Pakistan fought a war, and India and Pakistan did not fight a war." It is clear that war cannot be both what happens when two groups dislike one another. It is clear that India and Pakistan could not both fight a war and not fight a war. It is important to note that war could be defined as what happens when two groups dislike one another or not what happens when two groups dislike one another. In this case the term "war" would be a synonym for the word "everything." Similarly, one could truthfully claim that either India and Pakistan fought a war or India and Pakistan did not fight a war, though it might take some figuring out to determine why a person would make such a statement.

Scientists attempt to avoid contradiction in both their definitions and their claims. Given the examples above, this would seem to be an easy task. However, in difficult and complex studies contradictions often creep in, thereby rendering much of the work nonsense. For example, someone may claim that human beings seek pleasure and avoid pain. Discussion may proceed for a time on this basis until someone else asks, "What about masochists who seek to be hurt?" Perhaps the response will be, "Well, for that kind of person pain *is* pleasure." Is this response contradictory to the original statement that human beings seek pleasure and avoid pain? A yes-or-no answer to this question is impossible until definitions are checked. If by the term pleasure the person means "that which is sought by people" and by pain he means "that which is not sought by people" he is not in contradiction, for he has simply been arguing that people seek what they seek and avoid what they avoid. This kind of argument is tautological, or true by definition. If, however, by the term pleasure the person means a specific feeling and by pain a different feeling, then he is in contradiction.

Scientists attempt to avoid contradiction because they aim at accurate and systematic description of experience. Propagandists will attempt to employ contradiction whenever they believe it will serve the interests that they are trying to promote. For example, some religious promoters will define God as a supreme Person ruling the universe and then state that every person seeks God. If confronted by a person who claims that he does not believe in God nor seek God, the promoter will ask, "Well, do you seek anything?" The person may answer, "Yes, I seek social justice." Then the religious promoter will respond, "Well now, social justice is your God and so you do seek God after all." This kind of argument is contradictory, because the religious promoter will not usually admit that he means by God anything that human beings seek. However, though the propaganda is contradictory, it is sometimes successful in converting unsuspecting souls.

Even more serious than actual contradiction is the tendency of much propaganda to undermine the standard of consistency itself. Matching the misguided quest for "just the facts" are such phrases as "foolish consistency," "cold and unfeeling reason," and "life is larger than logic." When people use such phrases it means that either they want to avoid undertaking the task of self-understanding or that they want to prevent others from undertaking this task. It is obvious that if people can be persuaded that maintaining consistency is foolish, heartless, or stupid they will tend not to look seriously upon contradictions when they appear in propaganda. This does not mean that a person should never change his plans or intentions. There is nothing contradictory about planning to become an engineer and later deciding to become a sociologist, or vice versa, as long as one realizes that a plan has been changed. There is also nothing cold and unfeeling, or dead, about attempting to be consistent. In fact, the attempt to fashion a consistent image of the human condition can be one of the most exciting adventures in thought, because the very points where contradictions are detected are usually the points where one is most resistant to change and most self-protective.[25] A very good way of understanding oneself or another thinker is to track down the contradictions. They will appear at the points where a person is unwilling to surrender a principle even though it is confronted with a sharp challenge. Examples of such principles are the ideas that all people seek pleasure and avoid pain or that God is a supreme Person ruling the universe who everybody seeks. Since scientists aim at accurate and systematic description of experience, they are willing to surrender or alter principles when they stand in the way of attaining this aim. Since the science of human affairs is the process of self-understanding and clarification, everyone who would seek self-understanding must be scientific in the sense of trying to avoid contradiction.

EXERCISE

You are probably familiar with the views on society and social relations held by one or both of your parents. Are there any contradictions or inconsistencies in these views? (For example, do your parents proclaim a belief in equality and then say that you can only date people from certain groups?) If you can find any inconsistencies, can you account for them by some motive of self-protection? Can you account for them in any other ways?

A good indication of the importance of consistency in human existence is that a familiar way of dominating people is to make them and others believe that they are incapable of consistency. Thus, racist snobs have spread the belief that blacks are incapable of reasoned thought, and some people in the middle class have spread the belief that working people are incapable of reasoned thought.[26] A very large number of people believe that old people naturally become "senile" and, therefore, incapable of reason. Another large number of people believe that women are "basically" creatures of emotion. Many women seem to like this idea and claim a right to be inconsistent. In accepting this badge of inferiority they are playing a cheap trick on themselves and on other women in an attempt to be cute and win concessions in a fundamentally unequal relationship. As was pointed out in the first chapter, the greatest barrier to self-understanding is contempt for the mind. The invariable result of such contempt is exploitation.

Closely related to the standard of consistency is the standard of coherence. A coherent description is one in which the names used in describing the events exhaust the subject, are about the same thing, and do not overlap one another. For example, suppose that one was describing families and divided them into families containing more than one married pair and their offspring (extended families) and families containing no more than one married pair and their offspring (nuclear families). These categories would not overlap, would exhaust the subject, and would be about the same thing. Suppose the category of nuclear family was dropped from the system of classification and in its place was substituted the category of "happy family." Now the categories would overlap, would not exhaust the subject, and would be about different things. They would overlap because some extended families might also be happy. They would not exhaust the subject because some families with no more than one married pair might be unhappy. They would not be about the same thing since one category would define families according to happiness and the other category would define families according to the number of married pairs contained.

Scientists seek coherence in their descriptions of experience. It is only with a coherent system of names that facts can be accurately identified. Imagine a person doing research on the family with only the categories *extended family* and *happy family* available to him. Imagine further that this researcher could classify each family he observed in only one of the two categories. Where would he put the *happy extended family*? Where would he put the *unhappy nuclear family*? Coherence, of course, is not prized by the propagandist. In fact, he thrives on incoherence. For example, a popular form of propaganda is the statement that there are only two kinds of societies in the present world—i.e., capitalist democracies and communist dictatorships. Someone who accepts this classification system has a hard time classifying a capitalist dictatorship, a communist democracy, or some other form of society such as a socialist democracy. Usually the propagandist wants the individual to believe that all capitalist societies are democracies and all communist societies are dictatorships. Thus, he wants to cloak capitalism in the garments of democracy. This example shows how important it is to inspect carefully the coherence of one's categories. Without a coherent set of names many significant experiences will be lost to awareness and others will be hopelessly distorted.

ADEQUACY

Suppose that a person worked up a vision of the human condition that was factually accurate, precise, consistent, and coherent. Suppose further that another individual also worked up such a vision, but that it was different. How would someone be able to judge between these two visions? Both would meet the formal standards of science perfectly, but both would select out of human experience different facts and different categories. The first impulse might be to say that, as long as both visions are accurate and consistent, the choice among them is simply a matter of taste. That it is possible to take this position is proven by its popularity in the contemporary world. However, it is worthwhile to attempt to find out whether one can do any better than arbitrary whim.

One way of going beyond mere taste is to argue that the task of science is to explain the events that occur in experience. The general form of explanation is by a law linking two kinds of events together in time. An example of a law is that the volume of a gas increases in direct proportion to the amount of heat. This law allows one to explain particular cases of gases expanding in volume, as well as to predict when and how the volume of gases will expand in the future.

For most of its history, sociology has been a search for laws of human activity. Up until this time, few if any laws have been discovered. Despite, however, the lack of success on this score, the majority of sociologists continue to claim that their efforts are justified by the future possibility of a set of interrelated laws of human activity.[27] Sociologists point to physical science as an example of what they might accomplish. They are particularly impressed by two features of physical science. First, the physical sciences contain an interrelated body of generalizations that describe the succession of events accurately enough to be used for prediction of future events. This is the element of law in physical science. Second, the laws in physical science are derived logically from a small set of axioms. These axioms present a model of physical motion. Many sociologists hope for a future science of human activity that would be logically derived from a small set of axioms presenting a model of human behavior. In such a science of human activity, all the various generalizations about behavior would be tied together by this model. If sociologists have been thus far unsuccessful in discovering laws of human activity, they have been doubly unsuccessful in relating the tendencies that they have observed to a model of human behavior contained in a small set of axioms.

It is not our intention to question the presence of regularities and tendencies in human affairs. Without such regularities and tendencies human existence would be a mere chaos and we could not be even writing this book with the expectation that it could be read and understood. Thus, the search for trends, tendencies, and other regularized successions, even if it does not end in the discovery of universal laws, should be encouraged by those seeking self-understanding. Accurate description of such tendencies is of great help in supporting or casting doubt upon particular visions of the human condition. For example, suppose a person is organizing a vision of the human condition around the relations between men and women, and claims that the growing number of divorces is due to the fact that women have begun doing "men's work." The validity of this vision would be in doubt if it was found that the divorce rate was lower in marriages where the wife was doing work traditionally restricted to males than in other marriages. One need not adopt a physical science model of the human sciences to affirm that statements about regularized successions in human affairs should be substantiated.

While substantiated generalizations are valuable to a human science, the attempt to devise a small set of axioms about human behavior from which these generalizations could be logically derived contradicts the very principles upon which this book is based. The process of clarification, generalization, relativization, and commitment is a process of freedom. It is based on the premises that human beings can keep part of their experience detached from immediate social requirements, can say no to commands, can choose among alternatives, and can create new alternatives. It is this process that defines human existence rather than some axiom like "men seek pleasure and avoid pain." One begins work in the human sciences either with the principle of freedom or the principle of determinism. If one accepts the principle of determinism, one will seek a small set of axioms from which all human behavior can be derived. If one adopts the principle of freedom one will see the human sciences as opportunities to expand awareness of one's situation.

Adequacy: A Standard for Evaluation   If one adopts the principle of freedom, it becomes necessary to supply an alternative standard to logical derivation from a small set of axioms for evaluating images of the human condition. Such a standard can be called "adequacy." By adequacy is meant the degree to which the vision makes sense of one's situation by knitting the various parts of it into a meaningful whole. This is not the same as evaluating thought according to whether one "likes" it or not. One may like an image of the human condition which ignores such experiences as death, exploitation, and war, but such an image will not be adequate because it is not comprehensive enough to take account of these factors. Further, the judgment of adequacy only makes sense when applied to visions that tend toward factual accuracy, precision, consistency, and coherence. However, there is an element of "insight" in judgments of adequacy that is not reducible to the formal standards of science or to comprehensiveness. This kind of insight is similar to the appreciation of painting. In painting, the artist organizes parts of the visual field. He selects out certain colors and forms, and leaves out others. He puts some colors and forms in the foreground and others in the background. A similar process takes place in creating images of the human condition. The human scientist selects certain experiences such as economic production or religious activity to compose his vision, and he leaves out others. Given his selection from the whole mass of human activity, he places stress on these features in an order of significance. The result is an image into which the reader or listener can imaginatively enter and find a place for himself. For example, if Marxism is considered in this way, the individual enters into the image as the member of some economic class and is able to appreciate his situation with respect to others in a new way. By doing this he has gained an insight into the relation of his activity to the wider activities going on around him.

What does the term significance mean with respect to visions of the human condition? It is a judgment of what that image means for one's entire existence as a human being. Some images are grotesque in the sense that they appear to distort human existence even if they are relatively accurate and consistent. For example, we find the vision of the human condition presented by prohibitionists to be grotesque. It is difficult for us to make sense out of our lives by organizing all our experiences around the supposed evils of consuming alcoholic beverages. The same goes for visions of the human condition organized around the benefits of eating "organic" foods or of taking conscious-ness-expanding drugs. Yet some people find these visions, or others like them, to be more than adequate. From these differences in judg-ment we do not draw the conclusion that "beauty is in the eye of the beholder" or that "it is all a matter of taste." There will always be differences in vision, but some people arrive at their visions through rigorously undertaking the process of self-understanding, while others arrive at their visions somewhat impulsively. For us, it is this process that makes all the difference, because we are not so vain as to believe that our vision of the contemporary world is the most adequate one.

It is merely the most adequate one that we have been able to develop over time and through efforts at self-understanding.

Adequacy can be judged to some extent by the richness of a vision and its plausibility. One vision is richer than another when it provides a greater number of reasons why people might relate to one another in certain ways. For example, an account of conflict between ethnic groups which included motivations and reasons drawn from economic competition, power relations, religious rivalry, and language difference would be richer than one employing only language difference. A vision is more plausible than another when, through using imagination, one can make sense of the reasons given for a social relation in terms of one's own actual and possible experience. Plausibility is far less precise a standard than richness and should be used with care. One may find an account of human existence implausible merely because of one's own narrow experience or the limitations of one's imagination.

There is a way of making plausibility somewhat more precise—a kind of standard that one can use to approach a measure of adequacy. Suppose that two competing visions of the human condition are to be judged; suppose further that the advocate of one of these visions has understood only the image he favors, while the advocate of the other vision has understood both images. One would tend to trust the judgment of the person who had understood both images rather than that of the person who had understood only one.[28] This standard, of course, is merely a rough measure, because it is very difficult to judge whether or not one understands a vision of the human condition in its most important implications. The standard is most useful in picking out those who are making no effort at wider understanding, but who instead resist the process of self-understanding and prefer to rest content with whatever prejudices they happen to have. Ultimately, adequacy can be tested only through insight.[29] It should be obvious by now, however, that if insight is to be valuable it must be hedged by high intellectual standards such as factual accuracy, precision, consistency, coherence, and comprehensiveness, as well as by active commitment to the process of self-understanding. It is the use of such standards that distinguishes insight from taste. Perhaps the most important difference between the human sciences and propaganda is that the propagandist attempts to paint an image of the human condition based on wishful thinking, while the human scientist attempts to construct a vision based on accurate description of experience. Wishful thinking is the philosophy of the playpen and, unfortunately, of the board rooms of many corporation directors, military leaders, political bosses, and university trustees. From our perspective, the mark of maturity is the application of science to one's own life. Propagandists attempt to convince people that science is rigorous, dull and painful. They try to make them believe that to be scientific means that one turns into a robot or a human computer. Nothing could be further from the truth. While there is no doubt that science is rigorous, the rigors of a human science are both exciting and enjoyable.

FRUITFULNESS

A human science is not merely a description of human activity, but also an invitation to action. There is no sharp distinction between thought and action in human existence—one must act to gain knowledge. Thus, the methods discussed in the next chapter are really modes of action. One uses knowledge in acting. Within one's everyday activity are displayed certain assumptions about human relations that constitute an active vision of the human condition. This means that, when one clarifies his image of the human condition, certain modes of action seem more reasonable to undertake than others. For example, the prohibitionist will be directed toward action aimed at ending the manufacture and sale of alcoholic beverages, while the Marxist will be oriented toward action aimed at changing the system by which the means of production are owned and controlled. Each vision of the human condition situates the person in a wider domain of action, points out likely allies and opponents, and suggests measures to be taken for altering or preserving human relations.

The fact that each image of the human condition suggests courses of action leads to judging these images on the basis of their fruitfulness for action. While the physical sciences provide predictions, the human sciences provide possibilities. The physical scientist will predict that if a gas is heated its volume will expand. The human scientist will offer the possibility of, for example, changing the ownership and control of the means of production through revolution. There will be alternative possibilities to that one, elements of choice will enter, and future human beings will experience them. Thus, the possibilities provided by visions of the human condition are really invitations to living experimentation with human existence. This judgment leads to the question of whether there is any standard according to which possibilities should be chosen. This is a moral question, and an answer to it is implied in all of the preceding discussion. Visions of the human condition should not be judged merely according to the quantity of possibilities they reveal for action, but according to whether these possibilities promise to extend and reinforce the process of self-understanding.[30] Thus, the most fruitful images of the human condition will be those that provide the most possibilities for expanding clarification, generalization, relativization and commitment. This judgment is inescapable once one has adopted a human science based on freedom rather than determinism.

Much propaganda runs counter to a human science with regard to orientation towards the future. Some propagandists make believe that the possibilities they offer are predictions. They say that people have a "chance not a choice" to join the inevitable revolutionary movement or whatever other movement they are promoting.[31] Other propagandists tell people that they are already "free" and that they have no obligation to undertake the process of self-understanding. Both kinds of propaganda are attempts to bring the future under control through manipulating human beings. The "chance not a choice" appeal is an attempt to make people believe that they have no control over their own destinies, but that they are pawns of "history." The appeal to irresponsible "freedom" is an attempt to convince people to stay just the way they are so that they can remain easy pickings for existing power groups. Thus, the propagandist is ultimately out to make people into either mindless fanatics obeying the directions of a leadership group, or else grasping children manipulated by advertising and public relations technicians. The first technique is primarily used by the totalitarian political movement, while the second is mainly used by the conglomerate organizations of the West.

Figure 3.1. STANDARDS FOR EVALUATING A VISION OF THE HUMAN CONDITION

Natural Science Model	Human Science Model
1. Factual Accuracy	1. Factual Accuracy
2. Precision	2. Precision
3. Consistency and Coherence	3. Consistency and Coherence
4. Explanation (Under what conditions do specific events appear?)	4. Adequacy (Do diverse events fall into a plausible context?)
5. Prediction (Under what conditions will specific events appear?)	5. Fruitfulness (Does the image reveal new possibilities for action?

EXERCISE

What kind of image of the human condition would be most appropriate for getting people to obey a leader blindly?

What kind of image of the human condition would be most appropriate for encouraging people to act freely?

What kind of image of the human condition would be most appropriate for discouraging action?

Devise or find images of the human condition that would mobilize masses of people to follow a program of action, that would encourage them to reach independent commitments and that would discourage them from acting politically.

HUMAN SCIENCE

Sociology is the science of the human condition. As a human science it incorporates standards for judging its own products. These standards fall into four general categories—factual accuracy, consistency, adequacy, and fruitfulness.

A factual judgment is an answer to the question: Did it happen? There are no such things as pure "facts" separated from some framework of interpretation and some procedures for observing experience. Scientists attempt to make clear the frameworks guiding their search for facts and the procedures they are using to gather them. Propagandists pretend that their messages communicate the bare facts of the case.

Consistency is the avoidance of contradiction. Scientists aim for consistency in their descriptions by attempting to avoid saying that the same statement is both true and false. Propagandists will be inconsistent when they believe that it will serve their aims and that they will be able to get away with it.

Adequacy is the quality of an image of the human condition that allows it to make sense out of the various aspects of human activity. Human scientists aim for adequacy by attempting to paint an image of the human condition that is comprehensive, significant and grounded in consistent reports of fact. Propagandists aim for adequacy by appeal to wishful thinking.

Fruitfulness refers to the possibilities for action revealed by a vision of the human condition. Human scientists aim for a fruitfulness that will expand the process of self-understanding. Propagandists attempt to convince people that they should obey the orders of some elite group or that they should stay the way they are.

The practice of human science within everyday existence demands adherence to the standards of accuracy, consistency, adequacy, and fruitfulness. Adherence to these standards demands both respect for one's mind and knowledge of the methods of inquiry that are used to gain knowledge about the human condition. Gaining confidence in one's mind requires overcoming the barriers to self-understanding discussed in the first chapter. The methods of gaining knowledge about the human condition are discussed in the next chapter.

4

METHOD WITHOUT MADNESS

How does one arrive at a fairly complete vision of the human condition? Most people pick up information from their families and friends, and from the mass media such as radio, television, and newspapers. Along with this information come built-in interpretations and, without too much awareness, most people adopt a mixture of these interpretations as their image of the human condition.

Much of what is presented as news on the evening newscast can be seen as attempts to portray the human condition. Astronauts' wives are stoic and prayerful as their husbands fly through space; neighbors of a tragedy-stricken family are quick to rally and give aid; parents try to block the busing of their children aimed at achieving integration; people flock to football stadiums in frigid weather but tend to avoid voting if drizzles are predicted for election day; the President says that we all must sacrifice for the public good; the struggle for women's equality involves integrating bars and becoming jockeys. . . . Critics of the mass media claim that the human condition presented through them is partial and distorted, and meant to make people favor the status quo. William Ernest Hocking wrote that most people today gain their images of the human condition from "accepted moulders of crowd opinion," like propagandists, advertisers, and public relations men.[1]

The partiality, distortions, and prepackaged interpretations built into the most available sources of information about the public situation make it necessary for those in search of self-understanding to push beyond these sources. It also becomes necessary to use more active and reliable methods than merely watching the evening news to gather and interpret information. Since generalization, relativization, and, ultimately, commitment are based upon beliefs, the quality and type of information about the human condition are very important. The procedures used to gather this information are generally referred to as methods. Thus, method is a series of regularized acts pursued to gain previously unknown knowledge. The specific content of the knowledge is, of course, not known (documenting the obvious is a pointless activity), but the means of gaining the knowledge are fully in awareness.

In some ways, using a method is like fishing. Putting a baited hook on a string, attaching it to a pole to extend it further, dropping it into the water and retrieving it when a tugging is felt are all procedures in a method for catching fish. Where and when one fishes and the type of hook, line, bait, and rod one uses depend upon the variety of fish one is after. Although the method is known, the goal is at best only partly known. The method may be specific to a given species of fish, but the particular fish, or even the size or weight, cannot be specified in advance. In sociology, as in fishing, one chooses a method to suit one's goal. We do not need a sophisticated angler to tell us that we will not catch a barracuda by dropping a worm on a safety pin tied to a string into a pond. Likewise in sociology, certain methods are more appropriate for gaining some kinds of knowledge than are others. For example, one would hardly use a self-administered questionnaire to find out from which social groupings suicides come.

The analogy between sociological methods and fishing breaks down, however, because fishing is usually considered a diversion rather than an authentic activity in which the result matters. While a sportsman is not concerned ultimately with the uses to which his catch will be put, a sociologist should be concerned with the uses that are made of his findings. The sportsman will often allow his equipment to determine his goal. Sociologists, on the other hand, choose their goal, which in turn determines to some extent the method they employ. If one is a serious inquirer, a particular method is not used because it is popular or easily funded, or because the researcher is skilled in its use, but because it seems likely to help solve a problem, to give new information. To let the means determine the end is to fall prey to what Abraham Kaplan refers to as the Law of the Instrument: "Give a small boy a hammer, and he will find that everything he encounters needs pounding."[2]

Before any method is selected, the first step is to answer the question, What do I want to find out about? Responses to this question may be as varied as how many people agree with a given position, under what conditions people discriminate against others, the effects of worker self-management in factories on efficiency and job satisfaction, and what factors influence police rioting. There are, of course, a multitude of other possible responses.

A second question to ask oneself is, Why do I want to know this information? For some researchers, unfortunately, the answer is "to enable some people to manipulate others" or, more simply, "because I am being paid to find this out." For others, the goal is to reduce human behavior to a series of universal laws. A purer approach is to take neither of these two positions, and do research to make available information that will help ourselves and others clarify, generalize, and relativize images of the human condition. Such research is intended to provide fruitful possibilities for action or, in C. Wright Mills' terms, "To make private problems public."

METHOD AND PARADIGM

After deciding upon a problem that one wants to investigate, an appropriate method must be selected. In some sciences, particularly branches of physics and chemistry, there is general agreement on the problems that should be explored and, usually, general agreement on the methods that should be used. Sometimes the relation between problem and method becomes so close in these disciplines that if someone comes up with a problem that is not approachable by the approved methods, the problem is declared illegitimate rather than the methods being declared inadequate. For example, I. Velikovsky was concerned with determining the origin of the earth and, by implication, of planetary bodies in general. His thesis was that the earth was formed through catastrophic events, and to demonstrate this thesis he used ancient literature, reports of myths, and sacred books. His use of the historical method to demonstrate an astronomical thesis met

with derision and harsh attacks from the leaders of professional astronomy. Professional astronomers normally use methods based on
telescopic observation and other physical techniques to conduct their
investigations and to decide between competing interpretations of
astronomical events. Since Velikovsky's thesis could not be demonstrated by these methods, the majority of professional astronomers
declared his thesis illegitimate.[3]

The astronomers could laugh and scream Velikovsky out of court
(whether or not they were justified in so doing) because they agreed
upon the problems that astronomers should explore and the methods
that they should use. When there is such agreement on problem and
method in a science, that science is said to have a *paradigm.* Thomas
Kuhn in *The Structure of Scientific Revolutions* describes the process
whereby a paradigm is established in a discipline and then reigns
supreme. For example, Newton's paradigm of physical motion unified
the science of physics for a time because it accounted for a great deal
of work being done at the time on the problem of motion and showed
an impressive application of mathematical technique to this problem.
Almost all paradigms have emerged victorious from a battle against
competitors. Thus, revolutions that attempt to install a new paradigm
are sometimes successful. Unsuccessful attempts have on occasion led
to the founding of new disciplines. Paradigms unify the activity of
scientific inquiry through a division of scientific labor. Theorists work
on the most general principles of the paradigm and attempt to make
them consistent. Experimenters test the implications of the general
principles to see whether or not they are factually accurate. Applied
scientists devise ways in which the principles can be used in attaining
human goals. In this way, a scientific "community," or discipline,
forms around a paradigm. The existence of paradigms and of "scientific revolutions" should lead to the recognition that science is by no
means a repository of absolute and changeless knowledge. There are
always intelligent and informed people who do not accept the given
paradigm of a discipline, and who carry on a continuous war with the
dominant group. Some of them are reactionaries, attempting to carry
on a paradigm that has been discarded by most professionals, while
others are revolutionaries out to install a new paradigm. They are at
the fringes of the discipline and do not accept the going division of
labor. They are also an embarrassment to the dominant group, and
attempts are made to discredit them and ride them out of the profession. This situation is one more reason not to worship science, but to
attempt to understand it as a kind of inquiry.[4]

SOCIOLOGY'S APPROACH

Sociology has no single paradigm and, thus, has a number of different methods. This fact has been bemoaned by some and applauded by others. Among those unhappy with the situation are people who view the disciplines of the natural sciences as successful and worthy of emulation. They would like sociology to be based on a small set of axioms about human behavior and would like theorists to test these axioms for consistency, experimenters to test them for factual accuracy, and applied sociologists to use them in engineering the attainment of goals. As we pointed out in the last chapter, there is no way of wishing this kind of paradigm into existence and many good reasons (centering on the assumption of human freedom) for abandoning the quest for it.

At least for the present, sociology does not have a paradigm in Kuhn's sense of the term. Instead of paradigms there are visions of the human condition. There is a very important difference between a paradigm and such a vision. Adopting one paradigm rather than another (for example, adopting the wave theory of light rather than the particle theory of light) does not immediately change one's activity in everyday life. However, seriously adopting one vision of the human condition rather than another (for example, adopting Marxism rather than Christianity) does immediately change one's everyday activity. It is this immediate effect on action that makes it both unlikely and undesirable for sociology to have a paradigm. There is little worry that sociology will gain a paradigm in the near future. There is little consensus in the field either on the nature of what knowledge is to be sought or on the method to be used.[5] This is why we have not given a formal definition of sociology in this book. We hope that you will be satisfied to unify the field through the process of self-understanding rather than through any select list of problems and methods.

Besides those who would like sociology to have a paradigm are those who, disappointed by the many methods now in use in sociology, believe that once the proper method is found, all important questions could then be answered.[6] The very fact that so many methods abound indicates that the "right" one has not yet been discovered. Taken at its worst, the idea that there is one method that will provide the key to knowledge reminds one of Aladdin's quest for the magic words that would open the treasure-laden vaults. The process of self-understanding, which guides this book, is no such set of magic words. It will not answer all the important questions, but it will, we hope, help you to discover which questions are important.

DIVERSITY OF METHODS

Many sociologists are not only content with the diversity of methods within the field, but claim that this variety is necessary for furthering scientific inquiry. There are two arguments given to support this position. The first is that the goals sociologists seek are so diverse as to require different methods to attain them. La Piere's classic study of discrimination demonstrates this point well. La Piere sent out a letter to restaurants asking whether or not they would serve persons of Oriental descent (the study was conducted well before the passage of civil rights laws barring discrimination in public accommodations). Many restaurants replied that they would not serve persons of Oriental descent. This use of the questionnaire method, however, did not end La Piere's study. His next step was to visit the restaurants accompanied by Orientals. This use of a participant method disclosed that many of the same restaurants that had stated that they would not serve Orientals actually did serve them when they showed up.[7] La Piere's study shows that sociologists can have multiple goals. One goal could be to find out whether or not people are willing to predict their own discriminatory acts. A second goal could be to find out whether or not they actually discriminate. A third goal could be to discover whether or not predictions match actions. The first goal can be attained through a questionnaire method, the second goal can be attained through a participant method and the third goal through a combination of the first two methods.

The second argument in favor of a variety of sociological methods centers around the notion of validity, or the question, Is what has been reported by one method "the real honest-to-goodness truth"? This is not a question of whether the particular researcher has been honest and skillful, because studies using the same methods can often be repeated and can serve as a control for dishonesty and incompetence. The issue here is the object of study itself—human beings. Whereas a wooden block will slide down an inclined plane in the same way whether or not it is being watched, whether or not it has done so before, or whether or not the researcher wants it to do so, human beings can respond to given situations by altering their activities. Webb and his associates describe several ways in which the objects being studied, people, tend to react to research settings in such a way as to make the results of investigations invalid.[8] What ties these responses together is that the people do not act as they would if they were not in a research situation.

A general reaction is often referred to as the "guinea pig effect," defined as an awareness that one is on display.[9] Such an awareness frequently influences people to act in ways that they might not have acted had they not been conscious of an observer. For example, how "naturally" do people act when they are being filmed on home movies or when their conversations are being taped? A more specific reaction to being observed is role selection, where the research subject assumes a role that he considers appropriate to the situation, but which he does not assume in everyday life. For example, many people take the role of "expert" when responding to questions posed by a sociologist about which they know very little. They agree or disagree with policies that they have never heard of and praise or condemn men of whose positions and deeds they are ignorant. D. Smith has documented this tendency with respect to public affairs and has shown, in the process, how willing people are to take the role of "expert" when they are actually ignorant.[10]

A partial solution to the fact that people respond to research settings is the use of multiple methods. Instead of using one method to find something out, many sociologists urge that several different methods be used to cross-check one another. For example, in order to find out which individuals and groups are most powerful in a city, some sociologists will analyze newspapers and other documents, conduct interviews, and administer questionnaires.[11] However, while the use of more than one method to increase the validity of findings improves accuracy, it is unlikely that it eliminates the uncertainty of social research. This uncertainty is ultimately rooted in the fact that human beings are continually reshaping their situations. They make judgments upon their surroundings and then act to alter the surroundings or their responses to them. This creative activity is at a maximum when people are most free and most involved in the process of self-understanding; thus, the more people make human science a part of their lives, the less they will behave like robots whose movements can be perfectly calculated in advance. Perhaps the most ingenious way in which certain kinds of social research can be made questionable is for people to learn about the methods of research and how and why they are used. With such knowledge they are able to make a decision about whether or not to cooperate with the researcher, and the researcher may never know about that decision.

Most generally, methods of social research are complicated by the fact that both human science and human existence are changing simultaneously. In the natural sciences there is no assumption that changes in the science are due to fundamental changes in reality. Astronomers do not claim that during the Middle Ages the sun revolved around the earth and that in modern times the earth has been revolving around the sun. Instead, they assume that the earth revolved around the sun during the Middle Ages but that human science was not far enough developed to recognize this. No such assumptions about the uniformity of social existence can be made by human scientists. As human beings continually remake their existence, human scientists must alter their perspectives. The matter is complicated even further by the fact that human science is part of human existence and contributes to changing it. The historian E. H. Carr captured some of these difficulties, which are faced by all human scientists, in a striking passage: "The historian is like an observer watching a moving procession from an aeroplane; since there is no constant or ascertainable relation between the speed, height and direction of the aircraft and the movement of the procession, changing and unfamiliar perspectives are juxtaposed in rapid succession, as in a cubist picture, none of them wholly false, none wholly true."[12] The only change that should be made in Carr's description is that while he is observing the procession, the human scientist is taking notes on it, writing them up as interpretations and then throwing them down as leaflets. Those leaflets affect activity, and the human scientist becomes part of the procession.

CLASSIFICATION OF METHODS

Like patterns of social thought, methods of social research can be classified in many ways. One popular scheme classifies methods according to the degree that they incorporate precise measurement. "Hard" methods produce information that can be described in terms of mathematical symbols while "soft" methods produce information that can only be stated in terms of everyday language. Usually, those who employ this classification consider themselves "hard scientists," out to realize the dream of a science of human behavior based on a small set of axioms. Perhaps the more serious among them are less scientists than romantics like Don Quixote, forever tilting at windmills. In the process, they have gathered a tribe of Sancho Panzas around them who are along for the game.

The classification of methods used here is adapted to the aim of illuminating the process of self-understanding. Methods will be arranged according to the degree to which the researcher is involved in creating his information. Those methods that do not involve the creation of information by the human scientist are open for anyone to use. These can be applied immediately by anyone attempting to clarify his vision of the human condition. Those methods that do involve the creation of information by the human scientist are not available to most people because they are costly and often require the cooperation of organizations to be used. Even if one had the money, the cooperation can usually be bought only by a "licensed investigator" with an advanced degree in hand. For the purposes of self-understanding, methods relying on created information will be discussed mainly with the intention of informing you about their goals and uses, so that you will know about them when you encounter them. It will then be your choice whether or not you cooperate with the sociologist.

The general methods of investigation will be discussed here. They are not exhaustive of all sociological methods, but give some idea of the range of the discipline. The *historical method* is the one most available for use by people in their everyday existence. It involves the imaginative synthesis of information about the human condition which has already been gathered or created by others. The "founding fathers" of sociology, such as Karl Marx, Max Weber, and Emile Durkheim, relied heavily on the historical method.[13] They analyzed reports, past and present, about human existence, and wove the information into patterns illuminating the structure of social relations. Related to the historical method, and really a part of it, is the demographic method, in which statistical data (such as birth and death rates) gathered by official and other organizations are analyzed.

The *participant method* involves some creation of information because the human scientist is present in the group which he is studying. The aim of this method is to illuminate the structure of social relations by carefully observing what goes on in a group. While it is not possible for a person to gain entrance into every group in which he is interested, he can start using the participant method immediately in the groups to which he belongs. Related to the participant method is nonparticipant observation, in which the human scientist is present with the group he is studying, but not a part of it.

The survey method involves the researcher in asking specific questions to people about aspects of the human condition. Here the investigator is deeply involved in creating information. At the extreme, the research subjects may never have even thought about the questions they are being asked before being confronted by the interview or the questionnaire. Related to the survey method is the depth interview, in which the researcher asks open-ended and general questions to subjects in order to find out underlying attitudes about given questions.

While the survey method usually gets at specific attitudes, the depth interview plumbs the underlying perspectives supporting these attitudes.

The method of *experimental small groups* involves the greatest creation of information by the human scientist. These groups usually exist only for the purpose of social research and are manipulated and observed by the very people who have brought them together. The sociologists who do small-group research believe that, by organizing a group under controlled conditions, they will be able to discover general patterns of human behavior.

The discussion of these frequently used methods will proceed from those in which the data has not been created by the human scientist to those in which the information must be created by the human scientist.

THE HISTORICAL METHOD

The historical method was the first one practiced by those who were identified as sociologists. All of the "Fathers of Sociology"— Comte, Marx, Spencer, Durkheim, Weber, etc.—used this method extensively. Thus, the historical method was begun by thinkers in the monist and pluralist traditions of social thought, who attempted to discover the causes of human activity in historical "forces." Natural-law thinkers were far more interested in identifying the nature of the good life through speculative reason and argumentation than they were in discovering pattern in history. For them, history was a shifting and imperfect flux masking the social ideal that could only be known through contemplation. Thus, the historical method came into use only in modern times. Its use is carried over, however, into process thought, and many recent thinkers such as Sorokin, MacIver, Veblen, Riesman, and Parsons have relied heavily upon the historical method.

The historical method is the basic sociological method. It is basic because the knowledge resulting from its use takes the form of a general picture of a society or an age, or a vision of the human condition. Before an investigator can even use one of the other methods he must have a general idea of the social context in which he is operating. He may not be fully aware of this context, but it will shape his work anyway. The aim of the historical method is to bring the social context, or the kinds of human relations and organizations in which people act, into sharp focus. For example, it is certainly possible for someone to conduct questionnaire research asking people what brand of toothpaste they use without being fully aware of his vision of the human condition. The historical sociologist would say that unless the investigator was aware that this research would only have meaning in an industrialized and capitalist economy in which consumers were interested in cleanliness (perhaps because of old religious associations that have been forgotten), the investigator would be more like an automation manipulated by social forces than a free inquirer.

The Concept of Ideal Types The historical method provides a context through the construction of ideal types.[14] In forming an ideal type, the sociologist selects out of a human situation those elements that seem to him to be the most significant, and then knits them together into a coherent description. This process is not mysterious and is, in fact, carried on by most people every day. For example, most people have an idea of "dictatorship" that they carry with them and use at the appropriate moments in conversation and thought. This notion of dictatorship does not refer to any particular government, though it may be based upon knowledge of a particular government. Also, no government may ever have existed that had all the traits present in the notion of dictatorship. Thus, an ideal type varies from observed social situations in two ways. First, it does not include as much as any particular social situation. Social situations are infinitely complex, and if a person decided to describe every aspect of only one he could not do it in ten lifetimes. Second, an ideal type contains some traits that particular cases may not contain. There might be no government with all the aspects of a complete dictatorship. It is also important to note that the term "ideal" does not mean here "desirable." One may use an ideal type of a dictatorship without believing that any dictatorships are desirable.

Some of these points can be illustrated by the ideal type of totalitarian dictatorship. A totalitarian dictatorship is usually defined as a regime in which a single party composed of an elite attempts through force and propaganda to suppress all other political movements and to bring all social groups under its centralized regulation.[15] This definition certainly does not include everything that goes on in any government, nor does any government fully show all the characteristics of the definition. Also, for most people, it does not define a desirable form of government. What use is it? The ideal type of totalitarian dictatorship has been very useful in identifying and highlighting certain tendencies in twentieth-century politics by bringing them together and fusing them in a description. By doing this it has allowed people to better orient themselves to events in the contemporary human condition. Many people who warn of totalitarian tendencies in the United States are guided in their perception of public affairs by this ideal type.

Construction of a good ideal type is artistic work. Totalitarian dictatorship could be defined as a regime in which a single party composed of an elite attempts through force and propaganda to suppress all other political movements and whose members wear the same colored shirts and smoke more cigars than the average man. The defect of this ideal type would be the mixing up of significant and trivial characteristics. However, there is no easy way to determine which characteristics of a complex social situation are significant and which ones are trivial. A serious study of history and current affairs, as well as a study of social thought, gives some guidelines for determining importance, but the genius of those who have brought the historical method to its fullest development has been in creating new and imaginative syntheses that have illuminated the context in which human action was occurring.

Frequently, practitioners of the historical method compare two or more ideal types to one another. In the nineteenth century, monists and pluralists set the context for most contemporary sociology by formulating ideal types of whole "societies." Frequently these images of societies were meant to represent "the way things used to be" and the "way things are now." These ideal types were compared to one another with respect to the different forms taken by the family, law, religion, politics, various aspects of the economy, the fine arts, and any other aspect of human existence that the thinker judged to be important. Each "society" was seen to have a distinctive kind of some basic characteristic that greatly influenced the other aspects of human existence described.

This was particularly the case for monistic thinkers who sought to describe the human condition in terms of a single primary factor. For example, Karl Marx found the crucial characteristic in the ownership of the means of production. This led to the distinction between "feudal societies" based on ownership of inherited lands, and "capitalist societies" based on the private ownership of industrial property. For Ferdinand Toennies the crucial distinction was whether the human will was based on love or on calculation.[16] Toennies felt that, in the premodern age, human relations were organized around the feelings of solidarity while in the modern age cold and calculating reason had taken over. Emile Durkheim contrasted two types of society on the basis of their social solidarity, or what held them together.[17] The first human societies were based on the sharing of common beliefs (mechanical solidarity) while more modern societies have been based on the interdependence springing from a division of labor in which men must trade products with one another in order to survive (organic solidarity).

Durkheim's ideal types have been very influential in contemporary sociology and show how a wide variety of information can be synthesized into a compelling description. In the archaic societies founded on a mechanical solidarity of uniform beliefs, people generally had similar skills and life-styles. Criminal law was basically repressive, punishing the offender for the outrage caused to society. This repression and continuous attempt to secure conformity was based on the fact that only through conformity could the society be held together. Modern society, founded on an organic solidarity of division of labor, is characterized by a diversity of skills and life-styles. Rather than being repressive, criminal law is restitutive, aiming at restoring the disturbed situation to harmony or equilibrium. The focus on restitution is necessitated because modern society survives through interdependencies of specialists. This society is likened to an organism in which the organs and tissues (lungs, heart, stomach, and so on) can only perform certain specific acts and cannot maintain themselves without the help of the other organs. Durkheim's point is that only through pooling their skills are people enabled to obtain what they "require." This analogy might lead one to conclude that, just as the various organs in their interdependence function for the ultimate good of the body, so people in their interdependence function for the ultimate good of society. This kind of analogy is quite misleading, because a society is a human process incorporating freedom rather than a living thing striving to maintain equilibrium. Further, even if society is treated like an organism, it is necessary to remember that diseased tissues do not contribute to the ultimate good of the body. Thus, if one really took the organic analogy seriously he might have to admit that just as surgery is sometimes required on the human body so may it sometimes be necessary on the body politic. It is unlikely that these implications are in the minds of propagandists and politicians like John F. Kennedy who say, "Ask not what your country can do for you; ask what you can do for your country."

The method of historical sociology results in a broad picture of a given society. Essentially it attempts to describe the human condition at a particular time and place. One may criticize such images of the human condition on the grounds that all comprehensive visions are somewhat inaccurate. In attempting to contrast different societies, similarities are frequently overlooked. For example, in criticizing Durkheim's vision, one can note that in modern times the division of labor is not total. There are roles, and skills that go along with them, that most people in a society fill, such as the general role of human being, child or parent. This criticism, of course, is aimed at extravagant claims for the self-sufficiency of the historical method, not at the proper use of the method.

A second criticism, aimed at some of those who have used the historical method, is that the possibilities for future action disclosed by some thinkers are very narrow. This narrowness seems to result from monistic theories which trace social changes to the operation of a single "force." Pluralistic and process patterns of thought escape this difficulty by assigning importance to a variety of factors and to the diversity of commitments undertaken by human beings. This multiplicity of factors, however, does not prevent pluralistic and process thinkers from using the historical method to create general visions of the human condition. It merely makes the quest for common themes more challenging and the resulting product more complex.

DEMOGRAPHIC METHOD

Closely related to the historical method is the demographic method. While the historical method is qualitative in the sense that it issues in ideal types expressed in words, the demographic method is quantitative because it uses statistical data. The demographic method is the analysis of statistical data originally collected by government and other agencies for purposes other than scientific research. These numbers include crime statistics, voting results, tallies of membership in religious and other organizations, and vital statistics (births, deaths, and so on). This means that those who use the demographic method do not create their own information.

Demographic sociology, which began with the works of the Belgian Quételet in the nineteenth century, uses statistics to compare and contrast social groups. Durkheim, for example, used this method to show that the incidence of suicide was higher among people with few stable social ties than among those with many social ties.[18] This example shows the strength and the weakness of the demographic method. Its strength is that, as long as the statistics are somewhat accurate, this method can quickly dispel sweeping and misinformed generalizations about social groups and add support to some visions of the human condition rather than others. Thus, Durkheim's research cast doubt upon the idea that suicide was strictly a matter of "mental illness." The weakness of the demographic method follows from its strength. While it can detect trends and tendencies, it must remain mute about particular individuals and their projects. One cannot leap from statistical tallies to statements about what factors "cause" people to act in certain ways. The absurdity of such leaps is shown by the fact that they can be made in contradictory directions. Given the statistic that crime rates are higher in predominantly black neighborhoods than in predominantly white neighborhoods, some people draw the conclusion that blacks are inherently "prone to violence" while others draw the conclusion that "poverty and discrimination are the true causes of crime."[19] Neither of these interpretive leaps is warranted merely by the statistics. They must be judged in terms of wider visions of the human condition in which the statistics are merely one piece of evidence.

Uses The historical and the demographic methods are the basic procedures for carrying out social research without creating data. Their most important feature is that they can be used immediately by any human being who can read and count. If the aim of this book is to encourage people to embark on an adventure in self-understanding and to be responsible for their images of the human condition, a key step in realizing this aim is to encourage people to use the historical and demographic methods themselves. Perhaps the best way to begin · to use these methods is for the individual to take a look at his stock of ideal types and to see whether or not they stand up to inspection. This is simply another way of saying that the first phase of self-understanding is clarification.

PARTICIPANT METHODS

In the historical and demographic methods, the human scientist weaves information gathered by others into a pattern of which the others might not have been aware. He is generally not present at the events that were the source of this information. In participant observation, on the other hand, the researcher is present at ongoing social activities. For example, if a sociologist is interested in studying the characteristics of work and social relations on an assembly line, he might become an assembly-line worker for a time and gain firsthand knowledge of the situation. For a study of mental hospitals he might take a job as an attendant in a mental hospital.[20] For an investigation of the lower-class black man's way of life, he might hang out with such people at their haunts.[21] Thus, the participant-observation method involves the researcher more in the creation of information than do the historical or the demographic methods.

The general problem of the participant method is that, while the activities witnessed by the sociologist are generally not undertaken at his direction, there is a question of how much influence his presence exerts on the content of activity. There is no way of knowing what the precise nature of the activity would be with the researcher absent. This problem has led to several attempts at solution. Most of them involve the use of secrecy and sometimes of outright deceit. The simplest measure is for the sociologist merely not to disclose his purposes to the group being studied. For example, if he is working on an assembly line he does not tell his fellow workers that he is a sociologist, and pretends to be just one of the boys. More complicated measures involve the use of hidden tape recorders and cameras to transcribe "spontaneous" activities.[22]

These tricks have been devised to get around the problem that human beings are capable of altering their activities upon receipt of new information. They are of very dubious ethical standing because they only succeed by keeping the people being studied in ignorance of their actual situation. They may also be ineffective for two reasons. First, there is no way of insuring that nobody will suspect the fraud. This factor becomes increasingly important as more people learn about the "techniques" of social research. Second, with respect to the use of hidden recording instruments, the ultimate purpose of direct observation is to learn the meanings behind human actions rather than to impose meanings on these actions. By simply viewing a given social interaction, one may not correctly interpret the meanings given by the participants. For example, seeing a man giving a boy some money will not reveal whether he is giving charity, giving his son an allowance or placing a bet.

Participant observation was first perfected by anthropologists who were interested in understanding systems of action and the meanings of these actions in groups with unfamiliar cultures (including different languages from those known by the anthropologists).[23] Here there could be no question of outright deceit because the anthropologist was obviously different from those he was studying and had to win their confidence before he could attain his research goals. Obviously, an Englishman or a Frenchman could not pass as the member of a tribe in the Amazonian rain forests or the Kalahari Desert. The ultimate aim of field work (the anthropologist's term for participant observation) is not so much for the researcher to share directly in the experiences felt by those he is studying as to capture their existence as a whole through their own frames of reference. Thus, the goal of the anthropologist is essentially to clarify the image of the human condition held by those he is studying. It is, of course, often the case that the people he is observing are not aware of these frames of reference, just as many of those reading this book are not fully aware of their visions of the human condition.

An important consideration in using the participant-observation method is that the investigator give an accurate report of what he has observed, rather than a commentary colored by his original views, biases, and orientations. This means that good participant observation involves the method of self-understanding in all its phases. It involves clarification because, without knowledge of one's image of the human condition, it is impossible to pick out one's biases. Generalization enters when the anthropologist is able to identify himself as a member of a particular culture, and relativization follows with the recognition that the culture he represents is one among many. Finally, commitment comes when the anthropologist dedicates himself to understanding the meanings of activities for others and describing the general patterns of these meanings as they cut across different groups. The fact that good participant observation involves the process of self-understanding as both its precondition and goal means that everyone who is along the road to self-understanding has automatically become a human scientist. Thus, such a person will be studying each group to which he belongs at the very time he is acting within that group. If he is fully committed to inquiry he will make the results of his investigations known to his colleagues and thereby increase the awareness necessary for intensifying freedom. In this case, human science becomes collective self-criticism.

The result of participant observation is a description of a way of life. No other method results in an answer to the broad question, What is it like to be a member of this group? The researcher may find the life-style he is observing to be preferable to his own. There are stories of anthropologists failing to come back from their field trips because they became so involved with the groups they were studying. This can be viewed as either a hazard or a benefit of using the method. Short of conversion to a new way of life, the method enables a person to explore the possibilities of a life different from the one he is leading, either through undertaking research himself or reading the reports of research done by others. One can get an idea of what different jobs are like, or what it would be like to live under different family arrangements. Since the participant-observation method embodies the process of self-understanding, it is disturbing to realize that the majority of studies in sociology that utilize the method are concerned with either downtrodden or deviant groups.[24] Delinquents, the unemployed, drug users, and mental patients represent only a narrow spectrum of the possibilities for human beings. It is also important to note that, although what is commonly called participant observation involves physical presence in a group, many of the same results can be gained through *imaginative* participation in groups. Novels, utopian literature, and histories are all arenas for the observation of groups and the exploration of new possibilities. It is in such imaginative participation that the historical and participant methods fuse.

NONPARTICIPANT OBSERVATION

It is not necessary to become a member of a group to study it firsthand. Nonparticipant observation is the method in which the researcher is on the scene of group activity, but holds himself apart from that activity to study certain aspects of human relations. This method is not as easy for the ordinary person to apply as participant observation, because most groups will not invite a researcher to study their activity unless they expect to gain something from the research. Thus, much nonparticipant observation has been carried out in bureaucratic organizations where managerial groups have allowed sociologists to study human relations in work settings, perhaps with the idea that the resulting research will reveal the sources of inefficiency and the ways of reducing it.[25] Since the nonparticipant observer does not become a member of the group he is studying and often attempts to remain as inconspicuous as possible (to avoid the "guinea pig effect"), his aim is usually not to grasp visions of the human condition, but to describe patterns of social relations. For example, in studying a group of office workers, the nonparticipant observer may note when official rules are broken, for what purpose and by whom. He may uncover networks of "informal organization" through which tasks get carried out when the official rules hinder efficiency. Alternatively, he may uncover patterns through which work is avoided or sabotage is performed. Participant observers, of course, are also capable of focusing on patterns of human relations (for example, hidden power structures, friendship cliques). If the nonparticipant observer remains unobtrusive enough, he has the advantage of not disturbing the pattern of relations in the group by adding a new member to it.

For the ordinary person, nonparticipant observation can best be done in public places. One may study the relations among waitresses in a restaurant, the behavior of political demonstrators, the avoidance patterns of pedestrians on a busy street or the relations among mechanics at a garage when one's car is being repaired. Questions that one might ask would be: Who seems to ask for advice and who gives it? If conflicts appear, what are they about? Do the official authority relations seem to hold, or are they breached? How much of their time do people spend working and how much "socializing"? One might want to compare relations at different restaurants, different service stations, different demonstrations, or among different families at a public beach or park. Nonparticipant observation can be a broadening experience which opens up new sensitivity to the range of social relations. All bus terminals are not the same; each discount department store has a slightly different work setting, leading to more or less harmony, efficiency, and individual initiative. Making nonparticipant observation a part of one's existence not only reduces boredom, but also gives one knowledge of the complexity of what at first sight seem to be the simplest of human relations.

SURVEY METHOD

The survey method involves the sociologist in creating his information far more than do the methods previously discussed. This method, which basically involves asking people questions and recording the responses, takes several different forms. When a researcher records the reply, either in writing or with the use of a tape recorder, the method is technically known as interviewing. When the respondent writes his answer out it is known as the questionnaire method. In either case, the questions may range from those requiring a brief reply indicating such facts as one's age, marital status, or father's occupation, to those demanding a more extended response indicating such things as the reasons why one went to college or what one thinks of social equality for racial minorities. A further distinction within this method involves whether the question is open ended or forced choice. Open-ended responses allow the respondent to improvise his own answers to the questions in his own words. Forced choices require the respondent to select an answer from a fixed set of alternatives. Which particular type of survey method is used depends, of course, upon the problem guiding inquiry. For example, if one is interested in political-party affiliation, the forced-choice questionnaire with brief reply might be most appropriate.

The survey method is currently the one most frequently used in sociology (perhaps because of its apparent simplicity) and also the most misused method. The most important pitfalls are those that follow from the failure to clarify divergent frames of reference. Asking questions is a normal human activity. However, most inquiries take place between people who share common frames of reference, use language in similar ways and, in general, are quite sensitive to the specific intentions of the question. This is by no means necessarily the case when hundreds or even thousands of people are asked to respond on a questionnaire or to an interviewer. Many of the people questioned may have little in common with the background, style of language, and interests of the researcher.[26] Thus, they may give different meanings to the questions than the researcher intended. This means that the respondents frequently misinterpret the questions and that the researcher often misinterprets the answers, leading to a situation in which the "new knowledge" is of low quality. A second difficulty is that questions are sometimes phrased in such a manner as to bias the response. This is the social science equivalent of the "loaded question" which appears in propaganda and in everyday life. For example, someone interested in attitudes regarding future space exploration might betray his bias by asking, "Do you think that we should waste any more money on space flight?" In an attempt to avoid such bias researchers try to devise neutral questions. Propagandists and advertisers, on the other hand, try to devise loaded questions ("You do like our product, don't you?"). Then they can report that 95 percent of those questioned prefer their product.

Another danger in survey research is generalizing from an inadequate base of information. For example, it would probably be a mistake to question the people in your sociology class about their reading habits and then conclude from the findings that Americans in general read the same amounts of the same things; college students are of course unlikely to be representative of the rest of the population. The people in your sociology class, however, might be representative of college students in general on this matter and, thus, generalizing the findings to all college students might not be a mistake. Propagandists make it a practice to generalize from an inadequate base of information. For example, they will use striking cases of demonstrations turning into riots to argue that all demonstrations tend toward riots. For sociologists, however, whether one assumes that the sample surveyed is representative of some wider group, such as Americans, the middle class, or even "people," should depend upon knowledge of both the sample and the larger group.

While, like all other methods, the survey method can be misused, it enables one to gain significant information when wisely applied. It is particularly helpful in the processes of generalization and relativization, because it enables one to identify those with whom one agrees and disagrees. In reading the results of surveys, people are sometimes amazed and sometimes relieved to find that there are many who agree with them on certain issues. This recognition may stop a person from thinking that he is mentally ill or deviant ("If I am the only one in the world who thinks this I must be crazy, but if many other people agree with me maybe there is some truth in what I think"). Further, when people find that they are in agreement in criticizing the present order, this recognition may give rise to joint action for social change. Surveys also provide information about where support for and opposition to social movements can be expected.[27] Thus, surveys help make the private problems of individuals into public issues.

The current drawbacks of survey research do not arise from the method itself, but from the way it has been used. In general, survey research has failed to ask crucial questions, and has often allowed for only those answers the researcher considered to be possible.[28] The processes of clarification and relativization of beliefs are both enhanced when new answers are given to old questions. Respondents can also benefit directly from the research when they are asked questions they had never before confronted and when they are presented with alternatives they had never before envisioned. This kind of inventive use of survey research creates a new social reality.

Depth Interviewing

While the ordinary person is primarily hindered from undertaking survey research by the lack of funds and facilities (for example, a computer), depth interviewing is even more difficult for the nonprofessional to carry out. In depth interviewing, subjects are asked to speak about their ideas and experiences with regard to basic values such as social equality, civil liberties, marital and parental relations, ethnic identification, and religious commitments. The interviewer takes notes or tapes the conversation, sometimes letting the respondent determine the direction of the discussion (nondirective interviewing) and sometimes attempting to guide the discussion through pointed questions (directive interviewing). The aim of the researcher is to find underlying themes in the responses of the subject which reveal tensions and ambivalence about one's role in the social structure, conflicting values, and fundamental vision of the human condition. For example, one might conduct depth interviews with working-class whites to determine the extent to which they are willing to apply the value of social equality in their personal relations. Do they carry racial prejudices against blacks? Are they willing to let any prejudices they have influence their attitudes and activities with respect to equal employment opportunities, open housing and the integration of schools? If they are prejudiced and willing to discriminate, how do they justify their attitudes and actions? It is clear that many people would not submit to a depth interview unless they trusted the researcher personally or trusted his professional integrity.

Depth interviews differ from survey research and are similar to participant observation, because they allow for the analysis of visions of the human condition rather than particular attitudes. Thus, the best depth interviewers are those who have carried through the processes of generalization and relativization, enabling them to be conscious of their own world-view and sensitive to the world-view of the subject. Depth interviewing combines the difficulties of survey research and nonparticipant observation. Like survey research, it may involve asking questions about which the person has never thought deeply; and like nonparticipant observation, it may produce a "guinea pig" effect. Further, it is difficult to derive generalizations from depth interviewing, because the sample is usually small and the interviewer must be sophisticated enough not to impose his own agenda on the conversation. Like participant observation, depth interviewing demands that the researcher keep his own biases in abeyance.

In depth interviewing, the researcher is often concerned with identifying images of which the subject is not fully conscious. The subject may believe that he is committed to social equality, but his responses may show that in many cases he is actually committed to white supremacy. The aim of uncovering "covert culture" involves certain ethical dilemmas. To reach his goal, the researcher must conceal it from the subject in order to avoid defensive tactics and pat answers. Thus, the researcher must ask for trust at the same time he refuses to give it. This tactic involves a certain degree of manipulation.

If one is willing to forget the ethical dilemmas, approximations to depth interviewing can be made in ordinary life. On buses and trains, and at vacation resorts, people removed from their everyday social relations are often willing to speak freely about themselves, their problems, and their attitudes about social relations. They seek opportunities to converse in order to test their ideas against a neutral judge and because they feel more secure away from their normal social contacts. Also, in expressing themselves freely to a stranger they do not risk the tangible punishments they might suffer from expressing themselves freely at work, among friends or even in the family. It is possible to turn such conversations with strangers into depth interviews by guiding them toward the discussion of particular attitudes about society, and then looking for inconsistencies, tensions, and hidden motivations.

There is much to be learned about images of the human condition from such conversations, particularly if one makes sure to find out the social background data about the stranger (type of work, degree of education, religious affiliation, ethnicity, geographical residence, and family background). Then it may be possible to trace back some of the attitudes expressed to social factors, allowing one to reconstruct the stranger's image of the human condition. Whether or not one undertakes such a project will depend upon whether he is willing to manipulate people in this way.

EXPERIMENTAL SMALL GROUPS

The method of experimental small groups involves the sociologist the most deeply in creating his own information. In general, small-group research brings together people who would not otherwise form a group (and who may never have even seen one another before), and provides a situation in which these people interact. The basic assumption behind this method is that the behavior observed under the conditions contrived by the researcher is not significantly different from what would happen under similar conditions in everyday social life. For example, the behaviors observed in a contest set up by the researcher may be used as a model of what goes on in business competition.

The problems investigated through the experimental small-groups method have varied from trying to determine how a group can influence an individual's attitudes or beliefs, to attempting to find out how much pain one person will administer to another.[29] Many studies utilizing small groups are of particular interest to large organizations, especially business and military conglomerates. These organizations are interested in the question, How can workers (or soldiers) become more efficient? Some sociologists attempt to answer this question by having experimental small groups perform tasks under varying conditions.[30] They see how performance varies as conditions change (different lighting, presence or absence of music, varying styles of leadership).[31] Sociologists undertake these studies, not because they want to exploit the worker, but because they are being funded by the managements of the organizations. It would be interesting to find out what questions would be studied if researchers had a free hand in selecting their problems. It is also interesting to note that labor unions have not yet seen fit to support counter-research on such questions as, How can management be made to produce more humane working conditions?

The experimental small-group method has also been used in trying to understand international relations and relations between businesses (What are the causes and cures of conflict?). In such "simula-
tions of the real world" individuals are made to represent such units
as nations or corporations and then to play a game that supposedly
parallels what happens in actual conflicts.[32] This procedure rests on
the questionable assumption that organizations are "things" that act
like human beings. Further, and even more important, despite the use
of the game metaphor in politics ("Nixon's game plan") and business
("the money game"), games do not share many significant features
with other aspects of human existence. In a game, it is assumed that
the participants know the rules, the rules do not change in the midst
of the contest, all are aiming at the same goal (victory), the rules
declare a winner and an end to the game, and one person's loss is
another person's gain. None of these conditions seems to hold in most
life situations. Further, most games do not involve life-or-death decisions.

Much of the research utilizing small groups can be criticized from
the standpoint that most experimental situations do not reflect life
situations in important respects. Who cares to generalize from one
contrived situation to another? Attempts have been made to take account of this criticism by utilizing natural groups, that is, groups that
are already in existence, such as work groups, school classes and the
like. The validity of the results of these studies depends to a large
extent upon how real the participants viewed the situation.

The small-group method need not involve any separation between researchers and participants. In its widest sense the method
includes investigations where the roles of researcher and participant
are one. Utopian communities such as the Oneida experiment and
Brook Farm, as well as some hippie communes and radical collectives,
can be understood as experiments in seeing what life would be like if
certain principles and rules were put into effect. Small-group studies
of a more private nature frequently are undertaken, as when a married
couple attempt to live together with full equality and dignity for each.
In the case of such living experiments, the method of experimental
small groups becomes one with the method of participant observation
and the wider process of self-understanding. Every group situation can
be viewed as an experiment in human existence, and can be judged and
criticized by those participating. It is, of course, to the advantage of
elite groups to make people believe that group situations fulfilling elite
purposes are not experiments but are eternal parts of the human
condition.

Figure 4.1. THE CLASSIFICATION OF METHODS	
Least Creation of Data *by Sociologist*	*Most Creation of Data* *by Sociologist*

Historical Method
   Demographic Method
      Participant Observation
         Nonparticipant Observation
            Survey Method
               Depth-Interview Method
                  Experimental Small-Group Method

METHOD IN REVIEW

Sociological methods range from those in which the researcher analyzes and reshapes information gathered by others, to those in which he creates his own information. The basic sociological method is the historical and demographic method which uses available documents to construct images of the human condition (ideal types). These ideal types form the context in which more specific sociological methods are used. Participant methods involve the presence of the sociologist in group situations, attempting to grasp the meanings behind the behaviors of group members. Surveys require the sociologist to create his information by asking people questions and having them respond either vocally or in writing. Finally, the method of experimental small groups requires the sociologist to bring together people and contrive a situation in which they must act with respect to one another. While in its most narrow definition, this method involves the sociologist most deeply in creating his own information, in its widest sense every small group can be conceived as an experiment in human existence. This is because human beings are continually contriving the conditions of their existence, with or without the help of social scientists. Where the small-group method meets the historical and participant methods is where the sociologist makes people aware of their own experiments.

Despite the fact that the preceding overview of major sociological methods was brief, the diversity of methods is readily apparent. No one method is inherently better than another. Rather, a method is more or less appropriate to answer a given question. Certain prediction of future events is not possible using any of these methods, but it is human freedom rather than faulty method that is responsible for this situation. Certain prediction is valuable for engineers who want to manipulate things. Do we really want a class of human engineers who manipulate people for the ends of those who pay them? Fortunately, it is not even necessary to answer this question because sociological methods achieve an understanding of the present and of various possibilities for the future. Through the use of these methods one can choose with fuller awareness to commit oneself to a specific future and help to create it. The best way to block the emergence of a class of human engineers is to become a sociologist yourself.

THE HISTORICAL METHOD IN USE

Lipset, S. M.; Trow, M.; and Coleman, J.S. *Union Democracy.* Glencoe, Ill.: Free Press, 1956.

The historical method is best adapted to describing the general organizational patterns and processes through which human beings act on their projects. Any image of the human condition developed through the historical method draws some conclusions about the projects most likely to be successful in a given social structure. Those who dispute such conclusions have the alternatives of generating an entirely new image or of revising the existing image. The process of revision may be carried out through a "critical case study." In the critical case study, an organization is selected that does not display the characteristics defined in the existing image and then an attempt is made to explain the divergence from expectation.

An example of a critical case study is the analysis of the International Typographical Union conducted by Seymour Lipset and his associates. Lipset disputed the contention of Robert Michels that democratic decision making is impossible in large formal organizations. Selecting the International Typographical Union as an organization that had a two-party democracy rather than a single ruling elite, Lipset attempted to explain why this organization was not an oligarchy by seeing how its membership and social structure differed from the pattern within less democratic unions. He showed, among other things, that members of the ITU formed closer communities than other unionized workers because they worked in relatively small shops and often at odd hours. They also had a tradition of strong local organization and decentralized bargaining patterns with employers. Such factors encouraged concern with union affairs by members, the appearance of multiple power centers within the union, and built-in checks upon the seizure of power by small cliques. Added to these factors were the relatively high incomes, educational attainments and political sophistication of members. Thus, Lipset was able successfully to challenge and *revise* Michels' thesis that oligarchy is inevitable in large formal organizations. He did not argue against the claim that there is a *tendency* toward oligarchy in such organizations, but maintained that this tendency can be mitigated by particular constellations of social, cultural, and personal factors.

The kind of critical case study done by Lipset can be applied to challenge many sweeping claims about the nature of social organization. For example, some people claim that democracy is impossible outside a capitalist economic system. In order to challenge this thesis one might look for a nation in which democracy functioned in a socialist or semi-socialist economy, and attempt to see how the danger of using the economy as a political weapon was avoided. Or, one might challenge the thesis the grades are necessary to motivate learning by seeking out examples of successful experiments in ungraded courses and seeing how motivation was sustained.

THE DEMOGRAPHIC METHOD IN USE

Durkheim, Emile. *Suicide.* Glencoe, Ill.: Free Press, 1951.

Perhaps the most famous example of the demographic method in sociology is Emile Durkheim's study of suicide rates. Durkheim's major concern was to refute the claims that suicide was the result of variations in climate, hereditary factors, individual psychological disturbances or sheer imitation and crowd contagion, and to advance the thesis that rates of suicide are related to the degree to which human beings are integrated into social groups. Using publicly available statistics on suicide rates, Durkheim showed that explanations of suicide that did not take social integration into account could not be supported by the evidence. For example, some writers maintained that temperature had a direct effect on the number of suicides, but Durkheim showed that rate of suicide did not vary directly with temperature change.

In supporting his own claim that suicide is a function of the absence of social bonds, Durkheim linked suicide rates with three variables: religion, family, and political situation. He found that suicide rates were higher among Protestants than Catholics (Protestantism has an individualistic theology and Catholicism a more communal theology), among unmarried than married people, among childless married couples than married couples with children, and in times of political crisis and nationalist agitation than in times of political tranquility.

These conclusions helped support and advance Durkheim's central idea that social structure functions somewhat independently of individual personality characteristics in determining human activity.

Similar studies to Durkheim's can be done using publicly available statistics. For example, incidence of various kinds of crime, of automobile accidents, of divorces or of civil violence can be correlated with social structural factors to determine how far it is possible to explain these phenomena on the bases of personality, organic or environmental factors. Does the "long, hot summer" theory of civil violence make sense? What about the hereditary theory of crime? Such topics are continually studied by sociologists and you can begin to do research on them now if you are interested in any of them.

THE PARTICIPANT METHOD IN USE

Goffman, Erving. *Asylums.* Garden City, N.Y.: Doubleday, 1961.

While the participant method can be used in any social group to which the investigator can gain access, some of its most striking applications have been carried out in organizations closed off from the general public. An example of a significant and socially critical use of the participant method is Erving Goffman's study of the life and world-view of inmates in a large mental hospital. Guided by the assumption that "a good way to learn about (the world of the mental patient) is to submit oneself in the company of the members to the daily round of petty contingencies to which they are subject," Goffman took the role of assistant to the athletic director of the hospital and then "passed the day with patients, avoiding sociable contact with the staff and the carrying of a key." The top management of the hospital knew of his aims in advance, so he did not have to worry that his research would be cut off precipitously.

In penetrating the "world" of the inmate, Goffman found that mental patients attempt to maintain as much personal integrity as possible by appropriating property and space for their own uses and trying to keep up an appearance of dignity in a debasing situation. He also discovered that the official ideology of the hospital—that patients should cooperate with the staff in effecting a cure—was not shared by the inmates. Instead, the inmates showed "a self-justifying definition of their own situation and a prejudiced view of non-members, in this case, doctors, nurses, attendants, and relatives."

Goffman's research shows some of the strengths as well as some of the problems of the participant method. He was able to learn things about the "world" of the mental patient that could probably not be discovered through the historical, demographic, survey or experimental methods. However, he admits that his results were "partisan" (biased in favor of the values of the mental patients) and not amenable to verification by quantitative methodologies (statistical measurement would have been difficult for a participant observer). These difficulties, of course, are only significant if one believes that sociology can be "value-free" and should employ a natural-science model. More important, perhaps, is the ethical problem. Goffman was able to gather his information because people thought he was an assistant to the athletic director (when "pressed," he avowed to being "a student of recreation and community life"). He probably could not have been as effective an observer if he had announced his intentions in advance. This ethical problem of concealing intention haunts most participant research, and the choice is between gaining the insights and critiques produced by people like Goffman and making sociological research more honest.

THE NONPARTICIPANT METHOD IN USE

Blau, Peter M. *The Dynamics of Bureaucracy.* Chicago: University of Chicago Press, 1963.

Like the participant method, nonparticipant observation is useful in revealing patterns of social interaction that would be difficult to discover with more indirect methods. An example of nonparticipant observation is Peter M. Blau's study of a division of a state employment agency. Blau began with the idea that organizations do not always function according to the principles set down in the rule book. His observations confirmed in many different instances the existence of informal networks of relations that violated the spirit, if not the letter, of the official code. For example, employment interviewers were supposed to complete detailed forms on job requests for workers, provide counseling to those seeking employment and find the most qualified worker for a given job. However, the situation in which the interviewers actually found themselves did not lend itself to the fulfillment of these norms. Since requests for workers came sporadically and in large chunks, and since these requests were usually for relatively unskilled labor, there did not seem to be good reasons to spend time filling out detailed forms, deciding who was most capable of filling a position or counseling potential employees. Further, performance of the agency was judged according to how many people were placed, not according to the professional quality of counseling or to the level of accuracy in fitting individuals to specific positions. Thus, instead of living up to the spirit of the rules, interviewers placed people on a first-come, first-served basis.

From these observations, Blau drew the conclusion that informal relations functioning outside or even against the rules often fulfill formal organizational goals more efficiently. The state employment interviewers he observed were actually working to attain organizational purposes by more effective means than those prescribed in the rule book. Of course, behind this situation was a kind of organizational hypocrisy. While officially interviewers were supposed to be judged on the quality of their work, in actuality they were judged only on the quantity of placements. Such hypocrisy is probably responsible for a great deal of the kinds of informal organization Blau discovered. Workers grasp that what the rules prescribe is not what is really expected of them. This hypothesis, of course, can be tested by readers of this book as they observe formal organizations.

THE SURVEY METHOD IN USE

Stouffer, Samuel. *Communism, Conformity, and Civil Liberties.* Garden City, N.Y.: Doubleday, 1955.

One of the most important uses of the survey method is to determine how different groups in a society are aligned on given issues. By eliciting attitudes on various issues of public concern, the researcher can gather information on which groups are likely to favor and oppose certain policies. Further, attitude research can affirm or question generalizations about the perspectives of different groups. An example of this use of the survey method is Samuel Stouffer's study of attitudes toward the protection of civil liberties in the United States during the early 1950s—a time at which Senator Joseph McCarthy was attempting to mobilize public sentiment against the American left wing. Stouffer's study was based on two independently chosen random samples of the American people (a "national cross section") and two samples of community leaders (mayors and American Legion commanders). Stouffer was interested in determining which groups in the American population were most favorably disposed towards limiting such civil liberties as freedom of speech and association to diminish an internal communist threat. In order to reach his goal, Stouffer asked such questions as: "If a person wanted to make a speech in your community against churches and religions, should he be allowed to speak or not?" He found generally that the community leaders were more likely to express attitudes of tolerance to nonconformity than was the population in general. For example, while more than 60 percent of the community leaders claimed that a person should be allowed to make a speech against religions, 60 percent of the national cross section would not allow such a speech.

Stouffer's work has been used to support the theory of "democratic elitism" which holds that the protection of individual rights and democratic processes is best assured by the upper middle class and is somewhat endangered by the lower middle and working classes. This interpretation has been challenged by the claim that, even according to Stouffer's data, tolerance varies directly according to educational attainment, not directly according to class, and that most civil liberties issues are not of great importance to many lower-middle and working-class people. The use of surveys to support and undermine images of the human condition shows that they cannot stand alone as examples of "pure research" but that, instead, they have ramifications for the adequacy and fruitfulness of programs for social stability and change.

THE DEPTH INTERVIEW METHOD IN USE

Becker, Howard, et al. *The Boys in White.* Chicago: University of Chicago Press, 1961.

The depth interview is best adapted to probing ambivalence in attitudes and to uncovering sentiments that lie below the surface of socially accepted opinions and ideologies. An example of research using the depth interview method is Howard Becker's study of value conflict in medical students. While Becker was primarily conducting a participant observation study of the attitudes of medical students toward the medical profession, he spoke to individual students at length in conversations that approximated depth interviews. Becker notes that sociologists normally attempt to get "beneath" the idealistic ideologies of people and penetrate to their "latent" concrete interests. In his study of medical students Becker found himself confronting a reverse situation. He defines the subculture of medical students as one of "ritualized cynicism," in which a student who expresses any idealistic or altruistic sentiments will be ridiculed. Therefore, in his private conversations with students Becker attempted to pierce the conventional cynicism and bring out any idealistic motivations he could elicit. Rather than asking pointed questions that would reveal motives of self-interest, he encouraged expressions of idealism by speaking about topics in which they seemed to have "impractical" interests. He found that, despite the oppressive features of the role of medical student, many of the students maintained altruistic concerns that coexisted with their cynicism and concern for future security. This experience led Becker to the conclusion that sociologists should begin their research neither with the assumption that ulterior motives always underlie expressed motives nor with the assumption that people are as good as they say they are. Rather, they should begin with the hypothesis that people may have multiple motivations and that they may hold conflicting motives at different times.

Becker's use of the depth interview method raises some questions about its validity. How much does the interviewer have to intrude into the situation before the response he elicits is simply a function of his persistence? For example, how many of the medical students' altruistic responses were fabricated to please Becker? Further, how significant are suppressed motivations for actual social relations when the group structure imposes and enforces a conventional set of attitudes? Finally, is the hypothesis that people may be ambivalent any less dogmatic than the hypotheses that they mean what they say or that their expressed motives are screens behind which they hide their real motives? None of these questions renders the depth interview useless; they simply show the difficulties involved in understanding human motivations, attitudes, and sentiments.

THE EXPERIMENTAL GROUP METHOD IN USE

White, Ralph, and Lippitt, Ronald. *Autocracy and Democracy.* New York: Harper, 1960.

In the experimental group method the researcher creates groups and controls the environment so that he can determine whether certain consequences appear upon the introduction of given activities or relations. One of the more interesting series of small-group experiments was carried out by Lewin, Lippitt, and White on hobby and play groups of ten-year-old boys. While the designs of the various experiments are complex, the aim was to determine whether the quantity of work accomplished and the satisfaction of members with the group would be influenced by the style of the adult group leadership. Three types of groups were created according to three different styles of leadership—autocratic, democratic, and laissez faire (anarchic). Generally, the investigators found that in democratically organized groups the members showed the highest work motivation, the most originality in work projects and the greatest satisfaction with the group. Laissez faire organization, on the other hand, was characterized by lower productivity than democracy, poorer quality of work, and less satisfaction with the group. Finally, while autocratic organization resulted in the highest quantity of work done, originality was low, dependence was high, there was little satisfaction with the group, and, most important, there were high levels of discontent which were expressed by scapegoating, destruction of property, rebellion, dropping out of the group, and wild behavior when the autocratic leader was withdrawn.

The Lewin-Lippitt-White experiments demonstrate the manipulative character of small-group research, as well as its cultural boundedness. Is it ethical to impose autocratic leadership on a group of children who cannot understand why they are being subjected to this sytem? How much were the results of this research influenced by the fact that it was conducted in the United States, which has a democratic ideology, rather than in a society characterized by more authoritarian ideologies and institutions? While many small-group experiments show great ingenuity, use of the method raises moral questions and it is not easily applied, if it can be applied at all, in ordinary life.

5

HUMAN ACTION

The past four chapters have been devoted to describing the ways in which the human condition can be studied. They ranged from the most general consideration of how human beings can orient themselves to their situations as scientists to the more specific questions of the methods that they can use to analyze these situations. With this preceding discussion in mind, it is time to begin investigating the content of social existence. The presentation of the content of sociology will be, of course, from the viewpoint of process thought, and will stress the pattern of opportunities for human freedom present in the contemporary world, as well as the many obstacles to its attainment.

The content of sociology is the human condition, the basic components of that condition, and the relations among those components. Throughout the history of social thought, the major issues dividing competing perspectives have centered around different interpretations of the nature of these components and how they are linked together. In American sociology there are two general perspectives presently vying for dominance. Each is based on a view of which human experiences it is important for sociologists to investigate. One of these views is based on a restrictive interpretation of human experience, while the other is rooted in a more expansive understanding of experience. *Restrictive empiricism* has been the major current in American sociology up until recently, but now it is being challenged by a vigorous movement promoting *expansive empiricism.*

RESTRICTIVE EMPIRICISM

The root idea of all empiricism is that whatever can be known by human beings appears in their experience.[1] Therefore, according to empiricists, what is believed in but is not experienced (for example, many notions of God) is not an object of knowledge, but is an object of faith. Since factual accuracy is near the core of all science, scientific investigation is based on an empirical interpretation of knowledge.

Restrictive empiricism holds that only certain human experiences are open to scientific investigation. These experiences fall within the range of what is thought to be "publicly observable" or capable of being known independently by any human being with the full use of his senses.[2] Thus, restrictive empiricists argue that inquiry into the human condition should be limited to that area of experience that can be known through the five senses—sight, sound, taste, smell, and touch. This means that restrictive empiricists study human *behavior,* or that part of the process of human action which can be "externally observed."

Restrictive empiricism became popular in sociology mainly because many social scientists thought that it was the foundation of the natural sciences. They reasoned that, if natural science restricted itself to studying what could be observed through the senses, then social science could only be successful if it placed the same limitations upon itself. This decision to follow the lead of natural science led to the development of many of the methods discussed in the preceding chapter, particularly the demographic, survey and experimental-small-group techniques. Social scientists believe that by using these techniques they could avoid the difficulties involved in trying to find out what was going on "inside people's heads." Governmental statistics on suicide rates were seen as objective, in the sense that they referred to events that could be observed through the senses. The web of feeling in which the suicide was enmeshed could be factored out of the scientific description and left to the novelist or playwright. Responses to a questionnaire on political-party preferences were also held to be observable, at least by anyone who understood the language in which the responses were written. For many purposes, the meaning of this preference to the respondent could be ignored. This was particularly true if the aim of the social scientist was to predict the general trends in voting behavior. The results of experiments aimed at finding the factors influencing the output of work groups were considered objective. Meanwhile, the fundamental principles of economic activity operating within the contemporary human condition, such as organizational growth, could be held constant and put out of awareness. Finally, with feelings, meanings, and principles left out of social research, many social scientists concluded that their task was to find out the factors that determined human behavior rather than the structural limitations on the development of human freedom. This lack of attention to freedom was a direct result of adopting restrictive empiricism and trying to imitate the natural sciences.

Restrictive empiricism has, we believe, a built-in failing which has led to the development of opposing interpretations of experience. This weakness can be grasped by considering the claim that the responses to a questionnaire are scientific data because they are observable through the senses. It is apparent that the least significant feature of the responses is that they are publicly observable. The questions themselves are put in a language that must be understood by the respondent if his answers are to be useful. This understanding, essential to the purpose of the questionnaire, is not publicly observable. Further, the very purpose of the questionnaire is to gain knowledge of some aspect of the human condition. This purpose is not publicly observable, but is intended by the scientist. Finally, the observable responses to the questionnaire are merely symbols of the meanings that respondents have expressed. Thus, a complex network of understandings, intentions, and meanings is necessary to make sense of the questionnaire as a tool of research. From this viewpoint, the questionnaire is merely the tip of a vast iceberg. It is, of course, possible to ignore the rest of the iceberg and study only the tip. However, in choosing to do this, the scientist should realize that he is taking for granted large chunks of human experience in the absence of which his research would not be possible. This means that the results of his research will be indicators of underlying processes which he has cut himself off from studying. It also means that his thought about the human condition will be inadequate to account for his own activity as a scientist. Like all other human activities, scientific inquiry is enmeshed in a set of feelings, goals, principles, and choices which can only be understood by opening inquiry to the entire field of experience.[3]

EXPANSIVE EMPIRICISM

The weaknesses of restrictive empiricism were already apparent to some thinkers in the nineteenth century, but have only come to the attention of a large number of sociologists in recent years.[4] One response to these weaknesses is to appeal to principles outside of human experience, such as a deity or an absolute spirit that cannot be observed, but that are supposedly responsible for making sense of the "inner life." Similarly, appeal can be made to abstract entities such as the Self or Society, which do not appear directly in human experience except as words. From this perspective, some entity called the Self, or some object called Society, stands behind human experience and causes particular experiences to occur. For example, some people claim that "bad individuals" are the cause of crime, while others retort that the real roots of crime are found in "society." Anybody who has engaged in such debates can testify how arid they become and how they seem to dissolve into confusion. This aridity and confusion are the result of discussing human activity in terms of entities that are not experienced as "things." Neither the self nor society are things that cause other things to happen. They are processes into which particular human activities such as producing, consuming, learning, and deciding are knit, and are, therefore, much more like results than like causes.[5] What view of experience can one adopt in order to be aware both of the weaknesses of restrictive empiricism and unwilling to appeal to entities beyond experience? The answer to this question is really present in the preceding discussion. The scientific alternative to restrictive empiricism is an expansive empiricism which takes account of the full range of human experiences, including feeling, meaning, principle, and freedom. It attempts to link these experiences to one another and to the "tip of the iceberg"—publicly observable behavior. Thus, it is not a way of throwing out the vast amount of social science research that has been done in the twentieth century with the tools of demographic analysis, survey research, and experimental small groups. Instead, it is a way of trying to make sense out of this research and relating it to more fundamental human concerns. One way of understanding expansive empiricism is as an attempt to integrate the historical and participant methods with the other methods. The historical method has been the major means through which the meanings and principles of human activity have been revealed, while participant methods have been the means through which the feelings and choices in human activity have been disclosed. Thus, the historical and participant methods help to "make sense" out of the results of the demographic, survey and experimental-small-group methods.

Expansive empiricism is basic to a humanistic perspective on sociology and, therefore, to the process of self-understanding. In order to embark on the quest for self-understanding it is necessary to open oneself to the full range of human experience without any preconceptions about where it necessarily begins and ends.[6] Restrictive empiricists did not intend to place obstacles in the way of self-understanding, but they ended up doing so because their doctrine forced them to ignore significant phases of experience, or at least to slip these phases in through the back door and under the cover of "observable behavior." The case of restrictive empiricism shows how closely intertwined are the categories of human fact and human value. Through cutting off sociological inquiry at an arbitrary point, the restrictive empiricists also placed barriers in the way of attaining freedom. This is particularly ironic because the restrictive empiricists claimed that their "behavioral" human science would vastly increase the scope of human freedom by providing people with knowledge of the conditions under which particular kinds of events occur in social existence.[7]

Expansive empiricism has been developed by a number of philosophers and sociologists throughout the nineteenth and twentieth centuries, including such figures as William James, Henri Bergson, Edmund Husserl, Maurice Hauriou, and Georges Gurvitch. It has influenced American sociology through the works of Charles Horton Cooley, George Herbert Mead, Florian Znaniecki, Pitirim Sorokin, and Talcott Parsons. Its spirit has been strikingly described by Georges Gurvitch, who states that human experience breaks without cease its own frames of reference: "Like a true Proteus [experience] escapes us when we believe that we grasp it; we are made fools by it when we believe we have penetrated its secret, we are its victims when we believe we have freed ourselves from it, even if only for an instant."[8] The key to expansive empricism (called by James "radical empiricism" and by Gurvitch "hyper-empiricism") is that all human experience that can be described has a component of sense and feeling, is in process and is in some measure conceptually constructed. Thus, all experience has an element of immediacy (sense data and felt process) and mediacy (concepts and structured processes): "The effective experience that we oppose to arbitrary philosophical interpretations, such as lived experience, everyday experience or constructed experience, is always mediate to some degree. It is a point of intermediary spheres between the immediate and the constructed. . ."[9]

In order to understand fully the insight contained in expansive empiricism, it is necessary to perform a revolution in ordinary thinking. One helpful aid towards making this revolution is to imagine experience as a field—i.e., a somewhat amorphous moving mass rather than a specific and sharply defined object. You will notice that we did not say that you should imagine *your* experience as a field. For the expansive empiricist, the self appears *within* experience, rather than experience belonging to a self. This means that experience is the fundamental category and not the self. It is another way of stating the major point of the first chapter—that the self is process, not property.

Once you have grasped the image of a field, it is necessary to move on to the point that experience is a special kind of field. Experience is a field of happenings, expanding and contracting, sometimes moving quickly and sometimes more slowly, sometimes unified and sometimes diverse, sometimes smooth and sometimes jagged. Sometimes feeling predominates in the field, at other times relatively precise objects are dominant, at still other times the center of attention is relations among actions and actors, and at yet other times the very processes of change are at the forefront. Any complete description of a given experience will contain each of the major aspects of experience —sense and feeling, objects, relations, and processes. However, each given experience will tend to emphasize one of these aspects over the others. Thus, experience is always moving in the direction of one or another of its major aspects.

Each of the major aspects of experience can be given a name and made the basis of a type of experience. The more experience moves in the direction of sense and feeling, the more it can be called *lived experience*. Lived experience is the most primitive form of experience, and one may suppose that the closest human beings ever come to it in its pure form is when they are infants confronting a whirl of sense and feeling that has not yet been blocked out into objects. Sometimes people attempt to wrench themselves back into lived experience through taking hallucinogenic drugs (such as LSD or marijuana), or through encasing themselves in an environment of loud music, incense, and flashing lights. Whether or not such efforts are successful in liberating experience from well-defined objects, they show that a number of people in the contemporary world are looking for a foundation to their experience beyond the definitions that they have been taught.

The more experience moves in the direction of marked off objects, the more it can be called *cultural experience*. In cultural experience, parts of the field of experience are detached from the rest and made into more permanent features of existence. Unlike lived experience, which is a humming and buzzing confusion, cultural experience is relatively orderly and regularized. Most of the experiences of everyday life are cultural, in the sense that they are of objects that have names in an ordinary language and have usages that are known by those who identify them. Similarly, the experiences that scientists speak about in specialized languages are cultural, in the sense that those who understand the languages can identify them out of the total field of experience. For most people most of the time cultural experience is at the center of existence.

The more experience moves in the direction of ongoing relations between actions and actors, the more it can be called *social experience*. Social experience relates to such intergroup and interpersonal processes as competition, conflict, cooperation, exchange, and love. These relations are present wherever human activity appears and are not linked specifically to any set of cultural experiences. Nearly all human experience contains a social element, even those portions of experience which seem to be the most "private" and personal. Much personal experience is in the form of a conversation, a dialogue or an argument, in which the individual "talks to himself."[10] This internal conversation may embody such processes as conflict and cooperation between different tendencies towards action. Sometimes the conflict becomes so severe that it becomes difficult to speak of a single personality. Other personal experience, particularly creative activity, is undertaken with potential consumers, users, or appreciators in mind. In these experiences, the creator at least implies a possible future cooperative relation between his producing activity and the consuming activities of others.

Finally, the more experience moves in the direction of the processes of acting themselves, the more it can be called *creative experience*.

Creative experience makes sense out of the ways in which cultural experience arises from its lived and social matrix. As Gurvitch noted, human experience breaks without cease its own frames of reference. This aspect of novelty, freshness and dynamism is the creative component of experience. It is through creative processes, such as inventing and perfecting tools, creating new patterns of symbols, devising and appreciating products, and testing systems of rules for coordinating activity, that cultural experience becomes blocked off from lived experience. Thus, creative activity continually organizes and reorganizes the rest of experience. Since human existence takes place in time, and since time is irreversible, there are always new challenges, opportunities, and barriers appearing in human existence. In its purest form, creative experience comes close to the sheer intuition of change and process.[11] From there it shades off into the experiences of activity, effort, challenge and novelty.

Figure 5.1. THE TYPES OF HUMAN EXPERIENCE

		Subjective and Private	Objective and Public
Contents	/	Lived Experience	Cultural Experience
Processes	/	Creative Experience	Social Experience

DIRECTIONS OF HUMAN EXPERIENCE

Lived, cultural, social, and creative experience are the four directions in human experience. In the ever-shifting field of experience, one or another of these comes to the forefront and then fades away to make place for another. Viewing experience as a field makes it difficult to make hard and fast distinctions between the contents of experience and the processes of experiencing, or between subjects who experience and objects that are experienced. Of course, the four directions of experience are characterized by varying degrees of content and process, of subjectivity and objectivity. For example, lived experience has a primacy of content since its core is sensation and feeling. It is also relatively subjective because it is difficult to communicate and is closely related to specific states of the organism. Cultural experience also has a primacy of content since its core is the blocked-out and identifiable object. However, it is relatively objective, because it forms the basis of communication (language is an important phase of cultural experience) and is relatively independent of specific states of any particular organism. Social experience has a primacy of process, because it refers to interpersonal, interactional, and intergroup relations. These relations can be about any conceivable content. There can be cooperation in making weapons as well as in making medicines. Social experience is also relatively objective because it is generally centered around the interlinking of regularized activities, such as the competition between political parties, the conflict between warring states, the cooperation among members of an athletic team or the exchanges between buyers and sellers. Such relations are often quite independent of the particular organisms taking part in them. Finally, creative experience also has a primacy of process, because its core is the very flow of action. Like the relations making up social experience, the activity making up creative experience can work upon any conceivable content from a poem to a hammer. Creative experience, however, is relatively subjective because it tends to be highly individualized and, although its ultimate aim is usually a sharable cultural experience, it cannot be readily communicated before its completion. Thus, while there are no sharp lines that can be drawn between process and content, and subjectivity and objectivity, or between the four directions in experience, each direction has its distinguishing characteristics; these conceptual distinctions are rarely experienced separately.

The field of experience is always moving more in one direction than in the others. If you have been able to picture experience as a dynamic field, you will by now be able to grasp its ebbs and flows, and its changes in direction, as existence unfolds. Heightened awareness of the characteristics of experience is itself an immediate benefit of expansive empiricism. It is a benefit that cannot be provided by restrictive empiricism, because this view carves out certain phases of experience as being worthy of scientific attention and ignores the others. However, the importance of expansive empiricism goes far beyond its ability in aiding a person to make more immediate sense out of experience. It also provides a fundamental perspective for the study of human action.

EXERCISE

Try to experience your activities consciously as you go through the day. Which types of experience seem to predominate? When are you most immersed in cultural experience? lived experience? social experience? creative experience? What contexts seem to encourage each experience? What contexts discourage each type of experience?

HUMAN ACTION

Every science takes from the field of human experience a class of events, objects, processes or happenings that serve as its subject matter for analysis and description. The definition of this subject matter can be called the *scope* of the science. For example, restrictive empiricists have defined the scope of sociology as the class of "publicly" observable human behaviors, or even as the study of the "forms" of social relations (competition, domination, exchange, and so on), the investigation of groups, the study of rule-bound and purposive behaviors, and many other slices of experience.[12] There have frequently been heroic efforts to attempt to carve out a special niche for sociology that would distinguish it clearly from the other social sciences, such as political science, economics, anthropology, and jurisprudence. Thus, some have hoped that sociology would become the master social science, synthesizing all the results of the other social sciences into descriptions of the general patterns of historical development.[13] Others have advocated that sociology confine itself to investigating the linkages between different "areas" of human existence, such as the economy, the "political system," and the "culture."[14] Still others have observed that sociologists seem to study whatever the other social sciences have ignored in their investigations of the human condition.[15] According to this interpretation, since no other social science was taking an interest in such subjects as the family and race relations, sociology got to work on them. Related to this view is the idea that sociology arose as a result of the new problems created by the indirect consequences of industrialization and urbanization. Nobody specifically intended that industrialization and urbanization would bring on problems of juvenile delinquency, alcoholism, racial conflict, the displacement of religion from the center of human existence, the increase in impersonal crime, and the demand for organized measures to cope with mentally ill human beings. No specialized social science was uniquely equipped to study these problems and provide advice to elite groups concerning their solution, so sociology grew up to perform these services.[16]

The ideas that sociology is (or should be) the master science of historical development, the study of the relations between the various specialized areas of human existence and the investigation of the leftovers from the other social sciences are merely a few of the multitude of suggested definitions of the scope of the discipline. It is important to note that none of these definitions is arbitrary, but that each one of them reflects the way that its proponents view human experience. For those who believe that experience is divided up into neat boxes, sociology will have a special scope distinguishing it clearly from the other social sciences. On the other hand, for those who view experience as a field, there will be no clear lines of demarcation between the disciplines.

ESTABLISHING SOCIOLOGY AS A SEPARATE DISCIPLINE

One reason why a number of sociologists have been concerned to distinguish their discipline from the other social sciences is that sociology is one of the youngest human sciences. In the late nineteenth and early twentieth centuries, sociologists had to battle to gain their own departments and courses in the universities of the West.[17] They had to prove both that they represented a respectable science, that they were studying different contents, and were employing different methods than the existing disciplines. Their respectability was in doubt because some considered them to be social reformers while others thought of them as propagandists for the establishment. These attacks were probably one reason why many sociologists bent over backwards to prove that they were like natural scientists. Even more serious were the fears of scholars in the other social sciences. Some historians felt threatened by a discipline that appeared to cover the same ground as their own field. They argued that no new discipline was necessary to investigate human affairs comprehensively, and remained unimpressed by claims that historians could content themselves with describing unique events while sociologists would search for general laws of human behavior.[18] Meanwhile, political scientists, anthropologists, and economists were busy making their claims to represent the most significant "science of man." In such a competitive and hostile environment it is no wonder that sociologists felt called upon to prove that they had a specific and unique contribution to make to the advancement of human knowledge. Of course, they were unable to agree upon a common definition of the nature of that contribution.

The history of sociology shows clearly that other considerations than the quest for understanding frequently influence scholarly work. Like labor unions fighting jurisdictional battles and then reaching agreements about which trade does which work, academic disciplines have parcelled out human experience only after conflicts—often bitter ones. Definitions of scope have been used as weapons in such conflicts, with the more powerful disciplines making extravagant claims about the extent of their scope and the weaker disciplines making modest claims with the hope that they will be granted some niche in the academic marketplace. Thus, in its early years, sociology was a weak discipline that had to prove that it deserved a place in the university structure. Today, however, it is no longer applying for admission and need not prove that it is distinct in its scope from the other social sciences.

The subject matter, or scope, given to sociology in this book is *human action*. This is a wide scope, but it is the only one that will support the quest for self-understanding and the only one that is consistent with the idea of experience as a dynamic and shifting field combining feelings, objects, relations, and creative processes. Even if they have not always been anxious to admit it, since the beginnings of their discipline sociologists have ranged over the entire scope of human action and have studied it with a variety of methods. Sociology has been the one discipline besides history to take a consistently comprehensive view of human experience. Thus, the broad definition of scope that we have given merely makes explicit what many other sociologists have known but have left unsaid.

Human action is a process interrelating groups, relations, objects, and purposes. In its briefest definition, a full human action is a group of people in relation to one another, using a set of objects for the realization of purposes. It is not easy to grasp the whole meaning of this definition all at once, but certain points are relatively apparent. First, our account of human action does not have for its basis a single individual doing something. In fact, for the moment, the "individual" is left out of the description altogether. Instead of the common-sense way of thinking about action as proceeding from particular "actors" (individuals) sociologists think about action in a group setting. However, it would be a mistake to think that sociologists simply substitute the unit group for the individual and then go on to state that action proceeds from a group "will" or a group "mind." According to the sociological view of action, there is no group will or group mind. Rather, groups are only evident where human beings are in relation to one another and using objects to realize purposes. There are no groups apart from these activities, and it would not be inaccurate to say that the extent of the activity defines the extent of the group. For example, the group of undergraduate sociology students does not have a will or a mind of its own, but is defined by the activities involved in being a sociology student, such as registering for courses, taking examinations, listening to lectures, participating in discussions, and reading books and articles. What sense would it make to say that there was a group will standing behind these activities and determining them? Yet there are people who believe that such groups as the "American people" or the "black people" have destinies and "souls" which in some way can be separated from concrete activities.

A second point following from the definition of human action is that, among other things, the group is a network of relations. Among some sociology students there is competition for grades and among others there is cooperation in attempting to understand the human condition. In certain cases there is competition and cooperation going on at the same time. Sometimes, even among sociology students, there is outright conflict, as when someone with a revolutionary vision of the human condition encounters someone whose vision emphasizes the goodness of the present order. The relations that occur in the process of human action are sometimes fixed in advance by rules, sometimes they seem to arise spontaneously and sometimes they grow up around systems of rules, subverting these systems or reinforcing them. Often the people involved in the relations are not aware of them, as when professors in college are not aware that they are competing with one another for the student's time. Frequently the individual has little or no control over the relations in which he is enmeshed. Does the student preparing to enter graduate school have control over the competitive relation governing the distribution of the limited number of places and the limited amount of financial aid available? Whether he likes it or not, if he is seeking to enter graduate school he is engaged in a competition with others having similar purposes. This lack of control by individuals over many of the relations that they enter is another indication of why sociologists do not begin with the individual in their account of human action.

A third aspect of the definition of human activity also takes one beyond the individual. Interrelated group activities refer to meaningful objects available to a number of actors. Perhaps the most striking feature of human action is the one that is usually most taken for granted—the fact that the human world is a world of meaning.[19] For the most part, experience does not appear as a meaningless blur, but as a relatively well ordered array of objects linked to one another in significant relations. It is culture that makes this order possible. A cultural object is a human creation with a usage attached which, if used in the prescribed way, will provoke a relatively standardized experience. Examples of cultural objects are tools, rules, symbols, and products. A hammer used correctly will allow one to pound a nail into a piece of wood, a set of rules followed by a group of people will create a particular social situation, a word whose meaning is known will allow one to recall past events and tell others about them, a television set when properly adjusted will allow one to witness the evening news. Hammers, the rules of parliamentary procedure, words, and television sets are all cultural objects. They are human creations that can be used over and over again to provoke standardized experiences.

THE SWEEP OF CULTURE

When it is grasped, the imposing character of culture is very impressive. Any single individual is responsible for only the tiniest fragment of the objects available in the field of experience. A person's innermost thoughts are drenched in culture, because they are expressed in words that he has learned from others, rather than in symbols that he has thought up himself. The ways of processing and preparing the foods that he eats to sustain life are parts of culture and were not put into being by his individual activity. The systems for making decisions that he encounters when he is involved in disputes were in the process of development long before he was born. The very things that he finds beautiful are usually the creations of others and, at the very least, were identified by others long ago. It would be possible to go on endlessly pointing out how dependent human beings are upon culture. In most phases of existence, individual persons are far more representatives of culturally defined processes than they are freely creative actors. The genius at the game of chess, the master carpenter, the assembly-line worker, the housewife and mother are all representatives of a long history of cultural development. Perhaps the chess master adds his own individualized flair to the game, but he works within rules that he did not devise, he learned how to play from others, and he has usually studied the styles of the great masters of the past.

The immense, massive, and imposing character of culture is normally taken for granted in everyday life. People talk about "their" automobiles, "their" houses, "their" children. They forget that they only acquired the automobiles and the houses because others first designed and produced them, still others financed them, and yet others recognize rights of ownership. They forget that the ways in which they raise their children are not original, but were usually devised long ago. In short, they do not see themselves as mere points for the organization of culture. Perhaps one important reason why the significance of culture is generally ignored is that much of it seems to take care of itself. Most people, for example, do not worry continually about the language that they use in everyday life. They are not afraid that tomorrow the English language will not be understood. They expect that people will continue to give and receive messages in English and that children will continue to be taught the language. They only begin to worry about the language when they are confronted with specific problems.[20] For example, they will become concerned if people who should "know better" persist in misunderstanding them. The importance of language will come home to them when they are in contact with people who cannot speak English, or refuse to do so. They may become enraged when specialists insist upon speaking to them in words that they cannot understand. They may feel helpless and inadequate if they "cannot find the words" to describe the way they feel or to describe something unique that they have observed. Thus, people will begin to see the importance of culture when they are confronted with its inadequacies or when they have problems using it. However, such insights into the significance of culture are almost never carried over to a durable awareness of the person's dependence upon culture as a whole. Problems with language, for example, occur *within the context* of a given language. The context itself is normally not questioned, merely the specific thing that is responsible for the problem. Similarly, when a television set breaks down, it is usually not the entire system of electrification and electrical appliances which is brought into question, but merely a faulty circuit board.

In order to undertake the process of self-understanding, it is necessary for a person to wrench himself out of the everyday way of looking at the world and into a wider perspective that looks upon human action. Ordinarily, people look at themselves as the centers of the human universe and look at culture as organized around them. Rather than seeing themselves as representatives of long lines of historical development and as participants in complex chains of action beyond the grasp of any single person, they see themselves as the causes of human events. It is just this way of looking at things, of course, that makes a person most the slave of culture. People who believe that they are at the center of human affairs are unlikely ever to question the cultural context in which they are embedded.[21] They will believe that their most important activities are "natural" and could not be otherwise. They will believe that "God speaks in English," in the sense that any thought worth expressing can be expressed in the English language, and that "children need a mother at home if they are going to grow up to be normal." Thus, the people who are the staunchest individualists can at times also be the most abject slaves to culture. Their very individualism is part of a long tradition in Western economic and political life.[22] Conversely, the quickest way for a person to become free is to recognize his dependence on culture. Through such recognition he will be able to scrutinize the cultural context in which he is embedded, see its strengths and limitations, and compare it to other contexts. This is the idea behind the phrase "liberal education." For example, it has been a traditional goal of liberal education that people learn a language other than their native tongue. The reasoning is that learning another language will help allow one to gain a better understanding of communication. This understanding will be the result of clarification, generalization, and relativization with respect to language. Thus, liberal education, in its broadest sense, is carrying the process of self-understanding into as many areas of life as possible.

The importance of culture has been stressed so much in the preceding discussion because it is the key to understanding why the sociologist considers human action to be far wider than the movements of individual organisms. Awareness of culture has also been one of the primary means by which twentieth-century thinkers have liberated themselves from the notion that the self is property and have been able to grasp the idea that the self is process. While the group takes action beyond the organism, it is still easy to think of the group not as a field of activity but as a set of organisms. While the idea of relation brings home the interdependence of human beings, it is still easy to think of relations as happenings between two concrete organisms rather than as processes through which activities are interlaced. Similar evasions are more difficult to make with respect to culture, because culture is the content being organized by groups in their interrelated activities.

Bentley's Concepts of Space One of the most illuminating descriptions of the way in which culture opens out human action beyond the individual was done by Arthur F. Bentley.[23] Bentley's concern was to reveal the idea of space adequate to describing human activity precisely. While this problem appears to be somewhat abstract and removed from the quest for self-understanding, it has close connections with the major themes of this book. By following Bentley through the various ways in which space can be conceived in sociology, one will be able to make the transition from the everyday perspective to the sociological perspective.

The first idea of space discussed by Bentley is "movement-space." There are two varieties of movement-space. The crudest description of movement-space confines the description of human affairs to events that take place inside of the biological organism, such as nerve impulses. Restricting space this narrowly means that the sociologist could never account scientifically for his own activity of selecting a problem for investigation, observing relevant phenomena and reporting his results. A wider movement-space than the inside of the organism is the space formed by body movements. Many sociologists claim to use this space in their research when they state that they are studying "observable human behaviors." However, confining oneself to body movements creates a problem for the sociologist. Sheer body movements have no meanings in themselves. Is waving a clenched fist a sign of anger, a sign of the unity of a group, a greeting, or something else? The answer to this question cannot be determined by studying the body movement itself and confining one's observations to movement-space. Noting this difficulty, Bentley argues that there must be an idea of space adequate to take meanings into account.

The second idea of space discussed by Bentley is "action-space." Here, space is no longer defined by successive body movements, but is defined by the entire field of activity taken up by an organism over time.[24] Action-space is what most people assume in their everyday lives when they describe activities. They begin thinking of space as the field that they use for carrying out their daily activities, and then extend this notion to viewing space as a great container in which things go on. However, close inspection shows that action-space is not adequate for describing human activities. First, it is obvious that human organisms do not occupy action-spaces distinctly separate from one another. There is a great degree of overlap among action-spaces, and what accounts for this overlap is that human beings are engaged in common activities. For the most part, these activities are organized around complexes of cultural objects, such as factories and homes, rather than around biological organisms. Second, the extent of action-space seems to vary with the activity being performed rather than with any state of the organism. When a person goes off to college his action-space changes, not as a result of his organism changing, but as a result of his undertaking a new activity. Thus, Bentley argues that it is putting the cart before the horse to speak in terms of action-space. The space taken up by human events is not the sum of a number of action-spaces but, instead, action-spaces are merely the results of human activities.

Bentley's idea of a space adequate for describing human affairs is an attempt to overcome the weaknesses in the notions of movement-space and action-space. His "transactional space" is neither defined by body movements nor by the field taken up by an organism's activity, but by activities themselves in their spread over time and space. Thus, the activity of making automobiles has a certain spread that defines its transactional space. This spread is already longer than any single individual's lifespan, and wider than any single individual's comprehension (like the unification of France over several centuries). By adopting transactional space as his frame of reference, the sociologist is able to add an historical depth and a comparative breadth to his work. Bentley would argue that, whenever people have given accurate, consistent, adequate and fruitful accounts of human affairs, they have assumed the framework of transactional space whether or not they were aware of doing so. For example, somebody describing the development of the automobile industry and its consequences for the existence of organization does not conduct his analysis in terms of the particular action-spaces of specific individuals who have at one time or another produced or used automobiles. Rather, he considers the transactional space taken up by activities engaged in with respect to automobiles. He does not look at particular action-spaces both because they will overlap with one another in many cases and because they will contain much that is not relevant to his problem. Of course, if someone's concern is describing the activities of organisms, action-space is the appropriate notion of space to use. It is well to ask, however, whether human beings can be considered fruitfully merely as "behavioral organisms" or whether serious inquiry into the human condition demands that action be considered in its wider space and time spread.

Transactional space is the frame in which human action, as the sociologist considers it, occurs. In transactional space, cultural objects and the activities undertaken with respect to them are the center of attention, rather than individuals. These activities always involve groups, at the very least in the sense that for a cultural object to exist it must have a sharable meaning and the possibility of being available to more than one human being. Most cultural objects involve groups to a far greater extent, in the sense that they can be neither produced, used, managed, nor known without the involvement of a number of people. Similarly, the activities that take up transactional space always involve relations, in the sense that group activity is the interlacing of human relations. Producing, using, managing, and knowing all involve, at one time or another, one or more of such relations as cooperation, competition, conflict, love and exchange. By removing oneself from action-space and placing oneself in transactional space, one is enabled to appreciate a process of human action extending far beyond any particular individual and even beyond any specific membership group.

The discussion of groups, relations, and cultural objects as phases of human action, prepares the way for the fourth point contained in the definition of action. A full human action was defined before as a group of people in relation to one another, using a set of objects for the realization of purposes. The notions of group, relation, and object all take one away from the person as central focus. The idea of purpose reinstates the person into the process of human action.

The Purposefulness of Culture   While insight into the immensity of culture allows one to appreciate the dependence of human beings on a wide field of activity, it becomes at some point necessary to account for the existence of this humanized cultural world. Some sociologists have attempted to view culture as a "thing" which somehow determines human beings to act in preordained ways. According to this viewpoint, the person is a resultant of the intersection of the "organic" (biology) and the "superorganic" (cultural object).[25] From where, however, does this superorganic realm arise? A restrictive empiricist might argue that culture is a means by which human beings secure their biological survival as a species. While this may be a result of culture, it is quite difficult to show that all cultural objects have this consequence and even more difficult to show that all cultural objects are direct responses to the drive towards survival (if there is such a drive at all). An expansive empiricist, who is not tied down to movement-space as a frame of reference, need not reduce "culture" to "nature." Rather, since he takes the entire domain of experience as his province, he can note that cultural objects are inserted into human existence through the creative and purposing activities of human beings.[26]

Just as human action has a spatial dimension, it also has a time dimension. This time dimension does not include only the past and the present, but also extends into the future. Human beings project images of the future ahead of themselves and then attempt to bring some of these visions into existence. This futuring activity is responsible for the insertion of new cultural objects into existence, as well as for the more mundane acts involved in achieving culturally given purposes.[27] For example, the chess master who devises a new strategy and then attempts to put it to work is inserting a new cultural object into existence. However, the more general purpose that he has of winning the match is culturally given.

Figure 5.2. WAYS OF CONCEIVING SPACE

Movement-Space: The space taken up by a particular body movement (e.g., the wave of an arm)

Action-Space: The space taken up by the actions of an organism (e.g., the office where a person works)

Socio-Cultural-Space: The space taken up by human projects (e.g., all the places where this book was written, produced, read, etc.)

A Sociologist's View of Time A description of time parallel to Bentley's analysis of space can be developed to make more sense out of evolving human purpose. The most restricted frame of time is "movement-time" confined to present body processes or sucessive body movements. In this notion of time there is no idea of proceeding in a meaningful way from the present into the future. There is merely the notion that at a certain instant a certain movement took place. Movement-time sees human activity as a series of "presents" detached from one another. No attention is given to the fact that accumulated past experiences make a difference for present action.

A wider frame of time is "action-time," which takes account of the summed-up life history of the organism. The framework of action-time carries the recognition that human beings are continually accumulating fresh experiences and, to some degree or other, integrating them with past experiences. Each organism is a unique center for the integration of experience and, according to sociologists who use action-time, memory of past events is a key factor in shaping the course of present activity.[28] The common expression, "His past has come back to haunt him," shows recogntion of the importance of action-time in human existence. Just as action-space spread out to include the organism's activities, so action-time spreads out to include the organism's life history. However, while action-time has distinct advantages over movement-time, it is not adequate to describing human activity, because it does not contain a necessary future reference.

A notion of transactional time can be developed to remedy the deficiencies of movement-time and action-time. Transactional time expands the frame of time to include the future perspectives of human beings. Not only are human beings the organizers and integrators of present and past experiences; they are also the creators of the future through their decisions to carry on or alter ongoing activities in the name of projected purposes. Thus, human activity is prospective (forward-looking) as well as retrospective (backward-looking). Human beings are enmeshed in a web of groups, relations, and cultural objects, but present activities carry with them a future reference. It is through this future reference that human beings are enabled to reject the propagandist's claim that "things are as they have to be." It is also to this future reference that Gurvitch referred when he stated that human experience breaks without cease its own frames of reference. An appropriate motto for the sociologist using action-time would be, "Where there is life there is hope." The sociologist using a transactional perspective would have to deny this and say instead, "Where there is hope there is human activity."

Figure 5.3. WAYS OF CONCEIVING TIME

Movement-Time: The time elapsed in a particular body movement

Action-Time: The lifetime of an organism

Socio-Cultural-Time: The time of human projects—past, present, and future

Note the similarity to the ways of conceiving space in Figure 5.2.

Thus, the idea of purpose brings the person back into human action, not as the fundamental unit of analysis which "causes" everything to happen, but as the focus of purposive activity and as the gateway through which human activity enters the future. What purposes could there be without groups, relations, and cultural objects? Purposes have reference to activities involving a number of people, they relate to other purposes in a number of ways, and they are expressed in terms of plans for cultural objects. Yet what would groups, relations, and cultural objects be without purposes? There might be packs of organisms reproducing themselves in an endless cycle and changing only in response to changes in climate and vegetation, and to mutations in their germ cells. There might be blind and predetermined relations of conflict or collaboration, as in "wars" between armies of ants or in the feeding of the queen ant by worker ants in a single colony. There would not be cultural objects, because for these to reach their full development they must be designed to realize a purpose. There might, however, be such structures as beaver dams, made by organisms following a biologically determined program. In short, there could be life without purpose, but no human existence. There could be action-space and action-time, but no transactional space and time.

Figure 5.4. THE PHASES OF HUMAN ACTION

Group: People are observed acting together.

Relation: People interact with one another cooperatively, competitively, in conflict, and with love.

Cultural object: People act with respect to objects which have meaning for them.

Purpose: People act from motives and for goals.

A human act is a group of human beings, in relation to each other, oriented toward meaningful objects and entertaining purposes. Fighting a war and making love are examples of human actions.

Humanistic sociology is the study of human action in its fullest extent. It is not "humanistic" because it idealizes the individual, preaches the love of humanity, recognizes the emotional element in human existence, or commits itself to equality among classes, races and sexes.[29] It is humanistic because of its expansive empiricism, which takes account of the full range of experience and the complete extent of the process of action in time and space. The major idea of humanistic sociology is that the process of human action is far wider than the activity of any particular individual or group. This means that the human condition cannot be understood by describing it in terms of the needs or desires of individuals, or with reference to the interests or demands of groups. Both groups and individuals are aspects of activity, rather than entities or "things" standing behind activity and "causing" it to happen. Think for a moment about what you call your own activity. Have you ever found yourself completely at rest and then pushed a button to get yourself moving in a particular direction? Not if your experience has been at all like ours. We find ourselves acting whether we like it or not. Even when we are sleeping we have dreams. When we are fortunate enough to integrate our various activities, thoughts, and feelings into some kind of unity and thereby exert some control over them, we consider it quite an achievement, if only a temporary achievement.[30] Continuous organization and reorganization of existence is the price that people pay for having a future reference to activity. It is also the reward for being human.

Figure 5.5. TYPES OF HUMAN ACTIONS

Creative Acts: The meaning of the act is unknown until the act is completed (e.g., the composition of a new song).

Imitative Acts: The meaning of the act is known consciously throughout the act (e.g., practicing a dance step which one has been taught).

Habitual Acts: The act is touched off by an external stimulus and is performed without thought (e.g., brushing your teeth in the morning . . . if you are in the habit).

A full human action includes groups, relations, objects and purposes. However, all human actions do not combine these components in the same way. Florian Znaniecki has distinguished among creative, reproductive, and habitual actions: "Creative actions, reproductive (imitative) actions, and habitual actions differ mainly in the formation of their purposes. At one limit we find creative actions in which the purpose continues to evolve until the action is completed. At the other limit, we observe habitual actions, in which the purpose is formed at the very moment when the action starts. In between these limits fall imitative actions, in which stabilization of the purpose is achieved during the first part of the action and the purpose remains unchanged during its realization."[31] At the limit of habitual actions, future reference is at its minimum and human beings appear to behave like trained animals. The propagandist's dream would be to have all human action except the elite's become habitual and to be directed toward serving the elite's interests. One of the moral purposes of the sociologist is to expand the range of creative actions. However, the sociologist understands very well that, for creative actions to be more than childish play, they must be based on a disciplined appreciation of existing cultural objects. This means that the route to creative freedom involves making a large number of activities habitual and spending a great deal of one's life performing imitative actions. Many actions which are first imitative are usefully made habitual once they are learned. For example, what good would it be to deliberate about how to brush your teeth every morning? And, of course, the destiny of creative actions is to be made imitative. We are relieved that we were not called upon to reinvent the typewriter before beginning work on this book.

Understanding human action as a process involving groups, relations, objects and purposes saves one from the oversimplifications of worshiping such abstractions as "society" or the "individual" or "culture." The problem of human action is not deciding whether one should favor the "individual" over "society" or sacrifice individual rights to the collective good. Rather, it is a problem of which actions should be encouraged and which ones discouraged. It is, of course, also a problem of how actions can be effectively encouraged and discouraged, and how diverse actions can be organized into a harmonious whole. While these problems are far from solution, they are at least far more intelligible than the older dilemmas.

EXPERIENCE AND ACTION

The basis of a humanistic sociology is expansive empiricism. As opposed to restrictive empiricism, which limits sociologists to studying observable behavior, expansive empiricism permits sociologists to investigate the full range of human experience. A comprehensive view of human experience contains the elements of lived experience, or the life of feeling, social experience, or the processes of relation among human actions, cultural experience, or the experience of blocked-off and definable objects, and creative experience, or the very processes of change. None of these types of experience is shut off from the others by fixed boundaries. Rather, experience is a dynamic field, continually moving in the direction of one or another type of experience, but always including elements of all four.

Given a basis of expansive empiricism, the scope of sociology is the process of human action. Human action, from a sociologist's perspective, should not be confused with the behaviors of particular individuals or concrete groups. Rather, it is a process spreading out in space and time far beyond the range of specific individuals or groups. The process of human action contains the four components of group, relation, cultural object and purpose. The definition of a full human action is a group of people in relation to one another, using a set of objects for the realization of purposes. This view of human action assumes definitions of space and time that treat space as a field taken up by activity, rather than as an area circumscribed by body motion or the behavior of an organism, and of time as a process extending from the past into the future, rather than as a series of instants or the life history of an organism.

Expansive empiricism and the full human action define a humanistic sociology, which is distinguished not by its good intentions toward humanity, but by its willingness to investigate all facets of human experience without preconceived notions.

PART II
THE PRINCIPLES OF
SOCIAL ORGANIZATION

6

HUMAN RELATIONS IN A
MASS SOCIETY

In the fourth chapter it was pointed out that using the historical method of sociological research leads to a vision of the human condition summing up the major features of an entire age. In the modern age no one vision has been convincing enough to persuade all reflective people of its accuracy. A number of images have competed with one another, and this has made it possible for people to experiment with different ways of interpreting human existence. This means that in the modern age there are more opportunities to relativize one's view of existence than in preceding eras. It also means that interpreting the significance of one's actions in a broader context than immediate satisfaction or dissatisfaction is a more complicated task than ever before. There is no "normal" view of human relations against which one's own ideas can be judged for their adequacy. Each human being, whether or not he is aware of it, is continually testing assumptions about society for their accuracy and adequacy. It is easier to determine whether or not someone else's vision of the human condition is adequate than to determine the adequacy of one's own image. We may be painfully aware, for example, that someone's assumption that we believe in white supremacy is unfounded, but we can never be sure which of our assumptions about other people miss the mark. This is why we have come to believe that understanding a number of visions of the human condition is the best way to grasp the values and beliefs of others.

THREE ASPECTS OF A COMPREHENSIVE HUMANISTIC VIEW

There are three major aspects of any comprehensive image of the human condition. Perhaps the basic aspect is *a way of seeing oneself in relation to others.* Each vision provides an account of the significant groups composing the social order and the relations that hold among them. For example, in France before the Revolution of 1789, people frequently saw themselves as members of "estates." There were three estates of the realm, each supposedly performing an essential function for the good of the whole. The nobility was composed of landowners who gained their title through inheritance and also made key political and administrative decisions. The higher clergy was composed of the religious leaders of the Catholic Church, many of whom came from the families of the nobility. The "third estate" was composed of the merchants, professionals, and tradesmen. According to the doctrine held by the nobility and higher clergy, the three estates were supposed to cooperate with one another for the social good. When this interpretation was challenged by many members of the "third estate," who held that they were being denied freedom of enterprise by the nobility, a revolutionary conflict ensued that ultimately deprived the nobility and higher clergy of many of their former privileges.[1]

A second aspect of a comprehensive image of the human condition is *a set of values which supposedly are or should be realized in social life.* For example, harmonious cooperation of different social ranks and orderly fulfillment of traditional duties were the values supposedly realized in France before the Revolution. In its struggle against the Old Regime, members of the third estate charged that the claims of harmony masked unjust inequalities, and fought for the new values of individual freedom regardless of traditional and inherited rank.

The third aspect of a comprehensive image of the human condition is *an orientation for action.* Following the image of estates, the appropriate action for each person would depend upon the estate into which he was born or had entered through arduous efforts. Generally, proper action was defined as discharging the duties of one's station without interfering with others discharging their obligations. In this image there was no hope held out for changing the social order in its essentials, though groups could appeal to higher authorities that their traditional rights had been violated. Only in the nineteenth century did the idea that the very structure of society could be changed become widespread. Under the Old Regime, the official image held that the social order was backed by the divine order and, therefore, could not be changed without committing sin.

The three aspects of a vision of social existence are closely tied together. The key values are realized by the significant groups performing appropriate actions. For example, the values of harmonious cooperation were supposedly realized by the three estates discharging their traditional obligations. In the modern era, since it has been difficult to uphold any "official" version of social existence, all images have come into question. At the present time, in the West, three visions of the human condition mainly compete for the adherence of both sociologists and social actors. The images of class society, interest-group society, and mass society have broad followings both in the academy and in the public at large. A fourth image, of community, has gained a number of adherents since World War II.

CLASS SOCIETY

Jean-Paul Sartre has claimed that human beings today live in the age of Marx.[2] What he means by this is that Karl Marx was the first thinker to develop systematically a vision of the human condition in which people could find the meaning of their existence mainly in terms of the social groups to which they related. The image developed by Marx was one in which the broader significance of human action was in terms of economic classes. The human being was first and foremost a member of an economic class, and the values to be realized in society and the appropriate action to be taken by people in the public domain referred to the class structure.

In the second chapter Marxism was discussed as an example of monistic thought in which the primary factor of human existence was economic. Human beings were classified according to their relations to the means of production. In its simplest form Marxism holds that in capitalist societies (where the means for producing goods are owned privately and used for making a profit) there are two classes—owners and workers (bourgeoisie and proletariat in the Marxist terminology). According to the Marxist argument, where the means for producing goods are owned by a few, these few charge the many a fee for access to the tools. The fee is in the form of profits made by the owners. Thus, the Marxist argues that workers do not receive full value back for the labor they expend. The hallmark of capitalist society is class struggle. Workers fight to receive full value for their labor, while owners strive to keep back as much of the product as they can for themselves. In the Marxist view, one is a member of an economic class and, if one is a worker, one should view oneself primarily as a worker struggling to overthrow capitalism. Workers who view themselves as members of religious or national groups first have "false consciousness" because these affiliations are only keeping them from solidarity with fellow workers throughout the world. The goal of the Marxist is a fully "class-conscious" working class dedicated to instituting public ownership of the means of production (socialism).

The Marxist view is that the key value is justice, and that the primary evil of the capitalist order is exploitation. The most basic justice would be realized if workers received full value for their labor instead of having some of it taken away from them in profits. The core of exploitation is living off the labor of others while the others must sell their labor to live. Marxists are convinced that, once economic justice is established through public ownership of the means of production, the way will be open to the realization of creative freedom for all and the treatment of each according to his needs.

Marxists hold that the appropriate action for workers is revolution aimed at destroying the capitalist system and its ruling class of owners. They do not believe that owners will voluntarily surrender their privileges, so they hold that coercion is necessary to establish justice. Marxists argue that revolution will come with the sharpening of the class struggle, though they disagree on how to plan for revolution and the exact form that it will take.[3] Though it is not readily apparent to Americans, who live under an anti-Marxist regime, Marxism in its many varieties is probably the most widely believed in image of the human condition throughout the world. Much of its appeal resides in the fact that many people regard economic concerns as the most important in their lives and see in revolution the hope for a better future.

INTEREST-GROUP SOCIETY

If everyone believed in the image of class society, things would be simple for the Marxist. The workers probably would have overthrown capitalism long ago, and there would be no more need for Marxists because there would be no more class divisions. The Marxist could forget the revolution and enjoy the good life. However, since the appearance of Marxism in the mid-nineteenth century several other images have appeared to compete with it. The one most widely held in the United States is that of interest-group society.

In the image of interest-group society, human beings are not primarily members of any single class, but belong to a number of diverse and often conflicting groups.[4] A person may be a worker, but he may also be a Catholic, an American, a black, a home owner, and many other things. Some of his affiliations may reinforce one another, but others may pull him apart. For example, the fact that he is a black and a worker may make Marxism appealing to him, but the fact that he is an American, a Catholic, and a home owner may dispose him to reject Marxism. For those who hold the interest-group-society image, multiple memberships and cross-cutting cleavages make any monistic image like Marxism far too simple a view of human existence. Life appears more like a balancing act than a straightforward boxing match. People are continually faced with conflicts among loyalties, and they must make some sense out of their lives by choosing one horn or the other of various dilemmas.[5] One is lucky when one can strike a relatively harmonious balance among one's various allegiances. All too often the self is divided among conflicting interests.[6]

The values associated with the image of the multigroup society are diversity, autonomy, tolerance, and compromise. For the pluralist, social life is like an Oriental bazaar with a remarkable variety of sights, sounds and smells. The pluralist resists "reducing" the diversity of existence to any single interest, be it economic, religious, or any other. Amid this diversity, the individual gains a measure of autonomy because, wherever there is conflict among claims, there is room for individual choice and ultimately even creativity. Thus, the pluralist sees creative freedom emerging out of conflict, not out of economic justice. Within the pluralist scheme the problem arises of how society holds together. This is why those who hold the multigroup image value toleration and compromise so highly. They find these virtues necessary to maintaining an "equilibrium" of diverse interests and opportunity for exercising individual initiative.

The social action favored by pluralists runs to reform rather than revolution. Any attempt to change the social order wholesale will involve the imposition of a simplified and distorted image of the human condition. Thus, if one is concerned with realizing greater justice, the wisest action is piecemeal reform through established institutions. Those who hold the image of interest-group society usually affirm the goodness of representative democracy in which political parties compete through elections for government offices. They claim that the system of elections is a peaceful substitute for revolution, and that by working within this system justice can be progressively realized.[7]

MASS SOCIETY

The image of group society was developed towards the end of the nineteenth century in response to Marxism. In the twentieth century yet another image has attracted the attention of many social thinkers.[8] Those who hold the vision of mass society claim that human beings in the West are members of either masses or elites. The masses are composed of individuals who can relate to each other only on the basis of what they can get out of the other, not on any genuine sharing of experience. The masses are herded into vast organizations where they perform particular functions and do not get the chance to engage in creative work, make decisions about their destiny or inquire into their situation. Most important, the masses are manipulated through propaganda into doubting their ability to think independently. They are taught by advertisers that comfort is far more valuable than adventure, and by political ideologists that they are threatened by vicious enemies. They are convinced that only specialists understand the multifarious aspects of human existence, and that they are incompetent to judge what is good for them. Elites are those on top of contemporary organizations.[9] They gain wealth, power, and dignity when their organizations accumulate greater resources. For those who hold the image of mass society, the major principle of elite domination is manipulation through the mass media of communication. Elites in the United States project myths of the "communist menace" to keep control over the masses, while elites in the Soviet Union project myths of "American imperialism" for the same purpose. One of the major reasons for the appearance of mass-society theory is the growth of large organizations wielding impressive power in both East and West. The emergence of a manipulative elite in communist countries cast doubt on the idea that justice would be automatically realized in a socialist order, while the growth of enormous organizational complexes uniting government, industry, labor and the universities (for example, the military-industrial complex) cast doubt on the notion that diversity was a hallmark of Western countries with modified capitalist systems.

For those who hold the mass-society image, the values sought in such an order are wealth, power, influence and loyalty for the elite, coupled with security and transient pleasures for the mass. Life is seen as hollow, concerned only with the externals of existence. In a mass society, responsibility for public affairs tends to be shunned, creativity is cut off, and the appreciation of complex experiences is discouraged. More and more of life becomes organized, which means that contributions are standardized and the personal touch is lost. People are not so much faced with the problem of which side to choose in an ultimate struggle or how to balance a myriad of allegiances, but how to keep from being swamped by organizations.

The image of mass society is far more pessimistic than those of class society and group society with regard to social action. Revolution seems hopeless to those who see human beings as isolated from genuine relations with one another, while reform of mammoth organizations appears to be futile. Many of those who hold the image of mass society without realizing it view apathy and "going along with things" as the only sensible strategies. However, those who have written about mass society counsel rebellion. The individual, along with those few he can find to share experience, should resist the organizations by asserting the possibilities for realizing such values as free inquiry, justice and respect for others. When ordered by an organization to commit barbarous actions, such as slaughtering civilians in war, the individual should refuse to obey orders. Resistance is a last ditch effort to preserve dignity in a hostile world.[10]

EXERCISE

Analyze the contents of American television programs from the viewpoints of the three images—class society, interest-group society, and mass society. Can television be considered as a tool of dominant economic classes? Is it an arena for the competition of interest groups? Is it a means for elites to manipulate masses?

COMMUNITY

Since World War II, people who have generally agreed with the mass-society image have sometimes attempted to push beyond this view of the human condition. They have not so much come up with a new vision of the present as a possibility for the future. What would the rejection of mass society mean? Primarily it would call for the establishment of trusting and cooperative relations among people engaged in common endeavors. Such relations are the substance of community. Under the emerging vision of community, people would view themselves as cooperators in realizing a set of values to which they were committed.

The most significant question with regard to community is, of course, What values are sought? What is the principle that brings people together to cooperate? For the most part, the answer to this question has been the preservation or expansion of some particular tradition, or of the values of some restricted group. For example, the alleged rights of the "black community" have become a major issue in current political controversy. With the growth of the black movement, Jews, Italians, and "middle Americans" have "discovered" their group identities.[11] People have reacted against mass society by reasserting claims to cultural and even political autonomy as members of nationality groups. This has been evidenced by protest movements in the two great multinational states where the mass-society image best applies— the United States and the Soviet Union. The "ethnic revival" can be seen as an ingenious way of going beyond the lonely resistance of the rebel in mass society.

There is a second way of reacting against mass society in the name of community. This is to envision a rational and inclusive community which would not be restricted to any particular group of people formed by historical accident. The primary value of such a rational community would be furtherance of the process of self-understanding described in the first chapter with the aim of a critical synthesis of the contributions of various peoples throughout the world.[12] People would not attempt to affirm the superiority of their particular tradition, or even the independence of that tradition, but would attempt to appreciate the contributions of others and in turn show others what they might appreciate. Such a rational and inclusive community is far from being realized in the present world, but it is the commitment of the authors of this book. A rational community would not eliminate conflict, but at least people would know why they were opposed.

The image of the human condition guiding most of the following discussion will be that of mass society. However, since this image is not wholly adequate, some of the observations will be drawn from the perspectives of class society and interest-group society. Those who have reflected on the images discussed above will realize that each of them distorts experience by overemphasizing some relations that appear in everyday life and ignoring others. Such an understanding of the limitations of visions of the human condition is a beneficial result of relativization. However, one must still be committed to the general standpoint that one finds the most adequate, and modify it to take account of other insights. The image of mass society has been chosen by us because we find large organizations to be a very significant factor in everyday life. We find that, though we are members of a multiplicity of groups, the ones that determine our fate the most are highly organized, impersonal, and often knit into complexes. We find that, though we are workers in the sense that we do not own our means of production, we are separated from other workers by specialized function and difficulties in communication. Mass society helps us explain our situations better than the other images, just as rational community helps us express our goals. It is within this context that we interpret the various types of human relations. However, it is important to note that many other thoughtful observers have reached different conclusions than ours. We can only present the interpretation we have chosen as convincingly as we can, recognizing the existence of other perspectives. It is ultimately up to you to evaluate the adequacy of our interpretation to your own existence.

Figure 6.1. CONTEMPORARY IMAGES OF SOCIETY

Image	Major Group	Value-Quality	Appropriate Action
Class society	Economic classes	Justice and freedom to produce	Structural revolution
Interest-group society	Interest groups	Peaceful competition and freedom of choice	Legal reform
Mass society	Elites and masses	Authenticity and self-consciousness	Individualized and small-group resistance
Community	Communities	Creation and appreciation of culture	Institutional experimentation

THE CHARACTERISTIC RELATIONS OF MASS SOCIETY

Whether a collectivity of individuals is seen as a class, group, or mass society, the nature of the relations between the individuals is a crucial consideration for sociologists. What is the basis for the interrelation between people? Chemists ask a somewhat similar question when they try to account for the interrelation between molecules or atoms. Why do twice as many hydrogen atoms as oxygen atoms combine with one another in just this proportion to form the compound known as water? These chemical bonds, as any high school student can tell you, result from the different "shells" of electrons surrounding each type of atom and the resulting valence, or physical attraction, created. However, this analogy to human relatedness has severe limitations. The primary one is that the chemists' atoms have no ability to reflect upon their situation. Further, atoms cannot choose to interact. Human beings can inspect their activities and can, and sometimes do, change them. Whereas chemists today would tend to agree about the general mechanisms involved in chemical bonding, social thinkers have posed contrasting answers of different degrees of completeness to the problem of how social bonding occurs and its forms. Departing even further from the model of chemistry, those concerned with human relatedness are not even in agreement that there is a general solution to this problem applicable to all times and places. Of course, "common sense" is of no great help in solving this problem: note the contradiction in the proverbs "birds of a feather flock together," and "opposites attract."

Emile Durkheim, considered to be one of the more important of the late nineteenth- and early twentieth-century sociologists, viewed the task of accounting for the bonds between people as central to sociological inquiry. He called the presence of bonds of interrelation "social solidarity." Durkheim believed that the basis for social solidarity was dependent upon the extent of the division of labor (people doing specialized tasks, rather than all doing the same thing, such as farming).[13] Where there was very little division of labor the solidarity was termed "mechanical." Kinship and neighborliness acted as external forces holding people together. As jobs became differentiated, social solidarity could be accounted for by the interdependence of people. Durkheim termed this "modern" type of solidarity "organic." Applying this idea, society can be compared to a living thing in which the organs of the body, such as the heart, brain, and liver, are interdependent. Each organ is needed to contribute to the life of the whole organism, and thus to its own life as well. Thus, in Durkheim's model, people are seen as performing functions necessary to the persistence of the society. The personal meaning of their lives is not important to the social scientist, only what they do for the so-called social organism.

While Durkheim's idea points to a significant feature of contemporary life, it is not entirely accurate to think of society as an organism. Are societies such tightly knit wholes that everyone in them performs one or more functions necessary to the survival of the whole? The first reason to question the organic metaphor is the existence of widespread conflict in modern societies. The presence of diverse groups acting on incompatible images of the human condition (for example, the class and interest-group images) makes it difficult to determine just what is supposed to be maintained. Social conflicts frequently arise when some groups are accused of not making enough of a contribution to the whole, or even of trying to destroy the whole. Some people in the United States today believe that welfare recipients are destroying society by draining away money from those who have "earned" it while others hold that capitalists living off investments are parasites in the social body. The existence of these two divergent positions shows how difficult it is to characterize society as an organism.

A second and related reason to question the organic metaphor is the fact that in social existence some people gain benefits at the expense of others. It is not ordinarily thought that the liver is making a profit at the expense of the heart, or that the lungs are exerting arbitrary power over the big toe, but it is often thought that some groups and individuals are "getting the better" of others. Even if it was assumed that everyone made some contribution to the maintenance of the whole, could it also be assumed that everyone was being rewarded justly for their contributions? This problem of injustice and inequality does not usually arise with regard to biological organisms. Of course, the fact that human beings do debate about what is just is closely tied to the fact that they enter into conflicts. Perhaps an entirely rational society, in which everyone was convinced that all relations were just, would appear more like an organism than present societies. This, at least, is what utopians who have described static ideals of social perfection have felt. However, there is even question that the disappearance of conflict and injustice would make society more like an organism.

The third and most important reason to question the organic metaphor is that social existence, at least in modern times, is continually changing. If, as Durkheim thought, groups are the organs of society, Western societies have been discarding organs and adding new ones at a furious pace over the last several centuries. Certainly, biological organisms undergo change across generations. However, a given dog or cat does not throw away its heart and add something entirely different to replace it in a single life time. With the advent of automatic pin-setters, the pin boys have disappeared from the bowling scene. Meanwhile, the group of people who maintain snowmobiles has grown very rapidly. These relatively superficial changes are matched by more fundamental transformations, such as the emergence of groups of skilled technicians and the decline of the landed aristocracy.[14] There is no reason to believe that even with the advent of "justice" there would be an end to the formation and dissolution of groups. So long as people create new meanings, there will be no way of reducing society to an organism.

FURTHER VIEWS OF MODERN SOCIETY

Ferdinand Toennies would agree with his contemporary Durkheim that the type of social solidarity has changed from "primitive" to modern society.[15] According to Toennies, social relationships in earlier times were characterized by an emphasis on treating others as ends in themselves rather than as means to ends. This end-oriented type of relationship is called a *gemeinschaft* and it refers to the way family members or friends are supposed to treat one another. Toennies' modern *gesellschaft* relationships are of the "what's in it for me" and "you scratch my back and I'll scratch yours" variety. They are based on rational calculations of advantage. An important aspect of *gesellschaft* relationships is the need for a third party to maintain the stability of these relationships. Under a *gemeinschaft* people are united by bonds of feeling and sentiment, and tend to resolve their disputes through custom or mediation. Under a *gesellschaft*, the parties to the relationship do not necessarily have any bonds of sentiment uniting them and frequently even try to eliminate emotion from their dealings with one another. They confront each other trying to get the best bargain. Under these conditions there is no guarantee that promises and contracts will be honored if one of the parties finds out that honoring them will be to his disadvantage. Therefore, where *gesellschaft* relationships come to predominate, a strong state usually arises to enforce contracts through law and, if necessary, coercion.

The British social thinker Henry Sumner Maine was impressed by the importance of contract in modern life.[16] Like Durkheim and Toennies, he devised a classification scheme for human relations in which there were two major types. Maine termed his types "status" and "contract." Basing much of his conclusions on research about the family in ancient Rome, Maine described how one's position (status) in the family (father, eldest son, for example) was the major criterion for the way in which people behaved towards one another. With the expansion of the Roman Empire, and the concommitant decline in power of the patriarchal (father-dominated) family, relationships based on rational decision (contract) rather than who you were (status) became the predominant type.

In summary, then, many influential social thinkers have claimed that the dominant mode of relating in modern society is of an organic, *gesellschaft,* and contract variety.[17] How useful is this composite picture for understanding relations at present? How congruent is it with the mass society vision?

Figure 6.2. FROM TRADITIONAL TO MODERN SOCIETY

Theorist	Traditional Society	Modern Society
Durkheim	Mechanical Solidarity (Unity through homogeneity)	Organic Solidarity (Unity through interdependent functions)
Toennies	*Gemeinschaft* (Unity through shared sentiment)	*Gesellschaft* (Unity through rational exchange)
Maine	Status (Rights through birth and tradition)	Contract (Rights through voluntary agreement)

Are relations in mass society characterized by rational calculation? The sales situation has often been used to illustrate the rationally calculated relationships of modern society. In the pure form of the sale, the buyer and seller confront one another, each having the aim of gaining maximum advantage in the bargain. Where there are no other considerations, any means, including threats, fraud and other kinds of coercion, will be used by either party when he calculates that it is to his advantage to do so. Whatever one party gains, the other loses, and each party, knowing this, tries to make sure that he wins. It should be evident that the pure sales situation is not the most typical relationship in modern society. For example, an insight into buyer-seller relationships today is provided by an inspection of advertisements. Advertisers exhort people to make purchases on anything but rational grounds. "Use this hair cream and girls will find you so sexually appealing that you will have to fight them off!" "Chew this gum and boys will want to kiss you!" "Drive this car and everyone will be envious of you!" Such advertising does not encourage people to make choices on a rational basis, since it appeals to nonrational fantasies and, even more importantly, does not give the kind of information about the product relevant to making a rational choice about its merits when compared to competitors. A possible reason for the lack of information is that there is exceedingly little difference between one brand and another. From comparably priced American cars to innumerable varieties of detergents, not only are the differences among competing products miniscule and irrelevant (blue bleaching beads versus green whitening crystals) but the same companies frequently produce more than one of the "competitors."

RELATIONSHIPS IN ECONOMIC SITUATIONS

The interrelationship between the consumer and the producer can thus hardly be characterized as rational, although the calculating manipulation of the masses (consumers) can be seen as a rational activity for the elite (manufacturers). The sales situation in this case is only partial. The manufacturers have their eyes open and are clear about their aims, but the same cannot always be said for the consumers. The imbalance between manufacturers and consumers may be alleviated to some extent by the appearance of the "consumer movement," which calls for greater information about products, enhanced product safety and more rights for aggrieved consumers. However, it remains the case that even the face-to-face relationship of salesman and customer is frequently anything but a *gesellschaft* or rational type. Aside from outright lying (the image of the used-car salesman), salespeople often resort to a form of behavior that has been termed, borrowing from Toennies, *pseudo-gemeinschaft*.[18] The prefix "pseudo" means false, and the whole term indicates feigning *gemeinschaft*. In pretending to be interested in you as a person, the salesman will ask about your family, listen to your complaints about your job, or discuss the possibilities that rain may ruin your picnic tomorrow. As the customers usually realize, with increasingly less dismay about it, this "interest" is shown by the salesman only to make the sale; it is not genuine.

Pseudo-gemeinschaft is, of course, not confined to commercial relations. It is present in situations in which one person is attempting to gain another's cooperation in something that might be unpleasant for the other or against the other's interests. For example, the "bedside manner" of medical doctors is sometimes an aid in gaining the cooperation of the patient. Teachers sometimes pretend to conduct their classes on a basis of friendship and openness even though they must give grades, while administrators show great "concern" for office personnel who would be fired if they did not obey orders to the letter. *Pseudo-gemeinschaft* is a potent barrier to social change because it gives some people an excuse not to fight for greater rights. After all, if the boss is such a "nice guy" it would not be right to hurt him.

FURTHER EVIDENCE OF NONRATIONALITY

Thus, economic relationships are not the only ones characterized by a lack of rational calculations. The masses as citizens are treated in a similar manner to the masses as consumers. Individual politicians are packaged by advertising firms which also do market research to see what personal characteristics should be played up, manufactured, toned down, or hidden.[19] Political campaigns, like automobile advertisements, usually fail to give information relevant to helping the person (in this case the voter) make a decision as to which candidate would make the best officeholder. And, like the proverbial used-car-salesman's guarantee, the candidates' promises must be listened to without naively believing that there will be a real effort to fulfill them.

Racial, religious, ethnic, and sexual discrimination, as has been pointed out by civil rights workers, is not a rational activity either. One decides that a person is unfit to be an employee, a neighbor, a fellow club member, or some other kind of associate, not on the basis of characteristics relevant to the association (for example, work skills, friendliness, or special personal interests) but on the basis of some unrelated criterion. What has been termed reverse discrimination, that is, giving people preferential treatment because of their racial, religious, ethnic, or sexual characteristics, does not constitute a particularly rational relationship either. Although reverse discrimination has been prevalent for a very long time, it has only recently been publicly acknowledged. Slogans such as "Buy Black" exemplify this position.

Related to reverse discrimination is the entire "ethnic revival" which, under the impetus of the black civil rights movement, arose in the late 1960s. America has long been known as a "nation of immigrants," but it has also been known as a "melting pot" in which the particular customs and characteristics of the immigrant groups became fused into "the American way." During the 1940s and 1950s the attempts to assimilate into the dominant culture sometimes went as far as people changing their names to more Anglo-Saxon forms. In the 1960s many people began to acknowledge that there were "lumps in the melting pot." The reestablishment of ethnicity can be seen as an attempt to overcome another feature of relations within mass society —the atomization of individuals, which results in increasing isolation.

Atomization implies not only the lack of close relations with other individuals, but also no meaningful relations with collectivities.[20] One's relationship to the larger collectivity of the state is the only meaningful relationship, but it is only one way—from the state to the individual. Even relations within the nuclear family (parents and minor children) have become less intense and less meaningful. Other agencies can perform most of the traditional functions such as preparing food and clothing, child care, and education. A large proportion of women work and are capable of self-support. Geographic mobility due to shifting job opportunities reduces interaction with other relatives.[21] Divorce looms as a very real possibility. With over one in every three marriages ending in divorce, the husband-wife relationship is no longer seen by many as a lifetime commitment.[22]

DECEPTIVE UNITY IN INTEREST GROUPS

The pluralist or interest-group image of the human condition provides a very different view of contemporary, and especially American, society from the one discussed above. In the pluralist image, people relate to one another as members of groups of one sort or another. They also relate to the state as members of groups. America, in particular, is seen as a nation of joiners. Mass-society proponents give two complementary arguments to counter the pluralist's claim. First, they contend that sizable proportions of Americans are not members of voluntary associations. When a representative sample of adults was asked, in 1960, "Are you a member of any organizations now: trade or labor unions, business organizations, social groups, professional or farm organizations, cooperatives, fraternal or veteran groups, athletic clubs, political, charitable, civic, or religious organizations, or any other organized groups?," only 57 percent answered affirmatively, which means that approximately 43 percent of all adults are not members of any voluntary associations.[23] The second argument, which is the more crucial one, refers to the responsiveness of the groups to their members. Since the pluralist position sees the group as transmitting demands to the state (through lobbies and general pressure-group tactics), as well as interpreting the actions of the government to its members, groups must allow for the democratic input of their members. However, it has generally been conceded that most voluntary associations, particularly labor groups, are run by elites. The conclusions of Robert Michels' famous study of the German Social

Democratic party in the late nineteenth century, in which he found control by an oligarchy despite democratic procedures and beliefs, seem to hold true for many groups in the United States. Michels even formulated an "iron law of oligarchy" that related the increasing size and complexity of organizations to control by elites.[24] S. M. Lipset, an advocate of the pluralist position, has acknowledged that his analysis of the International Typographical Union, which showed it to be democratically controlled, points to an exception rather than the rule.[25] It is significant to note that, if one excluded unions, fully half of American adults are not affiliated with any organized group.[26]

DIRECTNESS IN COMMUNICATION

Linked to the atomization of individuals is the fact that relations in mass society are more often mediated than face-to-face. Mediation can be of two types, both of which are prevalent in mass society. First, mediation can refer to communication via some technology that allows people to relate to one another over great distances and time spans. For example, communication by telegraph can span continents. Second, mediation can refer to communication via a third party. For example, journalists often convey messages from politicians to their constituents. An important result of mediated relations of both types is their distortion. Even the telephone distorts. Have you ever felt frustrated by not being able to see a person's facial expressions while talking to him over the phone?[27] You have difficulty in judging how what you are saying is being understood. Messages are misinterpreted (communications analysts call this "noise in the system") and neither party is quite certain about the effects on the other. Relating to others via the written word (as the present authors are with you, the reader) is even more noise-producing, because authors of books and journalists (as opposed to letter writers) rarely obtain feedback from those to whom they are communicating. Radio and television also suffer from a general lack of feedback, especially immediate feedback, and thus serve as poor vehicles for undistorted communication.[28] Newspapers, radio, and television are often referred to as mass media because they are able to reach a mass audience. A mass audience is not only composed of a large proportion of the population, but also refers to the level of exertion and skill (both relatively low) needed to receive the medium.[29] For a number of reasons, including the fact that the more complex the message, the more possibility there is for distortion, the mass media have generally communicated only the simplest types of messages.

Figure 6.3. FACE-TO-FACE COMMUNICATION AND MEDIATED COMMUNI-
CATION

Face-to-Face	*Mediated*
Grasp of the total situation	Access to information through a limited number of senses
Chance to respond immediately to initiatives	Limited opportunity to respond to initiatives
Opportunity to cooperatively determine the relation	Terms of relation set at origin of message
Possibility to check effects of communication	Limited possibility for ongoing evaluation of effects

Because so many of our relations are mediated through the mass media (such as those with the President, the news commentator, the talk-show host), relations within mass society are often on a superficial and somewhat childlike level. Issues are oversimplified, possible solutions are seen as either right or wrong, people are classified as either good or bad, and much of life's richness and complexity is lost to people.[30] The implications of this stereotyping go beyond lamenting about the masses not being able to appreciate the fine points of experience. Of greater significance is that these oversimplifications allow the elite groups, who control the mass media, to distort "reality" and present a particular biased view. Manipulation of the masses through the media is accomplished not only in this way, but also by simply not allowing opposing views to be aired: "The idea that gets amplification and extension through the media—not necessarily the most reasonable idea—is the one which wins the endorsement of the people. Those who are in positions controlling access to media can take advantage of this fact to gain public support for ideas and policies which would not be accepted by the majority of people if they had to compete fairly in the open marketplace of ideas."[31]

IS LIFE A GAME?

Relations in mass society are also characterized by frequent reference to game and drama images of life. "All the world's a stage." "Life is like a game." Nixon had a secret "game plan" to end the Vietnam war. In one sense these images add a poetic quality to everyday speech.

Unfortunately, metaphors become reality to people, and life does become a game or a play.[32] These beliefs result in people acting inauthentically. Believing that they are but actors obeying scripts, they do not feel responsible for their actions. Their "real" selves would never kill others—but while playing the part of soldier one may kill because it is in the script. One may begin to wonder under these circumstances whether the "real" self ever makes its appearance, whether there is such a "real" self at all.[33] And what happens to those who cannot change parts rapidly enough? Ex-soldiers have been known to "go berserk" and shoot people in their home towns, confusing them with "the enemy." But, life is not all a play. Curtains do not come down and the bodies do not get up and walk off stage. If one believes that life is only a game, one's actions need not be taken too seriously—it is all merely an amusement. The game metaphor would have you believe that everyone has an equal chance of winning since the rules of the game are fully known to all, and everyone is striving for the same goal. One gets the idea that poor people simply are not really trying and one need not worry about them. If they want to become rich, they have the same chance as anyone. The life-as-a-game view is being challenged in contemporary life in a number of ways. Workers (for example, the United Auto Workers) have begun to bargain for meaningful jobs rather than only wage increases. More and more people are "dropping out of society," setting up experimental communities and refusing to play *the* game.

Figure 6.4. Is Life a Game?

Game	Life
Everyone knows the rules.	The rules are not clear.
Everyone accepts the rules.	Different people play by different rules.
Everyone obeys the rules.	Rules are made to be broken.
The rules stay the same during the game.	The rules keep changing.
The rules affect everyone in the same way.	There is discrimination.
The outcome is not a matter of life or death.	The outcome of life is death.
Can you really say that life is a game?	

EXERCISE

Do you ever use the "game" metaphor to refer to your social relations? If so, when? Do you use it accurately, or does it distort the situation? If it distorts the situation, in what ways does it do so?

An example of life-as-a-game beliefs affecting relations in mass society is the popularity of the put-on: "The put-on is not mere kidding or joshing, or even lying or telling tall tales. . . . The goal of the kidder is to pass off untruth as truth. . . . For the kidder, the joy comes from letting the victim *know* he's been gulled and in watching that realization sink into his consciousness. In contrast, the victim of the put-on is never really let in on the truth—if, indeed, the truth ever existed. The victim is constantly in a state of uncertainty and confusion."[34] The put-on's significance lies less in its effect than as a symbol of relations in mass society—inauthentic, manipulative, impersonal, and irrational.

Figure 6.5. MASS SOCIETY AND AUTHENTIC RELATIONS

Mass Society	Authentic Community
Cynicism	Trust
Anxiety	Confidence
Manipulation	Cooperation
Private Advantage	Public Contribution
The Put-On	Dialogue

EXERCISE

How often do you consciously engage in manipulating others by such means as the put-on? In what relations do you use such manipulative means? What are you trying to accomplish in these relations? In what cases do you attempt to be honest? Which do you find more satisfying—manipulation or honesty?

The impact of relations in mass society—a lack of real interest in you as a person, not being sure if the other is trying to manipulate you, not really understanding the whole interaction—leaves people bewildered, unsettled, and somewhat anxious about their entire situation. In extreme cases this produces a state of anomie in which a person does not know what he should or should not do.[35] The general reaction to mass society is one of looking to others for guidelines, since one cannot trust one's own judgment. Many sociologists have discussed this general phenomenon from a number of different approaches. In David Riesman's definition of the other-directed character-type, one's contemporaries are the source of an individual's goals and behavior, and cues from them are constantly being monitored to see that one is doing the right thing. Although Riesman discusses how parents mold their children into other-directedness, making them "feel guilty not so much about violation of inner standards as about failure to be popular or otherwise to manage . . ." relations with other children, *why* parents and educators feel that other-directedness is the ideal is a more basic question.[36]

A somewhat similar understanding about people in mass society is reached by William H. Whyte in his book *The Organization Man*.[37] Rather than discuss relations in general, he treats them within the setting of large business and governmental organizations. Whyte goes beyond the analysis of other-directedness by discussing the content of this orientation, which he calls "the social ethic." His analysis provides some indication of why other-directedness arises. The basic principles of the social ethic are the beliefs in belongingness as the individual's ultimate need, and the group as the major source of human creativity. The social ethic is an ideology in that it justifies the existing types of relations, particularly power relations, in mass society. In the middle levels of massive organizations, technicians and administrators must function as efficient "teams," carrying out the orders of top management. Other-directedness and the social ethic help create such team work, and play down the possible satisfactions that a person might derive from making basic decisions about the goals and conditions of his work. Demands for participation in major decisions are viewed as threats by organizational elites, and security-conscious parents and teachers seem to know intuitively that the road to the suburbs is traveled by those who understand "team work."

SUMMARY

Each image of the human condition contains a view of human relations. For those who hold the image of class society, modern life is characterized by bitter conflict among classes attempting to satisfy incompatible interests. Owners supposedly try to draw away as much of the worker's product as they can for their own uses, while workers attempt to wrest control of the economy away from the owners. In contrast, those who hold the image of group society believe that competition among a multiplicity of divergent interests is the dominant social relation in contemporary life. Human beings, according to this view, are often split apart by internal conflict among their diverse allegiances. Finally, those who hold the image of mass society claim that the dominant relations today are impersonal, mediated and manipulative. A potent symbol of the mass society is the "put-on" where the victim is never fully aware of the basis of the relation or its implications. In a sense, advertising is an enormous put-on because it uses rational methods to make people behave irrationally.

Writers like Riesman and Whyte have argued that the dominant character-type in the mass society is the other-directed person who derives his standards of action from those around him. This character-type is well adapted to the massive organizations of contemporary life, which demand a combination of team work, obedience, and initiative in handling details from their employees. Thus, behind the relations of mass society are hierarchical organizations channeling the various social processes and activities.

READINGS ON IMAGES OF THE HUMAN CONDITION

The following list of readings is a small sampling of representatives of the four images discussed in this chapter: class society, interest-group society, mass society, and community. It may be used as a beginning in the attempt to clarify one's own image of the human condition in the contemporary world. Select the image that seems closest to your own, choose a theorist from the list and, as you read the work, identify the points at which you agree and disagree with the presentation. Then sample some of the other images so that you can relativize your perspective.

CLASS SOCIETY

BACHRACH, PETER. *The Theory of Democratic Elitism.* Boston: Little, Brown, 1967. Bachrach criticizes the interest-group image and suggests a class image stressing participatory democracy at the work place.

BARAN, PAUL A., and SWEEZEY, PAUL M. *Monopoly Capital.* New York: Monthly Review Press, 1966. Baran and Sweezey apply Marxian economics to American capitalism and social structure.

DOMHOFF, G. WILLIAM. *Who Rules America?* Englewood Cliffs, N.J.: Prentice-Hall, 1967. Domhoff discusses the extent to which there is a ruling elite in the United States.

HAMILTON, RICHARD F. *Class and Politics in the United States.* New York: Wiley, 1972. Hamilton argues that the most significant political issues in the United States today are based on class rather than any other considerations.

MARCUSE, HERBERT. *One-Dimensional Man.* Boston: Beacon Press, 1966. Marcuse contends that capitalist society is maintained through the manipulation of human desires and the systematic narrowing of choices by elite groups.

INTEREST-GROUP SOCIETY

DAHL, ROBERT. *Who Governs?* New Haven: Yale University Press, 1961. Dahl argues that inequalities in the United States are "dispersed" rather than "cumulative."

DAHRENDORF, RALF. *Class and Class Conflict in Industrial Society.* Stanford: Stanford University Press, 1959. Dahrendorf argues that there are inequalities in power throughout the institutions of industrial society, not only in the economy.

GALBRAITH, JOHN KENNETH. *American Capitalism.* Boston: Houghton Mifflin, 1952. Galbraith argues that corporate power in the United States is checked by the "countervailing power" of unions and government.

RIESMAN, DAVID, et al. *The Lonely Crowd.* New Haven: Yale University Press, 1961. Riesman argues that rather than power elites, deadlocked "veto groups" determine public policy in the United States.

ROSE, ARNOLD M. *The Power Structure: Political Process in American Society.* New York: Oxford University Press, 1967. Rose presents a comprehensive defense of the interest-group image.

MASS SOCIETY

CARR, E. H. *The New Society.* New York: St. Martin's Press, 1960. Carr's vision of mass society emphasizes the importance of economic planning and manipulation through propaganda in determining social structure and policy.

JASPERS, KARL. *Man in the Modern Age.* New York: Doubleday, n.d. Jaspers presents the classic description of contemporary industrial society as a purposeless "life-order" in which human beings are merely cogs in a vast "wheelworks."

MILLS, C. WRIGHT. *The Power Elite.* New York: Oxford University Press, 1956. Mills argues that the tendency in American social structure is toward a mass society dominated by a "power elite" of wealth, military power, and high administrative position.

NISBET, ROBERT. *Community and Power.* New York: Oxford University Press, 1962. Nisbet maintains that in the modern world there is a tendency for "intermediate" organizations to disappear and for masses of individuals to confront power elites without the protection of solidary groups.

ORTEGA Y GASSET, JOSÉ. *The Revolt of the Masses.* New York: New American Library, 1950. Ortega describes the rise of the undisciplined "mass man" as the dominant social type in the twentieth century.

COMMUNITY

DEWEY, JOHN. *The Public and its Problems.* New York: Holt, 1927. Dewey argues that problems become a public responsibility when they affect people who are not directly involved in creating the original situation.

GOODMAN, PERCIVAL, and GOODMAN, PAUL. *Communitas.* Chicago: University of Chicago Press, 1947. The Goodmans describe various possible communitarian solutions to the problems of modern societies.

MCLUHAN, MARSHALL. *Understanding Media.* New York: McGraw-Hill, 1964. McLuhan proclaims the arrival of the "global village" brought about by the worldwide web of electronic media.

MUMFORD, LEWIS. *The Culture of Cities.* New York: Harcourt Brace Jovanovich, 1938. Mumford documents the decline of community in the contemporary megalopolis.

ROSZAK, THEODORE. *The Making of a Counter Culture.* New York: Doubleday, 1969. Roszak discusses the "youth revolution" of the 1960s in terms of cultural transformation and the quest for solitary communities in a technocratic and scientifically oriented society.

7
THE CULTURE OF
MASS SOCIETY

Human action is a process in which people relate to one another in terms of future plans in a world of meaningful objects. In the last chapter the kinds of relations appearing in mass society were discussed in some detail. That discussion, however, provided only a partial view of the quality of life in mass society. Relations are the form of human life; the meaningful objects of culture are its content. Just as mass society has its characteristic human relations, it also has its distinctive cultural objects that provide a kind of comprehensive environment for human life that frequently overshadows in significance the so-called natural or biological environment.

Human beings are continually creating meanings out of their experience. Cultural objects are such meaningful creations. They lend a certain stability to experience, by marking off or shaping parts of it so that the same experience will be available to many different people at different times. A cultural object, then, is something created by human beings with a standard usage that will make similar experiences available to different people at different times.[1] The usage of the object is its *meaning*. For example, a hammer is a cultural object, because if it is used correctly a person will be able to pound a nail into a wooden surface. Similarly, a roast duck is a cultural object, because if it is eaten a person will experience certain tastes and undergo certain changes in bodily functions. A word is a cultural object because its standard usage allows one person to share a thought with another, while a traffic regulation is a cultural object because if people follow it their relations will be coordinated in a certain pattern.

The examples of the hammer, roast duck, word, and traffic regulation point to four major aspects of culture—tools, products, symbols, and rules. A tool is a cultural object used to create other cultural objects—for example, the hammer may be used to produce a bookcase. For some writers, the human being is distinguished from other forms of life by the ability to make tools.[2] Other animals, so the argument goes, must adapt themselves instinctively to the "forces of nature," while only human beings can actively "tame nature" and "bend" nature to their uses. Through the use of tools people create an environment that supercedes the organic. Kroeber, in fact, coined the term "superorganic" to characterize culture as a whole.[3] Some people have taken this argument so seriously that they have concluded that tools are the most important factors in human existence and that they even determine the rest of human existence.[4] This position, which may appear to be reasonable at first glance, becomes much less plausible upon closer inspection. What would life be like if people were primarily tool-makers and tool-users? The bulk of existence would be spent in preparing to produce things or producing them. People would have their attention fixed on "nature" rather than upon one another. Everyone would be merely a specialist, performing some function in an enormous productive machine with no overall goal in mind. Certainly, human beings are tool-makers and tool-users, but they are other things as well.

A product is a cultural object used for the appreciation derived from it. For example, the roast duck is appreciated for its taste and the feeling of well-being derived from it. The distinction between tools and products is one of usage, so the same object may be a tool or a product. A master craftsman, like a cabinet maker, may deeply appreciate the qualities of the materials he uses in his work, while a person striving for success may consider the food he eats merely as a tool for strengthening his body to make it fit for the great rat race. These overlaps do not destroy the distinction between tools and products, but only point to the fact that cultural objects can have multiple uses.

It is a mistake to believe that everything created by human beings has one "correct" use. Newspapers can be used to wrap fish as well as for reading material. Is there anything "wrong" with using them to wrap fish? Some writers believe that human beings are distinguished from other animals by their ability to appreciate.[5] Animals supposedly do not cultivate standards of taste, and do not develop music, poetry, and other arts to be appreciated for themselves. While it is correct that human beings are appreciators, it is just as distorting to believe that appreciation is primary as it is to hold that tool-making is primary. A world in which appreciation dominated other processes would be one in which creative activity and special skills would be devalued. The connection between products and what was necessary to produce them would be destroyed.

A symbol is a cultural object used to convey information (or misinformation) about other objects. For example, the word refers to some object, idea, or relation. The importance of symbols in human existence can be demonstrated by a simple mental experiment. Try thinking without using any symbols at all. If your experience is anything like ours you will find that thought without some symbols (be they mathematical, the symbols of ordinary language or some other symbols) is very difficult. Thinking is a form of talking to oneself—and try talking without using a language! This pervasiveness of symbols has led some thinkers to claim that the human being is the "symbolizing" animal.[6] In fact, while in nineteenth-century thought the image of the toolmaker was dominant, in the twentieth century the image of the symbolizer seems to be displacing it.[7] Certainly, human beings communicate through the use of symbols, and without communication there would be little or no shared meaning, if there would be any meaning at all. However, the same kind of argument applies as was used with tools and products. Would life be human if people confronted a "natural" environment which they could not control, or if they had no way of ordering their life of feeling? Believing that symbolizing is the dominant human activity may be comforting to intellectuals, but it is a distorting belief that leads to placing those who specialize in knowing above those who specialize in making. But, in human life the "mind" does not exist without a "body," and knowledge is no guarantee of virtue.

A rule is a cultural object used to coordinate and order the uses of other objects. For example, the traffic regulation coordinates and orders the uses of automobiles. Like the other aspects of culture, rules are pervasive, and this has led many writers ever since Aristotle to proclaim that human beings are "political" animals because they are capable of self-consciously organizing their existence.[8] This belief, prevalent more in ancient times than in the present, is distorting because it tends to place ruling above other human activities. Those who make rules for others or who administer the laws are seen as somehow "higher" than those who make and use tools, or gain and transmit knowledge. The notion that human beings are primarily political animals is partial because without tools and products there would be nothing to regulate, and without symbols there would be no way of making the rules known.

Tools, products, rules, and symbols are all equally important in human existence. Eliminating any one of them would mean the end of human existence as people know it, because each of the components of culture is dependent upon the others. How, then, is the human being best characterized? At the very least, human existence is a combination of a variety of distinctive meaningful processes, no one of which can define what it is to be human. More ambitiously, human existence is capable of becoming a creative process in which people continually improve their tools, deepen their appreciation of products, inquire more extensively and intensively into their experience, and regulate themselves more harmoniously.

Sociologists do not study tools, rules, products, and symbols directly, but study primarily the relations among human beings that grow up around the uses of these cultural objects.[9] One might say very roughly that cultural anthropologists study systems of tools, rules, products, and symbols, the relations between these systems, and the relations of these systems to other phases of the environment. It is important to note that cultural objects do not appear apart from wider contexts. Tools form parts of technologies, products form parts of life-styles, symbols form parts of languages, and rules form parts of legal, moral, or customary systems. Further, at any given place and time, there is often a coherence between technologies, life-styles, languages, and systems of rules.[10] In the present day, this coherence does not go so far that all cultural objects are linked together into a system in which they fit together perfectly. However, each image of the human condition involves some view of how the various aspects of culture cohere. The image of mass society involves the interpretation and criticism of the notions that contemporary human beings in the West live in a "technological," "organizational," "affluent," and "scientific" society. Each of these adjectives describes respectively the system of tools, rules, products, and symbols that are supposedly found today. They are all widespread and have gained currency through repetition in the mass media. Critical examination of them goes to the root of how many people today think of their situation.

EXERCISE

Do you conceive of yourself as primarily a producer, a decision maker, a consumer, or a thinker; or do you think of yourself in other terms? Try to determine the activity you think is most important in the human condition and then try to interpret contemporary life in terms of that activity.

Figure 7.1. THE FOUR COMPONENTS OF CULTURE

Object	Example	Image of the Human Being
Tool	Hammer	Producer
Rule	A speed limit	Decision-Maker
Product	Candy bar	Consumer
Symbol	Sentence	Communicator

A tool is an object with which other objects are created.
A rule is a pattern for coordinating human activities.
A product is an object which provokes certain complexes of feeling.
A symbol is a means of referring to experiences.
A cultural object is a standardized means to experience.

THE TECHNOLOGICAL SOCIETY

The image of technological society, focusing on systems of tools and their consequences for human beings, depicts technology alternatively as creating the possibilities for either a heaven or a hell on earth. On the positive side, the increased efficiency of agricultural technology allows for fewer workers to feed more people than previously. The plow, tractor, and insecticides are some of the tools composing this technology. Those who are no longer needed to produce food can then work to produce other cultural objects—from automobiles to books. The tools of the automotive industry, including the much noted assembly-line conveyor belt, allow a worker to be more efficient. That is, for the same number of hours worked per man, more cars are produced. They also increase efficiency in the sense that highly skilled workers are not needed and, thus, the time that would have been used to train them can be used to produce the cars. The increase in efficiency due to the development of tools not only produces a wider range of cultural objects and a wider distribution of them, but also reduces the number of hours per week that a person must work in order to support a family. The four-day week is discussed as a possibility in a number of industries. In general, the positive view of technological society holds that, given sufficient resources, the technology to solve any problem, from curing cancer to preventing the strike of nuclear bombs, is within mankind's reach.

The negative view of technological society consists of a number of separate critiques. One concerns the organization of persons and tools in the process of production. The division of labor in the factory breaks down the manufacturing process into a number of very small steps and eliminates the need for highly skilled workers. Each worker repeatedly performs one task, such as tightening a bolt, all day long. Not only is this task boring, but it is meaningless to the worker as well. It is meaningless because the worker has little knowledge of how his activity contributes to the final product. Tools are not used to create, but only to obtain income with which one may buy products.[11] However, the worker's task is obviously meaningful to the plant manager who does understand how each job contributes to the whole. The division of labor, which was initiated for the sake of efficiency, may have gone too far. The boredom and frustration of jobs have resulted in high absentee rates, alcoholism, drug addiction, and even sabotage.[12] The quest for efficiency may be leading to inefficiency.

Technological society has also been under attack from the ecology movement. Air, land, and water pollution, as well as the depletion of natural resources such as minerals and topsoil, have been blamed on the improper usage of technological systems. Antithetical stands, often taken in conjunction with each other, have been taken with regard to solving the "crisis." On the one hand there are those calling for the abandonment of all but the simplest tools, advocating bicycling over driving an automobile, eating foods grown and manufactured without the use of chemicals ("organic foods"), and in general prescribing a "back to nature" life-style. Although some people are trying to adhere to this, to a greater or lesser extent, most are in favor of fighting the baneful effects of technology with technological weapons. Laws are passed to require manufacturers to produce less polluting cars. Complicated purification systems are developed to turn sewage into potable water. Garbage is now used as the basic ingredient in manufacturing certain construction blocks. The masses are urged to separate aluminum cans, glass, and other materials from the rest of their waste material so that these can be recycled.

Further criticism of technological society can be found in literature, particularly science fiction. Enlarging upon already existing tools, science fiction stories develop their consequences in extremes. Thus, computers or computerized robots take over the world, a "mad scientist" creates a pill which, when dropped into the public water supply, renders people incapable of making decisions, or any number of other nightmares. Aldous Huxley's *Brave New World* and George Orwell's *1984* are other examples of this genre. All have in common the domination of tools over human beings.

Whether technological society and its future developments are praised or damned, those who concern themselves with the vision tend to share a view of the relationship between human beings, tools, and other aspects of culture. In a somewhat extreme form, their view is that, although human beings are the creators of tools and technologies, once developed, these creations have a life of their own. They tend to dominate the other aspects of culture. They will produce what they were developed to produce—and rules and symbols will have to be altered to fit these new developments.

Many people are afraid of some of the technologies now being perfected. Their underlying assumption is that, once it is possible to create something, attempts will necessarily be made to realize this possibility.[13] Recently, the technology related to producing animals asexually through the process known as cloning has been given much publicity. Instead of a cell from each of two parents joining to form a fertilized egg that combines genetic material from both, cloning produces an individual genetically identical to its one parent—i.e., it has the same chromosomal composition. Rabbits and frogs have been produced in the laboratory through cloning, and the possibilities exist for producing human beings in this manner as well. The news media gravely (and very naively) weigh the consequences. There could be hundreds of Adolf Hitlers, or hundreds of Albert Einsteins produced, and the journalists wonder who will have the power to decide who is to be made into multiple copies. Totally forgotten is the effect of environment on human beings. People of identical genetic material, that is, identical twins, do not share identical dispositions and talents and, thus, cloned individuals would not be exact duplicates of the original person. Of particular interest, however, is the implicit assumption that, because something is possible, because the tools have been developed, they will be utilized. People have demanded that various types of research be stopped, because if successful the results would create havoc. For example, there have been movements to end the testing of nuclear weapons and to put curbs on experimentation with human beings and animals. Opponents of certain kinds of research have assumed that the results of the research (the tools developed) would definitely be put to use. If you had the tools to enable you to rob a bank, or kill someone, without being detected, would you use them? Many countries aside from the United States (which has the dubious distinction of being the only country to have used it) have the technological capability for nuclear attack. Must they use it? It seems reasonable to conclude that not all tools are put into use. This conclusion can be verified to some degree by noting the thousands of patents registered in the United States each year. Very few of them ever come into general use.

Tools can enter into a culture in either of two general ways. Either a member of the society invents the tool, or it is "borrowed" from some other culture. The process of invention raises several interesting questions. Were basic tools, such as fire and the wheel, invented only once or several times? Archeological evidence cannot refute either of these views conclusively, but for many of the simple tools multiple invention, rather than single invention and diffusion to other areas, seems likely.[14] Was a tool invented by a single individual or by several or a group of people? From what we have learned about modern inventions and what we can infer about prehistoric ones, the answer to this question would tend to depend upon the nature of the tool. The simpler the tool, the more likely one person only was involved in its "discovery." Complex or specialized tools (those requiring more knowledge than is possessed by the average member of the society to understand them) probably involve more than one person in their development. Frequently, the complex tools incorporate principles of several tools, simple or complex, within them. Is the inventor the one who puts it all together, or should he share the honors with those who invented the tools that help to make up this latest invention?

The process of borrowing tools (their cultural diffusion) and the process of inventing tools can be considered together when attempting to account for why some tools are adopted in a given culture, since many invented tools and many known foreign tools are never incorporated. Why, then, is a given new tool adopted? One answer may be "because it is usually possible to demonstrate the superiority of one tool over another for doing a particular job."[15] Anyone who has ever tried to start a fire in more "primitive" ways appreciates the invention of the match. A second explanation refers to need—necessity is supposedly the mother of invention. Would this explain the invention of the elevator once multiple-storied buildings were developed? Yet there are a number of tools that produce cultural objects for which there does not seem to be pressing need—for example, the butter curler or the automatic card shuffler. For these tools, and others like them, technological society must create needs both for the tool and the product.[16]

In general, however, there is no denying the importance of tools. Tools transform nature into cultural objects. Trees become houses, animals become food and clothing, iron ore becomes a car, and grapes become wine, all through the use of tools. It is somewhat ironic to see in modern society, with its pragmatic emphasis, other aspects of culture being conceived as tools. Products such as food are seen as tools to fuel us. Symbol systems such as mathematics are seen as tools to sharpen our minds. Rules, such as the Ten Commandments, are seen as tools to help us get to heaven. By transforming rules, symbols, and products into tools, we make ourselves into cultural objects, rather than creators and appreciators of culture.

THE ORGANIZATIONAL SOCIETY

While some commentators stress the importance of tools in contemporary mass cultures and analyze current affairs under the heading "technological society," others are more impressed by the development of complex systems of rules in modern social life. These analysts tend to use the term "organizational society" to refer to the human environment in which people in the West today live.[17] Comprehensive systems of rules which coordinate and guide the conduct of social life can be thought of as forms of organization, because they describe the patterns that organize human activities. When people use the term "organizational society" they are referring to a particular form of organization that has become important in modern life—the bureaucracy.

The first systematic description of the bureaucracy was done by Max Weber, who wrote in the late nineteenth and early twentieth centuries.[18] For Weber, the most important characteristic of the bureaucracy was that it divided an overriding task into a number of parts, each of which contributed to the fulfillment of the task. The principle of the bureaucracy is efficiency and the rationality of means —the holders of each job are given rights to demand the cooperation of others and the obligations to cooperate with others solely on the basis of what is thought necessary to accomplish the task. The bureaucracy is organized into a chain of command, in which those on top are ultimately responsible for seeing that the mission is carried out. Proceeding down the chain of command, each officeholder is responsible for playing his preordained part.

Examples of bureaucracies abound in contemporary life. An example would be any large business firm, like a bank. The purpose of the bank is supposedly to make a profit through acting as an intermediary between those who save and those who borrow, as well as performing other financial services. The principle of the bank is to pay savers an interest rate for their deposits and then to gain a higher rate of interest back from borrowers. Large banks are bureaucratized in the sense that the jobs involved in accomplishing their task are divided up in accordance with the aim of maximizing profits. There are loan departments staffed by specialists in assessing the risks of potential borrowers, trust departments staffed by specialists in caring for the financial affairs of others, and savings departments staffed by specialists in attracting and processing savings and checking accounts. Upper management is staffed by those who coordinate the various departments and make general policy decisions on interest rates and major loans, as well as the stands to take on public financial policy. In accordance with the distribution of rights and obligations by specialized function, those in the savings department, for example, have no right to grant or refuse a loan, while those in the loan department have no right to decide how to invest a client's trust fund. In accordance with the distribution of rights and obligations by chain of command, the bank teller has no right to decide what rate of interest the bank will pay on savings accounts or what kind of charge will be assessed on checking accounts.

In the perfect bureaucracy, workers would be reduced to functionaries, performing only their prescribed tasks and treating every problem according to the rules. However, as anyone knows who has spent time in "bureaucracies" (and these include most public and private school systems), no bureaucracy is perfect. One of the favorite tactics that workers use in disputes with management is performing all tasks in accordance with the letter of the rulebook. A short time of functioning under this tactic usually brings operations to a halt. Thus, observers like Peter M. Blau have noted that all organizations develop informal networks of rights and duties that by-pass the formal rules and enable the various tasks to get done.[19]

Blau's observation brings up the point that not all rules are written down (codified) or otherwise explicit. Rules vary from the explicit injunctions contained in handbooks of regulations and statute books (often more honored in the breach than the observance) to fully implicit rules of which nobody is aware but which an outsider can observe are guiding activity. In between there are the informal networks of rules, which sometimes depart strikingly from what is contained in the official regulations. One study of a social work agency revealed that the case workers were in almost all respects acting in violation of—or at least against the spirit of—the official job description.[20] This led the author to conclude that many bureaucracies may be merely symbolic. On the surface it may look like the principles of efficiency and rationality of means are in force, but in actuality the workers have invented entirely new job descriptions.

An even more serious weakness of the organizational society image is that many large organizations do not have clear overriding tasks around which the rights and duties of functionaries can be rationally organized. Many contemporary organizations appear to be less bureaucracies than conglomerates performing a multiplicity of functions, some of them in conflict with one another.[21] The enormous university can be considered a conglomerate. Is its main task teaching students, weapons development, holding conventions, providing mass entertainments, providing agricultural extension services, or some other task? No single task seems to predominate and, therefore, the rules cannot organize activity to accomplish rationally an overriding purpose. Efficiency seems less prized in the conglomerate than flexibility and growth. Of course, each unit of the conglomerate is supposed to be efficient with respect to its particular task, but such judgments of efficiency are clouded by power struggles over division of the budget and alliances between widely divergent agencies. The conglomerate and the "symbolic bureaucracy" with their networks of informal rules still contain the characteristics of mass society—manipulation, inauthenticity, and impersonality. However, they do not reduce the person to a simple cipher or cog in the machine; much more, they divide people into master manipulators and bewildered victims.

Another hallmark of the perfect bureaucracy is its independence from other organizations and the ultimate responsibility of its top leadership for accomplishment of the mission. Critical students of contemporary organization, like C. Wright Mills and Theodore Lowi, have pointed out that government agencies, business firms and universities are often linked into "complexes" or "whirlpools" which break-down the independence of these organizations and blur responsibility for failures.[22] Who is responsible for huge cost overruns on defense contracts? The manufacturer who may have purposely underestimated costs to get the contract? The budget officer in the government agency who failed to anticipate the higher costs? The university scientist who consulted on costs and came up with the low figure, perhaps simply to impress his employers? Top managers frequently claim that they are helpless pawns of the competing factions lower down in their organizations, while the middle managers excuse themselves by claiming that they take orders from "above." The "responsibility gap" is even more severe than the "credibility gap" at least with respect to the efficacy of formal systems of rules in contemporary life.

One aspect of the perfect-bureaucracy notion does seem to apply in contemporary organizations. Just as technologies have become more complex and specialized, so have rules. In societies characterized primarily by Durkheim's "mechanical solidarity" (where all do the same things) there tends to be a single system of rules guiding relations, with variation mainly centering on age and sex differences. However, in societies characterized more by "organic solidarity" there tends to develop a large number of different rule systems related to specialized activities and interests. Among these systems are the various by-laws of associations and clubs and the endless regulations of bureaucracies, not to mention systems of civil and criminal law.[23] Most people never become concerned with the vast majority of these rule systems and are not even aware of their existence. However, they are aware of many of the rules relevant to the activities they perform. The sum of the rules guiding a person's behavior with regard to a particular activity may be considered that person's *role* in the activity. When one realizes that roles are merely systems of rules from the person's viewpoint, one realizes how pervasive rules are in human existence.

Rules control access to the use of other cultural objects, or more simply, define rights and duties with regard to the use of objects. When people desire to use objects in certain ways, these uses become *values.* Thus far in complex social orders some people have had more rights to valued experiences (and have been able to enforce these rights) than others. Often these inequalities of rights have been organized into systems where some groups have had more rights than other groups to what were considered the good things in life.[24] Such systems of inequality are called systems of "stratification." Davis and Moore have attempted to argue that stratification is inevitable in social life, because people who perform more difficult or responsible functions than others must be rewarded more than others in wealth, power, respect, and loyalty.[25] The assumption is that people will not take responsibility and do difficult (and often interesting) work for its own sake. There seems also to be a concealed assumption that historical inequalities can be justified by differential contributions to social well-being. We find no proof that either of these claims is correct.

THE AFFLUENT SOCIETY

Related to the images of the technological and organizational societies is that of the "affluent society." Here the focus is on products rather than tools or rules; the basic idea is that, for the first time in history, masses of people are able to go beyond the daily struggle for biological survival and enjoy the blessings of leisure.[26] These blessings are usually thought to come in the form of mass-produced commodities and entertainments. Those who extoll the affluent society point to the fact that the "masses" now have access to Shakespeare in the form of paperback editions and to Beethoven in the form of stereo recordings.[27] Those who believe that the supposed blessings of the affluent society are really evils in disguise point out that Mannix reaches more people than Macbeth and that the Beatles outsell Beethoven. This debate, interesting as it may be to those who are first becoming aware of mass society, does not go to the central issues relating to products in contemporary life.

Just as tools have become specialized and based in scientific knowledge, and rules have become adapted to particular activities, products have become ever more complex and bewildering to those who use them. In earlier times people had a certain understanding of the products they enjoyed. They knew where the products came from and what was involved in making them even if they could not produce all of them themselves. The distance between raw material and finished product was relatively short, and people could see and feel the raw material in the product. It was also quite likely that people would be able to repair products if they broke down. Today none of this is true and there is a situation that might best be termed "alienation from the product." Not only are people unaware of the processes through which their products are made, but they are often incapable of using the products so that they gain full benefit from them. People must study owners' manuals with great care to learn what a product can do, particularly such products as sound systems and vehicles. Repair of one's products is frequently out of the question, especially when expensive facilities, expert knowledge, and a great deal of space are required for repair. Many products are made out of materials that are not found in nature but have been synthesized out of unfamiliar chemicals. Most people are unlikely to know what materials their products are made out of, and the term plastic has come into vogue as a way of naming a wide diversity of materials that the lay person cannot intelligently distinguish. Where products are simple and few, it is often not difficult to determine when and in what circumstances a product will be dangerous. Where products are complex and many, the reverse is the case, and people must be taught in school and through the mass media how to use products safely and must be warned when particular products become threats to life and safety.

With alienation from the product comes a particular mentality characteristic of mass society. It is closely related to the state of mind created by the "put-on" discussed in the preceding chapter. According to the folklore of the affluent society, the "consumer is king." The mass-man has become lord of the manor, catered to by manufacturers, service personnel, and big-name entertainers. However, this contemporary nobleman, able to summon his court jester by turning on the television, has become a veritable slave to his supposed servants. While one may feel temporarily on top of the world when one sits down in front of the television with a can of beer and a tin of new-fangled potato chips to watch a football game being played a thousand miles away, when the picture starts rolling and then disappears with a wisp of smoke, euphoria turns to impotent rage. It is not merely that one's pleasure has been interrupted by a mechanical failure; it is much more that one dimly senses that he is the victim of a massive put-on. There is the feeling of impotence because one cannot control the objects in one's own environment. There is the feeling that one has been taken advantage of because the television is an expensive and new model. There is the feeling of anxiety because one does not know whether or not the repairman will tell the truth about what is wrong. Faced with a succession of such breakdowns, the consumer feels less like a king than a fool. One begins to feel that things are continually on the brink of breaking down, and is thankful for the days when everything works properly.[28]

More important than mere breakdowns in dissolving the myth of the affluent society is the consciousness that one is being patronized and manipulated by sales and service personnel. Specialists, like medical doctors, are frequently reluctant to fill people in on what is being done to them. The human body is one of the most significant products, the sine qua non of appreciation. It is given in nature, but altered significantly by human activity.[29] Yet, paradoxically, modern medicine, which has helped prolong the human life span, has also contributed to alienation from the body. A similar situation holds in the arts. The "put-on" was made fashionable by artists who created seemingly incomprehensible works.[30] Were these works serious or were they merely haphazard conglomerations of material? The artists refused to tell, and many people could not be sure whether or not they should take the works seriously. Of course, the artists themselves were led to this extreme by a belief that mass culture (Mannix not Macbeth) made it impossible for most people to appreciate "serious" art. Whether or not this is true, the fact that many artists claim to believe it is evidence for the claim that relations in mass society are frequently inauthentic and depersonalized.

The proliferation of complex products has gone along with changes in the contexts for use and appreciation. In pre-modern times the appreciation of products was usually carried on in the family group and in a religious context. In the modern period there has been a progressive tendency for appreciation to be carried out on a mass basis and in a secular context. The most striking examples of this tendency are the mass entertainments, such as sporting events and rock concerts. The appreciation of art in the context of public museums and of symphonies in orchestra halls are also appropriate examples here. Appreciation en masse tends to "privatize" people in the sense that each person is directed toward the entertainment and does not respond to it in consonance with a small group of familiar others. Sometimes the crowd takes on a mood of its own and one is swept away with it. However, this is not the same as joint appreciation with valued associates. Perhaps a counter-tendency to the privatization of appreciation and the decline of the family unit as a setting for the appreciation of products is the growth of communal living units among certain segments of youth. Some communes attempt to carve out distinctive life-styles that their members can jointly appreciate.[31] Sometimes these communes are centered around religious themes, sometimes around drug-related experiences, sometimes around political activism, and sometimes simply around experiments in living together harmoniously. Whatever their ultimate fate, they are evidence that the appreciation of products has not become totally standardized.

One of the most popular criticisms of American life is that the majority of people have become mindless and self-satisfied consumers.[32] While this judgment ignores the fact that approximately one-fifth of the population is not incorporated into the affluent society (this segment has sometimes been called "the other America"),[33] it also tends to overemphasize the importance of products in contemporary life. Certainly, the image of the human being that one gains from mass advertising is of a stupid, suggestible, emotional and pleasure-seeking child. Yet the human beings that one meets in everyday life do not often conform to this image. They are concerned about their jobs, their health, their loved ones, and even about "impersonal" interests such as helping others, the state of the environment, and political change. It is one of the most debilitating aspects of advertising that it would reduce the richness of appreciation to simple and gross private pleasures.

SCIENTIFIC SOCIETY

In mass society, stress on the aspect of culture known as symbols leads to the image of scientific society. The term "scientific" is used because, in the large organizations of today, symbol systems are employed to control reality through systematic descriptions of experience, leading to prediction and the possibility of intervention on behalf of human projects.[34] Science has replaced religion as the dominant symbol system. In many respects the replacement has been on a one-to-one basis. Both the clergy and the scientists are expected to have a calling or commitment to their work. Each of them is trusted to act with integrity, especially since it would be most difficult to detect faking a religious experience or fudging results of an experiment. Both religion and science concern themselves with interpretations of reality, and each has had doctrinal disputes in which new orthodoxies often have replaced older ones.[35] Religious notions of reality were shared by the people and the clergy, and both were capable of discussing and taking sides when competing views (often called heresies unless they were adopted by the establishment) were put forward. However, this is not the case with scientific world-views. The masses cannot conceive of a negatively curved space, they attach no meaning to a neutrino, and they do not understand the theory of the expanding universe. Although science is the dominant symbol system, and the masses have faith in it, its contents are by and large alien to all but a few specialists.

Science, which was discussed in the third chapter, is a rather complex symbol system because it is composed of or utilizes a variety of symbolic forms. It is to these components that we now turn our attention.

The most important symbol system, not only for science, but for culture in general, is that of language. The words of a given language are symbols because there is no necessary relationship between a word (spoken or written) and what it stands for. For example, it is only a matter of convention or agreement that the word *chair* refers to something we sit on, or a "chair." We could call it a *beep* rather than a *chair*. We would then say, "Sit over here on this comfortable leather beep," or, "Don't you enjoy sitting in a rocking beep?" This bit of nonsense is only nonsense because there is no agreement that the word "beep" refers to what we know as a "chair." If you grew up in an English-speaking area, you learned to refer to a "chair" by the word chair. Spanish-speaking people do not share this agreement. They use the symbol *silla* to refer to a "chair." French speakers use the word *chaise*. Other groups of people use other symbols, but among themselves they agree about what the symbols stand for.

Language is not only made up of symbols; it is also a system of symbols. The term system implies that there is a relationship between the symbols. They are not haphazardly arranged. We could make a haphazard arrangement, for example, by randomly selecting ten words from a dictionary. However, there is a very high probability that utter gibberish would be the result. The arrangement of symbols in a language is known as its grammar. A grammar makes possible the expression of meaningful sentences.

Sociologists are not interested in the intricacies of various languages qua languages. Rather, they concern themselves with the various ways in which language usage varies among groups of people. For example, in many parts of the world a significant portion of the population speaks more than one language. This *bilingualism*, as it is called, varies with social class. That is, in any given area, such as Montreal, Canada, or San Antonio, Texas, a greater proportion of the lower classes than the upper classes will be fluent in two languages. This phenomenon is sometimes explained by the necessity to learn another language in order to obtain a job. The assumption, which seems to hold true in most areas, is that the employers (upper class) all speak the same language, which is different from the native tongue of the lower classes. (For example, the upper classes in San Antonio speak English, while many people in the lower classes speak Spanish primarily and English for economic reasons.) The tables are sometimes turned when the lower classes demand that in order to gain employment a person should be *bilingual*. If such a policy is put into effect at all levels of organization, the upper classes are placed at a disadvantage.[36]

Even when people are said to speak the same language, there are many variations of that language, some of which are unintelligible to other speakers of the language. On a rather obvious level, we are all familiar with different pronunciations or accents. In the United States alone, one can easily identify natives of Boston, the New York metropolitan area, the South, Appalachia, among others. However, if you listen to television or radio, even to programs that originate and are only broadcast to the areas named above, you will find all personnel speaking in the same standard American accent (non-accent?).

A given language may vary not only in pronunciation, but also in its symbol usage. Words may be given different meanings than the standard usage, or words may be employed that the general population does not use at all. The first case, where the same word symbolizes different phenomena, is exemplified in slang, hip talk, jive talk, and the like. "Lay some bread on me, Daddy" is not an order to one's father to place some baked goods on one's person. Drug users have always employed common words with meanings known only to those who were involved with drugs. Words such as pot, smack, mainline, nickel bag, upper, joint, and acid have meanings quite different than those understood by the general public. To some extent this utilization of language is functional for those who employ it. For one thing, it enables those who are participating in unlawful activity to discuss matters openly without fear of detection. Also, it allows drug users to detect phonies. Currently, drugs have become very popular, not only as things to consume, but also for the mass media to discuss. The record industry has discovered drugs and has found them to be invaluable assets for boosting sales. Song lyrics are composed with double meanings—one being drug related. Those who understand the double meanings feel "in." Gary Allen writes: "Drug lyrics are a mystery to most adults because of the Aesopian language used by the singers. . . . Youngsters pick up the meaning of the argot through disc jockeys, conversations with their peers, and the teenage and 'underground' newspapers and magazines. The hippy vocabulary allows verbal communication in code and separates those who are hip from the squares."[37]

The jargon, or technical language, used by various professions (academic, artistic, medical, for example) frequently employs unfamiliar meanings for common words as well as words peculiar to the area of specialization. The extent to which the restricted language serves to enhance investigation and communication is difficult to assess. In any event, it does serve other functions. For example, it allows for identifying the initiated and the uninitiated. This seems to be particularly important in those areas where folk wisdom and "common sense" can also be applied. Such is the case in the various social sciences, and to some extent in medicine. Calling hives "urticaria" sounds impressive and not only justifies the fee, but also prevents the patient from utilizing folk remedies. An interesting consequence of this is that a prescription written for placebos may help the patient, whereas if the doctor wrote the common equivalent, "sugar pills," it would be far less effective. The extreme of jargon is so-called bureaucratese through which administrators disguise ordinary situations in a fog of rhetoric. For example, when somebody is fired or dismissed from a job, the boss may call his action an "unavoidable termination of employment" and vigorously resent the use of the term "firing." Similarly, a union spokesman may use the term "job action" instead of "strike." Bureaucratese is normally used when the administrator is doing something others will oppose or is trying to glorify some activity demanding very little skill. A good project for those pursuing self-understanding is to become sensitized to bureaucratese and to expose it whenever possible in organizational situations.

There are a number of other symbol systems that are derivatives of or are dependent upon spoken language. The most common is the written language, as is used in this book. The letters of the alphabet can be substituted for one another, as in various codes, or they may be represented as various combinations of raised dots, as in braille. Visually, they may also be depicted as various hand positions as for communication among the deaf, or as the double-flag-waving postures in semaphore. Acoustically, letters can be delineated as long or short clicks, as the dots and dashes of the Morse Code.

Language, particularly in its alphabetically written form, is the most important symbol system of science. However, there are other systems of symbols that are independent of language, such as musical notation. Several of these nonlinguistic systems are used in science. Of these, the most important one is mathematics. The symbols consist of various quantities (for example, 1, 2, 3) and their relations (for example, $+$, $=$, $>$). Whether one speaks Urdu, Swahili, or Russian, the meaning of the symbols $2+2=4$ or $10>6$ is constant. Mathematics allows for more precise descriptions than ordinary language: 84 percent of all xs have ys, rather than many or most xs have ys. All branches of science use mathematics to some extent. The social sciences have been accused of overusing this system of symbols. Pitirim Sorokin has entitled this misuse "quantophrenia" and claims that its prevalence is partly due to the prestige of mathematically based research in other fields of science.[38]

Figure 7.2. IMAGES OF MASS CULTURE

Image	Primary Object	Characteristics
Technological Society	Tools	Tools developed through the application of scientific principles; specialized tools
Organizational Society	Rules	Bureaucratic and complex organizations; rules specialized according to social function
Affluent Society	Products	Mechanisms of products understood only by specialists; profusion of products
Scientific Society	Symbols	Specialized symbol systems for understanding different parts of experience; fragmentation of knowledge

SUMMARY

There are four major social processes: creating cultural objects, ordering the uses of culture, appreciating cultural objects, and conveying information about culture. Sociologists study the human relations involved in these processes rather than the intrinsic characteristics of the various cultural objects. A particular type of cultural object is associated with each social process. Tools are associated with creation, rules are associated with ordering and coordination, products are associated with appreciation, and symbols are linked to inquiry and communication. In mass societies, tools tend to be complex and specialized, systems of rules define bureaucratic organizations, products tend to be too complex for most people to understand fully and symbols tend to be linked to science. These tendencies have given rise to the ideas that today human beings live in, respectively, technological, organizational, affluent, and scientific societies. Each of these images is distorted, in the sense that an adequate characterization of contemporary living has to take account of all of them, and attempt to integrate them into a relatively consistent pattern.

In the remainder of this book there will be an attempt to discuss in some detail the relations that grow up around the various social processes in mass society. An understanding of these relations will be furthered by keeping in mind the idea of mass society, as well as the images of technological, organizational, affluent, and scientific societies. It will be useful to remember the limitations of these images.

PART III
SOCIAL PROCESSES

Creation and Production

8

THE QUALITY OF WORK IN MODERN LIFE

One of the basic social processes is the creation and production of cultural objects, or what is frequently called "work." Throughout history there have been a number of diverse interpretations of the role of work in human existence, some of them in stark conflict with one another. Is work a blessing or a curse? Does it give the human being an opportunity to widen and deepen experience, or does it snuff out the possibilities for human development? Is the goal of work its ultimate abolition and a utopia in which machines carry on all creation and production, or is the aim of work the expansion of opportunities for more satisfying work? These questions show a profound ambivalence (conflict of values) in the Western tradition. One way of making sense out of this conflict is to point out that interpretations of the meaning of work are relative to images of the human condition as a whole. A person's view of work is quite likely to be tied up with his views about other aspects of human existence. Since this is the case, it will be useful to review several perspectives on the meaning of work that have appeared in Western thought.

191

WORK AS A CURSE

The basic attitude toward work in Western culture is negative. Human beings are forced to work for a livelihood because of their sin against God, but this situation is not to be welcomed. De Grazia has summarized this attitude: "To the authors of the Bible . . . work is necessary because of a divine curse. Through Adam's fall the world has become a workhouse. Paradise was where there was no toil. This is the feeling about work one encounters in most of history's years. Unavoidable, but nonetheless a curse."[1] Not only the Bible but also Greek philosophy promoted this attitude. Plato set up his ideal state with three major social groups. On top of the pyramid were the philosopher-kings who governed on the basis of their knowledge of ultimate reality. They had come to this knowledge through contemplation, not action, and were fit to rule solely because they were not involved with the "imperfect" material world. Below the philosopher-kings were the soldiers and administrators who directly organized the activities of other human beings. Finally, at the bottom of this "ideal" state were the workers and artisans who had the lowly task of transforming nature into culture.[2] Aristotle shared this attitude and felt that those who were involved in manual work had neither the time nor the breadth of vision to make intelligent decisions about the conduct of public affairs. In Aristotle's ideal world, slaves did the work and citizens did the thinking and ruling.[3] It is interesting to note that physicians, who have high prestige in the contemporary world, were simply artisans in the eyes of thinkers such as Plato and Aristotle.

The fusion of Christianity and Greek philosophy in the Middle Ages only served to intensify the devaluation of work in Western culture. Even today, much of the doctrine of the Catholic Church values contemplation far more highly than work.[4] These early attitudes, however, carry over beyond the confines of Catholicism. The idea of a technological utopia in which people are the passive recipients of pleasures created by machines is a garish rewriting of the Garden of Eden myth. Also related to this tradition is the dream of getting "something for nothing," which motivates many people in capitalist economic systems.

WORK AS A DUTY

With the Protestant Reformation a new attitude toward work

arose in the West which was overlaid on the old one without displacing it. De Grazia summarized this new attitude: "Once, man worked for a livelihood, to be able to live. Now he worked for something beyond his daily bread. He worked because somehow it was the right or moral thing to do."[5] The new attitude toward work has been summed up as the "Protestant ethic." Martindale has noted that in the early Protestant sects the importance of the priesthood to salvation was minimized and the Christian life was no longer defined as withdrawal to contemplation. The person could no longer confess his sins to the priest and gain absolution, so he had to solve his problems in his own conscience. Everyday life, thus, became of utmost importance, because every act became potentially relevant to salvation. Individuals began to see their economic life as a divine calling: "Life acquired a new vocational significance as the drama of conscience was worked out in the solution of problems. Individuals tended to measure their religious worthiness in terms of exemplary conduct of life's practical affairs."[6] Hard work, in short, became an indicator that one might be saved, and economic success an even better index.

It is important to note that the Protestant Ethic, glorifying hard work and economic success, did not hold that work was a good in itself. Rather, work, though unpleasant, was an indicator of or a means to salvation. Over the past several centuries the strictly religious aspects of the Protestant Ethic have declined in importance while the notions of hard work as a duty and economic success as an indicator of human fulfillment have persisted. When people are no longer even certain that work is an obligation, a debased form of the Protestant Ethic may exist in the blind craving for more and more work regardless of its consequences or the satisfaction associated with it.[7] Jules Henry has called this phenomenon "drivenness" and he notes that many people seem to be driven by forces beyond their control to achieve according to organizational standards: "Ours is a driven culture. It is driven on by its achievement, competitive, profit, and mobility drives, and by the drives for security and a higher standard of living. Above all, it is driven by expansiveness. Drives like hunger, thirst, sex, and rest arise directly out of the chemistry of the body, whereas expansiveness, competitiveness, achievement, and so on are generated by the culture; still we yield to the latter as we do to hunger and sex."[8] There is, of course, a positive side to the Protestant Ethic in the sense that through work one may contribute to a common good and not be a parasite off the work of others. However, this argument contains the very questionable assumption that most work in contemporary societies contributes to a common good. Perhaps it is better to be unemployed and on welfare than to produce fragmentation bombs.

WORK AS AN INTRINSIC VALUE

During the past century yet another attitude toward work has appeared in the West which makes the Protestant Ethic appear as a transition between the traditional and contemporary world-views. The new attitude, which is shared by American pragmatists and Soviet Marxists, is that work at its best is creative activity—a value to be pursued for its own sake. John Dewey summarized this view by arguing that the "old tradition" held that "labor was an unavoidable evil to be minimized" and that "material comfort and ease was magnified in contrast with the pains and risk of experimental creation."[9] Dewey, however, holds that production is important "because of the intrinsic worth of invention and reshaping the world" and that through creative activity human beings expand and deepen their experience.

Figure 8.1. PHILOSOPHIES OF WORK IN THE WEST

Traditional Society	Modern Society	Mass Society
Work as a curse visited upon man by God	Work as a moral duty imposed upon human beings	Work as an opportunity for creative activity

The idea that work can be a good in itself is no less than revolutionary. It goes along with the emergence of a mass society in which the multitudes rather than a small elite are the citizens. Regardless of the domination of elites in the contemporary world, all must at least pay lip service to the dignity of labor, and the creative workshop rather than the cloistered garden becomes the philosophical ideal. This, of course, does not mean that all work in contemporary societies is to be valued for its creative opportunities. For social philosophers and critics such as Marx and Dewey, the great problem with modern societies is that the masses are given few opportunities for creative work and are instead regimented into boring and meaningless routines. Even current sociologists seem to have abandoned the ideal of the creative workshop for the ideal of the professional expert who rises above the mere worker. It is to the current sociological view of work that we now turn.

PROFESSIONS AND NONPROFESSIONS

The contemporary philosophy of work is basically concerned with the examination of the concept of profession, and as an extension of this, with comparing professions to other occupations. The fundamental principle of this pattern of thought is that a few jobs are professions and the remainder are simply nonprofessional. The residual category of "nonprofessions" is often divided into white-collar (people-work or, especially, paperwork, usually done in offices or stores) and blue-collar (machine work or work with "things," usually done in factories). However, in mass society the differentiation between blue- and white-collar jobs has blurred. Salary ranges overlap extensively, white-collar workers are being unionized, offices are becoming inundated with various machines, and increasing suburbanization has often made the life-styles of the two types of workers indistinguishable.[10] Even the "white-collar" is being replaced in various offices by company-supplied uniforms. Only differential prestige levels (which will be explored in the following chapter) remain. Thus, differences within the category of nonprofessional work are seen to be less than those between nonprofessions and professions.

In distinguishing professions from nonprofessions, interest has usually focused on the former. As a consequence of this interest nonprofessions are usually described negatively, as lacking those characteristics that professions have. There is a lack of agreement about what attributes are both necessary and sufficient to define a given job as a profession.[11] There seems to be some agreement on several of the features, but the question is whether there are but a few central elements from which others are derivable, or a whole constellation of them. Another question involves the classification of a job that has some professional characteristics, but lacks others. This question can be resolved by discarding the all-or-none approach and viewing a job as being more-or-less professional.

Expertise organized around specialized bodies of knowledge is one of the crucial attributes of a profession. Ideally this knowledge should be esoteric—it should not be available to everyone. Usually those outside the field are unfamiliar with the special knowledge, not because it requires a very high level of intelligence to understand it, but because of the myriad of details. Legal expertise, for example, is largely knowledge of laws and court decisions, and the ability to make analogies between situations. Although most people are capable of this type of reasoning, they are simply not familiar with the innumerable "cases."

The feature of expertise gives rise to several other professional characteristics. One is the rather obvious need to acquire the specialized knowledge. Professional training, "ideally" begun after a general college curriculum has been completed, involves both learning the theoretical knowledge and gaining practical experience. The training period, which may last for years, as with medicine, is supervised by members of the profession, rather than by knowledgable outsiders. This, in addition to the fact that laws have been passed making the training a prerequisite for practicing that profession, gives the profession an effective control over personnel. This training also permits the special interpretations of the profession to be passed on to new members. Part of this interpretation involves defining what is a legitimate or respectable problem for professional concern. Everett C. Hughes claims that ". . . professionals do not merely serve; they define the very wants which they serve."[12] He points out that, despite the fact that many women have wanted very much to bring their pregnancies to a premature end, the medical profession has not traditionally considered abortion to be a legitimate problem for it to solve.[13]

The expertise acquired through this specialized training gives rise to, or at least attempts to legitimize, another characteristic of a profession—autonomy. Professionals are to decide how their functions are to be performed, and any supervision is to come from fellow-professionals. In conjunction with claims for self-regulation, professional codes of ethics are drawn up. One of the oldest of these is the Hippocratic Oath which is said to have been imposed by the ancient Greek physician Hippocrates upon his disciples, and is now taken by students upon receiving their medical degrees. The code of ethics prescribes, explicitly or implicitly, the professional's commitment to the client's welfare over his own self-interest. This is in direct contradiction to the so-called business ethic which assumes a profit motive and warns the client or customer: *Caveat emptor* (let the buyer beware). It is argued that because ". . . the client is usually not in a position to judge the adequacy of the professional's advice (e.g., medical prescription, need for surgery, legal interpretation, etc.), the client's belief that the professional has the client's and not his own interests at heart may become crucial in determining the credibility of that advice and the likelihood that the client will follow it."[14] This line of reasoning seems more like a defense than an analysis because the same argument can be readily applied to many businessmen. The complexity of cultural products is such that consumers not only have little comprehension of how to create or repair them, but do not even know how to use them properly or judge their performance. Those who have had experience with stereo equipment, color televisions, or European sports cars have had to believe that the businessman would place the customer's interest first, or at the very least take account of it.

Professional associations, which coordinate and set standards for training, promulgate the code of ethics and attempt to assure autonomy in work situations, are also supposedly accompaniments of professional jobs. Professional associations also concern themselves with educating the general public about the nature of the profession and building the expertise of members through publishing journals and sponsoring meetings. Many types of jobs have occupational associations, but those on the nonprofessional side of the continuum are unions (representing "labor") and trade associations (representing "management"). Their basic activities in the United States supposedly revolve around their members' economic concerns. In Europe, however, unions frequently have broad political aims, sometimes encompassing social revolution. Possibly in an attempt to distinguish themselves from unions, professional associations seek to have no connection with the financial concerns of their members, although the political efforts of the American Medical Association against national health insurance are an exception to this rule. In addition, being interested in financial matters is viewed as unprofessional for the individual, since it is seen as a manifestation of self-interest. Professionals are thus urged not to advertise their services.

The professional association helps reinforce, and in some cases foster, still another characteristic of a profession—professional community. William Goode contends that, despite the lack of distinct physical sites, professions form communities because professionals share a sense of identity, values, and role definitions; few give up the work; they employ a common language not well understood by outsiders, and the community has power over its members. Unlike a traditional community, there are no geographic limits, only social ones, and the next generation is produced only socially, not biologically.[15]

Whatever characteristics one does propose for defining a profession, a continuum of sorts can be constructed. Given occupations can be placed on it and seen as more or less professional. Although this allows one to compare different jobs according to their relative professional status, the comparison is not usually perfect because the factors in "professionalism" do not always vary together in the same direction. A continuum also permits comparing an occupation to itself over time to see if it has become more professional. For a number of reasons that will soon be made explicit, many nonprofessions are attempting to transform themselves into professions. Some have met with more success in this endeavor than others. Despite unique circumstances surrounding any particular nonprofession, there seem to be a number of common procedures involved in the attempted transformation. The most fundamental step seems to be the establishment of a professional association. Not only is this the attainment of one specific professional characteristic, but, more importantly, organization permits the coordination of other activities in the pursuit of professional status. These activities include the formation or extension of formal training programs, often with the addition of special degrees and the upgrading of requirements (either only recommended or legally enforcable) for being able to practice. Such restrictions on practice and control over personnel often serve better than unionized collective bargaining to insure high incomes for the professionals. Although the sequence of initiating new operations differs from one nonprofession to another, formulating a code of ethics, publishing bulletins, and holding conferences are likely to occur. Numerous nonprofessions have been studied and their ventures toward professionalization have been detailed. They include the police, life-insurance salesmen, pharmacists, rehabilitation counselors, and librarians.[16]

There are several possible answers to the question of why so many nonprofessions are trying to professionalize. There is the desire for prestige, usually expressed by deference to professionals on the part of others. Another reason for professionalizing, consistent with the one just mentioned, is controlling competition. Competition is controlled by obtaining the recognition that a given area of concern is to be handled in one particular fashion and by one exclusive group. When this recognition is given by the government, the occupation obtains a license to practice and thus restricts competition. Professional standards established by associations often discourage undercutting fees of other practitioners and advertising, both of which control competition. Both controlling competition and increasing prestige may not be the only or final goals of those working to professionalize their occupations. Economic rewards, or privileges, cannot be discounted as possible aims.

Figure 8.2. PROFESSIONAL AND NONPROFESSIONAL WORK

Profession	Nonprofession
Expertise organized around specialized bodies of knowledge	Knowledge readily accessible to the general public
Need for specialized training	Little or no training necessary
Autonomy in determining how work is performed	Organizational direction on how work is performed
Regulation by code of ethics and professional peers	Regulation by organizational work rules and managers
Professional association	Trade union or no organization

Still another reason why a given nonprofessional group may adopt professional characteristics is the presence of other professionalized occupations in its work situation. That is, if the job requirements involve interaction with members of professions, those who are not professionals usually have little power, privilege, and prestige. Close contact allows those in the less professional occupation to see what steps are necessary to increase professionalism. Doctors and nurses are an example of this phenomenon. As each profession dispatches the "dirty work" elements of its task to another group, with time the latter group tries to do the same. Thus, nurses have sought to transfer the less appealing aspects of their jobs to nurses' aides and orderlies. This process seems to come to a halt when the lower group unionizes instead of trying to professionalize. A group may choose unionization over professionalization because of its members' educational level and their familiarity with unions gained from the experience of friends and relatives. Thus, the choice between unionization and professionalization may not be based on the characteristics of the job itself.

THE PROFESSIONAL IDEAL: A CRITIQUE

The description of professions by sociologists not only emphasizes an important trend in contemporary work, but involves an attitude toward work different from those defined by philosophers. For the ancients, work was a curse, and the highest human activities were contemplation and governing. In the Protestant Ethic, work is an obligation, while in the modern philosophies of creativity (process philosophies) work can be a value in itself. According to the professional ideal, only certain kinds of work are highly valued and they do not necessarily involve creativity.

Figure 8.3. BUSINESS AND PROFESSION

Business	*Profession*
Universalism (Business judgments are not based on family ties and/or other particular relations)	Universalism
Performance (Business judgments are made on the basis of efficiency, not the group to which a person belongs)	Performance
Self-orientation (Business judgments are made on the basis of profit)	Collectivity-orientation (Professional judgments are made in the interest of the client)

This is the way it's supposed to be. Use your own experience to determine how often it really is this way.

The values enshrined in the professional ideal are primarily the possession of specialized skills and knowledge, autonomy of decision within the supposed sphere of competence and, following from these, the right to make decisions for others within that sphere of competence. These are the very values denied to people in many other lines of work in mass society, and perhaps this is one reason why nonprofessional work is defined in terms of the absence of professionalism. For example, the proverbial assembly-line worker has little or no specialized skills and knowledge, no autonomy of decision about how to do his work, and no right to make decisions for others. The professional in a mass society often feels fortunate to have escaped from the drudgery and impotence associated with many other jobs, and gains a measure of satisfaction from the fact that others defer to him in at least one area of experience. However, has the professional escaped into paradise, or is there a serpent in his Garden of Eden?

The limitations of professionalism as a philosophy of work, and the problems created by professionalism in the society at large are not often stressed by sociologists, who themselves lay claim to professionalism. These limitations are of two kinds. First, while the professional has autonomy in one small sphere of existence, he is no better off than anyone else in coping with the rest of life. With regard to decisions of war and peace, race relations, and the fate of the economy, the professional has no more to say than the operator of a punch press.[17] Even if the professional is a specialist in economics, he is expected to follow policy guidelines developed by higher officials who are much more generalists than specialists. The same goes for specialists in military affairs and race relations. Along the same lines, with regard to specialities other than his own, the professional is just as much in the dark as the punch-press operator. The lawyer is no more competent to judge the quality of dental work than is the janitor. Further, by devoting himself to a narrow area of experience intensively, the professional is prone to distort the rest of experience by overemphasizing that area of life to which he is most accustomed. Engineers often believe that all problems can be solved by the invention of new machines, while medical personnel frequently hold that all human activity can be accounted for biologically. Specialists in the human studies are no more exempt from this failing than others. Psychiatrists, for example, sometimes claim that physical disturbances are really emotional in their origin. The battle of the specialities may be as damaging to the professional as to the society at large.[18] One might say that the professional has purchased a degree of autonomy in a single area in return for subservience in the rest of life.

The second limitation of the professional ideal flows from the effects of specialization on human relations. Professionals who cherish their autonomy do not make concerted efforts to allow their clients to appreciate their work. Thus, professionals tend to separate themselves from other human beings. Instead of taking the time and effort to inform patients about exactly what is being done to them and why, many medical doctors try to cut off questioning by being unresponsive and projecting a mystique. Lawyers would rather not waste their time with what they consider misdirected questions, and demand trust from their clients. Since professionals are often called upon for assistance in crisis situations, any tendency to shut the client off from appreciation of the work is usually intensified by the client's anxieties. The tendency to keep clients in the dark frequently leads professionals to look upon clients with a certain contempt. It is perhaps ironic that the professionals themselves are partly responsible for the ignorance of their clients, but the overall impact of professional snobbery is the intensification of mistrust and hatred in social relations. For the common man, deference to professionals frequently alternates with hatred for the "pointy-headed intellectual" who cannot distinguish a carburetor from a cam shaft.

This critique of the professional ideal should not be interpreted as an attack upon the widespread use of specialized knowledge in modern life.[19] It is not so much specialization (which often leads to intense creative acts whose results benefit others) but the drive toward autonomy that creates the most severe personal and social problems. When autonomy is purchased by subservience to power elites on general policy matters, strict demarcations of boundaries among specialities and the will to keep clients in ignorance, the ideal of service gives way to debilitating irresponsibility. Is the answer to this problem stricter self-regulation by the professions, greater legal controls over professionals, counter-pressure by organized client groups or some mixture of these? This is perhaps one of the central issues of our time.

EXERCISE

When you go to a professional for help what is it that you want? Do you want the professional to solve your problem with as little of your involvement as possible? Would you like to have some say about how the problem is treated? Does the kindness or sympathy of the professional mean anything to you? If you were a professional would you conform to the model of professionalism presented in this book. If so, why? If not, why not?

EXERCISE

Professionals, such as college professors, have elaborate codes and ideologies justifying their work. Do students have such ideologies? If so, what are their contents? How much cynicism does the ideology of the student have? How much idealism?

ALIENATION

In part because of the idealization of professional jobs, most criticism of work is aimed at those job categories that are on the nonprofessional end of the profession-nonprofession continuum. Another reason why negative views of the work experience are concentrated on industrial jobs is that these jobs were the ones primarily analyzed by early influential critics of work. The most important of these critics was Karl Marx. Within his overall project of demonstrating the moral bankruptcy and eventual demise of the capitalist economic system, Marx took a severe look at the plight of the nineteenth-century factory worker and concluded that the worker was alienated from his own labor, from the product of his labor, from other human beings, and finally from himself. By alienation Marx meant that a relationship that should be a natural and familiar aspect of life had become strange to the person or separate from him (alien). The worker becomes alienated from his own labor when he has no control over it. He must sell his labor in order to survive physically. He thus becomes dominated by his labor.

On the job the worker is told what to do and how and when to do it. Essentially, the work process eliminates any choice on the part of the worker. Quoting Marx, from an essay he wrote in 1849: "What do we mean by the alienation of labor? First, that the work he performs is extraneous to the worker, that is, it is not personal to him, is not part of his nature; therefore he does not fulfill himself in work, but actually denies himself; feels miserable rather than content, cannot freely develop his physical and mental powers, but instead becomes physically exhausted and mentally debased. Only while not working can the worker be himself; for while at work he experiences himself as a stranger."[20]

Figure 8.4. TYPES OF ALIENATION

Alienation from task:	The worker does not understand his contribution to the final product.
Alienation of labor:	Part of the worker's labor is taken by the owners in the form of profits.
Alienation from control over work:	The worker does not determine what to produce, how, and when.
Alienation from consequences of work:	The worker does not determine how his production will be used.

Since the time of Marx's writing, industry has engineered the work situation to be even more alienating in certain respects than it was in the nineteenth century. This increased alienation has not been a consciously intended effect, but has been an *unintended consequence* of the drive to enhance efficiency. In the early twentieth century, Frederick W. Taylor developed the principles of "scientific management" and subsequently efficiency experts such as Frank and Lillian Gilbreth (of *Cheaper by the Dozen* fame) have attempted to mechanize the workers so that they would behave on the job in the same way as a piece of efficient equipment. A machine has no control over its simple and repetitive actions. However, the actions of a machine are not monotonous, because a machine does not get bored. Much to the chagrin of managers, though, human beings do become bored. Boredom seems to be the result of preventing people from making choices, that is, from exercising some control over their labor. Not only do industrial jobs prohibit decision making by workers but, because they require some degree of attentiveness, they make systematic thinking about anything else all but impossible.

Robert Blauner has attempted to test the hypothesis, derived from Marx's theory, that the less control workers have over their jobs, the more they feel alienated. He found that different kinds of industrial environments were related to differing degrees of alienation. Printers, who had a relatively high degree of control over work activities, were much less alienated than automobile workers, who had very little control.[21]

Workers also are alienated from the products of their labor. The actual product of a worker's labor is whatever result he has contributed to in the process of production. However, the very physical object upon which the worker labors may be alien to him in the sense that he only knows a small part of its make-up. Further, not only is the worker frequently unaware of the part his labor plays in making the whole product, but he often does not even know what the final product is. Those who produce electronic circuitry parts on the assembly line may not realize that the ultimate product is a sophisticated bomb, though some managements have placed pictures of the final product in front of assembly line workers in order to stimulate morale and productivity. Finally, the physical product is alien because the worker has no control over its quality nor over who will use it and how it will be used. The ultimate result of alienation from the product of labor is that workers labor only in order to earn a livelihood rather than to make a contribution to a worthy effort or for the sheer joy of working.[22] The object of their labor is simply money. This problem is intensified in a capitalist economic system where management, too, has money rather than the product as its object. Thus, there is no intrinsic relation between the work and the motivation for undertaking it.

Contemporary inquiries into industrial labor support Marx's view that factory work does not allow human beings to express their essence and is viewed by them as a means to physical existence. Ely Chinoy has described midwestern automobile workers who despair of escaping the hateful and boring routine of the factory, but who live in hope that through the vehicle of the money that they bring home their children will attain a better type of job, perhaps in a profession.[23] Such workers concentrate, as they get older, on their growing seniority and steady pay, and learn to attend as little to work as possible.

A new generation of workers has entered the automobile industry since Chinoy conducted his study. While some of their fathers were also automobile workers, it does not seem that the members of this new generation can sustain the deadening aspects of the job by hoping for a better future for *their* children. Incidents of slashed upholstery in new cars rolling out of the factory, tools welded into the bumpers, banana peels sealed behind the dashboard, and other similar kinds of sabotage have been increasing. Recently it was announced that the Volvo car factory in Sweden was abolishing the assembly line in favor of twenty-five-man groups. This is perhaps recognition that alienation may sometimes decrease productivity.

However, experiments in decreasing alienation are often unsuccessful. Even in the very progressive Hormel meat-packing plant in Minnesota, where there is a twenty-year guaranteed annual wage, profit sharing, workers having the right to set their own pace and foremen functioning to keep materials flowing rather than barking out orders like drill sergeants, the workers indicate that they are alienated from their work. Fred H. Blum reports that the workers seem "well-adjusted, because they have reduced their level of aspirations to the rather low level of the job. They coast along, keeping busy, visiting, talking, making time go by, and getting the work done in order to 'get out of there' in order to get home!"[24] The idea that work is only a means to other goals rather than an activity with intrinsic value is also exemplified in the responses that a sample of American workers gave to a question asking them whether or not they would work if they had an option to choose. Although almost all chose to continue working, only 9 percent said they would do so because they found their work interesting or challenging. The others gave various extrinsic reasons for their choice to continue working, such as not knowing what to do with their time, maintaining self-respect, or justifying their existence.[25]

Although Marx's vision of the industrial work situation seems to hold true as much today as when he first expressed it, this image has been generalized to include many other types of work routines. Alienation from work is no longer seen as the special plague of the factory worker. Max Weber extended the concept of alienated labor to all organized work situations: "Marx's emphasis upon the wage worker as being 'separated' from the means of production becomes, in Weber's perspective, merely one special case of a universal trend. The modern soldier is equally 'separated' from the means of violence; the scientist from the means of enquiry, and the civil servant from the means of administration."[26] Except for some independent professionals who are not related to clinics, hospitals, or corporations, plus some farmers and neighborhood small businessmen, most people hold jobs within bureaucratic organizations. Even those few who have not been bureau-cratized live in the shadows of massive organizations. The independent medical professional is dependent upon large drug firms, conglomerate supply houses, and powerful lobbies; the independent farmer is dependent on mammoth farm-implement producers, chemical-fertilizer manufacturers, and government agencies; and the small businessman stocks his shelves with goods produced by America's five hundred largest corporations and has little control over what he pays for these goods. Those who have been bureaucratized, including social workers, insurance salesmen, army lieutenants, junior executives, and schoolteachers, share fully the automobile workers' alienative work setting. Thus, though there may be important differences in the context of work—cleanliness of surroundings, opportunity to interact with others informally, and so on—the fact of alienation as separation from ownership and control of the means to work remains. Since all authority comes from the top downward, there is little control over one's own activities. There is no real chance to choose what, when and how work is to be done. Although the product is not a physical object, but an insurance policy, an advertising campaign, a war, a course, or some other train of events, white-collar workers too participate in only a fraction of the total production process. Efficiency experts have invaded the office as well, dividing up work into small units which require as little choice and initiative as the tasks of factory workers, and are just as boring. People are made to act like machines and, as in the factory, machines are replacing people: automatic copying machines are replacing secretaries while computers are replacing executives. There are many jobs in which alienation is carried to even further extremes than the factory-worker experiences. These are jobs that require one to sell not only one's labor, but also one's personality. C. Wright Mills took the case of the salesgirl as an example of what he called "the personality market." In order to achieve a sale, the salesgirl must express insincere sentiments, such as concern for the customer's comfort and even interest in the customer's personal problems. She must be ruthlessly cheerful, and to carry the example forward to recent times, the smile on her face must be a mirror of the smile on the yellow pin she wears. The waitress, the stewardess, the con artist, the fundraiser, the salesman, and the prostitute are others who are prey to self-alienation because they must use their personalities to manipulate others.[27] The personality market, as defined by Mills, is yet another example of how the "put-on" characterizes human relations in a mass society.

EXERCISE

Take a job which you have had and trace the ways in which it was alienating. Does alienation trouble you or make you feel discontented? Can you imagine what a society would be like if alienation was eliminated?

EXERCISE

In what ways is the role of the student alienating? Can you imagine an educational situation that would not be alienating? Would such a situation be desirable? Why?

ALIENATION AND THE QUALITY OF WORK

It would be no exaggeration to state that the concept of alienation has been a central one in the history of sociology. Many consider Marx to have been the first sociologist, and certainly his image of class society has been the model for all others that have succeeded it, even though the successors have altered the model drastically.[28] Debates about alienation have usually taken its undesirability for granted and have concentrated on whether or not alienation must necessarily be a significant feature of the lives of the masses. A different approach will be taken here, based on the idea that the values embedded in the concept of alienation can be held up to serious question.

In defining alienation, Marx focuses on the idea that in some way the worker is not really himself. The worker feels miserable, does not develop his powers, becomes exhausted and debased, and does not feel personal involvement in his work. John Horton has summarized the thrust of Marx's analysis: "Freedom for Marx, as well as for Hegel, meant autonomous and self-contained existence."[29] The autonomous human being is always "himself," is contented and personally involved. Yet, it is fair to ask: What is this true self? If the true self is merely what the individual would like to be, there is no guarantee that the end of alienation would bring anything but a conglomeration of human beings seeking goals that might involve the destruction of others and perhaps self-destruction. If the true self is defined according to some set of needs that Marx can identify, how will human beings who have been debased by a corrupt system learn to seek fulfillment

of their "real" needs rather than the transient desires at present motivating them?[30] Further, Marx defines the absence of alienation in
terms of such feeling states as contentment and personal involvement,
and such abstract goals as control over the situation for its own sake
and the development of unspecified potentialities.

Feeling states are notoriously poor indicators of situations. One
can take a drug, for example a tranquilizer or alcohol, and feel much
better about participating in an inauthentic and manipulative social
situation. One may feel pangs of discontent in the midst of joy and
flashes of ecstasy in the midst of despair. Abstract goals always need
to be filled in with some content. What is desirable about controlling
the work situation? What is desirable about developing potentialities?
One can exert control over the work situation in order to develop the
potential of one racial group to exterminate another racial group. It
is important to ask: What is control being exerted for, and what
potentialities are being developed? Finally, is the goal of autonomous
and self-contained existence worth striving for, or even intelligible?
Part of the human condition is being related to others. Relations such
as love and cooperation imply that one is neither fully autonomous nor
self-contained. Marx, of course, emphasized the sociability of human
beings, particularly in his image of the class society. However, taken
by itself, the idea of alienation seems to lead to the position that the
self is property, not process. There is a tendency to view the self as
something "real," which is disclosed after alienation is removed and
false consciousness peeled away.

Drawing upon the discussion of space and time in chapter five, an
interpretation of alienation consistent with the idea of the self as process can be developed. Efficiency experts often try to reduce jobs down
to the confines of movement space and movement time. The worker
is not even treated as a whole organism, but instead as a series of
segmented body movements, such as those involved in putting a tire
on a new car.[31] These movements, repeated over and over again,
transform the worker into a machinelike being. The effects of reducing
work to the confines of movement space and movement time are the
boredom and discontent discussed in the preceding pages. In order to
overcome these effects, some efficiency experts become "enlightened"
and attempt to pattern jobs around action space and action time, in
which the worker is seen as a whole organism relating to other organisms in an environment. Music, pleasant colors, the opportunity to
chat with co-workers, and somewhat more challenging work are introduced into the factory situation. This sometimes increases job satisfaction, but the meaninglessness of the work often remains. This is be-

cause reducing work's movement-space and movement-time or action-space and action-time alienate the process of creation from its wider relations throughout the society. Does the work have a moral end? Does the product help people? Is this work contributing to realizing the goal of more creative work for all? Workers are not supposed to be concerned with socio-cultural space and time. This is the preserve of top management, which plans for the future. Perhaps the workers will gain more control over action-space in the future, even if industrial organizations remain bureaucratic. However, it is highly unlikely that they will be able to participate in decisions affecting the management of socio-cultural space and time unless drastic changes are made in the organization of work. Yet alienation from the kind of contribution made, the uses of that contribution and the possibility for creation in a just set of relations is ultimately more significant in the human condition as a whole than job satisfaction. Perhaps it is not too much to say that greater job satisfaction, without concern for the morality of work, would be an indication of barbarism rather than freedom.

Horton has pointed out that, in current American sociology, alienation is normally used to refer to feelings such as powerlessness, boredom, and dissatisfaction.[32] This approach to alienation tends to split the problem off from the rest of the social process and makes it appear that it is rooted in subjective feelings rather than in the mono-polization of socio-cultural space and time by elites. It is to the great advantage of these elites if they can convince the rest of us not to think beyond the action-space of our everyday relations and the action-time of our personal projects. When they are successful persuaders they are left to define the ultimate meaning of what we do.

ATTEMPTS TO REMEDY ALIENATION

Since alienation has been identified for several generations as the most serious problem in modern work, it is to be expected that many suggestions and attempts have been made to remedy it. These attempts have ranged from making minor changes in the physical work setting to full-scale social and political revolution. As was pointed out in the preceding section, no cure for alienation has yet been found. Particularly if alienation is defined in terms of alienation from ordering socio-cultural space and time, there can be no remedy for it in either the East or the West unless mammoth bureaucratic organizations can be dismantled or somehow democratized. This is why debates in both

East and West today frequently center around whether bureaucracy is necessary to the smooth management of complex technologies, and around whether greater participation in organizational decision making by workers and clients will lead to chaos and disruption or to the realization of the good life.[33]

THE HUMAN-RELATIONS APPROACH

The method most favored by managements in the United States for reducing alienation can be conveniently called the human-relations approach.[34] From the management's viewpoint, alienation is not desired because it may lead to reduced productivity and therefore to lower profits. Thus, management is not motivated by benevolence toward the worker, and has no interest in reducing alienation if this is likely to cut into profits. The human-relations approach became popular in industry when it was found that workers whose jobs had been reduced to the segmented body motions of movement space were often unproductive and even prone to sabotage production. Thus, there was a shift to viewing the worker as an organism involved in relations with co-workers participating in a segment of the production process.

An industrial sociologist, Charles B. Spaulding, has developed a "general design for harmonious productivity," which reflects the principles of the human-relations approach. Taking the viewpoint of the firm (which industrial sociologists often do), Spaulding suggests that wages, fringe benefits, safety, and general cleanliness of work place should compare favorably with firms throughout the industry. However, these are not the most important factors for insuring harmonious productivity. The worker "wants a job that is clearly defined and for which he has been given proper instructions." "The worker who does not know what is expected of him and what he may properly do in accomplishing his obligation is uncertain and unhappy."[35] Further, "the worker is likely to be happier if he can feel that he is part of a relatively small group of congenial fellow workers and if this small group has some opportunity for self-determination." Management should "let the workers talk and joke and engage in horse play, if it doesn't obviously interfere with production."[36] This doctrine helps explain why the Volvo company is experimenting with abandoning the assembly line in favor of small work groups.

Of course, there is a problem. When workers have the opportunity to form groups, they frequently set norms of production for themselves that are below those desired by management. This dilemma has been identified since the very beginning of research into industrial relations. In their famous study of the bank wiring room at Western Electric Company, Roethlisberger and Dickson pointed out how even on a piece-rate system (where people get paid according to how many units they produce rather than on a flat hourly rate) the work group limited production.[37] Spaulding points out that there may be no solution to this dilemma, and that the best that management can do is try to persuade the group to accept its viewpoint, let the group determine the "details" of its job and try to get the group to make a commitment to cooperate in raising production or accepting changes decided upon by management. In some cases the human-relations approach will increase productivity rather than impede it, while in other cases the reverse will be the case. The amount of "alienation" sought by the management will, therefore, be a function of the balance sheet.

The human-relations approach can be held up to serious question. It is based on a view of the human condition and human possibility which, when made explicit, may be surprising to those who thought the approach was enlightened. First, the human being is not seen as a person who seeks creative and challenging work, but who, instead, is most satisfied when he knows exactly what is expected of him. This means that management is enlightened when it is paternalistic (like a benevolent father-figure) and lays down the law clearly. Second, workers are implicitly seen as interested in joking and horseplay rather than in serious concerns. This is not meant to be a criticism of joking and horseplay, but a comment on the way that industrial sociologists and managers view the worker. Those reading this book who have been factory workers or who have known factory workers well know that discussions in the plant and during lunch breaks are often highly serious and concern politics, religion, economic policy, and personal tragedy and joy. Third, the human-relations approach assumes that the worst aspects of alienation can be alleviated by giving the work group a certain limited control over the action space of its members. This assumption ignores the possibility that workers might be interested in the wider socio-cultural context of their work, and might seek to have some say in determining it. The human-relations approach takes alienation from socio-cultural space and time for granted. Fourth, the human-relations approach assumes that the major problems at work are communications problems rather than sharp conflicts of interest. Management is urged to try to convince workers to accept its point of view on the assumption either that the "real" interests of labor and management are the same in the long run, or that labor can be conned into acting against its own interests by smooth talk. Thus, the image of the worker projected by the human-relations approach is one of a person in need of clear-cut rules to follow and who values horseplay highly, is not concerned with the wider aspects of his activity

---

Figure 8.5. THE IMAGE OF THE WORKER IN "HUMAN RELATIONS" THEORY

Needs clear-cut rules to follow
Values horseplay highly
Unconcerned with wider meaning of his activity
Can be persuaded to adopt the position of management
Does this image fit the workers you know?

---

and who can be persuaded to adopt the perspective of his superiors in power. Viewed this way, the human-relations approach seems to define the worker as a child. Children supposedly need limits, love fun more than serious things, have no concern with life beyond their immediate environments, and are best off listening to their parents. One wonders whether managers or industrial sociologists would be willing to apply this image of the human being to themselves. It is doubtful that they would, because they like to consider themselves as professionals, and the hallmark of the professional is autonomy and the possession of hard-won skills.

REVOLUTION

At the opposite end of the spectrum of methods for alleviating alienation from the human-relations approach is revolution. Karl Marx, who was the first social thinker to focus attention on alienation in its economic setting, prescribed revolution as the only way in which alienation could be eliminated. Under capitalism, he believed, aliena-tion was inevitable because the owners took part of the fruits of the worker's labor in the form of profits. In order to preserve this profit system, Marx reasoned, the owners had to keep control of the work situation and make sure that "labor discipline" (closely resembling military discipline) was continually enforced. At the heart of Marx's revolutionary prescription was the idea that no ruling class ever gives up its power and privilege voluntarily. Thus, the owners of industrial tools would not allow the workers to take over without putting up some kind of fight. Sometimes the resistance of the ruling class would be physically violent, calling for the "counter-violence" of militant workers and sometimes it would take the form of propaganda, manipulation, and political maneuvering. In all cases, since the capitalist system was, in its essence, a system promoting alienation, it would have to be abolished before the work situation could improve significantly.

Marx believed that a socialist order, in which tools were owned publicly rather than privately, would progressively eliminate alienation. There would no longer be any need for cutting the worker out of decision making because there would not be any more parasitical classes living off the labor of others. Human existence would be lucid because there would no longer be any need to convince the workers that exploitation was really a good thing. With exploitation abolished, not only would propaganda be a thing of the past, but the state would wither away because there would be no ruling class paying off police and officials to protect property rights. Thus, human beings would take responsibility for their own destinies and collectively plan for their future democratically.

Marx's prescription for revolution was based on the assumption that private ownership of the means of production was responsible for alienation. In the twentieth century, people have begun to think that this may not be true.[38] The Soviet Union had its socialist revolution, but alienation, in the sense of lack of control by workers over their situation, persists. The mammoth Soviet bureaucracies are subject to the same problems as their American counterparts, and the difficulties are perhaps compounded by propaganda proclaiming the end of alienation.

The failure of the communist world, particularly the Soviet Union, to overcome alienation has led to a new radical proposal for transforming the work situation. This proposal is workers' management of the production process. Experiments with democracy in the work situation, going beyond the mere filling in of details with regard to policies coming down from above, have been tried in Yugoslavia and in some industries of Great Britain since World War II. The results of these experiments have been inconclusive (workers sometimes behave like managers, attempting to maximize advantage at the expense of consumers and other industries), but they have not shown workers to be one-dimensional or irresponsible.[39] Democracy in the work setting might go along with organized checks by consumers, so that there would be a worker-consumer democracy. Spaulding argues that workers' democracy is not viable because of "the failures of various reform movements and co-operative colonies which expected human beings to co-operate 'naturally.' "[40] This objection, however, does not meet the argument in favor of a worker-consumer democracy, because such a system would incorporate organized authorities and checks and balances. The great difference from the present would be that controls would be horizontal, as they are between the branches of the United States government, rather than vertical, as they are in bureaucratic organizations.

Countervailing Allegiances

Short of the ultimate remedy, revolution, workers have attempted to reform the work situation by restructuring it in the presence of capitalism through affiliating themselves with unions and other occupational associations. The worker's lack of control over his own labor, along with his inability to decide what tasks should be done in what manner, are among the chief reasons traditionally given for alienation. If one focused attention on the increasingly bureaucratic work organization, there would seem to be little hope for the worker to increase control. However, a broader view of the work situation discloses the existence of various types of occupational associations that have the possibility, at least, of allowing the worker to have more control over his activities. Why this possibility exists can be understood by describing a situation similar to work in a bureaucracy—that of a child with parents who disagree with one another about what the child should and should not do. The skillful (conniving?) child can play off one parent against the other, obeying his mother when she agrees with what he wants to do and obeying his father when their views coincide. He can get his own way only as long as each parent concedes that the other also has legitimate control over the child and as long as they each have roughly equivalent power. Similarly, as occupational associations have received the recognition of the employer's organization, the worker's possibility for freedom has increased. The extent of this freedom is dependent upon how similar the organizations are in strength and whether they are at variance about what the worker should do.[41]

Both employers and unions regard one another's control over the factory worker as legitimate. Although there is little that he can do about the employer's decisions regarding his work activity, the union's views are supposed to be reflective of their members' opinions—in official propaganda at least. The propaganda in this case has little resemblance to the practice and, for the most part, union leaders and management are in agreement as to the way in which the worker is to perform his job. In part, this may account for why industry recognized the unions as legitimate. Any disagreement usually concerns wages and fringe benefits rather than job descriptions.[42] The majority of instances where unions and employers are in disagreement over the job itself occur in those industries where the unions have a great deal more power than the employers. An example is in the construction trades where unionized painters are usually not permitted to use rollers to apply paint nor brushes greater than a stipulated width. However, because of the union's strength, the worker cannot side with the employer and thus has no control. Although the blue-collar worker ordinarily cannot use the two organizations against one another to achieve more control for himself, and thereby lessen his alienation, he frequently does have the opportunity to give his allegiance to one or the other. Despite the fact that alienating conditions still exist, he does not have to identify himself with his direct "oppressor" (the employer), which reduces the sense of self-alienation.

In general, occupational associations of all types facilitate the identification of a person with the type of work he does, rather than with the organization in which he is employed. On the profession end of the work continuum, the views about work activities held by the professional association are frequently at odds with those of the employing organization. For example, scientists working in industrial organizations are asked to direct their inquiry into two generally opposite directions. Their employers want them to work toward developing products that they could profitably market. Their profession, speaking through the professional association's journals and at meetings, wants them to concentrate on "pure" rather than "applied" science; to discover general principles rather than glamorous products. Rather than obeying the dictates of the profession or the organization for which they work, most professionals give their allegiance to one unit or the other, depending upon which one coincides with their own independent scale of values. They either look to their colleagues in the profession, corresponding with them through research publications, or look to their employers and get into administrative tasks. Whichever side they choose, taking sides reduces their freedom. Many of those who attempt to choose both employer and profession find themselves to be the servants of two masters, and to be plagued by conflict.

Sociologists have studied professionals employed in bureaucratic organizations, such as scientists, engineers, and college professors.[43] Alvin Gouldner classifies professionals as either locals or cosmopolitans. Although there are variations within each of the two groups, locals are those loyal to the organization who tend to have a low commitment to specialized skills, whereas the cosmopolitans' basic commitments are to their job and its skills. Cosmopolitans have little organizational loyalty since they seek recognition from those in their occupation or profession. For a number of reasons, including lack of identification with any given organization, cosmopolitans move from job to job more than locals. Probably the primary reason for this mobility is the fact that, although employers wish their workers to be loyal to the organization, they hire and reward them on the basis of their cosmopolitan characteristics—their skill and the reputation they have in their profession, which is partly based on their skill. While this may appear to involve a contradiction, in reality the "freedom" of cosmopolitans follows from the employer's dilemma. The employer wants organizational loyalty, but he also wants efficient and profitable operations. Locals often have nothing to sell but their loyalty, and hiring only them would lead to disaster for the firm in a competitive situation. Therefore cosmopolitans, who are skill oriented, have more freedom than most workers to play the profession off against the organization.

COMPLEXITIES OF THE WORK SITUATION

While none of the devices suggested to remedy alienation has been fully successful, study by social scientists over the past several generations has shown that the work situation is far more complex than Marx envisaged it. This appreciation of complexity is probably due to several causes. First, with the growth of sophisticated technologies and elaborate organizations, the work situation has, in many cases, actually become far more complex than it was in the nineteenth century. Second, in the development of inquiry the first step is usually to sketch out a broad interpretation of significant features and then leave it to succeeding generations to refine this interpretation and show its limitations. In the preceding discussion it was shown that Marx defined most of the significant problems for the philosophy and sociology of work as they have developed through the nineteenth and twentieth centuries. This does not mean that industrial sociologists are Marxists (in the United States most of them are not), but that the problem of alienation continues to be a focal point for research. Those sociologists who have gone beyond Marx have shown that there seem to be certain factors built into the organization of work that at least alleviate alienation slightly. The worker is not entirely beholden to the organization because the organization itself faces dilemmas that it cannot seem to resolve decisively, workers generate sets of relations that are not reflected by the organizational chart, some people are able to choose among competing definitions of the work role and, even in extremely oppressive situations, people are able to conceal their motivations and projects.

ORGANIZATIONAL DILEMMAS

Blau and Scott have argued that each type of organization faces a dilemma in attaining its goals effectively. For the business firm under capitalism the goal is maximization of profit. Within a bureaucratic organization this goal generates a dilemma. On the one hand, in order to insure a smooth flow of work, people working in the business must have some stable expectations of job security and some basis for reasonably predicting what their associates will do from day to day. If such expectations are disappointed, morale will suffer and perhaps labor supply will be lost and those left in the firm will sabotage operations. On the other hand, in order to gain maximum profits, individual initiative, innovation, and ambition must be fostered. Yet these very qualities, so essential to gaining competitive advantage in a market situation, are apt to disrupt stable expectations and normal routines.[44] The existence of this dilemma opens up a certain degree of freedom for the employee who is not simply bound to an assembly-line job. He can attempt to be a go-getter continually firing new ideas at his superiors who, according to the folklore of management, must give them consideration. The superiors may give in finally and grant the go-getter freedom just to get him off their backs.

Alternatively, the person may play according to the rules, be a docile underling and finally accumulate enough organizational IOUs that he is assured of a secure future with little work. Of course, it is not always possible to exploit the organizational dilemmas. Turning contemporary organizations to one's benefit often involves becoming cynical, renouncing the possibilities for creative work and making alliances with people who one considers to be hopelessly corrupt. Also, there is the possibility of being dragged into vicious power struggles and the risk that one will be caught on the side of innovation and profitability when the top management has decided to go in the direction of consolidation and stability, or the reverse. The existence of organizational dilemmas gives some opportunity to the individual for maneuvers, but does nothing to alleviate alienation from socio-cultural space and time.

INFORMAL ORGANIZATION

A second limitation on complete domination of the work situation by the organization is what has been called informal organization. An example of informal organization was discussed earlier when reference was made to the way factory workers may limit production when they have the opportunity to form groups. However, the extent of informal organization is far greater than the mere limitation of production. In any organization, chains of command are continually broken by people who have special relations with those several layers above them. Some bureaus in the organization will get more supplies than they are supposed to according to the budget, and others will have their allocations slashed because of the "regrettable need to economize." As was pointed out in the discussion of symbolic bureaucracy, workers in the bureau may behave in ways having nothing to do with their official job descriptions.

Informal organization arises whenever groups of people within the organization act according to sets of rules different from those officially spelled out.[45] Depending on the circumstances, informal organization has different consequences for the organization. Sometimes it arises because the official rules do not allow employees to meet the organization's own goals effectively. For example, if the rules demand that certain decisions must be approved by a superior before they are put into effect, and that superior is regularly absent because of alcoholism, the workers in the bureau may by-pass the rules and decide collectively on what is to be put into effect. Sometimes informal organization arises to protect the workers from ambitious managers, as in the case of factory workers collectively limiting production. At still other times, informal organization may reflect power struggles between factions battling for control of the organization. Thus, like organizational dilemmas, informal organization may prevent total enslavement of the worker to the organization, but it does not ordinarily provide an effective vehicle for alleviating the most significant types of alienation. Informal organization frequently exploits organizational dilemmas. For the person engaged in the process of self-understanding, its existence everywhere is important for two reasons. First, it explodes the myth that the organization is a monolith that simply processes people and turns them into machines. Organizations may be brutal in many respects, but they are not always awesome and, for those who do not insist upon being Boy Scouts and following all the rules, informal organization can provide a way of alleviating the worst abuses of hierarchy. Second, informal organization often is the bearer of alternative role-definitions. Particularly for professionals and other skilled workers, the organization usually has an approved definition of work. Teachers are supposed to keep order in their classes and forego experiments that will infuriate vocal groups in the community. An informal organization of teachers in a high school may promote an alternative definition of teaching that approves of experimentation. Such an informal organization may help protect the individual teacher who wants to depart from the official definition of work from reprisals by the administration. The use of informal organization as a weapon for social change has not been widely discussed by sociologists who have tended to make sharp distinctions between working within the system and revolutionizing the system from without. However, in the coming decades there may be increased use of organizational guerrilla warfare and mutual aid by networks of informal organization.

IMPRESSION MANAGEMENT

Informal organization assumes that there is at least some opportunity for people to scheme and plot. When the work situation is so repressive that small groups have no chance to form, the last resort for the individual is to withdraw any moral support from the organization, hold himself apart from his job and do it as poorly as possible. In resorting to such rebellion the worker may indulge in "impression management."[46] He may pretend to be stupid, forget his orders, apologize abjectly for mistakes, and play the perpetual clown. He may pretend that he has a hearing problem or even develop a language unintelligible to his oppressor. These are the tactics of slaves and they were used for more than a century by black people in the United States. Such tactics make oppression expensive because the oppressor cannot count on the job being done well, or even done at all. Of course, in the long run impression management hurts the oppressed person the most, because he must behave like a dumb animal all day long and must hope that he will be able to recover some self-respect in his few private moments. When people resort to the tactics of slaves, it means that they have judged their situation hopeless and see no possibility for organizing. All that is left to them to alleviate alienation is cultivating a private self, which the oppressor can never touch. However, even this private distance from the oppressor is an added complexity to the work situation. As Frantz Fanon points out, as he obeys his orders reluctantly, the slave can continually "sharpen his knives" in his mind, preparing for the day when he will rip the oppressor to shreds.[47]

SUMMARY

There have been three dominant philosophies of work in Western culture. Traditionally, work has been considered a curse visited upon human beings as punishment for sin, or as an activity fit only for slaves. In modern times this attitude was revised and to some extent replaced by the view that work is an obligation of all human beings. More recently a third attitude toward work has appeared, in which the possibilities for creative work have been emphasized.

In mass society, the most favored form of work is professional. Professionalism is defined according to the possession of expert knowledge and the autonomy of the specialist. Nonprofessions, the less favored kinds of work, are defined in terms of the absence of professionalism. Those who enter nonprofessional work need not possess expert knowledge and do not have control over how they do their work.

In his analysis of work in industrial society, Karl Marx identified alienation as a central problem. For Marx, the worker was alienated because he did not have control over his work situation. Remedies for alienation that have been suggested are the human-relations approach to work (where management gives labor some control over the details of the work situation); revolution; worker management of industry, and strong union or professional organizations to pose counterweights against management. None of these remedies has met with great success. However, within the work situation itself there are some built-in complexities that alleviate alienation slightly, such as organizational dilemmas, informal organization and, as a last resort, impression management.

9
INEQUALITY AND ITS DIMENSIONS

The preceding discussion of work in mass society introduced the notion of inequality in social relations by showing that at the present time there are wide differences between jobs with respect to the control that someone doing work has over his situation. Professionals were seen as having a large measure of control, while those in other types of occupations were seen as having little, if any, control. Inequality, of course, can appear in many dimensions of human existence beyond control over the work situation. There can be inequalities in the possession and use of products, inequalities in the possession and use of knowledge, and many others. It has seemed that throughout recorded history, when widespread and visible inequalities have existed, those benefiting from the conditions have attempted to justify them in one way or another. Traditionally, the justifications of inequality have been rooted in concepts from philosophy or religion. Inequalities were seen as divinely ordained or in some way rational. Among the most famous justifications of inequality are the ideologies of caste, estate, and class.

The caste system in ancient India was characterized as one in which the individual was born into a certain group (caste) and could not leave it. Each caste was associated with a particular occupation, and the castes were ranked according to their religious excellence. The Hindu belief in reincarnation (rebirth on earth after death) was the powerful underpinning of the system. One could only hope to rise in caste by being reborn in a higher caste. One could only be so reborn by having fulfilled the obligations of one's present caste perfectly and without complaint. According to the Hindu justification of caste, the members of the highest (Brahmin) caste were closest of all human beings to spiritual purity. The warrior caste was next in line to the Brahmins, followed by the workers, peasants, and artisans, and finally came the untouchables who performed tasks concerned with sanitation and other activities deemed impure. It is clear that anyone of a lower caste who believed in the justification of inequality would be a good servant of those with the privileges. There is perhaps nothing better for a privileged group than for those on bottom to believe that their situation has been divinely ordained and that their hope for the future resides in some afterlife. It is also important to note that, tightly bound up with the elaborate religious justification of caste, was a more mundane ranking of occupations based on the disdain for manual labor.[1]

Different from the caste system was the system of estates which characterized Western Europe in pre-modern times. In broadest outline, membership in estates was based on land ownership, with the hereditary nobility constituting the owners and the peasantry constituting the labor force. This distinction is, of course, exceedingly simplified, since there were tradesmen, artisans, the powerful clergy and free peasants in medieval Europe.[2] As with the caste system, the system of estates was justified religiously. The nobility was viewed as performing the essential social function of protecting the safety and good of the rest of the people, and this function was traced to divine command. Those who were not privileged were counseled to obey their rulers and were reminded that in the afterlife the poor might find their reward. While there was no hope of rising socially through reincarnation into a new estate, there was hope of eternal happiness in heaven. The Christian myth, unlike the Hindu myth, was universalistic and promised salvation to all. However, there was an emphasis on obedience of subordinates to superiors ("Render unto Caesar the things that are Caesar's . . .").

In modern times the class system described by Marx supplanted the system of estates. Marx did not justify the class system, but instead vigorously criticized it. However, the system in which the few owned the tools and the many worked for the owners found its philosophical and religious defenders. The most familiar defense of classes is based on the supposed "natural right" to own property.[3] The individual is considered a "self" isolated from others and possessed of the capacity to convert nature into culture. In a society in which all are free to exchange the fruits of their labor, those who are the most efficient producers will eventually come to own more property. The end result of this process will be that the few most efficient will own the tools and the rest will work for them. Of course, this defense of classes can be criticized on the grounds that there never existed a world of such "selves" all starting equally and freely exchanging the fruits of their labor. The inequalities of the system of estates were carried over into the modern period. Further, is free exchange the most important human value? The theory of natural rights merely assumed that it was.

Figure 9.1. SYSTEMS OF STRATIFICATION

Caste System	*Estate System*	*Class System*
One is born into a caste and cannot change castes.	It is difficult to move out of the estate into which one is born.	One attains class position through inheritance or success in the market.
Castes are ranked by religious purity and social function.	Estates are determined by ownership of land.	Classes are determined by ownership of capital.
Castes are justified by theology.	Estates are justified by theology and natural law.	Classes are justified by the "natural right" to acquire property.
Hindu Castes	*European Estates*	*Modern Classes*
Brahmins (Ritually pure)	Landowning Nobility	Bourgeoisie (Own the means of production)
Warriors	Higher Clergy	Petty Bourgeiosie (Small property-owners, shopkeepers)
Commoners	Lower Clergy and Freemen	Proletariat (Workers)
Untouchables (Ritually impure)	Serfs (Bound to work the land of a particular noble)	Lumpen Proletariat (Unemployed, unemployable)

The defenses or apologies mentioned above have in common a notion of the justice of inequality. There are other theories that view inequality as an inevitable condition rather than as something good or rationally defensible. These so-called scientific justifications can be divided into two groups. The first is composed of those arguments that state that human beings are born with distinctly different abilities. Social Darwinists, who enjoyed great popularity in the late nineteenth century, subscribed to the belief in the survival of the fittest as the explanation of evolution, for humans as well as for the flora and fauna.[4] Financial success was an indicator of fitness, and ne'er do wells, according to the principles of Social Darwinism, should not be helped lest they breed and corrupt the quality of the human race. More recently, racial and sexual inequalities have been justified by those who claim the natural superiority of whites over blacks and of men over women. Arthur Jensen, a Berkeley educational psychologist, stirred up a hornet's nest in the early 1970s by his attempts to document the intellectual inferiority of blacks, using several studies based on IQ tests. He suggested, despite the overlap in IQ score ranges (that is, there are blacks who score higher than some whites, although the average scores of whites are higher than those of blacks) that the two groups be given different types of education. Blacks would be trained for manual trades and whites would be educated for the professions.[5] This would result in continued inequality, since virtually only whites could obtain college educations and the higher-salaried jobs that such education commands.

Sexual inequality, the dominance of men over women, is seen by its defenders as the result of biologically controlled male superiority. Lionel Tiger refers back to prehistoric bands of *homo sapiens* for his argument:[6] Hunting requires men to work with one another (though only for certain types of game), and those bands that survived and evolved into modern man were the ones in which men formed stronger bonds with one another than they formed with women. Men stick together because it is in their genes to do so, and because they stick together they run the world. This, at least, is Tiger's argument.

CRITICISMS OF NATURAL SUPERIORITY

Critics of these natural-superiority arguments employ a number of approaches. Sociologists frequently hark back to the influence of nurture (social influence) over nature. Some refute the evidence that a given group is superior, others bring counter-evidence to show that the inferior group is superior in other qualities. Many refer to the overlap in the ranges of ability of the two groups. Also popular is the contention that people, within broad ranges of ability, have the legal and/or moral right to equal treatment.

The second type of justification that is based on the inevitability rather than the inherent justice or goodness of inequality is usually referred to as the functionalist argument. Based to a large extent on the works of Talcott Parsons,[7] the most frequently cited exposition of this position is Kingsley Davis's and Wilbert E. Moore's 1945 article entitled "Some Principles of Stratification."[8] Stratification is a particular type of inequality, in which people are grouped together on certain characteristics, and these groups are then ranked as higher or lower than one another. Briefly stated, Davis and Moore defend systems of inequality because they insure the fulfillment of society's essential needs: "In general those positions convey the best reward, and hence have the highest rank, which (a) have the greatest importance for the society and (b) require the greatest training or talent. The first factor concerns function and is a matter of relative significance; the second concerns means and is a matter of scarcity. . . . Actually a society does not need to reward positions in proportion to their functional importance. It merely needs to give sufficient reward to them to insure that they will be filled competently. . . . If a position is easily filled, it need not be heavily rewarded, even though important."[9]

CRITICISMS OF THE FUNCTIONALIST VIEW

The critics of this functionalist justification of inequality are numerous as well as vigorous.[10] One starting point for the controversy involves the question of who defines the needs of the society. The functionalist's assumption of a consensus about the needs of society —i.e., that everyone holds the same values—is highly questionable. In addition, there have been numerous instances in which values have been manipulated through propaganda, such as advertising, especially the commercials that appear on television. One can also point to various other means for manipulating the needs of society, such as the military provoking a war, which creates the need for a large army. The functionalist theory also suffers when confronted with examples of artificially created scarcity, such as the quota restrictions of professional schools and professional licensing arrangements. Davis and

Moore contend that high rewards are necessary to motivate people to take jobs that would not otherwise be filled, due either to stringent requirements for training or need for above-average ability. They do not give great attention to the argument that people might undergo the extra training, for example, because the intrinsic qualities of the job attracts them. The high rewards given to seemingly insignificant (nonfunctional or dysfunctional) roles, such as rock-and-roll entertainer, call girl, and race-car driver, also cannot be easily accounted for.

Walter Buckley challenged the theory by pointing to data indicating that family or lineage is a more important determinant of status than is role performance.[11] Tumin, in the classic rebuttal to Davis and Moore, questions the inevitability of systems of inequality for all future societies. Both the justifications of inequality in the functionalist theory and in the arguments involving the natural superiority of some people over others seem to have touched a raw nerve, both in society at large and within the social sciences. Perhaps this is because of the strain toward an ideology of equality in mass societies.[12]

Figure 9.2. JUSTIFICATIONS OF INEQUALITY

Theological: Social inequality is somehow approved by God.

Biological: Social inequality is a result of inherent racial, sexual, or other physiological differences.

Evolutionary: Social inequality is the result of the best adapted organisms or groups securing their survival.

Functional: Social inequality is the result of differential rewards for different contributions to the maintenance of society.

Mass societies tend to be characterized by functional justifications of inequality.

OCCUPATIONAL PRESTIGE: THE WORKING MODEL OF INEQUALITY

One of the most important distinctions between mass society and the forms of social order that preceded it is the lack in mass society of any authoritative or official justification of inequality.[13] The official justification of the caste system was rooted in Hinduism, while the official justification of estates was rooted in Christianity. Class society was upheld by such metaphysical concepts as "natural rights," though the philosophical defense of capitalism never gained the wide acceptance that the religious justifications of previous systems had. Mass society, of course, is no less defended by myths than are previous systems, but there is a change in the kinds of myths put forward by privileged groups. The hero of propaganda in mass society is the "common man."[14] According to prevailing myths, nobody can tell the common man what is good for him, and nobody can claim special privileges on account of some divine or metaphysical principle. The common man must decide who is to gain privileges and who is to be deprived of benefits. Thus, in both East and West the official propaganda stresses the value of equality. Even if governments and organizations recognize the existence of inequalities, they generally claim to be dedicated to eliminating them.[15] Those inequalities that are to be maintained are seen as inevitable, in the sense that Davis and Moore saw stratification as part of the human condition. Yet it is clear to everyone that inequalities exist in mass society, and that these inequalities are not random. The working philosophy of inequality in mass societies has, in a sense, been defined by the "common man" himself through the prestige that he accords various professions and occupations. While there may be no explicit justification of inequality in mass society, there is certainly an implicit one rooted in the relations and judgments of people in everyday life.

In mass society, prestige itself can hardly be said to exist. Prestige is the way people feel toward you, the honor they accord to you, on the basis of the various positions you occupy, such as mother, waitress, girl scout leader, PTA member, and Sunday school teacher. Prestige should not be confused with esteem, which is the way people evaluate you as a result of the manner in which you discharge the duties of these positions—a devoted mother, a bossy scout leader, a complacent PTA member, and so on. Prestige, as well as esteem, is not so much a characteristic that people have or lack; rather it refers to a person's place in a hierarchy. One has more or less prestige than someone else. Prestige can be evaluated best in a small town where people can know the multiple positions with which each individual is involved. Numerous studies of prestige were carried out by sociologists in the 1930s and 1940s. Under pseudonyms like Yankee City, Old City, Jonesville and Elmstown, hierarchies of prestige were measured in small towns in New England, the Midwest, and the South.[16] However, in mass society in general, and in cities or the nation in particular, prestige hierarchies were impossible to obtain. However, the studies just noted indicated that a person's prestige rank in the local community was most highly associated with the variable of occupation. The prestige ranking of one's occupation has thus come to be the equivalent of a person's general standing in mass society.

One of the most frequently used methods for the study of occupational prestige is that developed by the National Opinion Research Center in 1947.[17] A representative sample of the adults in the United States composed of almost three thousand people was given cards which stated: "For each job mentioned please pick out the statement that best gives your own personal opinion of the general standing that such a job has."[18] The possible responses ranged from (1) (excellent standing) to (5) (poor standing). A single score for each of the ninety jobs mentioned was devised by translating the percentages of each possible rating for that occupation—if it received all ones, its score was 100; while if it received all fives, the score was 20. Those jobs with the highest scores, such as Supreme Court justice (96), physician (93), state governor (93), college professor (89), not only have highly specialized training and relatively high salaries, but are also those involving the most control over other people. The low-prestige occupations, such as night watchman (47), janitor (44), and garbage collector (35) are those requiring little training, paying poorly, and generally allowing no control over other people.

This study has been repeated by other research teams. In addition to disclosing that people have a definite tendency to overrate their own occupations, the various studies done on American samples indicate a stability in the rankings over time.[19] Even more interesting are the findings that occupations are given the same relative positional rankings in many other countries.[20] Inkeles and Rossi compared rankings of samples from England, New Zealand, Germany, USSR, Japan, and the United States.[21] They explain their results in functionalist terms by suggesting that the rating of jobs within the factory (that is, the higher the pay and authority, the higher the rank) are functional to the factory system and thus would be transported to any industrial country. An alternative explanation might be that, in adopting the industrial system, countries also adopt certain values. Among these values is a specific prestige ordering of occupations.

CRITIQUE OF THE PRESTIGE HIERARCHY

The concern with occupational prestige as an indicator and even a definition of inequality in mass society can be criticized in several ways. First, the notion of prestige itself is built upon what David Riesman called "other-directedness."[22] The hierarchy of occupations is defined by the differences in respect accorded to various positions. In a sense, all that people would have to do is lower their respect for certain occupations and raise it for others and the system would change. Yet most people are not willing to do this and look to those around them for standards of what is more and less valuable. Thus, there is a circular process in which people validate one another's standards and thereby appear to enslave themselves. How is this circle broken? Where do the standards originate? Those occupational and professional groups with greater access than others to the mass media have the best chance of imposing their definitions of prestige on the rest. Thus, the common man does not decide the ranking of positions in a vacuum.

A second criticism concerns the values built into the ranking. People in Western societies seem consistently to value control over one's own situation and the situations of others more highly than anything else. Officials, professionals, and managers all have in common the possession of greater power and control than those ranked lower. This worship of control by the "common man" is perhaps an index of how impotent people feel in mass society. However, high estimation of control over the fates of others does not ultimately reveal very much confidence in the ability of human beings to shape their destinies cooperatively. Creative work seems to be far less valued than telling other people what to do. Perhaps the reader should see whether he rates the various kinds of work the same way as the "average man." When we looked at the categories we rated skilled laborers far above owners, officials, business agents, managers, and clerical workers. You don't have to go along with the crowd, nor along with us.

EXERCISE

Draw up your own ranking of occupational "prestige." How does it compare with the findings of researchers reported in this book? Can you justify your ranking?

OCCUPATIONAL IDEOLOGIES

Regardless of where in the prestige hierarchy a given occupation is located, from physician to janitor, there exists a system of beliefs that serves to enhance prestige. These beliefs, or occupational ideologies as they are called, are directed, in part, to members of the occupation. The beliefs interpret the work activities to make them appear meaningful, important (functional to society), and challenging.[23] A consequence of occupational ideologies is thus the overranking of occupations. Occupational ideologies are also directed toward the general public. Some make narrow claims about specialized competence and are termed "parochial" while others involve a number of related occupations and entire life-styles, and can be called "ecumenic."[24] An example of an ecumenic ideology is the entire notion of professionalism, which was discussed in the previous chapter. It claims that professionals are more concerned about their clients than self-interested, that they possess high levels of expertise because of long training, and that they govern themselves through rigid codes of ethics. The prestige of professions, in general, is high, and high prestige is associated with high income.

In addition to the extrinsic prestige-enhancing functions, occupational ideologies serve an even more important purpose of giving the worker more control over his job. Ideologies can thus be seen as directed at superiors, customers, and clients, in addition to members of the occupation and the public in general. Legitimizations of monopoly practice are obvious controls against competition. Occupational claims of expertise prevent clients from questioning the worker's judgments, and in bureaucratic settings also reduce control by superiors. Occupational ideologies frequently contain negative stereotypes of clients or customers, characterizing them as stupid, greedy, overdemanding, beyond help, and so on. The waitress in a busy restaurant and the doctor with a large practice need not exert themselves so much if they have the view that those they serve are demanding services unnecessarily. Howard Becker describes the contempt jazz musicians have toward most of their audience because the audience is viewed as being incapable of judging good music.[25] Audience reaction is not an effective control on how and what they play. The ideology of the arts is concerned with the freedoms needed by the artists in order to create. This allows the painter, writer, and others to dress, act, and in general have a style of life that is less controlled than the life-styles of other workers. The image of the unimaginative rule-following bureaucrat enables those who work in public bureaucracies to have more control, because their clients will be less likely to ask them to reinterpret or bend any rules for them. Even the stereotype of the lazy Negro servant added to the control servants had over their work activities in that it reduced the expectations held by their superiors of how much work they were capable of doing.

SOCIALIZATION

Occupational ideologies are learned by workers just as they learn the job's technical and social skills and other values associated with the position. This learning is often referred to as part of adult or role socialization, the adjectives serving to distinguish it from the general process of socialization in which a human infant is taught to be a member of a community. All occupations have some period of socialization but differ according to duration, formality, and intensity. Obviously, the longer the period of socialization, the more effectively the skills and values tend to be transmitted. In those societies where boys follow in their father's occupation, such as in traditional societies where most are farmers, or in a caste system, skills and values seem to be transmitted effectively. Although motherhood has not been recognized as an occupation in the United States (a mother receives no remuneration nor is the value of her labor calculated into the gross national product), girls are socialized into this role from infancy. They learn how to take care of babies and are taught the "appropriate" values through playing with their dolls. Boys are not allowed to play with dolls, and ambitious parents give them doctor's kits or junior scientist's labs to help shape their career aspirations.

In describing the military academy, Sanford Dornbusch indicates that its effectiveness is due in part to the organization's exclusive access to the person during training and in part to having the person's peers assist in the process.[26] The socialization of doctors in medical school and internship has many similarities to that of the Coast Guard cadets described by Dornbusch.[27] In both cases, learning technical knowledge and associated skills, such as shooting a rifle or suturing a wound, is not sufficient. For the socialization process to be considered successful, the entering student must emerge with a standardized self-image of a doctor or an officer.

Members of an occupation who do not share all the same job-related values as the majority are seen as having had faulty socialization. The salesman who tries to be abolutely honest with his customers, the factory worker who keeps producing more than her co-workers, the doctor who favors socialized medicine, the junior executive who declines invitations to attend his boss's dinner parties, and the politician who refuses to compromise her principles even slightly are all seen as having learned some of the facets of their jobs incorrectly.

Improper socialization is also called upon to explain why those calling for the reform of their occupations are usually the newer members—the *young* Turks. The socialization model accounts for this by indicating that one still is learning the appropriate values and skills for the first few years on the job, particularly if the job involves dealing with other people.

This model of occupational socialization is severely flawed because it does not allow for the possibility that people would rationally choose to reject some portion of the occupational role. According to this model, occupational values can only change through error (faulty socialization is often compared to a computer programming error), not through reason. Do people really sell their souls to a given occupation?

CAREERS

Once the person has been socialized into a certain occupation or profession by learning its ideology as well as the skills associated with it, he is, according to the conventional wisdom, ready to start his career in that line of work. A career has been defined by sociologists of work as "a consensually agreed upon sequence of appropriate work activities."[28] As in socialization into a job, there is a problem defining *who* agrees upon *which* sequence is appropriate. This is particularly the case when there are alternative definitions of the job, which may not be consistent with one another.

Even if the problems of defining the appropriate sequence are by-passed, it is clear that there are a wide variety of career patterns in mass society and that a large number of jobs do not really have careers associated with them in the strictest sense of the term. Assembly-line work, for example, does not really have a sequence of appropriate work activities over the years. Day after day the factory worker does the very same work regardless of his age and experience. Thus, careers are associated most closely with the more professional side of the work continuum and the higher rungs of the occupational-prestige hierarchy.

The person beginning a career in professional or managerial work frequently has an expectation of what the future will hold in terms of a sequence of activities. If properly socialized he has learned these expectations in his training period. The ideal career pattern in mass society views the person as rising with his age group up the ladder of organizational wealth, power, and prestige.[29] Both the person and the organization supposedly will have problems if the person falls behind his age group too much or rushes ahead of his age group too rapidly through overachieving. Since all organizations in mass society have a resemblance to armies, one might say that the ideal career is one in which the person rises through the ranks in decent step with his generation. Of course, not everybody has a "marshal's baton in his knapsack," and for the majority hopes of success must be dashed when the person approaches middle age. At this time, there is frequently a career crunch when the person begins to face the fact he has gone as far as he ever will, and that this is not at all as far as he had once hoped to go.[30] Psychologists say that the person at this point should face the music gracefully and perhaps take up a hobby. This, perhaps, is somewhat empty advice in a social order where occupational rank is the key to one's social status and self-esteem. Other aspects of career crunch occur when the person finds that the organization has changed either its goals or its means and that he is no longer capable of functioning in the new order, either through lack of skill or emotional strain.[31] Finally, Laurence J. Peter has observed that in many organizations people seem to be promoted up to just the level at which they are incompetent to function well, wreaking havoc both on efficiency and personal fulfillment.[32] All of this should be fair warning that the person who devotes herself to the organization or profession, and seeks the ideal career, will often be disappointed. Perhaps it is better to prepare for this disappointment, and thereby avert it, than to face the music suddenly at middle age.

EXERCISE

Select a career you might like to pursue. Find out through reading and interviewing people in the field the stages of career development in that field. Find out what proportion of people who enter reach each rung of the ladder and what characteristics the successes and failures have. When you are done, make some judgment about whether it is worth your while to strive for success in that field.

DIMENSIONS OF STRATIFICATION

The prestige of a person's occupation is frequently taken to indicate his standing relative to other people. Is the occupation's prestige only an indicator of where the person stands or is it the cause of his overall position? Is there, perhaps, some other dimension that is more fundamental than occupational prestige? Karl Marx claimed that if people did not own the means of production they were equal to one another, and were in an inferior position with respect to the owners. The owners, or bourgeoisie, were equal to one another too, in most relevant respects. The workers (proletariat) constituted one layer (or class) and the capitalists another, more highly ranked, layer. These layers are referred to as strata, and their relationship is called stratification.

Max Weber, partially in rebuttal to Marx, held a more complex theory of stratification. He conceived of three ways, rather than just one, in which people are ordered: class, status, and party.[33] Weber's notion of class is much broader than Marx's, and refers to an individual's economic opportunities. One's skills in an occupation or one's supply of monetary capital determines "life chances." People who share the same life chances, whether or not they are aware of one another, constitute a class. A second type of stratum is the status group, which is based upon social estimation of honor. Weber states: "With some over-simplification, one might say that 'classes' are stratified according to the production and acquisition of goods; whereas 'status groups' are stratified according to the principles of their *consumption* of goods as represented by special 'styles of life.' "[34] Power as a basis of stratification gives rise to strata which Weber calls parties. They are groups which are oriented "toward influencing a communal action no matter what its content may be. . . . Their means of attaining power may be quite varied, ranging from naked violence of any sort to canvassing for votes with coarse or subtle means. . . ."[35]

Ever since Weber's work was popularized in the United States by Talcott Parsons and others, American sociologists have been debating whether or not there is more than one independent basis for stratification. Those who hold that there is a single basis point out how money is convertible into, or at least can attract, power and honor. Others, who take a multidimensional view of stratification, cite counterexamples of wealthy gangsters with little prestige, or prestigious college professors with low incomes. A way of resolving this debate is to state that the question is one to be resolved by observation in each case. This would mean that any group's particular system of stratification might be uni- or multidimensional, and that one would have to find out which pattern held through empirical research. One should keep in mind, however, that different methods of measuring stratification have the possibility of confirming opposite conclusions for the same population.

EXERCISE

Find a stratification system in your local community or university and describe it. (It can be the stratification system of a formal organization, a small group, a voluntary association, a team, etc.) What is the basis of the stratification system? How is the system justified? Can you defend these justifications on any grounds?

Various studies have measured where individuals stand on a number of different variables. Kaare Svalastoga attempted to find out how closely these different measures of stratification were associated with one another. Such association, which is called "intercorrelation," would be highest (+1) if each person was in the same relative position on each dimension of stratification. The intercorrelation would be low (approaching 0) if any given person was likely to be high on some variables (for example, wealth and power) and low or intermediate on others (for example, honor and education). Svalastoga found "that the average intercorrelation between major stratification factors, as observed in the United States, is about +.5, ranging from +.6 or +.7 for the relationship between occupational prestige and education to somewhere between (+) .3 and .4 between education and income."[36]

The finding that the intercorrelations do not equal one indicates that some people are in different positions on different dimensions, or show status discrepancy. Do those in status-discrepant situations differ from those who are status consistent (are in the same position on all dimensions)? Gerhard Lenski, who calls status consistency "status crystallization," has found that it is related to social participation and political behavior.[37] For example, those classified as having low status crystallization tended to take more politically left-wing stands.

Perhaps an even more basic question than whether or not stratification is multidimensional is whether strata exist at all in a given population. Are there collectivities of people sufficiently similar to one another in terms of privilege to demarcate them from other groups? How many significant groups are there? Marx claimed that there were basically two important groups in industrial society: the proletariat and the bourgeoisie. Lloyd Warner found six groups, ranging from upper upper class to lower lower class,[38] while the Lynds, who studied the stratification system of Muncie, Indiana (which they renamed Middletown), followed a more Marxian approach and saw two groups: the business class and the working class.[39] Those who hold that there are sharp breaks between strata account for low status crystallization by stating that the individuals showing it are in transition from one group to another. Whatever the nature of ultimate social "reality," whether or not one perceives distinct groups or classes is often related to one's political orientations. Defenders of current social arrangements generally tend to hold that there are no sharp breaks between strata. Such a continuum theory of stratification is defined by "the idea that there are several prestige, power and status ranges, more or less continuous from top to bottom with no clear lines of demarcation."[40] Those who hold the continuum theory may refer to groupings, but only as statistical ranges. The poor are those whose income is less than some stipulated amount per year. The well educated are those with at least a college degree.

The continuum theory places everybody in the same boat; some merely have more of the "good things" than others. While this may not be the intent of continuum theorists, who are attempting to "describe phenomena," it is one consequence of their thought. Thus the continuum theory does not take account of the possibility that some people may be in far different situations than others, and may have entirely different kinds of opportunities than others. The official entitled to make decisions about the fates of human beings he does not even know is in a different position from the person, who, as a mother or father, may have some power over the fate of several children. The continuum theory also disregards the possibility that some groups may have dreams of constructing a different *kind* of society from the one presently existing, rather than merely redistributing some of the fruits of the present society. Thus, the continuum theory is a prop for the established order because it does not open the possibility of basic conflicts between groups in different social situations. Of course, our very criticism of the continuum theory betrays a negative judgment on important aspects of the status quo.

Those who argue for the existence of sharp breaks between strata often hold that people in the same stratum do or should develop an awareness of common bonds between them. Marx spoke of class consciousness in this connection, and indicated that solidarity of the workers could develop through treating the owners as an actual or potential enemy. Of course, those who hold the continuum theory do not focus on the possibilities for common bonds among members of particular strata. How can one decide whether a person earning twenty thousand dollars per year should identify with the middle class or the upper class? The continuum theory runs into some difficulty when racial, ethnic, or sexual affiliations are ranked according to status; for example, when whites are ranked higher than blacks, or Anglo-Saxon Protestants higher than Italians, or men higher than women. Also, it fails to account for the group consciousness that emerged in the 1960s among segments of racial, ethnic, age, and sex groups.

Despite the various debates on stratification, there does seem to be some agreement that the dimension of prestige (or honor as Weber called it) is becoming more important in the contemporary United States.[41] Prestige groupings are characterized by their differential consumption patterns or life-styles.

LIFE-STYLE

Along with social rank, particularly occupational prestige, go distinctive life-styles. Everyone is familiar with the fact that people with different incomes usually live in different neighborhoods and that some groups consume different products than others. Some of these differences are merely a function of the possession of different amounts of income or other wealth. The rich can afford more expensive products than the poor or those in the middle. However, the notion of life-style goes far beyond differences in income and even differences in consumption patterns. In the most comprehensive sense, life-style refers to the entire way in which people conduct their social relations.

Joseph A. Kahl states that "to the extent that the various classes live apart from one another, they develop recognizable subcultures with values that give a special and unique flavor to life."[42] He has identified five life-styles characteristic of the contemporary United States. For the approximately one percent of very wealthy people who have inherited large amounts of property or have otherwise become large-scale owners, the unique flavor of life is provided by the value of "graceful living." One who has been accepted into "high society" is expected to speak in a certain way, adhere to certain forms of etiquette, consume certain high-quality products, belong to exclusive clubs, and participate in certain charities and public services. In order to participate in this life-style, one must be accepted by those who define what gracious living is. This creates problems in a mass society, where people with great wealth are free to invent their own definitions of gracious living if they are excluded from the traditional charmed circle. Baltzell has argued that the exclusionary policies of the old

Protestant upper class in the United States have created a fragmented
and irresponsible upper class, divided into mutually suspicious ethnic
groups.[43]

For the approximately 9 percent of professional and managerial
families, the typical value quality is career. Progress up the organizational ladder and the prestige coming from high official position in a
bureaucracy are cherished by this group. The values of control, expertise, and autonomy, as well as the snob appeal of having supposedly
superior understanding to that possessed by the common man, are
sought by the upper-middle class.

The lower-middle classes, whose members compose approximately 40 percent of the population, cherish respectability, in the
sense of proper religious behavior, education for their children as a
way of allowing them to rise up the ladder to success, and home
ownership. These people are the ones satirized by television's Archie
Bunker of "All in the Family." Archie tenaciously defends his respectability and his home, and helps support his son-in-law through college.
He resents being looked down upon by the "liberals" of the upper-
middle class, but displays an awe of professionals when he meets them
face to face. Next time you laugh at Archie, remember that your laughter may represent the prejudices of the upper-middle class, to which
you may not even belong.

The upper-lower class of the less skilled, whose members compose another 40 percent of the population, are less concerned with
respectability than merely "getting by." Their concerns are with maintaining continuing employment and not getting too deeply into debt.
They would like some of the consumer goods possessed by members
of more fortunate classes, and frequently feel frustrated that they do
not have many of such conveniences.

Finally, the poor, who comprise 10 percent of the population, are
described by Kahl as apathetic. They have so little opportunity for
improving their situation that they have frequently simply resigned
themselves to a life of relative misery and deprivation. Kahl's description of the poor, and of the other classes, appeared in 1957, before the
social movements of the 1960s made many poor people conscious that
they might improve their position through collective action. Thus,
segments of the poor are no longer apathetic and are organized into
such bodies as welfare-rights organizations. Further, segments of the
upper-lower and lower-middle groups are demanding greater rights
and respect. How much these tendencies will eventually change life-
styles and effectively challenge the professional ideal and the hierarchy
of occupational prestige cannot now be determined.

Figure 9.3. AMERICAN LIFE-STYLES

Wealthy: Graceful living. Exclusive clubs, charity work, elaborate codes of etiquette

Professional/Managerial : Careerism. High organizational position, pride in expertise, autonomy, control over others

Lower-Middle Class: Respectability. Religion, home ownership, patriotism

Upper-Lower Class: Getting by. Job security, some consumer comforts

Poor: Apathy. Little hope for improvement

EXERCISE

Try to appreciate a life-style other than your own. Visit a neighborhood composed of a different class from your own. Go into the local shops, have a drink in a neighborhood tavern and strike up some conversations with people. See whether or not their concerns and values are any different from your own.

The most privileged groups have often used their life-styles as tools for preserving dominance. In the early twentieth century Thorstein Veblen pointed out how wealthy groups indulged in "conspicuous consumption" of luxuries to demonstrate their high status and inform everyone else that they deserved recognition. The "leisure class" would indulge in such activities as polo, which demanded both skills inaccessible to those who had to spend their time working for a living, and wealth. The leisure class and conspicuous consumption go along with a class society in which some people own the tools and others work for them.[44] The owners demonstrate their superiority by showing everyone that they do not have to sully themselves by participation in the workaday world. In a mass society, where there is a strain toward equality, new kinds of means arise through which privileged groups use life-styles to maintain dominance. First, there is a tendency to lay great stress on status symbols such as educational attainment which cannot simply be purchased by those who have accumulated a certain amount of wealth. Even if everyone had a chance to get a college degree, dominance would still be maintained by creating prestige hierarchies of schools. Second, there is a tendency to use status symbols characterized by "one-way visibility" rather than perfect con-spicuousness.[45] One-way symbols are those only understood by the in-group, and they are used to distinguish outsiders from insiders. Two-way symbols are understood by both insiders and outsiders, and, in mass society, can usually be purchased in the marketplace if one has enough money. One-way symbols are highly developed in professional groups, particularly in the use of specialized languages and fine grada-tions of prestige. They are taught in the process of professional sociali-zation, and are embedded in the professional ideology. The impor-tance of one-way symbols in maintaining dominance is seen by the fear that upper-middle-class groups have for the imposter who can master the speciality without the proper credentials. The same kinds of fears appear in groups of officials when opposition groups master the proce-dures and the bureaucratic jargon, and then turn "legality" against the defenders of business as usual.

One-way symbols are also used by oppressed groups seeking to maintain their integrity and solidarity against dominant strata. For example, drug users have developed a distinctive vocabulary that is constantly in flux and relatively impenetrable to outsiders. These one-way symbols aid drug users in identifying friends and foes and in developing a sense of community. Racial minorities, criminal groups, those adhering to unpopular life-styles, teen-agers, prisoners of war, and many other groups deprived of power have developed one-way symbols as means of defense and as means of keeping the enemy off balance. Private languages ultimately constitute a kind of effort to preserve the autonomy of individuals and groups from attack.

An interesting variant of the one-way symbol is the code word used by politicians to speak to a particular constituency through the mass media. For example, the appeal for "neighborhood schools" is seen by some as a code word for racial segregation in education. Code words are used to clothe policies that might be morally dubious in acceptable language, and they function to rationalize support of such policies by potential beneficiaries and to pick up unsuspecting converts to the cause. At its most successful the code word communicates its message to the desired constituency and leaves others in the dark.

EXERCISE

Analyze a system of one-way symbols with which you are familiar. What purposes does this system serve for the people using it?

EXERCISE

Listen to the television news or read the newspaper and attempt to pick out code words. Who are the code words aimed at? Who is supposed to be excluded from understanding the message? What policy is being promoted? Do you ever use code words? If so, against which groups or people? Can the use of code words be justified?

DEPRIVATION

The other side of privilege is poverty. Wherever there is stratification there are those who are placed socially at a disadvantage to others. If those who practice professions are accorded a great deal of respect, those who are in nonprofessions gain less respect. In order for some people to make decisions for large organizations, many other people must be deprived of the opportunity to participate in such decision making. During the 1960s many of those on the lower rungs of the social ladder began to demand more favorable treatment in many respects. For example, some so-called middle Americans began to express resentment publicly against specialists who look down upon them. However, perhaps the most widely discussed issue with resepct to deprivation has been economic poverty. Spokesmen for the poor have called attention to the inequalities in income distribution characterizing mass society.

Poverty is one of the most difficult terms in the vocabulary of social relations. What does it mean to be poor? For some people poverty is an absolute term. A person is poor when he does not have a certain level of calorie intake and a certain level of clothing and shelter fixed by an outside observer. For others, a person is poor if he defines himself as being poor. For still others, poverty is a relative term, defined by one's standing on the social ladder. Those on the lowest rungs with regard to the possession of economic goods are defined as poor. Thus, Herman Miller can claim that the United States has the "richest poor in the world," because in Tunica County, Mississippi (the poorest county of the poorest state in the United States), 52 percent of the families had a television set, 46 percent had an automobile, and 37 percent had a washing machine in 1964.[46]

The debates over how to define poverty have never been resolved in favor of any one of the competing definitions. As in the case of many other terms in the vocabulary of social relations, people often choose the definition of poverty they use according to their political views—

specifically their views with regard to social change. Those in favor of the status quo in the United States tend to define poverty absolutely, as a condition in which sheer physical survival is imperiled. Then they can argue that there are very few poor in the United States. Those in favor of reform and redistribution of income tend to define poverty relatively, as a disadvantaged economic position. Then they can argue for dividing the economic product more equally. Of course, those in favor of change sometimes define poverty in absolute terms by pegging the level of a decent and humane standard of life far above what many people at present enjoy.

Many Problems of the Poor   Regardless of the shifting definitions of poverty and the consequent difficulties in clarifying the meaning of the concept, there are demonstrable economic inequalities in the United States. In 1967, 34.3 percent of American families had incomes of over $10,000; 24.3 percent had incomes ranging from $7,000 to $9,999; 16.1 percent had incomes ranging from $5,000 to $6,999; 12.8 percent had incomes ranging from $3,000 to $4,999; and 12.5 percent had incomes of under $3,000.[47] At least for those in the bottom two groups, and probably for many of those in the middle group, the United States does not at all appear to be an "affluent society." The concrete meaning of these figures in terms of life-style can be grasped by referring back to Kahl's descriptions of the upper-lower class and the poor. He characterized the upper-lower class as being concerned with "getting by" economically, while the poor were so downtrodden as to be apathetic. Some of the reasons for these general attitudes are found in the multiplicative aspects of low-status position. Just as advantaged and privileged groups tend to concentrate benefits of all kinds (wealth, power, status, and skill) into their own hands, so those who are disadvantaged tend to have few benefits of any kind. Commenting on the situation in education, James B. Conant has claimed: ". . . the expenditure per pupil in the wealthy suburban school is as high as $1,000 per year. The expenditure in a big-city school is less than half that amount. An even more significant contrast is provided by looking at the school facilities and noting the size of the professional staff. In the suburb there is likely to be a spacious modern school staffed by as many as 70 professionals per 1,000 pupils; in the slum one finds a crowded, often dilapidated and unattractive school staffed by 40 or fewer professionals per 1,000 pupils."[48]

The multiplicative aspect of low-status position appears in many other ways. Patricia Sexton has noted that diptheria rates of the poor are far higher than they are for other groups. She found that in a sample of children, those whose families' incomes were between $3,000 and $4,999 were fifteen times more likely to get diptheria than those whose families' incomes were between $7,000 and $8,999. Those whose families' incomes were higher than $9,000 did not show any cases of diptheria. Further, Sexton found that when a school nurse diagnosed an illness, the children in the lowest income category were only half as likely to receive treatment as those in the highest income category.[49] Sexton's study is simply one example of a general tendency for the poor to have worse health and less access to health care than those more advantaged economically. These differences carry over to mortality rates, and there is a persistent tendency for the poor to die at an earlier age than the more wealthy.[50]

The cumulative disadvantages of poverty penetrate to the very core of the individual's aspirations. The poor tend to expect far less from life than the more wealthy, probably with good reason. However, this tendency toward low aspirations feeds upon itself with the result that it becomes a self-fulfilling prophecy. Expecting little, the poor do not try to get more, perpetuating a vicious circle. During the 1960s those who attempted to organize the poor as a political force had to confront this vicious circle and try to do something about it. They attempted to instill pride and self-respect in poor people, and mobilize them to demand better schools, housing, employment opportunities, and income. The results of these efforts, which continue with vigor at present, have been mixed. Welfare-rights organizations, tenants' unions, and strong parents' organizations have appeared in a number of poor neighborhoods. However, incomes of the poor remain quite low, unemployment continues, and slum housing and low-quality education persist.

The poor are caught in an environment in which a series of obstacles reinforce one another as barriers to improvement. Low standards of health and health care make it more difficult for children to achieve in school. Poor schools do not provide people with the skills to get better jobs than their parents and also do not inform people about the wider society. Lack of knowledge and information make for a home environment in which children do not learn how to take advantage of whatever opportunities schools might offer. Overcrowded and dilapidated housing creates the conditions for ill-health and does not provide the privacy necessary for intellectual and emotional development. The list of factors in this whirlpool of poverty could fill several pages. The end result is a situation in which it is very easy for a person to lose hope and, in Kahl's terms, become apathetic.

SYSTEMATIC DISCRIMINATION

The distribution of income and of "life-chances" does not exist in a vacuum apart from other social relations. Along with concerns about poverty in the 1960s came increasing interest in the inequalities associated with race, sex, age, and other variables. Perhaps the greatest attention was devoted to inequalities associated with race because of the strong black movement for equality which emerged in the 1950s and grew to be far more vigorous in the 1960s.

The phrase "black and poor" has become a familiar one on the American scene. While the majority of poor people (if poverty is defined as having an income below a certain figure) are not black, the proportion of poor blacks is far higher than the proportion of poor whites. Economic discrimination against blacks is not difficult to document, and evidence of such discrimination fills the columns of newspapers and opinion magazines, as well as the propaganda of spokesmen for the black movement. For example, in 1968 the unemployment rates for blacks were higher than those for whites, even when education was controlled for. While 4.6 percent of white high-school dropouts were unemployed, 9.8 percent of nonwhite high-school dropouts faced the same situation. While 2.7 percent of white high-school graduates were unemployed, 6.7 percent of their nonwhite counterparts were unemployed. The unemployment rates for college alumni were 1.7 percent for whites and 2.8 percent for nonwhites. Thus, a white high-school dropout was more likely to have a job than a nonwhite high-school graduate.[51] Given the importance of occupational prestige in the status system of mass society, another indication of systematic discrimination against blacks is that in 1964, 30 percent of the white high-school graduates who did not go on to college were able to obtain white-collar jobs, while only 8 percent of the nonwhite high-school graduates were able to obtain such jobs.[52]

Racial inequalities are, of course, not the only indicators of systematic economic discrimination in the United States. The example of the black movement led to members of other groupings reaching an awareness of their disadvantaged situations. Perhaps the most important of these groups was women. The most striking evidence of economic inequality with regard to women is the fact that women earn an "average of $3,000 per year less than men for performing exactly the same work."[53] The median income (that income below and above which half the people earn) for white males in 1970 was $7,164, while for white females it was $4,152. The median income for nonwhite males was $4,528 and for nonwhite females it was $2,949. Further, the situation of women has not been improving in comparison with that of men. In 1950, 40 percent of professionals in the United States were women, while in 1966 the corresponding figure was 37 percent.[54]

One of the most significant trends in the structure of work is closely tied up with systematic discrimination. Recently, there has been a tendency for "paraprofessional" jobs to proliferate in many categories of work. In education, these paraprofessionals are teacher's aides, in medicine they fill a wide range of positions from medical technologist to jobs involved directly with patient care, in dentistry they are "hygienists." Often the paraprofessional does many of the tasks performed by the full-fledged professional (physician, teacher, dentist, for example). However, the paraprofessional earns only a fraction of the income that a professional in the same field earns.[55] In considering social stratification, the important point about paraprofessionalism is that those who hold these new jobs tend to be members of racial minorities and women. Most professional associations have welcomed the emergence of paraprofessions. By hiring medical assistants, for example, physicians can expand their practices economically and also limit the amount of people who practice their profession. For those in disadvantaged groups, the paraprofessions offer some improvement in economic situation and security, particularly in the light of increasing automation of factory and office work. However, since paraprofessionalism tends to perpetuate existing systematic inequalities and perhaps intensify consciousness of prestige differences, it may ultimately intensify social conflict.

The existence of the vicious circle of poverty and the systematic economic discrimination against certain groups tend to weight the chances that individuals have to maintain and raise their status positions. Such change in status is termed mobility and concern about it has traditionally been great in mass society among sociologists and many segments of the general public.

MOBILITY

Like poverty, mobility is a term that is difficult to define to everyone's satisfaction. First, in the most general sense mobility can mean any change in social position whatsoever. A person is mobile if he moves from the job of automobile mechanic to the job of air conditioner repairman just as much as if he moves from automobile mechanic to president of General Motors. Sociologists usually distinguish the first type of mobility from the second by calling the first horizontal mobility and the second vertical mobility. In addition, the person who goes from president of GM to auto mechanic is distinguished from the person who goes from auto mechanic to president by stating that the first is downwardly mobile and the second is upwardly mobile. All of the changes discussed thus far refer to the career of a single individual —i.e., they are examples of intragenerational mobility. When a person's social position changes from that of his parents (sociologists usually compare the occupation of the son to that of the father) one speaks of intergenerational mobility. The prime concern of American sociologists studying mobility has been intergenerational (vertical) mobility.

The study of vertical mobility contains several concealed assumptions. First, there is the assumption that there is one agreed-upon ranking of social status that allows the sociologist to measure who has gone up and down the ladder how much. This assumption was questioned earlier in this chapter when we stated that our own ranking of occupations was by no means the same as the one that emerges from opinion surveys. Is a file clerk whose father was a skilled cabinet-maker upwardly mobile? The assumption of some ranking system is necessary to conduct any study of mobility, or even to discuss or think about mobility at all. One must conceive of the "society" as a giant apartment house with the plushest apartments on the top floors and the rat traps in the basement. One must further conceive of elevators continually stopping to discharge and pick up downwardly and upwardly mobile people, as well as people scurrying around between apartments on each floor. Simply thinking about this image will show how tentative any discussion of mobility must be in a society characterized by competing visions of the human condition.

Other assumptions have to do with the American stratification system in particular. Most sociologists assume that mobility is to be judged by occupational prestige. This is merely another indication of how important occupational prestige is seen to be in mass society. Further, intergenerational mobility is judged by comparing the father's occupation to the son's. This does not take account of the mother's status, and generally leaves women out of consideration with respect to the study of mobility. Such factors as these show how weighted interpretations of mobility are likely to be toward particular visions of the human condition.

Yet despite its difficulties, the idea of mobility has exerted a profound attraction for sociologists, propagandists, and the general public in mass society. The key to this attraction is that there is no official philosophy of inequality in mass society. All advantages and deprivations must ultimately be justified according to achievement and contribution to the maintenance of society. Thus, the official propaganda of mass society is geared toward perpetuating the myth that all careers are open to talent, and that those who rise the highest in the scale of occupational prestige are those who are the best achievers. This means that, in a mass society, people are not entitled to high position just because their parents happened to be successful. This does not mean that careers really are open to talent in mass society, only that the propaganda of large organizations tends to hold that they are.

The underlying myth of mobility is the ideal of a completely permeable society in which there is no relation whatsoever between the father's occupation and the son's. Yet the realization of such a society, or even a tendency toward it, would remove one of the major motivations for mobility—the desire to give one's children a better break in life. Further, the inability to pass on benefits from father to son would probably tend to weaken the family severely. We do not necessarily disapprove of reducing the ambition for upward mobility nor are we staunch defenders of the family. However, many people who hold the ideal of a completely permeable society may not grasp all its likely consequences.

Of course, there is very little likelihood that anything resembling a fully permeable society will be realized in the United States in the foreseeable future. The vicious circle of poverty and the various systematic deprivations discussed earlier in this chapter insure that the mobility elevator does not stop on the ground floor of stratification house very often to pick up passengers for the trip upstairs. James S. Coleman has noted that equal educational opportunity depends upon more than merely formally equal schools: "The equality of educational opportunity implies, not merely 'equal' schools, but equally effective schools, whose influences will overcome the differences in starting point of children from different social groups."[56] William H. Sewell has documented Coleman's point: ". . . a high SES (socio-economic status) student has almost a 2.5 times as much chance as a low SES student of continuing in some kind of post-high-school education. He has an almost 4 to 1 advantage in access to college, a 6 to 1 advantage in college graduation. . . ."[57] These differences translate into a social structure that is far from being perfectly permeable. Peter M. Blau and Otis Dudley Duncan note that there is more short-distance mobility than long-distance mobility (puncturing the rags-to-riches myth) and that there is a positive association between the occupations of fathers and sons.[58] The same findings have been shown for women.[59]

Upward mobility has been an important, perhaps the most important, part of the American dream. If you share this dream, how can you mold yourself to be the most mobile individual possible? First, you are out of luck if you are a member of any of the main groups against which systematic discrimination is directed—blacks, Hispanic-Americans, American Indians, and women. If you are fortunate enough to be a white male you should get as much higher education as possible at the most prestigious university. Probably by the time you read this, you already have one or more strikes against you. You are probably not at a high-prestige university and you probably have not learned enough self-discipline to pursue a course of study ruthlessly. But, if you are bent on upward mobility, you will prime yourself to get into the most prestigious graduate school possible in an expanding field and learn to forego much of your leisure time. However, this will not be enough. Your parents and friends have probably filled your mind with a good many preferences that will prove to be obstacles on your climb to success unless you change them. You should get married, because you need someone with whom to let off steam and share your tragedies and successes. But, you should not have any children, because they will be a drag on your time, diminish your energy, and divert your attention from professional success. You should turn a deaf ear to your parents if they want you to live near them, because you should be ever ready to switch jobs and homes as soon as better opportunities present themselves. You should get involved deeply in your professional organization, but shun involvement in friendships and organizations that are unlikely to give you esteem in your profession. It would also be a good idea not to be one of the young Turks in your profession, but to put yourself under the wing of a prestigious elder who will provide you with connections for better jobs. If the young Turks begin to make a dent there will always be time for you to get on their side and dump your protector once you have gained some independent prestige. Does all of this sound like the kind of life you would like to lead? Probably not, and even most of the upwardly mobile probably do not conform to this pattern in all respects. Yet it is a kind of composite picture of what sociologists and psychologists have found to be positively associated with upward mobility. The aspect of truth in it resides in the kind of tendencies toward the destruction of social bonds that were referred to in the notion of the completely permeable society. In order to be the perfectly upwardly mobile man, one must give up attachments to family, region, a possible family of one's own, interests wider than one's speciality, and ties with mere friendship circles. Those who do not give these attachments and interests up may still be upwardly mobile, but they will take the slow elevator rather than the express.

The description of the perfectly upwardly mobile man reveals some fraudulent aspects of the American dream. In that dream the successful man has his cake and eats it too. He has the joys of career as well as the other aspects of the good life. You should realize that this is a trick only the very rich usually turn.

THE MERITOCRACY

The tendencies in mass society toward specialization, professionalization, and the destruction of official philosophies of inequality can all be summed up in the master myth of the meritocracy.[60] The meritocracy describes a mythical future society in which all inequalities are based on achievement of specialized tasks. At the very beginning of childhood people begin taking "intelligence" tests to determine what they will learn and what kinds of jobs they will prepare for. As they proceed through life and enter careers they are continually tested, and are promoted and demoted according to the test results. Only functional competence counts, and nobody can determine what the final goal of all the specializations should be. The elite is composed of those who have achieved the most according to the standards of the meritocracy, and its members can be sure that their superiority is justified and scientifically validated. While present mass societies are far from approaching the model of the meritocracy, there are many pressures for its progressive establishment. Perhaps the most important pressure stems from leaderships in mass societies attempting to make their rule legitimate by claiming to utilize fully the talent in the society for the welfare of all. Thus, Svalastoga notes that ". . . to the extent that the welfare of a society depends upon a high level of utilization of its collective talent, mobility becomes of vital concern to the society."[61] In the effort to utilize talent fully, the "best" must be selected out early and encouraged by all means to develop socially useful skills. Nobody who can make a contribution to society should be able to avoid working. The rich should perform public services and the poor should be gotten off welfare and into jobs. The only problem is, Who defines which skills are socially useful and which ones are not? In the mass societies of today the elites of large organizations make these decisions without consulting the vast majority of the population. A meritocracy presided over by the elites of today would probably be even a worse nightmare than our brief description of it betrayed.

What, then, is the answer to the problem of talent utilization? While the meritocracy has its disquieting aspects, at least the work gets done. Certainly, we are not in favor of intensifying the extent to which family connections determine one's place on the status hierarchy.

Also, we do not favor the abolition of specialization and a return to nature. Rather, we would like to separate the cultivation of specialized excellence from extreme differences in prestige. We believe that there would even be more specialized excellence if professionals were disciplined by knowledgable clients rather than rewarded by irresponsible elites. In communities of creators and appreciators the quality of the product or service would take precedence over the prestige of the profession or occupation. Such communities, of course, seem no closer to realization today than the meritocracy itself or the fully permeable society. However, as a beginning one might reconsider the relations between hierarchy and craftsmanship.

EXERCISE

What would happen if specialists were checked by clients rather than regulated by managers? Would such a system be feasible. If so, why? If not, why not?

SUMMARY

The study of social inequalities, or stratification, in mass society is structured by there being no official philosophies justifying inequalities in mass societies. There is a strain toward equality in social relations and a consequent attempt to make inequalities appear to be the result of scientifically demonstrable "necessary conditions." For example, Davis and Moore tried to show that inequalities in rewards for various jobs were necessary in order to get people to do the jobs most vital for maintaining society. While the Davis-Moore argument is flawed because it does not recognize that work may have intrinsic value, there is a working philosophy of inequality in mass societies based on a ranking of the prestige of jobs derived from opinion surveys. In this ranking, jobs that involve control over the destinies of others, such as high political, managerial, and professional positions, are ranked the highest, and jobs involving unskilled manual work are ranked the lowest. The quest for prestige by professional and occupational groups is often pursued through the development of ideologies glorifying the job and trying to prove that it is vital. Neophytes learn these ideologies, along with any skills related to the job, during their period of occupational socialization. Once socialized, they are ready to embark upon a career which may be filled with unexpected pitfalls.

Occupational prestige frequently is associated with other variables such as wealth, power, and life-style. Advantaged groups often use life-style as a weapon for maintaining dominance, indulging in conspicuous consumption to demonstrate their superiority or developing one-way symbols to ward off interlopers from lower strata. Those who are least advantaged have their own distinctive life-style built upon the vicious circle of poverty in which poor health, inferior education, limited job opportunities, and dilapidated housing reinforce one another to block opportunities for improvement. Also certain groups, such as racial minorities and women, face systematic economic discrimination. Given the vicious circle of poverty and systematic discrimination, the idea that all careers are open to talent appears to be more myth than reality. The fully permeable society in which there is no association between father's and son's occupations is not even close to realization, and, were it to be realized, familiar institutions such as the family would probably undergo radical change.

The tendencies of mass society toward specialization and achievement orientation lead to the nightmare of the meritocracy in which standardized tests determine one's status. An alternative to the meritocracy is the construction of communities of creators and appreciators, whose criterion is quality of the product or service rather than prestige.

Control and
Coordination

POLITICS AND SOCIAL
CONTROL

The human condition is multidimensional, and human beings cannot be separated from other aspects of the world by any single faculty. The importance of work and economic stratification in the human condition was discussed in the preceding chapter. These facets of human existence relate to the human being as tool-maker and tool-user—the "creative" activity through which people transform the materials of experience into new objects promoting a multitude of ever-changing experiences. However, while the dimension of work was the first one discussed, it is neither the only significant kind of human activity nor necessarily even the most important one. In addition to making and using tools in diverse social relations, human beings make, follow, and break rules that order their uses of culture and their relations with one another. Thus, while the activity of work refers to the productive and creative dimension of human existence, the activity of social control (politics in its broadest sense—from the politics of Great Powers to the politics of the playpen) refers to the dimensions of order and coordination.

THE PROBLEM OF COORDINATION
IN SOCIAL THOUGHT

The ways in which social control has been discussed throughout history by social thinkers parallel the discussions of work. From ancient through modern times, philosophers attempted to account for why people had to work and how their having to work could be morally justified. They assumed that work had no value in itself. Similarly, with regard to social control, philosophers attempted to account for why some people had to obey rules made by others, and how this obedience could be morally justified, or even become a strict obligation. Arising from this basic problem that one group made the rules and another followed them were the problems of when the use of force is justified in disputes over rules or their application, who is best qualified to make the rules, what are the best procedures for making the rules, and what content the rules should have.

The results of deliberation on these issues were many elaborate justifications of the rule of some over others. Such justifications can be viewed usefully as attempts to make such rule "legitimate," or morally worthy of being obeyed. "Legitimation" of the split between rule-makers and rule-followers is frequently seen as the way of transforming power into authority. In these terms, power is defined as the ability of a group or person to get another group or person to act according to its will, regardless of opposition. Similarly, authority arises when obedience is based upon the "belief that the power or domination of him or those by whom the order is imposed is in some sense legitimate."[1] Some examples of legitimation should help make this idea more clear. The most common way historically of justifying rule by the few over the many has been by appeal to divine will. The King was in his throne by divine right, and disobedience to his commands was a sin. Another frequent justification of rule has been that the rulers have some inborn characteristic that makes them fit to lead. Whites have used this kind of ploy to defend their domination of blacks in the United States, and in ancient times Greeks sometimes used it to defend the enslavement of "inferior" barbarians.[2] The use of divine will as a legitimation has been standard practice when rulers and subjects identify themselves as members of the same group, while the use of inborn characteristics is the standard operating procedure when the rulers come from one group and the subjects from another. Social categories, such as women, are frequently subjected to both kinds of justifications at once.

A third kind of legitimation defends the rule of the few by claiming that they possess superior knowledge of how to govern best in the interest of all. From Plato, who proposed that kings be philosophers (or the reverse), to contemporary technocrats who advocate a "sociocracy" in which social scientists would rule the unwashed masses, visionaries have devised plans by which the "best" could make the rules and enforce them.[3]

Legitimation by claims to superior knowledge appears frequently in the contemporary world. Government officials claim that they alone have the necessary information and perspective to make reasonable decisions affecting the lives of millions, while teachers, guidance counselors, social workers, psychologists, and other assorted professionals claim that their "scientific" knowledge of human behavior gives them the right to decide what is best for the "deviant" or "delinquent" youth. At the present time, legitimation by knowledge seems to be more pervasive than legitimation by divine will or inborn superiority.

The growing importance of justifying the split between rule-makers and rule-followers by possession of "scientific" knowledge or privileged information is very compatible with the observations on stratification made in the preceding chapter. In mass society, all inequalities (not only those having to do with access to economic rewards) must be justified as necessary to the maintenance of society rather than merely morally obligatory. Those who make rules for others may only do so on the pretense that they are fulfilling an essential social function for which they are qualified by possessing knowledge of what is best for the people. Of course, the question arises of how what is best for the people can be determined. This question is never explicitly answered in any mass society, because there is a myth that the people themselves determine, in the most general sense, what is best for themselves. So, the process of determining ends becomes a vicious circle, and the working standard of policy seems to be the maintenance and expansion of established organizations. A bigger budget is better than a smaller budget, regardless of what it is used for.

Figure 10.1. LEGITIMATING OBEDIENCE

Appeal to Divine Will: God has given the leader the right to rule.

Appeal to Inherent Superiority: Some inborn trait has given the leader the right to rule.

Appeal to Superior Knowledge: Superior knowledge of statecraft has given the leader the right to rule.

Do you believe that only public officials have the information and wisdom necessary to make political decisions?

The preceding description of mass society does not seem compatible with the ideas of democracy most children in the United States are taught. They are taught that in a democracy the majority decides what is best and the officials carry out the majority's will. Much of political sociology in the twentieth century has been devoted to challenging these myths and, along the way, implanting the newer myths of rule by the experts—the professionals.

FORMULATING POLICY

In human affairs, rules are embedded in wider conceptions of social relations—the images of the human condition discussed in preceding chapters. Applied to the processes of ordering and controlling human activities, these images of the human condition can be referred to as *ideologies.* Ideologies play a multitude of roles in human existence, four of which are particularly important in activities of coordination and domination. First, and most important, *ideologies define possibilities for human relations.*[4] Each ideology has a distinctive view of the rules that should guide people in performing social tasks and, even more fundamentally, a view of what tasks should be performed. For example, those who hold a traditionalist ideology of the role of the clergyman state that clergymen should generally abstain from involvement in political causes and confine themselves to performing rituals and ministering to the spiritual needs of the congregation. Those who hold a more activist concept of the clergyman's role state that clergymen should be involved in political causes. Militant atheists do not believe that there should be clergymen at all.

In addition to defining possibilities for human relations, a second feature of many ideologies is *their attempt to transform power into authority.*[5] For example, the claim by a leader that only he has the necessary information and perspective to make important decisions is embedded in an ideology that holds that only those directly involved in an activity (in this case governing) can judge best how to perform that activity. Those who believe that this principle is true are more likely to obey the leader's commands unquestioningly than those who believe that it is possible for people to relativize their perspectives and gain some grasp of the problems encountered by the leader and the adequacy of his solutions for them. In the contemporary world, administrators of all sorts attempt to convert power into authority by claiming that only the decision maker is qualified to judge decision making. Sometimes their appeals are successful.

A third function of ideology is as *a weapon in group conflict.*[6] While the use of ideology to convert power to authority aids the internal stability of a group (rebellion is less likely when the followers believe that the leaders have the right to rule), the use of ideology as a weapon enables some groups to gain advantage at the expense of others. For example, Smith has noted that most groups in the United States seeking privileges from the government couch their appeals in terms of the public interest. He calls this phenomenon the "public interest distortion" because the vast majority of these groups have no broader conception of the public interest than getting privileges for themselves.[7] Of course, when a powerful group succeeds in convincing many people that its policies are in the public interest, the ideology takes on the function of legitimating inequalities as well as its function as a weapon.

The fourth role of ideology is related to *its use as a weapon.* When groups are embroiled in conflicts, leaders often attempt to persuade their own followers that the cause is holy or just, and that all of the world's problems will be solved when victory is won. Sorel called the belief in a decisive victory which would solve all problems a "myth." Working in the Marxist tradition, but revising it drastically, Sorel claimed that the guiding myth of the twentieth century would be the general strike. Workers would participate avidly in conflicts with owners, not because they had rationally chosen to do so, but because they were possessed by the myth that one day capitalism would fall of its own weight due to a massive general strike.[8]

IDEOLOGICAL COMMITMENTS OF THE MASSES

According to the democratic ideals children are taught in the schools, citizens in democracies are rational human beings in the sense that they have a clear idea of what they would like the society to be and are willing and able to work efficiently to realize their visions through established procedures like voting. Sorel is one of the many social thinkers and sociologists who have challenged this belief by submitting evidence that many people in mass societies have no coherent image of the human condition, but merely a series of more-or-less disjointed beliefs which frequently have little to do with their actions. Attitude and opinion surveys by social scientists have documented "the apathy, inconsistency, and material self-interest of mass publics."[9] For example, vast majorities of people in the United States will proclaim adherence to the principles of the Bill of Rights, such as freedoms of speech and assembly, but when asked specifically about whether these free-doms should be granted to specific groups (for example, communists) they will respond with a resounding "No."[10] The amounts of information that most people have about public affairs gives equally little reassurance to those who would like to hold democratic ideals. Don D. Smith has summarized a long list of studies documenting the low levels of political information characteristic of United States citizens. For example: "In 1957, 39% of the public did not have the slightest idea where one might start looking for the Kremlin. . . . Twenty-three percent of the national total could not locate correctly a single European country on the outline map."[11]

If members of mass publics are characterized by neither consistency nor very much information in their images of the human condition, they lack two of the most important requirements of the rational citizen. They cannot be said to have their own ideologies, but, instead, if they are mobilized to act politically in any sense, the meaning of their action has probably been provided by the members of some elite who do have coherent ideologies.[12] One of the most significant consequences of this fact is that, at least with regard to public affairs, many people are unable to engage in the process of self-understanding. They have not even clarified their visions of the human condition, much less relativized them. Unable to make self-created commitments, they may pretend that they are free as others go through the processes of manipulating them.

PUBLIC OPINION

The findings that most people in mass societies do not have coherent ideologies about their public situation and do not critically evaluate the perspectives that they hold throws into serious question the doctrine that public opinion is the most powerful force shaping policy in contemporary democracies. It would seem, rather, that the opposite is true. Public opinion is shaped by elites, and then elites turn around and claim that public opinion is guiding them.[13] This is the process that officials are referring to when they claim that they are leading public opinion. The ways in which public opinion is shaped can be grasped by viewing public opinion as a process. Kimball Young has identified three phases in the dynamics of public opinion formation: "(1) the rise of the issue; (2) the discussion about the issue and proposed solutions pro and con; and (3) the arrival at consensus."[14]

According to democratic mythology, issues emerge from the concerns of the citizens at large and are taken up by sympathetic spokesmen. Then reasoned debate takes place about whether or not the problem demands attention and, if it does, which side has the best solution. Once the debate has been carried to its conclusion, the best solution is implemented with the cooperation, or at least the acquiescence, of the minority. At a minimum there is agreement to support the experiment to see whether or not it works.

The mythology can be challenged on each of its major points. Edelman notes that in many cases "democratic" regimes spring drastic changes in policy on the citizens without allowing for full debate.[15] Such decisions are faits accomplis, in the sense that they cannot be reversed easily whether or not a majority approves of them. A stunning example of decisions reached without the preparation of public opinion were the foreign-policy initiatives taken by President Nixon toward the People's Republic of China (Communist China). The idea of improving relations with Communist China and downgrading relations with Nationalist China was not proposed by President Nixon during his campaign for presidential election, nor was it given full public airing before it was announced. There was no chance to debate the pros and cons of Nixon's particular way of shaping the Asian policy of the United States, nor was there any attempt to allow a consensus to be reached on the Nixon solution. Tens of millions of people who through most of their lives had been taught to loathe Communist China as the very embodiment of political sin were now asked by the President to revise their entire estimation of that nation. Matters were made no easier by President Nixon having billed himself as a staunch anticommunist throughout his career in public life.

It is not of great importance for this discussion that Nixon's decision proved to be popular with many American people. Officials can act in ways that will win them the approval of their subjects. The significant point is that Nixon's decision was not the result of democratically formed public opinion, but of factors about which the general public may never be informed. Once the decision was made, however, immense efforts began to sell the policy to the public by a wide variety of means. Newspapers and magazines were filled with human-interest stories about Communist China. Much was made of the possible benefits of traditional Chinese medicine (acupuncture) in which needles are inserted into the human body to relieve pain and alleviate supposedly baneful pressures. Suddenly people in the United States learned that the mainland Chinese were not starving after all,

that they firmly supported the communist regime (once thought of as
a band of ruthless tyrants), and that, of all things, they were generally
happy. Less than two years after the event, many people were probably
only dimly aware of the silence that there was about China in the news
media before Nixon's decision, and of the general belief that prudent
and responsible statesmen would go slow on such an explosive issue
as China. The example of Nixon's decision to improve relations with
mainland China serves as a useful case study in the ways in which
public opinion is molded. It would perhaps be useful for you to keep
your eyes open from now on for major decisions that are sprung on
the public. Then you will be able to trace, as you consume the media,
how the decision is sold. If you also keep an eye on the opinion polls
you will be able to see how effective the salesmen are.

Figure 10.2. THE IDEAL CITIZEN AND THE MASS MAN

Ideal Citizen	*Mass Man*
The ideal citizen is well-informed on public affairs.	The mass man takes little interest in politics.
The ideal citizen takes well-defined stands on public issues.	The mass man is unclear about his position on many public issues.
The ideal citizen is critical of leaders.	The mass man either obeys leaders blindly or lapses into apathy and cynicism.
The ideal citizen changes his opinions slowly in response to evidence and knowledge of opposing positions.	The mass man changes his opinion abruptly in response to manipulation.
The ideal citizen has a long memory.	The mass man was "born yesterday."

Which model describes you better?

The Nixon decision on China was a clear-cut case in which every
principle of democratic public-opinion formation was violated. The
issue did not emerge in the general public, the pros and cons of
solutions were not debated, and a consensus to see how the majority
solution would work out was not reached. Most cases are not as extreme as this one, and there is usually a blend of reasoned discussion
and manipulation. In issues of foreign policy there tends to be more
manipulation than in issues of domestic policy, one reason for this
being that domestic issues are usually under constant scrutiny by pow-

erful nongovernmental organizations with vested interests in certain policies. Binkley and Moos point out: "In a multi-group society public opinion tends to become a resultant of the competing influences of the various groups."[16] The presence of organized interest groups, of course, does not mean that debate is rational and that opinion is not manipulated. Leaders of interest groups are frequently as expert in manipulation of opinion as government officials. However, at least on many domestic issues, such as economic policy, there are standard positions that one can learn. The vast majority of people do not learn these positions and, thus, allow the issues to be framed for them by others.

Figure 10.3. HOW ISSUES ARE DEVELOPED

Ideal Democracy	*Mass Society*
Issues originate when citizens identify a problem.	Issues originate from the projects of elites.
Issues are developed through public debate on the merits of solutions.	Issues are developed through propaganda and media campaigns.
Solutions to problems are decided upon openly.	Solutions to problems are decided upon secretly and then announced to the public.
Solutions are monitored by a critical public.	Solutions are monitored, if at all, by competing elite groups.

EXERCISE

Through listening to television or reading the newspaper, see how an issue is "sold" to the public. Follow the steps through which the issue is first introduced and then the means used to secure public acceptance. Carrying out this project will involve paying attention to the news over a period of several months. Are you willing to make the effort to become informed about public affairs and the ways opinion is molded?

Does the preceding discussion mean that the mass of people should be blamed for their "apathy, inconsistency, and material self-interest?" Perhaps they should not be condemned. If decisions are going to be sprung on them anyway, why should they take the trouble to care about public affairs? We get paid for thinking and teaching about public issues, so we know something about them. Is it reasonable to spend the time on public affairs if they are not involved with one's work?[17] You will have to answer that question for yourself.

POLITICAL PARTICIPATION

Whether they like it or not, nearly all people participate in some kind of political activity nearly every day of their lives. The process of coordinating human actions is not the sole province of governments, but goes on each day in families, schools, hospitals, and every other kind of human organization. The small child appealing for the right to stay up later to watch TV is quite similar to the businessman appealing to Congress for higher tariffs on foreign competitors. Both are participating in politics to further their own interests, perhaps at the expense of others (the parents may want the child out of their hair and consumers may desire lower-priced goods). Similarly, a family cooperatively deciding upon what kind of house to buy resembles greatly the deliberations of a cohesive community planning its future design. Both are examples of participation in politics to achieve a joint end, part of which may be continuing the process of participation itself. Many people view participation as a cost, just as they view work as a curse. This viewpoint is most likely to appear where politics are based on narrow interest, and the process of making decisions is one of pulling, hauling, manipulating, and generally trying to take advantage of others. Participation is more likely to be sought for its own sake where relations are more cooperative and the standards of critical inquiry are embedded in the relations among the participants.[18]

In the contemporary world, participation based on cooperation toward joint ends is mostly limited to small groups and to decisions affecting very few people. Therefore some work groups, some families, and some societies for the appreciation of a facet of culture (for example, neighborhood groups in a local tavern or coteries of chess enthusiasts) may make their decisions cooperatively. With regard to decisions affecting large numbers of people, however, participation in decision making is frequently based on special interest and confined to very few people. Thus, a special kind of political alienation characterizes many areas of decision in mass democracies—alienation from the means to decision.

VOTING DELUSIONS

According to the democratic mythology, alienation from the means to decision is alleviated by the vote. Through voting, people supposedly gain the opportunity to select their leaders and thereby to gain some in-put into policy-making. The effect of any single person's vote is, of course, open to serious question, and even massive majority bloc votes may have little effect. For example, in 1964 the Democratic presidential candidate (Lyndon Johnson) pledged that the United States would not get involved in a land war in Asia if he was elected. He was elected and proceeded to involve the United States further in the Vietnam war. In addition to the minute effect of any single person's vote and the fact that breaking campaign promises has become a fine art, the vote is further diluted by the multitude of issues raised in any major election. When one votes for the mayor of a large city, is he voting to have certain policies on schools realized, or is he interested in law enforcement, housing policy, consumer rights, health maintenance, parks and recreation, race relations, attracting new business, tax policy, the candidate's leadership qualities, the candidate's appearance, or any one or more of a great number of other possible issues? It is by no means clear that, when a particular candidate wins an election, he has a mandate to accomplish anything. One of the most interesting devices that leaders use to manipulate followers is to play some of their constituencies off against others. The poor blacks cannot get construction jobs because the leader is also responsible to the white workers, but the white workers cannot get tax relief because the leader is responsible to the poor blacks.

EXERCISE

What standards would you use to determine whether to vote for one candidate rather than another? Can you defend these standards? Is it worth voting at all in this society?

The dilution of the vote is compounded in one direction by the lack of reasoned and coherent ideological commitments in many people, and in another direction by varying levels of participation in large-scale politics. There are many other ways to participate in politics besides voting. One can engage actively in campaigning for a candidate, work for an interest group lobbying in favor of some policy and even attempt to run for office. Such activities beyond voting tend to be engaged in most by those with relatively high social and economic status—the professionals and the managers. These are the people who also belong to the most organizations.[19] From another viewpoint, they are the "actives," most likely to inform themselves about large-scale issues and also most likely to influence and shape the perspectives of those with whom they come in contact.[20] Thus, there is a kind of vicious circle operating with regard to participation in broad-gauge politics. Those with the highest status tend to be the ones with the most coherent ideologies and also the ones who participate the most in the widest variety of political activities. At the same time, it is likely that participation itself aids one in clarifying a coherent perspective on public affairs, while a coherent perspective may direct one to opportunities for participation and give one the confidence to participate.

The factors discussed above have led some sociologists to conclude that the act of voting is not so much a way of influencing policy as it is a support for the existing system of making decisions. So long as people vote, they are proclaiming that they believe that their problems can be solved within the system.[21] When they participate in such ways as guerrilla warfare, violent demonstrations, and other revolutionary activity, they are proclaiming that the system no longer seems adequate to them. Once the myths have been critically questioned, it remains up to the person to decide upon which modes of participation, if any, he will choose to engage in.

DECISION MAKING AND POWER STRUCTURES

There is general agreement among social scientists that the people at large do not rule in the United States.[22] Given this consensus, the major question about political life investigated by American social scientists since World War II has been, Who governs? During the 1950s and much of the 1960s there were two major answers given to this question. One answer was that a relatively small group made decisions affecting the lives of many others. This was the elitist answer. The other was that a large number of groups competed with one another in the political arena, and decisions were the result of their competition. This was the pluralist answer. Elitists tended to be highly critical of the status quo in the United States, while pluralists tended to defend the status quo.

Elitists and pluralists fought their battles with regard to both the local and national political arenas. The opening guns in the conflict were sounded on the local front by Floyd Hunter, a sociologist who stated he had discovered a ruling elite in Atlanta, Georgia (named by him, "Regional City").[23] Hunter discovered this elite by using the reputational-method—i.e., asking people to list the names of those who they thought ran the town. He then did more intensive field work to determine how the people on the lists related to one another and to other people, as well as the kind of leadership they provided. Hunter's local power structure was composed primarily of wealthy businessmen, although wealth was not sufficient to be included in the power structure. One also had to take an interest in participating and be affiliated with one or more of the crowds where the fate of the city was regularly discussed. Social clubs were centers for such crowds, and their membership policies effectively excluded the vast majority from participation. The informal power structure described by Hunter had the greatest influence with respect to deciding upon which civic projects would be undertaken. As to issues handled by the formal structures of government, Hunter had little to say.

Response to Hunter's salvo was not long in coming. Dubious of claims that hidden elites governed cities, the political scientist Robert Dahl undertook to study power in New Haven, Connecticut, by a different method than the one used by Hunter. Dahl used the issue-area method whereby key issues are examined and an attempt is made to determine who participated in their resolution. He argued that Hunter's reputational method was faulty because it both assumed that there was an elite before research ever began and that reputation was somehow necessarily associated with effective action. Dahl chose as his issues such visible conflicts as those over housing policy which directly concerned the formal structures of government.[24] He discovered that New Haven did not have a clear-cut power structure in which the few decided policy for the many. Rather, politics in New Haven were characterized by "dispersed inequalities" not "cumulative inequalities." In a system of dispersed inequalities those concerned most with particular issues have the greatest say in resolving those issues. Since concern will vary from issue to issue, decision making is carried on by a series of shifting elites. Thus, inequality of influence is "dispersed" among large areas. In a system of cumulative inequalities the same elite group would make the decisions on all issues. Hunter had implied that local communities were characterized by cumulative inequality.

The raging battle over local power structure (sociologists tended to be elitists and political scientists pluralists) was mirrored in a similar conflict about the structure of national power in the United States.

Here the first blow was struck by C. Wright Mills, who in his *Power Elite* argued that major decisions in the United States were made by a relatively small ruling class composed of high military officials, wealthy corporate businessmen, and high political officials.[25] Constructing his argument with evidence obtained from publicly available sources (for example, newspaper articles and speeches), Mills concluded that decisions concerning such issues as war and peace were effectively in the hands of the "power elite." The battle was quickly joined against Mills by numerous social scientists from all disciplines. With a thrust similar to Dahl's, Suzanne Keller argued that there was no one power elite, but a set of strategic elites deciding policy in a multitude of different areas. She concluded that: "The proliferation and partial autonomy of strategic elites, their variation in composition and recruitment, and differing moral perspectives decrease the likelihood of an omnipotent oligarchy. In addition, these elites critically examine—and thereby check—each other's actions and decisions. Thus limited power leads to limited abuses."[26]

The battle between elitists and pluralists lasted more than a decade without leading to any conclusive results. Today the debate is ebbing and new conflicts are taking its place. Disregarding all the charges and counter-charges about method (the reputational method does not study actual decision making, while the issue-area method does not study the processes used to limit decisions from ever getting on the public agenda) there should never have been an attempt to answer the question of "Who governs?" dogmatically. It is probably more useful to conceive of a continuum of power ranging from cumulative inequality through dispersed inequalities to equal participation than to think of choice between one model and some other. It seems likely that both nationally and locally neither the model of a single power elite nor the model of multigroup competition is realized fully. Instead, there seems to be a situation where a mix of the models of cumulative inequality and dispersed inequality holds. Peter Bachrach has referred to this mix as "democratic elitism," and has shown how both pluralists and elitists depict a system in which participation in broad-gauge decisions is highly restricted.[27]

In a significant sense, journalists and commentators preceded social scientists in describing the mixed elitist-pluralist power structure. The mixed structure has its own distinctive design differing from either the dispersed or cumulative models of inequality. The centers of power in the mixed structure can be called complexes. One of these complexes is the military-industrial complex referred to so often in political debate. The military-industrial complex, which Mills mistook for the power elite, does not make decisions on every issue significant to someone, but neither is it composed of competing groups that check one another in a free interplay. The military-industrial complex is composed of mutually supportive groups in business, government, the military, and labor, and they all dampen any internal conflicts they might have in order to gain a greater share of national resources.[28] This translates into demands for bigger defense budgets at the expense of other activities and attempts to see that these demands are met. The most significant feature of complexes is that they cut across traditional barriers that were supposed to provide checks on arbitrary power. For example, according to pluralists, business, government, and labor are all supposed to check one another. When they all work in concert on a particular line of policy, the only check is the formation of a counter-complex. Thus, the military-industrial complex today faces a challenge from a "social-industrial complex" with interests in urban renewal, urban transit, education, medical care, and other such domestic issues. Thus, the new debates in social science about power do not concern the question of "Who governs?" but relate instead to questions of what policies are put into effect (Who benefits and at what cost?). Should the defense of the nation have the highest priority or should we devote our first attention to the crying needs at home? These are the terms in which complexes fight out their battles for larger shares of resources. Behind every cry to "reorder priorities" or "maintain a strong . . ." is some complex, and behind every complex are social scientific specialists, bringing up the rear as they calculate costs and benefits.

Complexes, of course, are not any more democratic in the mythological sense than are power elites or strategic elites. Essentially, they are mutually reinforcing combinations of strategic elites. Thus, their vision of the political world is one in which the degree of democracy is determined by the response of people to the outputs of government. If there is rioting in the streets, the trouble is not denial of participation, but either inadequate law enforcement and too little respect for law, or dilapidated housing, inadequate medical facilities, and other aspects of poverty curable by enlightened programs fashioned by elites. If the system improves its outputs, people will be satisfied and the legitimacy quotient will rise. There is certainly some truth in these claims. However, they exclude the possibility that political decisions will ever be managed cooperatively and that a system will ever be devised in which people seek to participate in making decisions for the sake of participating.

Figure 10.4. WHO GOVERNS?

Elite Theory: America is ruled by a single "power elite" composed of the wealthy, the top-ranking government and corporate executives, and the top-ranking military leaders.

Pluralist Theory: America is governed by shifting coalitions of interest groups which change their composition according to issue.

Complex Theory: America is governed by powerful complexes of interest groups organized around key activities such as military affairs and social welfare. These complexes often clash on particulars, but are committed to the maintenance of large bureaucratic organizations.

SYSTEMS OF RULES

The final results of the various conflicts over policies and processes of decision making are systems of rules. Usually when politics are discussed, that system of rules called law is taken as the prime example of a rule system. According to democratic myths, the elected representatives of the people make laws in accordance with the people's will, and then the officials of the state enforce those laws with efficiency against violators. Like the rest of the democratic mythology, this principle does not seem to be realized in practice. During the twentieth century, a succession of social scientists has pointed out that law is merely the tip of an enormous iceberg of rules.[29] One of the most serious mistakes made by many people who first learn about democracy and the rule of law is to believe that, whenever some problem arises, the proper solution is to pass a law against undesired behavior or pass one to require desired behavior. They seem to assume that, as soon as a certain behavior is prohibited by law, people will not engage in it any more, or that as soon as a certain behavior is required by law people will engage in it. The existence of widespread crime shows that this assumption is unfounded in many cases. The most important consideration here is that when laws or administrative rules promulgated by governmental agencies conflict severely with other systems of social rules, or injure groups of people, they will usually not be obeyed voluntarily. They may be obeyed, of course, because the police enforce them coercively, but where the conflict with other social rules is severe, even the police are ineffective.[30]

The most important of the other rule systems to which law is related are the very social roles performed by people daily. Normally people do not think of their roles, such as student, consumer, father, or driver as systems of rules, but they are in fact the most pervasive rule systems.[31] Many roles are defined in the law of the state (such as congressman or dog-catcher) while others are defined partially in the law (student, consumer, father, driver). However, even those roles spelled out in detail by the law (for example, the mayor of a city) often change drastically as more informal rules are developed in coping with events. Further, in roles partially covered by the law (for example, parent) the law has frequently only summarized preexisting facets of the roles. These observations are essentially the same ones that were made in the earlier discussion of informal organization. The only difference is that informal organization grows up in the context of formal organization while law usually grows up in the context of more informal rule systems.[32]

The third important kind of rule systems are moralities, or critically defended and explicit standards of right conduct. Moralities were discussed previously in connection with the codes of ethics drafted by many professional organizations. Gaps between behavior prescribed in moralities and behavior prescribed in everyday roles are notorious. Moralities play a similar role in social existence to ideologies. They define future possibilities for people, integrate groups around common ideals, are veils for attempts at domination and help spur people to fight for causes. Their relations to both everyday roles and laws are variable, and many moralities contain theories of the proper connections between law, common sense, and morals.

METHODS OF ENFORCEMENT

Rule systems do not enforce themselves. This principle is not true because the human being is a savage beast or a pleasure-hungry child, capable of murder and mayhem as soon as the lid is off, but because social inequalities are breeding grounds for conflicts of interests, because alternative systems of rules are often in competition with one another, and because given rule systems are not always enforced equitably. Some see law and the state as necessary instruments for taming the blood lust of the savage human animal, but their arguments can never be proven because, by the time the beast is ready to destroy and despoil, he has already learned how to use tools, rules, symbols, and products.

The most basic method of social control (getting people to adhere to rule systems) is "socialization," which means teaching or training people that it is right to obey certain rules. If socialization proceeds without any hitch, the child grows up committed to living by the moral program instilled in him by his trainers.[33] The presence of competing rule systems, the possibility of creating new rules and contradictions within any given program all combine to make it unlikely that socialization will produce automated Boy and Girl Scouts. However, it is successful enough to make many people experience intense guilt when they break one of the rules drummed into them by their parents at age five, or, alternatively, to experience inordinate pride when they stick by such rules to a tee.

Figure 10.5. FORMS OF SOCIAL CONTROL

Socialization: People obey the rules because they believe that they are morally right. People feel guilty when they break the rules.

Coercion: People obey the rules because they are afraid of being physically harmed if they step out of line.

Inducement: People obey the rules because they are offered some material benefits in return for obedience.

Approval: People obey the rules because they are praised by others when they stay in line and are ridiculed when they do not conform.

Fraud: People obey the rules because they have been deceived about the actual nature of the situation.

Stacked Procedures: People obey the rules because they do not understand the procedures for challenging them.

Reasoned Argument: People obey the rules because they have been rationally persuaded that it is in their interest to do so.

EXERCISE

Make an inventory of the ways in which methods of social control are used on you. In which relations do the different forms of social control predominate? Is there any way in which you can avoid being controlled? Make an inventory of the ways in which you use methods of social control to regulate others. Which methods do you use the most? In which situations do you resort most to methods of social control?

When socialization fails, there is always the possibility of using force or the threat of force to get people to obey rules. The monopoly of "legitimate" coercion supposedly resides with the state, but in actuality large segments of social relations are honeycombed with force. Force is a staple of family relations in many homes, it is used to resolve differences among members of many youth groups, it is used (though sparingly) to enforce agreements in organized crime and it sporadically characterizes racial and labor relations. It is probably best for discouraging actions rather than encouraging them—for encouraging actions rewards are probably better.[34] These may come in the form of goods or money, or in the form of praise. To get a child to go to sleep at the right time it may be more expedient to offer a candy bar than a spanking. Even better (and cheaper) is to say, "You're a good little girl. Now good little girls don't go to bed late." For many parents, the age of rebellion arises when praise does not work any more. Governments, of course, use exactly the same means on unruly subjects as parents use on recalcitrant children. During a race riot, police are brought in to administer the spanking, but in the following week the candy bar comes in the form of some government programs. Praise is lavished on the "responsible" leadership of the minority community. Of course, the child does not get to stay up late and the minorities do not get justice.

Rewards and punishments by no means exhaust the methods of social control.[35] Force and bribery, self-contempt and flattery, often take a back seat to manipulation. Manipulation comes in two forms— fraud and stacked procedures. In fraud, people are brought to obey rules by a false belief that doing so will bring them some expected benefit. When the benefit is not gained, those imposing the fraud may live to exploit another day by claiming that situations beyond our control, evil cliques or some combination of the two prevented success. If such excuses are believed, subjects will continue to obey the rules. Stacked procedures are used when outsiders try to claim rights that insiders do not want them to have. Perhaps the American Legion has been parading through a town for years without paying for a permit or posting a deposit for damage and clean-up costs. However, when Gay Liberation decides to have a march, the town fathers may throw the book at them, burying them in regulations. By such means the march may be effectively stopped. Many poor people know what stacked procedures mean when they try to claim rights which seem to be due to them under law from public agencies.

A final means of social control is reasoned argument and critical reflection. This entire book may be viewed as an attempt to exercise this kind of social control by encouraging commitment to the rules of critical reflection.

DEVIANCE

Breaking a rule is generally conceived of as deviance. The concept of deviance is one of the more controversial notions in sociology, because it is frequently biased in favor of a particular image of the public situation. Deviance is a relative, not an absolute notion, and actions are deviant only in terms of a broader context than the simple violation of a rule. This context of action involves the group whose rules have been violated, the type of rule violated (law, role, moral code) and the social position of the violator. Anthropologists have a storehouse of instances of groups whose rules are diametrically opposed to one another. It was mandatory for Egyptian and Incan royalty to marry their siblings, but Europeans would consider such behavior by their royalty as incestuous and, thus, illegal, sinful and, perhaps, disgusting. Prior to English conquest, upper-caste Indians expected widows to kill themselves on their husbands' funeral biers. This practice, known as the suttee, was declared illegal by the ruling (rule-making) British. As Robert Nisbet states: "Deviance, in sum, is not something inherent in any particular type of behavior; it is a property *conferred* by social definition upon behavior."[36]

Not only is deviance relative to social groups; it is relative to social positions within groups. The upper-caste widows were the only ones expected to perform the suttee. In the United States the actions of a two-year-old may be seen as normal while similar actions performed by his father would be viewed as deviant, and vice versa. The father would be seen as deviant if he removed his bathing suit at a public beach, but would not be viewed as deviant if he had a martini every night. The very reverse would hold true for the two-year-old son. In a discussion of justice below, it will be shown that the sanctions meted out by a group differ on the basis of who committed the deviant act, even where there is an ideology of equal treatment under the laws.

The major difficulty with using the term deviance involves the assumption that there is widespread agreement within any given group on the rules, or norms, of conduct in that group. In mass societies, where vast majorities live in cities and are under the laws of nation states, this assumption seems to be naive. With regard to which or whose rules is behavior to be judged as deviant? Social scientists, politicians, and the communications media frequently take the norms of those who hold power as the standard against which deviance is to be measured. But, as Gresham Sykes claims: ". . . this does not mean that other bodies of contrary norms are not regarded as legitimate by large groups of people."[37] Smoking pot, committing voluntary homosexual actions, remaining seated when the flag is saluted at public gatherings, engaging in public nudism, and refusing to kill Vietnamese people are all deviant actions when held up to the norms of the "powers that be." But, the readers of this book surely know people, at first- or secondhand, who would view these acts as correct, and consider their opposites as deviant. If one does not make explicit reference to the group whose norms are being employed as the standard, usage of the term deviance tends to have a strong conservative bias.

Another problem with the concept of deviance is the implication that people who commit deviant acts are in the distinct minority and are somewhat weird. Labeling itself is a form of social control. Tagging someone as a deviant, for example, may constitute a personal injury to that person, because it may deprive him of self-respect and close off social opportunities for him. Likewise, labeling someone as courageous or brilliant may enhance self-respect and expand opportunities. Whatever group is considered, the majority of members do behave, to a greater or lesser extent, in a deviant manner. Exceeding the posted speed limits, padding expense accounts, or failing to read all the assignments for a given course are not only frequent behaviors, but are expected by the very groups that judge them as deviant. The police will not usually give you a ticket for exceeding the speed limit by five miles per hour.

Deviance has a definite negative connotation. Some sociologists, however, including Emile Durkheim, claim that it sometimes has positive benefits in that it may help a group define its identity and provide a sense of solidarity.[38] The idea is that, by publicly holding up the violator to trial and punishment, the rest of the community expresses its collective indignation and reaffirms its commitments to the rules.

In any case, whatever the view of deviance, most sociologists view the group's integrity as a good in itself (explicitly or implicitly). But, are the norms of any group morally unquestionable?

Although the concept of deviance has usually been employed in a conservative sense, all views of rule violation have political implications. These vary with respect to which system of norms is considered to be legitimate. As was stated above, when the norms of those with power are seen as the only legitimate rules, the political bias is conservative. A more liberal position is one that tends to reject any one system as the standard of judgment and, instead, judges behavior as deviant or "normal" in terms of the current standards in the individual's own particular group. Like conservatism, radicalism considers only one system of rules. However, rather than being rooted in present power structures, the standards of radicals are derived from some future desired system. Finally, one can distinguish an anarchistic view which allows legitimacy to no set of norms and thus rejects any notion of deviancy or rule violation.

Several varieties of deviance, or rule violation, can be distinguished on the basis of whose norms are being violated, and the type of sanctions that have the possibility of being applied. The term "possibility" is used here because, except for sanctions applied by omniscient and omnipotent beings in charge of eternal salvation, many rule violations go undetected and many that are detected go unpunished. Sanctions are meted out by those whose rules have been broken, or by their agents. Arriving late for work, you may have your pay docked by your employer. If you cheat on a school examination, you may fail the course. Wear pointy-toed shoes when your clique of friends declares round-toed ones to be "in" and you may be ridiculed or even ostracized from the group. If you kill your brother, your freedom of movement may be restricted by the legal authorities through incarceration in a prison or mental hospital.

Figure 10.6. INTERPRETATIONS OF DEVIANCE

Deviance may be defined as nonconformity to an absolute moral standard.
Deviance may be defined as nonconformity to the society's norms.
Deviance may be defined as nonconformity to the standards of some group.
Deviance may be defined by a subjective decision about what is deviant.
What are the strengths and weaknesses of these interpretations of deviance? Is the category of deviance worth using at all? What kinds of interests would each definition of deviance promote?

EXERCISE

What behaviors do you engage in that would be labeled deviant if you were of a different age, sex, race, ethnic group, or class?

CRIME

The form of deviance that most concerns people, including sociologists, is crime. Crime entails the violation of rules enacted by some government, and like other norms, the law varies widely from one place to another. Even among the states of the United States there are great differences in the laws regarding abortion, divorce, property ownership, and gambling, to name but a few. As with the more general term of deviance, the category of crime is usually taken to refer to a social problem by both politicians and sociologists. This view has a conservative bias because laws are constantly being promulgated and abolished by legislators, and many laws are themselves seen as problems by dissenters.

An alternative to the deviance interpretation of crime is the idea that laws tend to be made in the interests of the most powerful pressure groups in a society, and that crime is often a bid by less advantaged groups and individuals to obtain a more favorable allocation of resources for themselves. This perspective is particularly appropriate with respect to crimes against property. Those who stand to benefit most by laws protecting private property are the wealthy and others who have a stake, or expect to have one, in the economy. Those who do not have much property may find it advantageous to attain resources through such crimes as mugging, burglary, theft, and robbery. Similarly, laws against the disclosure of government documents tend to favor those who hold political power at the expense of opposition groups. For example, the copying and release of the Pentagon Papers by the social scientist Daniel Ellsberg was aimed at helping the anti-Vietnam war movement. Laws against abortion, homosexuality, and other breaches of public morals favor powerful religious groups, and laws requiring professional licensing favor established functional groups. In what ways does it make sense to brand as a deviant someone like Ellsberg who was fighting for a change in public policy on explicit and reasoned grounds?

Much of the interest in crime has been centered on its possible causes. No longer do explanations of crime in terms of sin hold sway. They have been displaced by the popular notions that individuals are driven to criminal activity by various aspects of their environment, such as poverty or residence in areas where many people engage in criminal activities. When one considers the extreme diversity of actions that are called criminal, from murder and forcible rape to embezzlement, marijuana possession, and draft evasion, it would seem that more than one theory is needed. It is also difficult even to study any one type of crime, since the information about those who commit it is probably biased. The bias arises because knowledge can be obtained only from those who have been caught. Even more important is the limitation in giving strictly causal explanations for crime. Criminal activity cannot be fully understood without referring to the purposive choice-making aspect of activity. Though it is hard for law-abiding citizens to accept it, crime does pay. The official crime statistics indicate that only for a minority of known crimes is anyone arrested, and of those arrested only a fraction are imprisoned or fined.[39]

Whatever position is adopted on the question of why crime takes place, there is agreement that criminal activities are ubiquitous. Only considering those crime categories that are the basis of the FBI's Crime Index (murder and non-negligent manslaughter, forcible rape, robbery, aggravated assault, burglary, larceny of over fifty dollars, and auto theft) there were 4,990,000 separate reported criminal acts committed in the United States in 1969.[40] This figure amounts to 2,471 of such crimes for every 100,000 people.[41] Although there has been debate about the accuracy of reported crime rates,[42] an even more serious question concerns the inclusion of certain categories and the exclusion of others in the FBI Crime Index, since this index is the standard used by social scientists to devise measures of "social disorganization" and to test "causal" theories. It is also used by law-enforcement agencies to justify budget requests. The Index excludes the crimes associated with businessmen and business organizations (for example, price fixing), among others. Those included are the most publically visible crimes, which probably represent the violations feared most by the general public.

The FBI Index classifies crimes as either violent or involved with personal property. Many other typologies which classify the various types of criminal behavior have been proposed, some as simple as the FBI's, others quite complex.[43] Typologies are constructed according to one or more principles, such as motivation for criminal activity, goal of the crime, life-style of the criminal, among others. Like other classification systems, such typologies can be judged according to their precision and the insight they give into one's situation.

The typology that will be used here defines four major categories of criminal behavior: crime as an occupation, crime as part of an occupation, political crime, and expressive crime. Within each category there is a further dimension based on whether the criminal activities are organized or free-lance.

Figure 10.7. CLASSIFICATION OF CRIMES

Crime as an Occupation	Crime as Part of an Occupation	Political Crime	Expressive Crime
Bookmaking	Price fixing	Assassination	Rape

CRIME AS AN OCCUPATION

Criminal behavior that is considered here under the category of crime as an occupation can be best understood as business activity. The major goal of such crime, whether carried out by a single entrepreneur or a large organization, is profit. As with other occupations, different individuals possess different degrees of skill in criminal tasks, and the least successful must find other means of self-support. However, while the legitimate businessman who fails may file for bankruptcy or become unemployed, the criminal business failure may very well wind up in prison. Some criminal occupations require a high degree of skill (safe cracker, counterfeiter, for example), while others (mugging) do not. The concept of professionalism can also be fruitfully applied to certain criminal activities: "Being professional means not only earning a living by crime, but the following of a way of life with a full set of attitudes and rationalizations in support of such activity. . . . Training in the required skills, the instilling of 'professional attitudes,' the subscription to a 'code of conduct' . . . "are seen to characterize many criminals.[44]

Like most occupations today, very few criminal trades are plied on an individual basis. Burglers, shoplifters, pickpockets, prostitutes, counterfeiters, and those involved in confidence games may sometimes free-lance, but they frequently find it more efficient to work in groups. Although gangs are generally more successful than individuals, the most profitable and secure criminal occupations are those within organized crime. Functioning basically to provide illegal goods and services, the various crime syndicates organize capital and skill with a degree of rationality. Attaining much of their strength during the Prohibition Era through the manufacture and sale of alcoholic beverages, the syndicates have found a great demand for gambling services, such as the numbers game and wagering on sporting events. Other profitable activities include prostitution, narcotics sales, and sales of other illegal drugs. Like legal businesses, organized crime must gain the confidence of people (for example, bettors must have some assurance that they will be paid off if they win) and engage in competition. There are sporadic attempts by organized criminals to establish monopolies. For example, the famous St. Valentine's massacre was part of an effort by Al Capone's organization to establish a monopoly on certain crimes in the Chicago area. Rivals, such as Bugs Moran's group, had to be eliminated. Such competition most frequently does not involve the physical destruction of rivals, but as with legitimate business, such as the auto industry, rivals may be incorporated into the larger organization.[45] Unlike businesses conducted fully within the limits of the law, but similar to businesses engaging in some illegal activities, organized crime has special overhead costs deriving from the inability to call upon law-enforcement agencies for assistance and the need to pay bribes to law-enforcement officers. What would legitimate finance companies or banks do if they were deprived of legal recourse in collecting bad debts? Thus, organized crime has to pay for its own muscle since it cannot rely on the muscle of the state. Organized criminals gain some compensation by not paying taxes on their profits, but often legitimate businesses avoid taxation through getting loopholes written into the law.

Organized crime is a large industry in the United States, with estimated profits in the billions of dollars, employing tens of thousands of persons, and serving millions of people, all without the aid of advertising in the mass media. Not only do organized criminals lack the positive image given to other businesses by advertising, but they must combat the effects of the decidedly negative image projected by the communications media. On television shows like "The FBI" or "Mannix," the "organization" (formerly called the Mafia) is depicted as entrapping innocent people and always resorting to violence. According to Frederic Homer, a student of contemporary organized crime, this is a basically false picture. As businessmen, most organized criminals would rather minimize violence than escalate it.[46] It is interesting to speculate about whose purposes are served by the perpetuation of myths about organized crime. Although it is frequently denounced, the services provided by organized crime are apparently desired by large numbers of people who do not regard them as immoral even though they are prohibited by law.

PART-TIME CRIME

The second category of crimes refers to illegal activities that are not complete occupations, but which are more or less integral parts of "legitimate" occupations. These crimes are usually violations of the civil or administrative law, rather than the criminal law, and are not judged harshly by either the general public or the legal system. Almost every occupation has the possibilities for this type of crime, and the organizational freelance spectrum applies here too. Blue-collar occupational crime practiced by individuals is particularly rampant among repairmen. Charges are made for parts not replaced, and it is not unknown for service station workers to cut fan belts or add pellets to the battery to make it fizz over. Crimes within occupations conducted by one or only a few people include embezzlement by bank employees, bribe taking by public officials such as the police, building inspectors, or legislators, and the practice of any form of medicine without a license. Occupational crimes performed by organizations, like most crimes in this category, frequently evoke mild reactions from the public at large, despite the fact that their effects may be harmful to those who seem to care little about them. Included among such crimes are illegal actions on the part of corporations to fix prices, restrain competition through various means, misrepresent products in advertising, and knowingly produce defective goods. An example of the last kind of activity is the marketing of an anti-cholesterol drug by a manufacturer who knew of its negative side effects, which included hair loss and cataracts. At least 5,000 people suffered from this drug, yet the courts only fined the company about $80,000 and gave some of its officials suspended sentences.[31]

POLITICAL CRIME

Although all crimes have a political aspect, in the sense that the laws that are violated have been enacted through political process, political crime as a category is unique for a number of reasons. The general goal of those involved in the two kinds of crime previously discussed is profit. For the most part those who commit political crimes are not motivated by the prospects for financial gain, but are committed to realizing some change in the rules themselves, or the abolition of rules altogether. Those arrested in the civil rights demonstrations of the 1960s are examples of those who commit political crimes in order to realize a new or revised political system, while spies are frequently motivated by the desire to defend or extend an existing system. Political crimes are frequently violations of laws that have been enacted to preserve in some way the integrity of the political structure. This is particularly the case for violations of "unlawful assembly" laws in demonstrations. However, bank robbery may be a political crime when it is carried out to finance a revolutionary movement. Most of those who commit political crimes are not full-time operatives, although spies and professional revolutionaries commit their lives to political crime. The political criminal may act alone or in concert with others. The assassination of John Kennedy was supposedly committed by Lee Harvey Oswald alone. Mass protests and demonstrations are examples of more coordinated efforts. Draft avoidance and military desertion, sabotage and treason, may be carried out by groups or by single individuals.[48]

EXPRESSIVE CRIME

The fourth category in this typology is expressive crime. Whereas crimes in the previous three categories were largely a result of rational thought processes, in expressive crime feelings and emotions predominate. Some of these crimes are "victimless," such as narcotics usage and homosexuality. Others decidedly have victims, such as rape and murder. One does not make money through committing expressive crimes and, thus, like most political crimes, they do not constitute occupations. Many activities which legally define minors as juvenile delinquents can be classified as expressive crimes, although youth does not bar the commission of many other kinds of criminal acts. Gang warfare and stealing automobiles for joyrides are examples of delinquent activities. With exceptions like gang violence, expressive crime, which requires little or no skill, is usually committed by one or two individuals. Child molesting, drunk and disorderly conduct, traffic violation, and vagrancy are not aided by elaborate organization.

The typology of crimes discussed above reveals the extreme variety of acts that are lumped together under the concept of crime. It would seem more reasonable, as well as more useful, to refer to the four basic categories, than to the general term "crime."

EXERCISE

Devise a classification of crime different from the one presented in this book. Then classify crimes which are reported in the newspaper according to both schemes. Which classification is most precise? Which one seems to be most adequate and fruitful?

EXERCISE

To get some idea of the magnitude of "criminal" behavior, particularly that which does not appear in the crime statistics, consider how many criminal acts that have gone undetected are known to you (committed by yourself or acquaintances), such as shoplifting, speeding and illegal parking, fraudulent income-tax filing, possession of narcotics, and so on. How do you and/or your acquaintances differ from criminals?

SOCIAL DIFFERENTIATION OF CRIME AND ENFORCEMENT

Statistics indicate that, for most crimes, certain social categories provide more violators than their mere proportion in the population would lead one to expect. There have been a number of explanations put forward to account for the social differentiation of crime, many of which seem to be supported by the data. Some of these explanations are quite compatible with one another, rather than mutually exclusive. Those who are less well integrated into the social order (those called "anomic" by Emile Durkheim) are more likely to deviate from its norms. Durkheim argued that in general women are better integrated than men, and those with children are better integrated than childless couples or unmarried people.[49] In the United States, men commit 87.1 percent of the crimes for which there are arrests and young people (those under twenty-four years of age, and more likely to be childless) account for 50.3 percent of arrests. Both these figures are much higher than the proportions of these two groups in the population.[50]

Other explanations of the differential arrest rates make reference to the characteristics associated with different social categories. Women are brought up to be less violent than men and not to evaluate themselves by the amount of money they have. Indeed, crimes of violence (16.1 percent of those arrested for murder are women) and theft (24.4 percent of those arrested for larceny are women) are not committed by women with the frequency one would expect by their proportion in the population.[51] American men tend to view control of an automobile as more important to their self-definition than do women. The official figures indicate that 95.1 percent of those arrested for auto theft are males.[52]

It was mentioned above that violations of rules are not always detected. Murder can be confused with suicide, marijuana can be smoked in privacy, and embezzlers can cover their theft by falsifying the company's books. Citizens often fail to report crimes, such as rape, incest, or assault, particularly when they are committed by relatives or friends. Even when a crime is discovered, such as theft or murder, the violator may not be apprehended. And if the violator is found, the police may not make an arrest. Thus, another explanation of differential arrest rates may be biased crime reporting and police bias in arresting violators. In a report concerning police on skid row, the researcher concluded that the decision to arrest a person was made by the police, not on the basis of perceived guilt, but on the basis of the perceived risk of the person creating a disorder.[53] Donald Black reports that "when an offender victimizes a social intimate the police are most apt to let the event remain a private matter. . . ."[54] He adds that further bias results because "the police officially recognize proportionally more legally serious crimes than legally minor crimes."[55] Arthur Niederhoffer goes as far as to claim that "the police function to support and enforce the interests of the dominant political, social and economic interests of the town, and only incidentally to enforce the law."[56]

Bias has also characterized the courts in deciding upon sanctions imposed upon those brought to trial. For example, rape charges by white females against black males have in the past been punished far more severely than those brought by black or white females against white males. Questions have been raised as to the fairness of juries, which are preponderantly white and middle class, judging defendants (their supposed peers) who are lower class and/or black.[57]

INCARCERATION

Deviant acts, whether they are violations of law or of other rules, can result in removing the offender from general society. Breaches of law can result in imprisonment. Breaking other rules (for example, behaving hysterically in public) may result in being placed in a mental hospital. Although perhaps it is not apparent on the surface, both prisons and mental hospitals have a great deal in common. Each tries to achieve two somewhat conflicting goals—that of helping the inmates (rehabilitation) and that of protecting the rest of society from them. Both organizations are what Erving Goffman calls total institutions.[58] In total institutions people move around en masse and eat, sleep, and interact in general with the same group. Personal identities are stripped away: people are made to wear the same clothing, are given similar hair styles, and are usually forbidden to have personal possessions. Inmates soon learn that life is more pleasant if they do not make trouble. Mental patients who are disorderly are often sent to the back wards, which are generally locked rooms supposedly for severely disturbed people. Prisoners are punished with solitary confinement. In both prisons and mental hospitals good behavior is rewarded by earlier release and increased privileges. The staff has a strict hierarchy of authority, with those of lowest authority having almost the only contact with the inmates. These prison guards and ward attendants are placed in a difficult position, and are poorly paid for their services. These jobs have very high turnover rates. Sykes helps explain why in his description of the prison guard: "[He] . . . is in close and intimate association with his prisoners throughout the course of the working day. He can remain aloof only with great difficulty, for he possesses few of those devices which normally serve to maintain social distance between the rulers and the ruled. . . . He has no intermediaries to bear the brunt of resentment springing from orders which are disliked; and he cannot fall back on a dignity adhering to his office—he is a *hack* or a *screw* in the eyes of those he controls and an unwelcome display of officiousness evokes that great destroyer of unquestioned power, the ribald humor of the dispossessed."[59] The guards and attendants allow inmates to break many of the rules in return for their compliance in keeping a semblance of order, because their job performance is evaluated on the basis of how quiet they keep the inmates.

In the early 1970s the face of one type of total institution, the prison, changed. In a number of prisons there were outbreaks of riots and protests by prisoners, particularly members of racial minorities. The demands of the protesters ranged from the older issues of poor living conditions to newer demands for better job training and educational facilities, and the right to practice the Black Muslim religion and gain access to literature in black culture. These outbreaks show that the conflicts within the wider society seep into total institutions, despite the efforts of those who control these institutions to keep their environment stable and sealed off from social change.

Although total institutions are not very appealing places, they do not discourage people from remaining deviants. Statistics show that in 1969 44.2 percent of those sentenced to federal prisons had been there before.[60] The total institution, which represents the very antithesis of the values of critical self-examination, is a commentary on the operative values of mass society.

SUMMARY

The coordination and control of human activities centers around systems of rules. The rules by which people conduct themselves emerge out of ideologies which describe the human condition and project desired futures for it. According to democratic myths, the masses have coherent ideologies by which they judge competing policies. Studies have shown that this is not the case, and that many people are neither consistent nor informed in their beliefs about public affairs. This lack of coherence in opinion, as well as the management of major decisions by elites, deprives public opinion and the vote of much of their supposed meaning in contemporary democracies. Few social scientists believe that the people rule in mass societies, and usually divide themselves into elitists who believe that a single small group makes major decisions, and pluralists who hold that multigroup competition is responsible for policy. Currently, the elitist-pluralist debate is being reconciled by the notion of complexes of interests which pyramid power in broad issue areas.

Regardless of who governs, rule systems are enforced by a variety of means of social control ranging from coercion, through bribery to manipulation. The major types of rule systems are laws promulgated by governments, roles and moral codes. Rule violators are often called deviants, a term usually biased in favor of some particular rule system. The most widely studied kind of deviance is crime. Criminal activities appear in many varieties, some of which are widely dissimilar. One can speak of crimes like bookmaking that are occupations, and crimes like consumer fraud that are frequently integral parts of occupations. Such crimes are usually committed with financial profit as the goal. Different are political crimes, which aim at the maintenance or revision of rule systems, and expressive crimes, which have emotional aims. Each type of crime may be freelanced or organized.

Arrests and convictions for crimes are not distributed randomly among the population. Women are arrested less than men, adults less than youths, and whites less than blacks, proportionately. Part of this is explained by differential enforcement on the part of police and some of the rest by differential socialization and integration into the social order. Violators frequently wind up in total institutions, such as prisons and mental hospitals, where they are stripped of their identities and made part of a herd. The total institution is perhaps the epitome of mass society at its worst.

11

PATTERNS OF INTERGROUP RELATIONS

One way of looking at the relations between human beings and systems of rules is from the perspective of social control and deviance. Despite efforts to make this perspective comprehensive, it involves a person, almost unavoidably, in viewing human activity from the position of those who support existing officially sanctioned rule systems. The prime example is, of course, that crime is judged by the standards incorporated in the law. For those who represent the state, law violators are defined by their nonconformity to the official rules, not by the reasons for their activities. A bank robbery is a crime whether it is committed to support the robber in a plush life-style or whether it is committed to fill the war chests of a revolutionary movement. Yet one of the hallmarks of life in mass society is the existence of multiple and competing images of the human condition, each with a way of classifying human beings and each with a model for conducting human relations. Any particular system of law incorporates imperfectly only one or several of these images and, thus, excludes from official sanction

285

many alternative ways of conducting relations. For example, theories
of monogamous marriage are incorporated in Western legal systems,
while other notions of marriage are excluded. Is it adequate to consider those in favor of polygamy on principle as "deviants" or criminals if they violate the laws regulating marriage? In a strict sense, of
course, they are criminals. However, they represent an alternative way
of organizing human relations rather than a mere desire to gain advantage over others by violating certain regulations.

An alternative to the social-control perspective on human activity
is one that views human relations, at least in mass society, as a continuous competition between different conceptions of human relations.
For example, a police officer who arrests a person for committing
homosexual acts may consider that person to be a law violator, and
consider him just like other criminals; the officer may hold an image
of the human condition in which people are divided into law-abiding
citizens and offenders. On the other hand, the homosexual may consider the police officer to be just another member of the "straight"
world, imposing on his freedom to conduct his relations according to
a desired pattern. The homosexual's image of the public situation may
divide people into the categories of "straight" and "gay." In this case
the two parties to the interaction bring different conceptions of the
relation to their encounter. The policeman is normally able to make
his conception of the relation prevail because he has a gun and other
trappings of authority. However, the off-duty policeman without his
gun, who stumbles upon a homosexual night club, may have to accept
the homosexual definition of the situation because he is outnumbered
and is on unfamiliar turf.

Most people make the assumption in everyday life that they share
the same definitions of relations with those they encounter. This assumption is often ill founded, but it is frequently helpful for imposing
one's definitions on others. The insensitive person who believes that
his image is the only one sometimes can bulldoze others into acting
according to his definitions. Of course, in the long run this deprives
the bully of any wider experiences than the ones that he has already
programmed into his life.

For many people who hold different definitions of relations from
the ones that are officially sanctioned, the entire system appears to be
a bully. Any particular group that desires to exert domination over
another group will attempt, among other things, to eliminate any
competing definitions of the human condition. If successful, they will
be able to deprive those who are being bullied of any rallying point
against their system of domination. Thus, where some are more pow-

erful than others, perfect social control exists where the stronger are able to impose their definitions of the situation on the weaker. For example, under slavery before the American Civil War, perfect social control would have existed if the slaves believed that they were inferior beings best fitted to do drudge work while the whites were superior beings born to rule and to develop their "higher faculties." Of course, perfect domination is extremely hard to obtain, and there are various degrees of freedom in most human relations, even those characterized by inequality.

FOUR RESPONSES TO PERCEIVED INEQUALITY

The most elementary form of freedom for an exploited social group is taking refuge behind a facade of obedience and servility. Slaves might have to accept the physical domination of their oppressors, but they could resort to the tactic of pretending to be dumb animals and thereby being very inefficient in performing for the master. Behind the facade of the dumb animal they could live in their private worlds and dream of the day when they would replace the master. The greatest limitation of taking refuge behind a facade is that one is prohibited from combining with other oppressed people for liberation on the basis of a new image of the human condition. One's life is circumscribed by the oppressor's image and one's brute reaction against it.

A second degree of freedom is gained in rebellion, where a number of the oppressed openly refuse to cooperate with the masters, and demand freedom. Rebellions are almost always reactions against those who dominate the relation rather than activities aimed self-consciously at realizing an alternative image of the human condition. The riots that occurred in the black slum neighborhoods of the United States during the 1960s are examples of such rebellions. Those who took part in them did not seem to have any clear goals in mind, but were reacting against the police and other authority figures. Rebellion is most likely to occur where people do not have keen awareness of alternative images of the human condition, but do begin to have hopes for improving their situation.[1]

A third degree of freedom opens up where alternative definitions of the human condition openly compete with one another. In such situations there may be severe inequalities but those in the less favored position have the opportunity to organize around a different way of conceiving human relations than those in the dominant group. An extreme case of such alternative definitions was found in Europe during the latter part of the nineteenth century when observers spoke of two nations—the middle class and the working class.[2] The middle class was generally committed to the perpetuation of capitalism and relations based on private ownership of tools, while the working class was supposedly committed to socialism. These two nations existed side by side in cold and sometimes hot war. Today many blacks in the United States apply a similar two-nations concept to American race relations.[3] The presence of alternative definitions of social relations widens individual freedom and expands personal consciousness far beyond what is possible in refuge or rebellion.

The fourth and final degree of social or collective freedom is revolution, in which existing official definitions of social relations are overtly challenged and there is active experimentation with new definitions. Revolution in this sense does not necessarily involve violence, though violence frequently accompanies attempts to change the operative definitions of human relations. What kind of revolution would it take to overturn the hierarchy of occupational prestige based on control over others and specialized expertise, and substitute for it a set of relations based on maximum opportunities for creative work? Perhaps violence would have very little to do with such a revolution, and fuller development of the process of self-understanding would have a great deal to do with it. Whatever the answer, merely posing such a question shows that revolution should not be equated with violence. Making revolution synonymous with violence is a tactic of defenders of established rule systems who are quite happy to spread fear of drastic changes in social relations.

Figure 11.1. DEGREES OF FREEDOM

1. Taking refuge behind a facade of obedience and servility: Freedom to live in a private world
2. Rebellion against role-definitions: Freedom to say no to the oppressor through active resistance
3. Choice among alternatives: Freedom to select from among alternative life-styles
4. Creation of new alternatives: Freedom to create a new life-style

At which degree of freedom do you ordinarily live?

GROUPS

Throughout the preceding discussion the term "group" has been used without being defined. In much of contemporary sociology groups are seen as the basic units for describing human activity. The widest group is often called a *society*, and is defined as that group performing all of the functions necessary for its own survival.[4] Thus, "America" is a society because it has its own state (with a supposed monopoly on legitimate force), its own economic system, its own system of stratification and its own set of ultimate beliefs about the nature and destiny of man.[5] Within this many-splendored thing called America are a variety of other groups, far more specialized than the all-encompassing nation to which allegiance is pledged. Professions, political parties, age groups, racial groups, clubs, and many other collectives cannot perform all the functions necessary for their own survival. But they have their own special contributions to make to the good of the whole.

It is obvious that we have not used the above conception of groups in our preceding discussion. Rather, we tend to doubt that "societies" are anything more than mere shorthand terms for describing widely varied and imperfectly coordinated activities. We think of groups as being defined by human beings in relation to one another. There would be no "black people" as opposed to "white people" unless human beings decided that this distinction was important for the conduct of social relations. Certainly, there might be differences in skin color, but these differences would not necessarily have any bearing on how people treated each other or identified themselves. Anyone who can see will quickly realize that the variation in skin coloration among "whites" is very wide. The same goes for sex differences. Physiological differences between men and women do not necessarily lead to differences of rights and duties in social relations. Humans, not hormones, are responsible for the exploitation of women by men and the so-called battle of the sexes. Where people do similar kinds of work, appreciate similar products, follow the same sets of rules or use the same symbols, they already have a perceived basis for common action, though they may not recognize themselves as a group.

Whether or not any group is selected out of all the possibilities to be a focal point around which social relations are organized is determined by human beings holding images of the human condition. Thus, groups are always in the making. In mass societies people are continually being asked or forced to give their allegiance and effort to a wide variety of groups. These groups do not exist beyond the allegiance and effort given to them and, therefore, ultimately depend upon human commitment.[6] This dependence on human choice often becomes obscured when large numbers of people are intensely committed to a given group. Then the outsider may feel that he is confronting an enormous "thing" rather than a maze of activities. Thus, when nationalism is rampant in a small town and the vast majority are wearing flag pins, flying flags from their homes, affixing flag decals to every movable object and steadfastly proclaiming their allegiance to Old Glory, the minority of internationalists, anti-nationalists, and skeptics painfully feel the "reality of the nation." Yet the withdrawal of allegiance and effort would spell the end of the nation. Perhaps the greatest paradox of social life is that the most imposing collectivities are held together by the slender thread of commitment. Continually renewing this commitment is the full-time job of politicians and propagandists the world over.[7]

TYPES OF INTERGROUP RELATIONS

Given the understanding that groups are not things like automobiles or galoshes, one can speak of various kinds of intergroup relations. Cross-cutting the attempts of some groups to establish domination over others (to impose social control) and of some groups to win their liberation from others are such relations as conflict, exchange, cooperation, and competition. Perhaps the basic dimension of intergroup relations is that of conflict and exchange. In conflict, groups vie with one another for domination. At the extreme of conflict one group attempts to exterminate the members of the other group physically (genocide), while more moderate forms of conflict involve attempts to exploit in one way or another or to maintain a position of dominance. The conflict arises where the attempts to exploit, maintain dominance or gain liberation run into opposition. Struggles can take many forms ranging from debate through violent action. In fact, the very same methods used to establish social control are the methods used to fight out conflicts.

Most human relations are not pure conflicts where one group is attempting to wipe another out. Conflict is usually mixed with exchange. In an exchange, one group provides a good or service to another in return for some other good or service. Most social relations are built upon unequal exchanges.[8] At the limit of inequality the slave exchanges his labor for the bare opportunity to remain alive. According to Marx, workers in capitalist economic systems exchange their labor for only a percentage of what they produce, the surplus value being appropriated by the owners. Conflicts usually end with some groups improving their exchange positions at the expense of other groups, and thereby increasing their opportunities for exploitation.[9] At the other end of the spectrum are exchanges based on mutual benefit where each group takes the desires of the other into account and tries to pattern a relation in which both will benefit. Such mutual aid assumes that the members of each group are capable of relativizing their situations with respect to the circumstances of the other group.[10] Thus, the process of self-understanding is a precondition of mutual aid, though not a guarantee of it.

The other major dimension of human relations is that of competition and cooperation. In competitive relations, groups strive to attain some object at the expense of one another. For example, under competitive capitalism firms are supposed to vie with one another for the market. What one firm gains in sales the others lose. At its extremes, competition becomes indistinguishable from pure conflict, and there is an attempt to drive one's competitors out of existence. As opposed to competition, cooperation occurs when different groups contribute toward the realization of the same goal. Of course, just as with exchange, cooperation has its oppressive and equalitarian varieties. In the more oppressive forms of cooperation, some group or groups decide the terms on which the others cooperate without even consulting them. Such paternalistic cooperation may or may not result in equal exchanges (though almost always the exchanges are unequal in favor of those who set the terms), but, most important, it eliminates democratic participation. Those in control define who is to do what and even what the ultimate goal is to be. The most familiar example of paternalistic cooperation is contemporary business. Top management sets the terms of the cooperation and others are supposed to go along. In exchange for going along the workers receive wages.[11]

The opposite of paternalistic cooperation is democratic participation. Under democratic participation all of those who are to cooperate have a voice in determining the terms of the cooperation (both the ultimate goal and the allocation of tasks to reaching that goal). A work situation governed by the principle of democratic participation would be quite different from one guided by paternalistic cooperation. It would embody the ideas of worker management discussed in chapter 8 rather than the idea that the worker should be satisfied with his wages and leave decisions about the terms of cooperation to management. Democratic participation by itself would not necessarily result in relations characterized by mutual benefit. People committed to hierarchical notions of prestige and status could democratically decide to engage in unequal exchanges. However, the discipline of participation in determining one's situation encourages relativization and the process of self-understanding, and is in that way bound to relations of mutual benefit.

Intergroup relations can be characterized by any of the kinds of relations discussed above. A convenient way of studying these relations is to divide the topic by the kinds of groups involved. The division here will be based upon the four social processes of creation, coordination, appreciation, and inquiry. Thus, the first intergroup relations discussed will be those among economic groups, the second will be those among political groups, the third will be those among communities (such as racial and ethnic groups) with a special section on sex and age groups, and the fourth will be those among ideological groups. Throughout this discussion it will be well to keep in mind that groups are always in the making, not fixed entities.

Figure 11.2. TYPES OF INTERGROUP RELATIONS

Conflict vs.	*Exchange*
Groups vie with one another for domination.	One group provides something to another in return for something else. Exchanges may be based on exploitation or mutual benefit.
Competition vs.	*Cooperation*
Groups strive to attain some object at the expense of one another.	Different groups contribute toward the realization of the same goal. Cooperation may be based on elitism or democratic participation.

RELATIONS IN THE ECONOMY

A wide range of diverse and cross-cutting relations characterize economic life in mass societies, particularly those in which modified capitalist systems exist. The very foundations of capitalism are sets of competitive relations that are supposed to hold between producers and between buyers and sellers. In the capitalist myth, such competitive relations are extended to relations between buyers and between labor and management, as well as between members of the labor force.

COMPETITION BETWEEN FIRMS

The basic relations under capitalism are those that are supposed to hold between the units (individuals or firms) that offer goods and services for sale in the market. The ideal capitalist market is one in which competition is both pure and perfect.[12] Under pure competition no one seller is large enough to affect the price of what he offers on the market. Prices are determined by buyers who seek out the lowest prices and, therefore, drive all the sellers down to the price of the most efficient producer. Those who can offer the good or service most cheaply and still make a profit are those who remain in business. The others are forced to leave the competition because their income does not cover their costs. Under perfect competition goods and services are uniform. Products are not differentiated by brand names or by minor changes in style and design. For example, corn flakes are simply corn flakes, not Post Toasties or Kellogg's Corn Flakes. Thus, under perfect competition the decisions of buyers are based solely on considerations of price.

In the contemporary American economy, neither pure nor perfect competition characterizes the relations among firms. First, there is nothing worse from a businessman's point of view than too much competition. The thought that some day a rival will take away one's share of the market by means of some innovation that increases his efficiency is the businessman's nightmare. Thus, under capitalism throughout the world, firms have devised a wide range of means to limit competition. Pure competition, in which a large number of firms ceaselessly strive merely to keep their heads above water, is limited through a process in which a few of the more efficient, dynamic, or crafty firms take possession of large shares of the market and then proceed to exert controls over quantity of production and prices.

Overt price-fixing agreements among "competitors" are prohibited by antitrust laws in the United States, but there are various ways in which firms can cooperate to keep prices higher than they would be under pure competition short of signed agreements or even informal understandings. Firms can specialize in serving certain geographical areas, keeping off one another's turf. There can be a situation of price leadership in which firms in an industry fall in line with the price policies of one large firm. Such devices are on the boundaries of the law.

Perfect competition is drastically limited in the American economy by product differentiation. In product differentiation a relatively standardized item is made to appear different from its competitors by means of devices having little or nothing to do with the use of the product itself. The most extreme form of product differentiation occurs when the only distinctions between the products are those of image and advertising. For example, the actual differences between competing brands of corn flakes are minimal, if existent at all. More subtle forms of product differentiation occur when certain differences are built into the products themselves. The question here becomes: When does some change in a product become important enough to make it a different product in relevant respects? For example, all the large automakers in the United States produce six-cylinder compact cars. Each producer attempts to create a special market for the automobiles through product differentiation, ranging from style differences through engineering differences to differences in warranty and servicing arrangements. In this way the automakers can compete for larger shares of the market without engaging in price wars. Are their products different in relevant respects? The answer to this question depends upon one's definition of relevant factors.

Figure 11.3 FORMS OF ECONOMIC COMPETITION

Pure Competition:	No single seller is large enough to affect the price of what he offers at market.
Perfect Competition:	Goods and services marketed by different firms are uniform.
Oligopoly:	Some sellers have such large portions of the market that they are able to exert some control over prices.
Monopolistic Competition:	Goods and services marketed by different firms are differentiated by brand names and minor style changes.

EXERCISE

Go into a supermarket and choose ten products at random. Comparing the different brands of each product to what extent do you observe the effects of competition? Do you see any evidence of a lack of "pure competition" (compare prices)? Do you see any evidence of a lack of "perfect competition" (compare the way the goods are marketed)?

The backbone of relations between firms under capitalism is supposed to be the goal of attaining the largest possible profit. Since World War II, increasing doubt has been expressed that this goal focuses competition among firms. Galbraith has noted that the enormous capital expenditures required by firms to produce and market new products drives them to seek control over their markets by elaborate planning and massive advertising campaigns. Under such conditions, maximization of profit is pushed aside as the overriding goal and the aim of a stable rate of growth takes its place.[13] In order to insure such a stable rate of growth, businesses attempt to insure a steady flow of supply and a guaranteed demand. One way to do this is for firms to buy up their suppliers and their outlets. Such integration, which is also the subject of antitrust laws, has spawned giant conglomerate corporations. Thus, in many ways, the tendency of contemporary business is to control competition and confine it mainly to product differentiation.

LABOR-MANAGEMENT RELATIONS

The perfect capitalist labor market is one in which individual workers bid against one another for jobs, and firms bid against one another to attract workers. The result of such competition would supposedly be a situation in which the firms offering the best wages and working conditions would attract the most efficient workers. Inferior workers would have to take less desirable positions or be thrown out of the labor market altogether. This model of labor-management relations applies in today's economy no more than does the model of pure and perfect competition between firms. As firms became more and more concentrated during the nineteenth century, the balance of power tilted sharply in their favor and against the isolated worker confronted with corporate power. The response to this situation by workers was to mount counter-organizations that would present a united front to management and, therefore, alleviate isolation. Labor unions, which fought a long uphill battle to gain recognition as bargaining agents for workers, are today permanent fixtures of the economy. In large industries the labor market is almost fully controlled by giant unions representing the work force and large corporations bargaining with the unions for contracts covering, sometimes, hundreds of thousands of people.

Early attempts to organize unions, especially among less skilled workers, were marked by intense conflicts. Arnold Green notes that in the nineteenth century American unionism was frequently marked by a commitment to Marxian ideas of implacable class conflict: "When the AFL was founded in 1882, the preamble to its constitution included Marxian clichés of class warfare, such as 'A struggle between the capitalist and the laborer, which grows in intensity from year to year.' "[14] He continues that today these notions of conflict have been replaced by bargaining within the capitalist system for higher wages and fringe benefits: "The preamble to the proposed amalgamation of CIO and AFL [proclaimed] allegiance to 'our way of life and the fundamental freedoms which are the basis of our democratic society.' Terms such as 'struggle,' 'oppressed,' 'capitalist,' and 'laborer' were missing."[15]

There is even reason to argue that contemporary labor unions are beneficial to large corporations. The same conditions (large capital investments, long-range planning, need to control supply and demand) that lead businesses to place stable growth ahead of maximum profit also encourage businesses to seek a guaranteed and disciplined labor supply. The unions provide such a labor supply, and they cooperate with management by making sure that their members do not break the contract by mounting wildcat (unauthorized) strikes and slowdowns. This, of course, does not mean that the relations between labor and management are fully cooperative. Often intense competition takes place between unions and managements over the terms of the contract, such as wages, hours, and working conditions. Unions call strikes, in which they withdraw their labor and bring operations to a halt, while managements resort to lock-outs in which the workers are prevented from doing a day's labor. However, with the growth of complexes, such as the military-industrial complex discussed in the preceding chapter, unions and corporations (for example, in the aerospace industry) frequently bury their differences and cooperate to gain advantage over foreign competitors, governmental agencies, and environmentalists.

BUSINESS-CONSUMER RELATIONS

According to the folklore of capitalism, the consumer is king. Suppliers respond to spontaneous demands, and buyers call the tune by purchasing only what meets their specifications. To a great extent in the contemporary economy, spontaneous demand has been replaced by the manipulated market. Through advertising, businesses attempt to create demands for products that few, if any, consumers had ever envisioned, such as electric tooth brushes. Manufacturers also indulge in product fixing in which products are made to break down in a certain amount of time so that they will have to be replaced.[16] Of course, the most prevalent kinds of manipulation are more subtle. Generalized demands, such as the compulsion that many people seem to have for absolute cleanliness, are focused by businesses into highly specific demands for a bewildering array of deodorants and detergents. In such cases, businessmen claim that they are merely responding to a spontaneous demand when they market high-powered detergents that will supposedly make wash come out pure white. When these detergents are found to destroy lakes by encouraging the growth of plant life, there is no talk of sacrificing the "value" of a whiter-than-white wash. Instead, there is a frantic search for substitutes that will maintain the purity of the laundry while eliminating the overgrowth of the plant life.

INTEREST GROUPS

Economic units, whether business firms, labor unions, or consumer organizations, normally would like to have the power of the state backing up their interests. Thus, these units often support or act as interest groups lobbying government for laws or administrative actions that will bring them greater strength. Such interest groups compete or cooperate with one another depending on the issue at hand. The existence of interest groups is an indicator of how far the present economy is from the principles of competitive capitalism. Perhaps the most noteworthy development of interest groups has been their penetration into government agencies. The federal and state commissions, which regulate various industries (for example, communications, transport, power), are frequently "captured" by the very interests they are supposed to control. Commissioners on such agencies are often drawn from the regulated industry.[17] Further, interest groups are sometimes given the right to administer government programs. This is in addition to their efforts to influence legislation and administration through campaign contributions, public relations efforts, mobilizing blocs of votes, providing useful information to officials, and doing favors for politicians.

RELATIONS IN THE POLITY

Economic relations are those that concern the production and distribution of goods and services. These relations, frequently marked by conflict and competition, give rise to efforts aimed at bringing the power of governments to bear on sustaining or altering the rules by which economic activity is ordered. Further, in other human activities there are often efforts made by various groups to have governments support certain systems of rules. For example, churches may agitate for laws prohibiting abortion or allowing grants to parochial schools. Within this maze of clashing demands and various attempts at cooperation, political relations are formed.

PARTY COMPETITION

According to the folklore of democracy, the predominant political relation is competition between parties. Paralleling the myths of the capitalist economic order, the idea of democratic politics is based on the supposition that political parties offer voters a choice between competing candidates and programs.[18] The structure of choice is very much like the one projected for the marketplace. Just as soap companies supposedly strive to make the best detergent so that they can maximize their sales, political parties are supposed to try to come up with the most popular mix of candidates and programs so that they can win a majority of votes.[19] This means in practice that parties are supposed to try to satisfy the most influential and intense interests so that they will generate a winning coalition at the polls.[20]

The dynamics of democratic politics under this notion contain a paradox. For those who have a special interest to further, the best strategy is to be as extreme and uncompromising as possible up to the point of losing legitimacy altogether. The special-interest group should attempt to push its issue as far up on the agenda as possible at the expense of all other issues. Meanwhile the best strategy for the party is to compromise and to arrange bargains among interests. This process of pulling and hauling becomes paradoxical when the party contains special-interest groups within it, as all parties do. At one and the same time the spokesmen for these interest groups must try to push their pet issues as far up the agenda as possible and arrange compromises that will aid in victory at the polls.

The propaganda devices used in such processes tend to obscure clarity on any issues. For example, many labor leaders at the Democratic Party National Convention of 1972 chastized spokesmen for minority and women's rights, the peace movement, and the environmental and consumer movements for their extremism and unwillingness to compromise. They kept repeating the refrain that compromise was necessary to insure a winning coalition. The Women's Caucus was derided by many for failing to compromise for a united front; those in favor of the legalization of marijuana, rights for homosexuals, and the rights of women to terminate their pregnancies by choice were told that they were ruining the Democratic party's chances of winning the presidential election in November. Then, once Senator McGovern was chosen as the party's presidential nominee, the labor leaders who had hitherto called for compromise abandoned the candidate of their party. This repudiation of compromise was in turn derided by the backers of McGovern.

This kind of situation is bound to recur frequently in a system in which both compromise and extremism are indicated strategies. The usual propagandist's ploy, of course, is to call strongly for compromise when one's opponents are making their claims and to defend stoutly an adherence to principle when one's own demands are involved. This was what the labor leaders did at the Democratic convention. The important point to note about the dynamics of "democratic" politics is that the very system of competition is mainly responsible for this double-faced behavior. Many people believe that all would be well in the Republic if only the rascals were thrown out and good men elected. However, it is not at all a question of good men and bad men. Rather, in order to be most effective in promoting a special interest, the political actor must blow the importance of the interest out of all proportion and simultaneously deflate all other interests. Anything less would be treason to the cause he represents. Thus, party competition does not tend to focus issues clearly or to encourage critical scrutiny of policies. The blurring of issues is compounded by the fact that interest groups often attempt to play both sides of the street and, therefore, eliminate competition altogether.

EXERCISE

Compare the positions of the two major political parties on a given issue. Can you devise different positions and solutions from the ones generated by the parties? Can you defend your positions?

EXTRALEGAL ACTIVITY

The system of building coalitions among interests has another unintended consequence besides the one of distorting political debate. What happens when an intense interest of a particular group is continually denied within the process of party competition? According to democratic myths, all interest groups are supposed to remain within the rules of the game—appealing to public opinion, working within the parties and governmental institutions, and focusing their hopes on elections—and accept any losses without resorting to violence in the hope that some day they will be able to win a majority over to their side. However, persistently frustrated groups are unlikely to remain convinced that they should play a game they continually lose. Thus, contemporary democracies are continually threatened by the extralegal competition of groups that have been excluded from realizing the benefits they desire.[21]

One way in which an interest that has been thwarted can gain recognition and some fulfillment of its demands is through raising the stakes of the political game. This can be done by resorting to violent action such as riots and conspiracies aimed at destruction of symbols of authority. This does not mean that riots are planned in advance by small cliques of agitators, but rather that they function to call attention to the plights of groups that have not gained entry into the winning coalitions.[22] Resort to violence puts the established groups on warning that the out-groups will not sit still for exclusion any longer, gives moderate leaders of the excluded the opportunity to offer one last chance to the establishment before the whole situation gets out of control, and shows apathetic members of the excluded that it is possible to fight for one's rights.[23]

Of course, in the long run violence by groups with very few resources aimed at groups with great resources has very little chance of success. Faced with violence, the authorities can make concessions only up to the point at which they begin to lose the support of privileged groups whose members begin to believe that a revolution is imminent and that the government is collapsing through failure of nerve. At the point at which the government loses the support of dominant groups and can only gain it back through suppression, the movement of the excluded is likely to be squashed. Thus, for disadvantaged groups the most effective strategy is to intimidate the authorities enough to drive them to make concessions, but not enough to drive them to repressive measures.

It is quite useful to view politics in mass democracies as a vast bargaining process in which groups use a mixture of means, legal and illegal, violent and nonviolent, to gain their objectives.[24] In this bargaining process, one of the most important weapons is propaganda, and one of the most effective kinds of propaganda is the kind that appeals for an absolute commitment to legally approved methods of competition. Such legally approved methods almost always favor those groups that are best organized and best endowed with financial resources. Thus, members of less advantaged groups are always faced with the choice between participating in a system that is stacked against them and courting disaster through resorting to highly visible extralegal actions.

INTERSTATE RELATIONS

Many of the behaviors that defenders of established institutions deplore when they are enacted by excluded groups are applauded by them when undertaken by their national governments. Relations among nation-states, each one supposedly endowed with a monopoly of legitimate force within its territory, cannot be conducted through the processes of competitive parties and elections, because there is no supreme authority in the international domain. However, aside from this difference the relations among nation-states run the gamut of the bargaining process from violent conflicts (the various kinds of wars) to cooperation among close allies. E. H. Carr noted that international conflicts tended to follow the very same patterns as conflicts between interest groups and classes within nations. Those nations with the greatest control over international trade and the greatest wealth tend to be the staunchest defenders of international law and the peaceful resolution of disputes between nation-states. Those nations rising in strength tend to be far less committed to the rhetoric of peace and far more prone to justify the violent defense of national rights and honor. Deplorably weak nations tend to scramble for the crumbs that they can get from the tables where the great powers sit and negotiate.[25]

THE MILITARY

Perhaps the most striking aspect of contemporary international relations is the presence of superpowers such as the United States and the Soviet Union deploying vast and specialized military forces. The most impressive technological breakthroughs of the twentieth century have come in weapons development. Nuclear energy was freed first to construct atomic and hydrogen bombs, not to light cities. Sensing devices were developed to snuff out the enemy and were only later used to monitor diseases. In order to use these technologies effectively, military forces have undergone a reorganization from the pre-industrial dependence on infantry and cavalry to a present emphasis on specialization and professionalization. The most highly technological military organizations are supposedly manned by specialized officer corps whose members are no more interested in seizing political power than the members of the American Medical Association. However, military organizations do differ from other contemporary bureaucracies in their necessary dedication to the ideas of nationalism and particularism.

Perhaps a volunteer army will further "professionalize" the military (easing the special problems of maintaining discipline associated with a forced draft), but the vested interest in the nation-state system, with its continuous threat of war, is not likely to lessen in the foreseeable future. In both superpowers, the military organizations are important and influential interest groups, linked with other groups into powerful complexes. In the United States, the military-industrial complex has only faced serious challenge since the late 1960s.[26] It is thus too early to determine what the military might do if it was threatened with a significant loss of influence.

INTERCOMMUNAL RELATIONS

Intergroup relations exist between communities, or peoples, as well as between economic and political groups. The term "community" as used here does not refer to geographically bounded territories based on governmental control, but to groups of people who share a common life-style and who have a sense of identity due to some common bond. The common bond may be one of a religious, racial, linguistic or national-origin type; frequently communities are multi-bonded, including more than one of these ties. The more that the bonds are fused together to form a common life-style, the more a community can be referred to as an ethnic group. Like all other groups, and perhaps more so, ethnic groups are continually in the making rather than fixed in advance. It is frequently difficult to draw the line as to where they begin and end. For example, in the United States the Spanish-speaking community can be subdivided into a number of smaller communities on the basis of national origin: Mexican-American (Chicano), Puerto Rican, Cuban, and Hispanic (composed of descendents of colonists from Spain).

Some political entities are composed primarily of one ethnic group, such as Iceland. Most large political units, particularly great powers, however, consist of a plurality of communities, and the relative sizes of these communities is an important factor in determining the pattern of intercommunal relations. Superpowers such as the United States are marked by a great diversity of ethnic groups. Even prior to the arrival of the Europeans, the territory of the present United States contained many communities of North American Indians. Immigrants, coming from Europe, Africa, and Asia, singly, in groups, or as families, have made the area one of the most ethnically diverse in history. Most Americans, including government officials and scholars, did not intend that the existence of multiple communities be continued indefinitely, at least among those of European descent. Logically, there are two ways of reducing the number of different communities. One is to get rid of the members of weaker communities, either by killing them or transporting them elsewhere. The other is to devise a process whereby the differences between communities, their separate ways of life, are eliminated. This second process is called assimilation, and there have been two basic theories of assimilation in the United States. As Milton Gordon points out,[27] it is not clear whether these theories attempted to explain what was happening or to predict (or suggest) what would happen. The earlier of the two theories was termed the Anglo-conformity theory;[28] the second has been called the melting pot theory.

WAYS OF ASSIMILATION

Assimilation via Anglo-conformity meant that communities would retain none of their unique traits. Their members would learn to speak only English, cook, dress, and in general behave in the English manner. They were to regard English institutions (somewhat modified by the American Revolution), such as democratically elected government and trial by jury, as the superior forms of organizing existence. To a great extent, free public education, established in the mid-nineteenth century, and compulsory education laws (over 75 percent of the states had them by 1900) served to teach the "ideal" way of life.

According to the melting-pot view, the common way of life that will eliminate diverse communities is to be some kind of amalgam rather than a reduction of the rest of the communities into the English community. The separate communities are to spice the English language with some of their phrases, spice the palate with their ethnic food, and so forth. Those born in the United States, regardless of their parents' community affiliations, are all to live the melting-pot life-style and thus diminish ethnic diversity. Essentially the theory of a single melting pot does not differ very much from the Anglo-conformity theory, because even if the spice is exotic, the meat is English. Revisions of the melting-pot theory have indicated that there might be more than one pot. In a study of intermarriage rates in New Haven, Connecticut, in the early 1940s, Ruby Kennedy concluded that there was a triple melting pot.[29] Catholics of diverse national origins shared one, Jews another, and Protestants the third.

Which theory, Anglo-conformity or melting pot, best accounts for the pattern of inter-communal relations in the United States? Arguing for Anglo-conformity, one may point to the official language and the political and legal systems of the United States. Mention might also be made of the WASP (White Anglo-Saxon Protestant) names that Hollywood stars choose to replace their own ethnic names for stage purposes: Doris Kapplehoff, Bernie Schwartz, Dino Crocetti, and Joseph Levitch became known as Doris Day, Tony Curtis, Dean Martin, and Jerry Lewis.[30] For supporting evidence for the melting-pot theory, one may cite, for example, the variety of ethnic dishes in the American cuisine or the politicians with such names as Kennedy, Muskie, Javits, Abzug, and many others.

However, there is a great deal of data that would lead one to conclude that both of these theories are quite inadequate. There are communities in the United States that have existed for at least several generations and that show no signs of abandoning their ways of life. For example, there are the Amish and Hutterites, who shun the use of automobiles and modern styles of clothing, and who live a nineteenth-century farming life. There are communities within cities such as New York and Chicago where Polish, Italian, or Chinese is the everyday language rather than English. Further, assimilation includes not only the behavioral similarities of people who once belonged to diverse communities, but also their complete interaction with one another. Segregated housing patterns and the low rates of intercommunal marriages also cast doubt on the amount of assimilation that has taken place.

EXERCISE

In the city or town where you live or go to school what evidence is there of unmelted ethnic groups? If there are such groups, how have they managed to escape assimilation?

Assimilation, therefore, cannot account for all types of intercommunal relations in the United States, nor in other areas.

THE AVOIDANCE CONCEPT OF COMMUNAL RELATIONS

A second type of relation to characterize relations between communities of equal or unequal relative power is avoidance; it can be the goal of one or both of the communities. Avoidance can be partial, allowing for interaction in some spheres such as work, while refusing interaction in other areas such as marriage. It can also be total, like the general isolation of the Hutterites. A well-known measure of prejudice utilizing the idea of avoidance was developed by Emory Bogardus almost a half century ago.[31] In this technique people are asked whether or not they could tolerate a member of a given community (Chinese, black, German, for example) as a visitor to their country, as a citizen of their country, as a co-worker, as a neighbor, as a personal chum, and as a relative through marriage.

The following diagram indicates important variables to consider when describing avoidance relations between communities.

Figure 11.4. INTERCOMMUNAL AVOIDANCE TYPES

	Whose Goal of Avoidance		
	Goal of Both Groups	Goal of More Powerful Group Only	Goal of Less Powerful Group Only
Partial	a	b	c
Extent of Avoidance			
Total	d	e	f

The relations between the black and white communities in the United States have generally been of type *b*. Whites have generally been willing to interact with blacks who are in menial occupational positions, such as janitor, domestic, or porter, but have not sought

interactions with blacks on an equal plane, such as neighbor, school-
mate, or fellow worker. This desired pattern of avoidance was not
reciprocal—in general the black community wanted interaction on an
equal plane with whites. Partially in reaction to repeated frustrations,
some black groups such as the Black Muslims advocate a policy of black
separatism in which blacks are supposed to avoid any relations with
whites. A different pattern of relations holds between Jews and Protestants in the United States. At present these relations can be classified
generally as type *a*. Neither group desires intermarriage or even
friendship, but members of both groups generally tolerate one another as colleagues. Figure 11.4 should only be viewed as suggestive,
since there are many instances where one group desires partial avoidance and the other total avoidance. One such example was the interaction between the Japanese-American community and the American
government (not a community in the sense used here, but all intergroup relations are not always between the same kinds of groups)
during World War II. The Japanese-Americans wanted a partial-
avoidance relationship with other communities, but the government
put them in detention camps, thereby effectuating nearly total avoidance.

     When two communities disagree as to the amount of avoidance
they desire in their relations, a frequent result is violence. Numerous
examples of intercommunal violence can be cited, including the struggles between the Protestant and Catholic communities in Northern
Ireland, the conflicts between French- and English-speaking communities in Canada, the war between the Ibo and Hausa communities
of Nigeria, and the conflict between the Tutsi and Hutu communities
of Rwanda. Broadly defining violence as the systematic denial of equal
rights to the members of one group by another group, violence can be
seen to characterize intercommunal relations between groups such as
the Bantu and Afrikaaners of South Africa. In this case, the Afrikaaners
restrict the freedom of movement, employment opportunities, and
access to justice of the African peoples. At present the Afrikaaners are
attempting to complete a program of apartheid (apartness or separation), which requires the African people to remain on camplike reservations.[32] The most extreme form of intercommunal violence, however, is that known as genocide, where one community seeks to
annihilate the members of another community. For a number of years
in the nineteenth century the whites in Western North America practiced a genocidal program against the Indians. The Aryan community

(one can debate its existence, although it can be defined as German-speaking non-Jews) under the leadership of Adolf Hitler put in motion a plan of genocide against the Jewish and Gypsy communities. Before they were stopped, several million people had been killed, mainly in gas chambers or ovens in concentration camps.

CULTURAL PLURALISM

In addition to assimilation, avoidance, and violence, intercommunal relations can be characterized as aiming for cultural pluralism. Similar to the pluralist theory of competitive parties described in the discussion of political life, cultural pluralism views intergroup relations as a series of communities with distinctive cultures and identities competing and interacting in the public arena. The communities supposedly share certain general features of life-style and an agreement on the rules of the game, both of which permit their interaction. Ideally, each community is committed both to its own preservation and to the continuation of the other communities. Horace Kallen, an early and frequent exponent and prophet of cultural pluralism, affirmed that ". . . ethnic groups contribute elements from their cultural heritage to the total national culture, making it richer and more varied"[33]

But, if everyone is a member of a separate community, whose culture is the national culture? And if only some people are members of special ethnic groups, are they simply being used as entertainment for the masses? When Pat Nixon was in Chicago to witness a Lithuanian folk festival in the summer of 1972, she asked the folk dancers to keep up their culture so that she, as well as other Americans, could enjoy it. Some cultural pluralists would have communities freeze their cultures and therefore remain static, rather than have them develop their cultures further through internal creation or exchange with other groups. Native peoples in many parts of the world, including some on Indian reservations in the United States, set themselves up for display to tourists. This drives them to freeze their cultures and in some cases to learn about traditional ways for the first time. Sometimes rituals are simply invented on the spot to please the tourists. Within the framework of cultural pluralism, communal groups are not valued for the intrinsic worth of their activities, but rather for what they contribute to some larger system. The live-and-let-live policy of cultural pluralism tends to make all communities equal, regardless of the quality of their cultural objects.[34]

RELATIONS BETWEEN AGE AND SEX GROUPS

Although age and sex groups may resemble racial and other communal groups because their membership requirements are biologically rather than rationally determined, they differ from communities in one important respect. Those belonging to communities usually find their most significant relations within their communities, while for members of age and sex groups many of the most significant relations are with people from outside of the groups. This difference influences, to some extent, the nature of the intergroup relations between sex groups and between age groups. Since members of sex and age groups often live with "the enemy," intergroup conflict cannot be as extreme as it often is between other kinds of groups.

The popular view of relations between sex groups depicts a battle of the sexes: women want consumer goods and financial security; men have lustful aims. Each tries to outsmart the other to get what is desired without fairly exchanging what the other wants. In some degree this absurd scenario is accurate, largely because people believe it is true and act accordingly. In a sense, the two groups can be seen as having separate cultures. Women supposedly like to cook, sew, clean, take care of children, primp, gossip, and shop. Men like to watch or participate in sports activities, read the newspaper, strive for success in a given occupation, look at pretty women, and generally dislike things that women like. So far as power is concerned, the groups are very unevenly matched, and the competition between them in the public arena is neglibible. The overwhelming majority of those in the professions, almost all those elected to public office, most high level administrators, and creative artists are men.[35]

The popular explanation for sexual inequalities is based on the belief in biologically determined differences in abilities. Many sociologists, however, utilize a more functionalist defense of inequality and try to show that the role of female (the submissive and emotional housewife) and the role of male (the dominant and rational worker) are the most efficient patterns for organizing relations between the sexes.[36] Other scholars, including many female sociologists, attribute the relative lack of achievement by women to a pervasive ideology justifying inferiority.[37] This ideology, consistently reinforced by parents, the media, school textbooks, and similar means is directed at girls from infancy and never ceases. Essentially, it states that motherhood is the highest, most noble goal, and that women get their greatest satisfaction through the success of their husbands and children. Sometimes this ideology is fortified by street-corner psychology, and claims are made that women who wish to achieve in a man's world (the public arena of creativity, work and politics) are mentally unbalanced since these desires reveal penis envy. Women who refuse to be submissive (although not striving to be dominant) are viewed as castrating bitches. Men who wish to dominate others are simply called men. As long as women did not seriously question the ideology, the relations between the two groups were somewhat harmonious, and the battle of the sexes was seen as a game.

THE GROWTH OF THE WOMEN'S LIBERATION MOVEMENT

The movement for black civil rights and equality of the 1960s gave rise to critical inspection of the status and role of women in the United States. Many women had worked in the black movement, and in time some of them began to recognize that the conditions opposed by the blacks (inequality of opportunity in the economy and polity) were also suffered by women. Judging that collective action might further greater equality, the women's liberation movement began. This movement paralleled the feminist movement of the nineteenth and early twentieth centuries which grew out of the movement to abolish slavery. Both the blacks and women had won the right to vote, but they had secured neither equality nor dignity.

The various organizations that comprise the women's liberation movement vary widely in aims, membership, and tactics.[38] Some are stridently anti-male, such as the Society to Cut up Men (SCUM). Others, such as Betty Friedan's National Organization for Women (NOW), actively seek male membership and support. Intermediate groups, such as the New York Radical Feminists, take a "realist" position: "While we realize that the liberation of women will ultimately mean the liberation of men from the destructive role of oppressor, we have no illusion that men will welcome this liberation without a struggle."[39] Consciousness-raising, where members attempt to rid one another of the ideology of inequality and its effects upon their personalities, is the sole aim of certain groups. Other groups, such as Women's Equality Action League (WEAL) seek "to exercise a positive influence on legislation and practices regarding the work and education of women."[40] Abolition or reform of abortion laws, development of child-care centers, and reform of state laws regarding women's control of their property are aims of a number of organizations. The media delight in the guerrilla-theater antics of groups such as WITCH (Women's International Terrorist Conspiracy from Hell), but pay little attention to the lobbying tactics of NOW or the women's caucuses that are currently present in almost every professional association. Although the majority of the members of women's liberation organizations are middle class, some organizations are based on occupation (Federally Employed Women, National Coalition of Nuns, Sociologists for Women in Society), and others have a wide-ranging membership. In addition to, and often in conjunction with, the various organizations has been the proliferation of articles, books, magazines and newspapers arguing for equality and demonstrating conditions of inequality.[41]

The women's liberation movement has added a great deal of complexity to relations between sex groups. There are men as well as women who are in favor of the movement's basic aims, and there are both men and women who are opposed to them. This opposition is hardly organized, (except around specific issues, such as various anti-abortion groups and those organizations devoted to preventing passage of the Equal Rights Amendment) although the media devote a great deal of space to whatever does exist, such as the international Anti-Women's Liberation League or NEVER whose stated "sole purpose is to keep women in the kitchen."[42] Thus, the complexity of intergroup relations is increased by the conflicts among the various women's liberation groups and their conflicts with foes.

AGED-BASED COMMUNITIES

Although the divisions between sex groups are readily apparent, there is little agreement about the number of age groups or the criteria for membership in them in mass societies. However, allowing for many gray areas, four major age groups can be identified: children, youth, the middle aged, and the elderly. The middle-age group has undisputed power over the other three, though its relations with each one are different. As in relations with women, dominance by adult males over other age groups is maintained largely through the use of ideology, though the ideology has been challenged in recent years. Leaving children aside, the ideology aimed at youth makes reference to sowing one's wild oats when young, and associates responsible decision making with older people. Youth is in a more favored position than women, because as they grow older young males will assume power. However, a youth movement began in the 1960s, also in response to the civil rights movement, which has rejected the prevailing ideology. The claim of this youth movement is that all people should have the power to make decisions that affect them. Lobbying for lowering the voting age, refusing induction into the military, working for political candidates (for example, the Children's Crusade of young people working for Eugene McCarthy's candidacy in 1968) represent challenges to middle-age authority. The counter-culture of some of the young (marijuana smoking, communal living arrangements, hard rock music, cooperatives), described by Theodore Roszak, is a rejection of many aspects of the life-style of the middle-age group.[43] Unlike the women, the youth group has not generated any large organizations concerned particularly with its cause. There are a number of groups that are political in nature, such as the Yippies, Black Panthers, White Panthers, and Students for a Democratic Society; they embody, in part, the youth group's aims. The music industry, which will be discussed in the following chapter, also publicly announces the goals of youth as counter to the middle-age group's goals. The middle-age group often appears to be ignorant of the nature of the youth group's challenge, and hides behind such slogans as the generation gap. This saves them the trouble of recognizing that power is at stake.

The ideology aimed at the aged consists of remarks to the effect that one does not need to have power when one has honor. Intergroup relations between the middle-aged and elderly groups are characterized by segregation and legal maneuvering. Laws are passed that require one to retire at age sixty-five despite the desire and ability to continue working. The elderly are segregated into old-age homes,[44] mental hospitals, and decaying city slums. The lucky members of this group get to live in retirement villages in Florida or Arizona. Not only are more and more people swelling the ranks of the elderly, but they are generally better off (physically, mentally, and financially) than they were years ago. Perhaps spurred on by the model of other groups, the aged are beginning to organize and lobby for power. (There is now a group calling itself the Gray Panthers.) Recent increases in social security payments have been attributed to their efforts. In sum, then, intergroup relations of both age and sex groups are characterized by challenges to traditional inequalities, achieved through organization and pluralist politics, as well as through counter-ideologies.

EXERCISE

Although you are, by definition, a member of age, sex, and ethnic groups, to what extent do you identify with these groups? Do you feel yourself to be in opposition to members of "opposing" groups? With which groups do you most highly identify? Why? Are the groups with which you identify consistent with your image of society?

IDEOLOGICAL CONFLICTS

A final category of intergroup relations centers on the conflicts among adherents to belief systems. In all the varieties of intergroup relations there are important ideological elements. The capitalist economic system has its ideological expression and foundation in the doctrines of pure and perfect competition, while the system of competitive party democracy is defended by a body of ideas stressing the abuses of absolute power and the virtues of electoral choice. Anglo-assimilation, the melting pot, and cultural pluralism all refer to systems of ideas as well as to possible patterns of social relations. Thus, in nearly all intergroup relations there is a component of beliefs describing the nature of the relations and defenses of particular interpretations of these relations.

Relations between adherents to beliefs can take a wide variety of forms. According to the myths about science, scientists engage in relations of critical cooperation. All scientists supposedly have the goal of discovering truth (frequently defined as the accumulation of empirically grounded and logically related systems of general statements about experience).[45] When a scientist develops a new interpretation of experience it is supposedly subjected to severe scrutiny by other scientists and then accepted if it accounts for the pattern of experience better than preceding interpretations. Kuhn has argued that this ideal of critical cooperation is not always realized, and that scientists range themselves into groups based on divergent interpretations of experience and struggle for supremacy.[46] Frequently those adhering to discredited theories do not give up their ideas, but cling to them till they die.

In the way science is usually defined, its method of critical cooperation can only yield statements about what is happening, not what ought to happen. Thus, an entirely different ideal from the one characterizing science is projected for the relations among adherents to belief systems concerning what ought to be. Questions about what is the best way of life, what is the best way of organizing social relations and what beliefs about the nature of reality one should hold are supposedly left up to the individual's conscience and judgment.[47] Groups of believers are supposed to engage in a peaceful competition to secure converts, much in the way parties compete for votes, businesses compete for sales and women compete in the marriage market. The free market of ideas is extolled as the best way of managing relations between groups of believers who would otherwise be at each others' throats, attempting to get the power of the state to back up their particular conception of the ultimate good.

Unfortunately, the free market of ideas is no more open than economic competition is pure and perfect. Those who have the greatest access to the mass media of communication have an important advantage in the competition over those who are blocked from print or the air waves. Further, the very notion of a free market of ideas demands an overriding public commitment to the principle that the state should not attempt to enforce belief or even to regulate the process through which beliefs are expressed. In addition, it means that the state is supposed to intervene to prevent some groups from enforcing their beliefs on others. These principles carry a built-in bias in favor of those beliefs that are held by those who can afford to disseminate them. Of course, the state does not remain neutral in the battle of ideas. It actively propagates nationalistic interpretations of the human condition, often to the point of making internationalism appear to be treasonous. In the United States, the federal government sometimes enforces "equal time" laws aimed at giving less well financed candidates an opportunity to express their views on the electronic media. In all, however, the market of ideas is heavily weighted in favor of the propaganda mills of the established organizations.

An important, and unintended, consequence of the market of ideas is that there is no control over the quality of reasoning that characterizes public debate. Nineteenth-century defenders of free expression, such as John Stuart Mill, counted on reason to separate out the well-founded from the ill-founded ideas.[48] However, he did not reckon on the systematic adulteration of public debate by propaganda, which encourages people not to trust their thought processes. Ideologies, faiths, and movements competing for adherents often do everything possible to snuff out the process of self-understanding. Typical is the Black Panther party which based much of its appeal to lower-class black Americans on a "Ten Point Program" which could be easily memorized and parroted, but which in no way encouraged critical reflection.

One way of reacting to the market of ideas is to have the state back up by force an official definition of the human condition. This device has been tried, with varying success, many times throughout the twentieth century and has given rise to the term "totalitarianism." The two most familiar varieties of totalitarianism are communism and fascism. Communist totalitarianism, which grew up in the 1920s and 1930s in the Soviet Union under Joseph Stalin's reign, was an attempt to enforce conformity to a simplified and crude version of Karl Marx's class interpretation of the human condition. Adherents stated that Marxism was a science and that it allowed the ruling elite to make the correct policy decisions; dissenters against those controlling the Communist party were deprived of career advancement and sometimes jailed or executed. The fascist variety of totalitarianism is associated with Mussolini's Italy and Hitler's Germany, but has appeared in milder forms wherever extreme nationalism has been tied to anticommunism. The Fascists of Italy and the Nazis of Germany attempted to enforce conformity to their beliefs in national superiority and historical mission. As in the Soviet Union, dissenters were terrorized or murdered.

Frequently defenders of the market of ideas point to fascism and communism as indications that any attempt to control the expression of ideas must necessarily lead to the kind of barbarism characteristic of totalitarianism. This claim, however, may not be correct, because controls enforcing accuracy and consistency of presentation might actually lead to greater freedom through encouraging critical reflection. At present, slander and libel laws give individuals some control over what is said about them, and since the late 1960s there have been appeals for constitutional protection against folk libel (claims that the members of a community are inferior beings). Such principles could be extended further into regulations over public debate, and there seems to be no necessity that they lead to totalitarianism. However, though controlling the expression of ideas might not necessitate totalitarianism, it would give an advantage to those groups with the most articulate individuals. These groups are also the ones whose members have the highest standing in wealth, power, and prestige. Thus, while controls might lessen propaganda, they might also inhibit less powerful groups from political participation.

The history of the twentieth century has shown that the most vicious intergroup conflicts are those which arise when economic, political, and communal conflicts are capped by struggles between believers. Eric Hoffer has described a personality-type he calls the "true believer" who feels that his life is wasted and who seeks the regeneration of his identity by committing himself absolutely to a militant faith.[49] For all those who maintain their rational processes, the vision of armies of true believers spearheading intergroup conflicts strikes terror into the heart. The true believer is defined by his unwillingness or inability to relativize his image of the human condition. Blind conflict with other groups becomes a way of life for coteries of true believers, because only when competing beliefs are eliminated will complete certainty of faith be attained. However, should one let the specter of the true believer scare one into embracing an insipid tolerance of all ideas?

SUMMARY

From the perspective of those exercising social control, rule violators are deviants. However, groups in an inferior situation may view the violation of rules as a means of gaining equality and liberation. When groups are very weak, their members often take refuge behind a mask of pliant conformity. Sometimes, however, there are bursts of rebellion. Where there are competing images of the human condition, tactics ranging from reform to revolution are possible. Cutting across domination and liberation are relations of conflict or exchange and competition or cooperation. In conflict, groups vie for dominance, while in exchange they trade goods and services. In competition, groups vie for larger shares of a good, while in cooperation they work together to realize an aim. The substance of human relations can be divided according to economic, political, communal, and ideological kinds of activities.

The prevailing view of economic relations is that they are characterized by competition. However, in actuality competition is severely limited by management of prices and product differentiation. Similarly, political relations are supposed to be marked by competition between parties and interest groups. Such competition is limited by vast complexes pyramiding their power. Intercommunal relations, too, are thought to be characterized by pluralistic competition, but frequently this idea masks patronization by the Anglo community. Relations between sex groups and age groups have tended toward greater conflict since the 1960s, due to the emergence of women's liberation and youth movements repudiating images that depicted only middle-aged males as being fully responsible. Frequently conflicts between groups spawn conflicts over belief systems. As in other relations, the prevailing myth is that belief systems compete for adherents in a free market of ideas. The market, however, is not so open as the myth would lead one to believe, and the major issue may be what kinds of controls there should be over expression, not whether there should be controls at all.

The general theme of this chapter has been that any view of free

competition between groups of all kinds should be seriously questioned, both as a description and a prescription. As a description the
competitive model fails, because all the so-called markets are weighted
in favor of entrenched complexes of power. As a prescription the
model is at least open to question, because it does not make equal
participation and mutual exchanges the goals of social relations.

Consumption and Appreciation

12

APPRECIATION OF THE HUMAN CONDITION

Human beings create with tools, and order their conduct through systems of rules. The social processes of creation and production give rise to what is often called the economic order; in turn, the social processes of coordination and domination lead to what is frequently called the political system. However, though creative work may be thought of as an end in itself, just as participation may be sought for its own sake, where there are just cooperative efforts, it is always possible to ask: What are we working for and why should we have these rules? In capitalist societies the answer to this question often is that people work for money and that rules are made and enforced so that lives and property will be protected. In communist societies the answer is frequently that people work to build a just order that will emerge in the future and that rules are made and enforced to insure progress toward this order. Neither of these answers probably reflects what the vast majority of people in these societies work for and why they ordinarily obey rules. Both answers are faulty because they focus on what

317

many people think of as the means of life rather than on the ends. For example, to state that people work for money obscures the fact that people use money to purchase a certain kind of life-style, to obtain a certain quality of life. This life-style is not simply measured in dollars and cents, but incorporates a wide range of experiences, some of them highly valued. Similarly, to state that people work simply for the realization of some distant goal ignores the fact that they, as well as members of future generations, have the capacity to enjoy aspects of their present existence. This does not mean that there are no people whose primary goal is to accumulate money or no people who dedicate themselves to the fulfillment of grand historical designs. The ideologies and reward systems of capitalism stimulate money madness, while the propaganda and incentive systems of communism stimulate overt commitment to the programs of the Communist party. However, neither economic nor political myths are usually strong enough to override concern with all other aspects of existence, particularly when there are plentiful counter-myths.

What is it that makes some work more meaningful than other work? Challenges provided by difficult problems, opportunities for creativity, and chances to exercise skill certainly are some of the reasons why certain work is highly valued. High pay, control over other people's lives, prestige, and the opportunity to be a snob are other reasons. However, these reasons do not exhaust the characteristics sought in work. While some people believe that the challenge of going to the moon is worthwhile meeting just because the moon is there, many people seek work that will provide results beneficial to others. In other words, the work is sought because others will be able to appreciate it.

The act of appreciation is thus bound up with that of creation. Without at least a potential appreciator, the creator's efforts seem to be nearly absurd.

The hallmark of mass society is that appreciation, as well as work, has been fragmented into specialties. One central part of the human condition, the human body, has been severed from the rest of existence and given over to the various specialties of medicine, physical education, recreational counselors, food-service personnel, the fashion and beauty industry, and many other cross sections of activity. No unified theme binds together one's awareness of the body and its wholeness. There is no standard of health that includes both normal functioning and the exploration of physical possibilities. Similarly, there is no unified appreciation of the physical environment. Communities are not arranged with an eye to integrating diverse experiences into harmonious wholes, but are the results of a crazy-quilt of bargains among interest groups.[1] Environmental pollution is viewed as a cost to be counted in with other costs of doing business. If the cost gets too high (if enough people scream loudly enough) remedial measures will be taken. In addition, entertainments are calculated not to reveal to people new perspectives on their situation, but to elaborate on the familiar and the acceptable in order to sell products or political ideologies. The products themselves do not add new dimensions to experience, but simply automate or make more convenient familiar experiences such as witnessing staged murders. In all, people appreciate only the surfaces of products and services, having little or no understanding of what went into creating them or why they work (when they do). Thus, appreciation of existence has become both fragmented and superficial in mass societies.

Appreciation is the social process of experiencing the products of human creation and the physical and biological environments of human activity. While it is frequently the activity that all other human actions aim at, it has not been singled out for as much attention by social scientists as economic or political activity. Perhaps this is because in the modern period there was great emphasis on industrialization and perfecting the processes of production.[2] Work determined life-style, as it still does to a great degree, rather than the other way around. It was thought, at least in the United States, that appreciation was private, in the sense that individuals were left to determine how to organize their leisure time (leisure being mere recuperation from work) so long as they did not intrude on the equal freedoms of others to do the same. With the rise of mass entertainments, mass production of goods, competition for scarce land, and threats to health and well-being from the processes and products of industrialism, the quality of life as experienced day by day has become a major issue in the contemporary world. Perhaps as time goes on, this issue will grow into a concern about how to combine the various aspects of human existence harmoniously into communities, but for now the specialization of appreciation seems to have proceeded so far that the first efforts to make appreciation public will probably come from clients of the specialists demanding higher quality.[3]

RELIGION AND APPRECIATION

Prior to the modern era the central focus for the appreciative life was religion. Religious ideas, practices, and symbols unified the various aspects of human existence by placing them into a context of myth and giving people's everyday lives broader and sometimes infinite meaning. Festivals were centered around occasions with religious importance, worship brought together communities in acts of common commitment, and knowledge was embedded in a supernatural framework. Religion can be conceived of as a kind of social cement that held the various aspects of human existence together by fitting them into a single framework during the pre-modern era in the West.[4]

The Decline of Religion's Hold on Mankind

One of the dominant themes of the last four centuries in the West has been the growing tendency for religion to decline as a unifying perspective. Progressively, various human activities have been detached from the religious perspective and context, gaining their autonomy by developing special sets of standards.[5] For example, in political affairs the will of the people increasingly came to be substituted for the divine right of kings as a myth of legitimacy. Similarly, science came to replace theology as the most highly valued kind of knowledge. First the natural sciences, such as physics and chemistry, split themselves off from a supernatural framework and became systematic descriptions of various phases of experience. Then the biological sciences gained their independence through widespread acceptance of the hypothesis that human life developed out of other forms of life rather than being created by an act of God. Finally, human sciences, such as psychology, sociology, anthropology, political science, and economics, began to claim their independence of the religious worldview. Once this process had been completed (only a very recent development), religion was left with no special claim to knowledge about any phase of human experience. Finally, with the growing mastery over the environment brought by the technologies of industrialization, work became less a matter of adapting to a divine order in which human beings had a fixed place than a matter of using human intelligence and energy to recast the environment towards ends projected by human beings.[6] Capitalism's glorification of the profit motive posed a direct challenge to religiously based doctrines of just price and the supremacy of worship over other human activities.[7] Socialism's assumption that the good society would be realized by attaining an economy of abundance and eliminating scarcity flew in the face of religious claims that human beings depended upon God for their salvation. Thus, religion lost its predominance in Western life through a complex process of secularization through which human activities were freed from their dependence upon a supernatural context.[8]

As the economy, polity and systems of knowing became detached from the religious world-view, religion became increasingly an appreciative activity. However, the fact that it could no longer unify diverse human activities around a comprehensive tradition necessarily weakened its appeal as a focus for appreciation. Mass entertainments, sporting events, the arts, and recreation also grew apart from religion and developed their own standards. Under these conditions religion became simply one image of human existence among many. This, of course, constituted a profound revolution in human affairs. For those who did not choose to commit themselves to a religious faith, religion became simply another possible human activity rather than the single human activity that made all other actions meaningful. Such people judged the worth of religion by standards that were not religious in origin. On the other hand, adherents to religious faiths became aware that their images of the human condition were not the dominant ones, and that they would have to "sell" faith in a competitive market of ultimate meanings. Where religious images of the human condition are the dominant ones, leading a life of faith is consistent with prescribed action in economic, political and learning institutions. Where religious images of the human condition are not dominant, those who would live according to their faiths are not assured of social support and often must hide their commitments in order to avoid ridicule or impediments to organizational advancement. Students who hold deep religious convictions are often made painfully aware of their defensive position in their encounters with atheistic or agnostic professors.

Figure 12.1. THE SEPARATION OF HUMAN ACTIVITIES FROM RELIGIOUS CONTROL

---

1. Economic activity gained independence through stress on the profit motive in capitalism and hopes for a just society on earth in socialism.
2. Political activity gained independence through stress on popular sovereignty and natural rights instead of on the divine right of kings.
3. Inquiry gained independence through the development of the natural sciences which substituted analysis of observable events for supernatural causation.
4. Much social activity gained independence through the development of mass entertainments.

What is religion? It is not possible to give a definitive answer to this question because every religion contains its own definition of religion, just as every antireligious or nonreligious view contains a definition of religion. Some people would consider us to be religious because we believe in rational criticism and self-examination—i.e., they would say that our religion is rational criticism and self-examination. This only means that such people define religion as any serious belief whatsoever. We do not happen to accept this definition, because we hold that the differences between reason and faith are significant, and we choose to uphold reason. We therefore define religion as the comprehensive organization of human experience in terms of principles and causes which supposedly lie beyond human experience, and we contrast religion to science, and faith to reason. Science, as the comprehensive organization of human experience in terms of principles and causes lying within human experience, relies upon rational inquiry. Religion, which attempts to look beyond human experience, relies upon faith. Not all the readers of this book will be satisfied with this definition of religion, but their definitions of religion will be just as rooted in particular images of the human condition as ours. As with most important human concerns, there is no neutral definition of religion that will be satisfactory to all.

Given the definition of religion as an organization of human experience referring to factors beyond that experience (and this definition includes Christianity, Judaism, and most other world religions), one can identify the functions of religion from a sociological viewpoint. A sociological perspective on religion suspends judgment on whether or not religious faiths actually refer to realities beyond human experience, and simply describes the consequences that religious activities have on the rest of human experience. Thus, sociology views religion as a phase of a social process rather than as a standpoint from which to describe and judge social processes.

LEGITIMATION

According to Talcott Parsons, the primary function of religion in society is to legitimate other human activities.[9] By drawing on the standards of an "ultimate reality" religious beliefs frequently support established definitions of right and wrong conduct in a wide variety of contexts. For example, in Catholic countries, religious institutions have been used to defend the institution of marriage by pressure on the state to make divorce difficult. Religious language is used by political leaders as a prop to nationalism and an aid to the continuation of particular regimes. "In God we trust" is stamped on American coins, the phrase "one nation under God" appears in the pledge of allegiance, and the American Revolution was justified by the claim that the Creator endows men with inalienable rights.[10] Public officials are not in the habit of questioning God's existence and will frequently appeal to God in a pinch. Of course, the use of religious legitimations does not necessarily involve action according to the moral codes of religions. Politics has its autonomous standards, which, in the United States, include the virtues of competition among interest groups (Christianity, in contrast, preaches love) and the goodness of compromise (Christianity preaches unwavering faith). Of course, one must render unto Caesar what belongs to the state, and through this loophole have passed a multitude of legitimations.

The importance of religion as a legitimator of other social institutions has been greatly lessened in contemporary mass societies. First, throughout the communist world, Marxism rather than any religious beliefs is called upon to legitimate institutions. Second, many people do not care whether institutions have the blessing of religious figures and may even find such blessing a negative factor in their judgments on institutions. Third, the autonomous standards that have grown up to regulate and legitimate activities during the process of secularization make religious legitimations both redundant and difficult to apply. For example, the professional ideal in the sphere of work depends upon science rather than religion for its legitimation.

THE MANAGEMENT OF HUMAN RELATIONS

For those who are firm believers, religious faiths perform certain functions that have direct bearing on social processes. Within the Western tradition the problem of evil has been a central personal dilemma. Why is one fated to live in a world where death and sorrow appear inevitable? Why is good so often rewarded with evil and evil so frequently rewarded with good?[11] Why is there no immediately apparent ultimate meaning to one's action? Why should a person obey moral codes, legal rules, and role requirements when so many people who violate the rules gain such great success? Those who seriously ask such questions sometimes find solace in religious faiths which announce that only those who obey the rules will gain eternal life and that all actions are part of a divine plan beyond mere human understanding. Further, myths such as the one recounting the fall from grace in the Garden of Eden are used to account for the presence of evil and for the necessity of discharging such duties as the obligation to work.[12] Hope is held out for the dutiful poor because it is easier for a camel to pass through the eye of a needle than for a rich man to get to heaven, while hope is held out for the rich because their success is proof enough that God holds them in high esteem. At the extreme, the problem of evil is solved by the belief that moral bank accounts are squared in heaven, where decisions are made on who will be granted eternal life and who will suffer eternal damnation. More sophisticated approaches hold that worthy deeds contribute to the divine plan for goodness, while evil deeds are devoid of such universal value. Whatever approach is used, however, religious solutions to the problem of evil tend to support established institutions by giving people reasons to fulfill role requirements. Of course, despite religious propagandists, not everybody craves ultimate meanings or worries about why human existence does not conform to human fantasies. Evil can be accepted as a fact and steps can be taken to diminish its frequency.

Stemming from the function of inducing people to fulfill their role requirements by "solving" the problem of evil is the function that religion has in crisis management. For those who contemplate suicide, mourn for dead friends and relatives, face perilous situations, and are under severe competitive pressures, religions have various solutions. One can recognize that suicide is against God's law, pray for the souls of the dead (and get on with the business of living), pray for divine guidance and strength, and pray for the resources to vanquish the competition. All these functions relating to crisis management bolster established institutions because they protect against the possible erratic behavior of people under great strain.

Of course, religions need not bolster the status quo. When their commandments are at variance with other role requirements, some people may use a religious base for mounting attacks on other social institutions. For example, the Berrigan brothers used a religious basis to oppose the Vietnam war, while Martin Luther King used religious appeals to promote racial equality. If religious codes require justice and mercy, and economic roles require exploitation, those who perceive the disparity may choose to follow the religious injunctions and seek comprehensive change in economic institutions. Yet those who intend to use contemporary religious institutions in this way must fight against the tendency of these institutions to adapt themselves to the wishes of established power concentrations in the economy and polity.

STATUS CONFIRMATION

Religion in the United States frequently serves as a badge of status. Religious affiliation and occupational prestige tend to be associated with one another. For Protestant denominations, 46 percent of Episcopalians are professionals, owners, managers, or officials; 33 percent of Presbyterians, 21 percent of Methodists, 18 percent of Lutherans, and 13 percent of Baptists fall into these categories. Fifty-one percent of Jews and 19 percent of Roman Catholics are similarly situated. On the other hand, 10 percent of Episcopalians, 15 percent of Presbyterians, 22 percent of Methodists, 22 percent of Lutherans, 25 percent of Baptists, 30 percent of Roman Catholics, and 10 percent of Jews are unskilled or semi-skilled workers.[13] Changing churches can be a mark of upward mobility as well as a way of forming social relations with people of one's status position.

RITUAL

The central focus of religion in the appreciative life is ritual, which gives depth and perspective to significant events in people's lives, as well as binding them into a community. In Christianity, baptism often marks birth, confirmation the emergence out of childhood, wedding the assumption of independent family responsibility, and funeral rites the deaths of family members and associates. These ceremonies are related to sacred myths and, when successful, cause people to reflect upon the beauty and profundity of much in everyday life. In addition, they serve to legitimate the person's passage from one status to another. There are recurrent rituals, performed at religious services, in which attempts are made to symbolize dimensions of existence beyond human experience and their effects in giving purpose to human life. Is such ritual a necessary part of a full appreciative life? Can beauty, profundity, and a sense of tragedy come only from institutions based on belief in powers and principles beyond experience? Recently many people have attempted to answer these questions in the negative by seeking out direct religious experiences, whether based on the use of drugs or meditational techniques, rather than founding their religious lives on conventionalized symbols and rituals. Others have been encouraged by the ecumenical movement to unite at least the various Christian churches. Both those engaging in the quest for direct experience of new dimensions of consciousness, and those wishing to unite the various churches have rejected established rituals and powerful religious bureaucracies as focal points for the appreciative life.[14]

The ritual function of religion has not succeeded in unifying the appreciative life in mass societies. For some people who work day after day in jobs that have little or no relation to religious precepts or practices, faith is highly important and gives some guidance to personal relations. Rituals may be sought for the comfort that they give that something is stable and that continuity can be maintained after all. However, such faith is purchased at the price of closing one's eyes to the day-to-day operating principles of complex organizations, which are not so much antireligious as simply independent of religion. The hierarchy of occupational prestige and the myth of professionalism have little or nothing to do with the ways in which religions organize the appreciative life. Thus religion, when taken seriously at all, tends to become a specialized corner of life.

NATURE

With the onset of secularization, religious conceptions of human existence were progressively challenged by ideas based upon the category of "nature." In the sense that all images of the human condition that are not rooted in ideas about supernatural realities can be considered naturalistic, this book has nature as one of its fundamental categories. However, like religion, definitions of nature differ according to images of the human condition. Some people believe that there is a fixed order to the universe and that nature is defined as whatever accords with this order. Standards of right and wrong are supposedly part of this order, and people who do not live by the standards of natural law are somehow unnatural as well as evil.[15] Others hold that nature is defined by what is studied by the so-called natural sciences, such as physics, chemistry, and biology. These people usually do not include standards of right and wrong within the bounds of what is natural. More popular definitions of nature in everyday life interpret nature as whatever is untouched by human hands, whatever is spontaneous rather than devious and fraudulent, and whatever is an unshakable boundary to human projects. Thus, people speak of "unspoiled nature," "acting naturally," and "the forces of nature," respectively. This diversity of definitions should show that "nature" is by no means a fixed category in human experience, but is continually being reinterpreted through social and cultural processes. For the purposes of the following discussion, we will define nature as that aspect of human experience centered upon the human body and that part of the physical environment that has not been shaped by human beings into tools or products. Of course, the boundaries of this definition are quite vague, because the human body is continually in the process of being modified through social and personal action, and those parts of the environment that are neither tools nor products serve as a context for cultural objects or are maintained in their condition through the use of cultural objects.

The preceding definition of nature is different from the most popular definitions in an important respect. Unlike most definitions, it does not make a sharp distinction between nature and culture. The anthropologist Lévi-Strauss is representative of those who do make such a sharp distinction. His idea is that "cultures are coded screens which enable us to organize the facts of nature, as a projector is needed to make sense out of a film strip."[16] This view that there are facts of nature and interpretations of culture tends to sever human existence from nature. This split between human existence and nature can lead to two very different attitudes toward nature, both of which are significant for the process of appreciation.

Two Contrasting Attitudes to Nature

First, one can value culture far more highly than nature and attempt to do everything possible to create a thoroughly man-made world. Under this attitude, nature is something to be conquered. Sometimes it is conceived of as a hostile force, throwing obstacles in the way of people's conquest of happiness, while at other times it is conceived of as a neutral field upon which human beings perform their exploits. In either case, mastery over nature is the object of activity, even if there is an effort to learn the ways of nature through scientific inquiry before turning those secrets to the fulfillment of human ends. At the extreme of this attitude, nature is viewed as a vast machine to be manipulated by human masters.[17] Alternatively, nature is seen as a woman, either pliant or wily, to be conquered or ravished by "man."

The second way of conceiving of nature, under the nature-culture split, is to value it more highly than culture. Here, human creations are viewed as artificial, while unspoiled nature is idealized.[18] Human beings are seen as throwing nature out of balance, despoiling species, filling the environment with their waste material, and generally showing insufficient respect and appreciation for the beauty and bounty of the gift they have been given. Sometimes this attitude leads to appeals for dismantling complex technologies and going back to the simple and natural life, while at other times it results merely in romantic idylls or back-to-nature fads. In any event, the guiding idea is to adapt to nature rather than to master it.

Neither of the two major attitudes toward nature that follow from the nature-culture split takes into account that the very category of nature is humanly defined. Whether one would prefer to conquer nature or to adapt to it is frequently a question of which human experiences are being defined as parts of nature. It is most likely that the majority of people would prefer to have rabies conquered through the innoculation of dogs rather than adapt to the disease by having numerous people die from it. Similarly, it is also quite likely that the majority of people would prefer to adapt to the fact that streams are not immediately cleansed of chemical wastes by limiting the dumping of such wastes than to drink water that would poison them. Broad generalizations about nature are of no help whatsoever in deciding which technologies should be used and which ones should be suppressed. However, such generalizations are of enormous help to propagandists.

Environmentalist Propaganda

In the United States at the present time there are two main kinds of propaganda about the environment. The propaganda that follows from the idea that nature should be conquered states that, while there may be some harmful side effects following from the use of certain technologies, the only way to get rid of these side effects is to perfect even better technologies. The core of this argument is that people are definitely unwilling to give up any of the blessings (products) of contemporary industry and that they should not be encouraged to make such sacrifices anyway. Thus, ways must be found to keep the glut of products flowing and still keep the environment from being thoroughly poisoned. Those in charge of business enterprises and certain labor unions are particularly fond of this line of argument. The problem with the argument, of course, is the assumption that it is neither morally nor practically justified to attempt to curb technological development in certain directions. Perhaps in most cases controls are not justified. However, the claim that such controls are never justified merely closes the issue in advance of inquiry.

The propaganda that follows from the idea that human beings should adapt to nature holds that severe controls must be applied immediately to limit population, regulate land uses, and bar the expansion of technology. Sometimes the claim is made that the very survival of the human race is at stake, while sometimes more peripheral arguments about vanishing species of wildlife are brought to the fore. The ecology lobby is a complex movement containing diverse special interest groups. Some, like the Sierra Club, are concerned with maintaining lands unspoiled by industry, others are concerned with individuals picking up litter off the street (a kind of meaningless gesture in the shadow of belching smokestacks), others are out to protect the interests of hunters and campers (for example, the National Rifle Association), while still others promote controls limiting industrial wastes. Insofar as environmentalist propaganda states that technology *must* be dismantled, it is as dogmatic as the opposing propaganda. However, the ecology movement has contributed to an increased concern about what it means to appreciate the physical environment.

The hallmark of attitudes toward appreciation of the environment in the United States is their fragmentation and general lack of coherence. For many people, appreciation of nature is a mystique. There is supposed to be something sacred about getting out of the human orbit and into a situation where one faces the elements alone (though usually with clothes on and some camping equipment).[19] For others, appreciation of nature simply means getting out in the country or in a park where they can camp. Still others believe that it means eating organic foods (grown without pesticides and chemical fertilizers). Still others simply see it as preserving their quaint towns and comfortable suburbs from invasions by the unwashed masses. A distinct minority does not draw a sharp boundary between nature and culture, and looks for ways of harmonizing all phases of human experience into coherent communities.

During the era of industrialization, debates took place over the issue of whether nature was an infinitely exhaustable detachable resource to be used unsparingly to satisfy human wants, or whether it was a finite gift to be husbanded and conserved for future generations. Thus, the debate about nature was oriented toward the social process of production. Today the debate is shifting, at least for the middle classes, to how nature can be best appreciated. It is important as one listens to and participates in this debate to clarify one's image of nature and to recognize when one has made a fetish out of nature by severing it from the rest of human experience.[20]

Figure 12.2. PERSPECTIVES ON NATURE

1. Nature Is Something to Be Conquered. More technologies should be developed. The abuses of technology should be curbed by inventing better technologies. Culture is superior to nature.
2. Human Beings Should Adapt to Nature. Dependence on technologies should be lessened. Nature is superior to culture.

Where do you stand in this debate and why?

HEALTH

One of the most important parts of nature for human beings is the human body, and the category most relevant to the appreciation of the body is health. Just as nature is socially and culturally defined, so is health. Many people believe that a standard of good health can be scientifically defined without any recourse to choices among values. However, a moment's reflection on what is meant by health will show one the complexities involved in defining it. Is good health to be defined in terms of a feeling ("feeling well")? This is the way most people evaluate their health and appreciate their own bodies day by day. Yet one can feel very well and still be in the early stages of a major disease that will later ravage the body. So, is health to be defined according to the more objective standards of medical science, such as normal pulse rate and blood pressure? Certainly some of these measures may put boundaries on the idea of good health, merely because if one deviates from the norm too far one will soon feel poorly. However, beyond such boundary markers, no science can specify how strong one must be to be healthy, how one's skin and features must appear to look healthy, or how well coordinated one must be to be healthy. All of these considerations, and many more, are not defined scientifically but through value choices. For example, why must people who have lost limbs or have noticeable scars often feel stigmatized? Why do they often attempt to mask these physical characteristics whenever possible?[21] Certainly there is no scientific or purely medical judgment behind these feelings. Rather, these people and many of those around them feel that such physical characteristics render one ugly or unnatural. Thus one cannot escape the values implicit in the notion of health merely by pretending that they have been in some way scientifically validated.

One of the most marked tendencies in the appreciative life in mass societies is a progressive alienation from the body. As knowledge about the body has become specialized and a large number of professions and semi-professions have arisen to care for (or abuse) various aspects and parts of the body, people have come to depend on others to inform them about whether or not they are healthy and, if they are unhealthy, what should be done to remedy the situation.[22] Beauticians, barbers, rehabilitation counselors, chiropracters, podiatrists, dentists, physicians representing all specialties, nutritionists, physical educationists, physical therapists, nurses of all kinds, and a host of others, have divided the body among themselves, staking out special claims and fighting out jurisdictional battles. Given this situation, two types of alienation arise. First, the person is alienated from understanding the body as a whole, since it has become the object of many different institutions. The ideal of a sound mind in a sound body, or better, of a fully integrated self-process (a wonderful sociologist's phrase!), is a mere abstraction when conflicting interpretations of the body abound (think of how differently the candy manufacturer and the dietician view the problem of overweight, or of how differently the dentist and the bubble-gum manufacturer view the dental needs of children). The second kind of alienation centers on most people not understanding what is happening to them and why when they are treated by specialists in various aspects of the body. This kind of alienation extends from the seemingly trivial instance of a woman relying upon her beautician to tell her whether or not she is attractive, all the way to the tragic plight of someone seriously ill who continues with a prescribed treatment as he feels his strength ebbing from him as the days go by and is too intimidated by the professional image to question his doctor or change doctors.

Figure 12.3. ALIENATION FROM THE BODY

Beauticians and barbers take care of the appearance of the body.
Physical educationists take care of muscular development and coordination.
Chiropracters, podiatrists, dentists, and various specialized physicians take care of curing the body.
Nurses, physical therapists, and other paramedical personnel assist physicians.
Nutritionists dictate what the body should be fed.
Rehabilitation counselors and occupational therapists fit the body for work.

The epitome of alienation from the body is the contemporary general hospital. Just as the mass army bureaucratized military life, the general hospital bureaucratizes health care.[23] The patient is faced by an array of functionaries, each one with a particular task to perform and each one caring for only a fraction of the entire case. The first object of the staff is to get the patient to comply willingly with directives, so that the flow of work will not be interrupted. The patient is at a disadvantage, because of illness and fear about the future, and he has little choice but to go along and cooperate with the staff. Financial resources are of great moment in determining the extent of alienation from the body and loss of control over the situation, since money can buy private rooms, special nurses, and more time from physicians.

Going along with alienation from the body is the sick role supposedly prescribed for people who are ill.[24] According to Parsons, the sick role has four aspects: "First, the sick person is exempt from normal social role responsibilities. Second, the sick person can expect assistance and care from other people. Third, the sick person should be motivated to get well. And, fourth, the sick person should seek medical help and cooperate to the fullest extent possible."[25] Other sociologists have pointed out that this interpretation of the sick role does not cover all illnesses, since "chronic illness by definition is not temporary, so that role-expectations predicated on the assumption of the temporary nature of illness (for example, 'motivation to get well') are clearly inapplicable"[26] Barring chronic illness, however, the significant feature of the sick role is that it requires the person to cooperate with medical personnel to effect a cure that will make it possible for the person to resume his social functions. This means that, according to conventional wisdom, sickness involves recourse to medical personnel.

It is not at all clear that the sick role is generally followed in mass societies. First, the very poor frequently do not receive much medical care. Second, people continually resort to do-it-yourself medicine and all sorts of health fads ranging from health foods to various patent medicines. As organized medicine continues to become more alienating, one can expect health faddism to fill a gap in appreciation of the body as a whole.

LEISURE AND ENTERTAINMENT

Curing oneself of actual or imagined ailments is merely one of many possible activities that can make up the appreciative life in mass societies. Leisure, of course, is not exclusively a privilege of elite groups. As working hours have become limited for large numbers of people, and labor-saving devices have become prevalent in the home, time has been freed for a wide variety of appreciative activities. Perhaps the hallmark of leisure in mass society is that it is increasingly directed by large organizations. Television is an obvious example of such organization and standardization, and a glance at TV program listings will reveal that the various networks differ very little in what they offer in terms of content (one season Westerns predominate and the next season doctor or detective shows take the spotlight) or depth (the shows are not demanding of great concentration). Even reading books is organizationally influenced by publishers who select works to print (primarily with mass sales potential in mind) and by book clubs which select given books to be offered to members. Bridge is played in bridge clubs,[27] travel is structured by agencies in the form of tours, and dating is arranged through computer-matching firms or in swingles clubs which are mushrooming in large cities. Much of children's leisure is organizationally directed, too, from Little League baseball, football, and hockey, to the Boy Scouts, 4-H Clubs, and Campfire Girls.

The problem of leisure in mass society is not so much the *fact* of organizational control as the *consequences* of such control. Essentially, organizations tend to direct the leisure activities of individuals toward one end alone—entertainment. Although no one but a rather uptight snob would deny that fun and laughter are an integral part of the human condition, pursuing entertainment exclusively precludes the attainment of other important values. One of these alternative (or at least additional) goals is the attainment of new perspectives on one's existence through finding out about other ways of life. Leisure activity, through such media as the theater, films, novels and television *could* portray other patterns of living which might then be taken by viewers as viable possibilities to be tried or to be vicariously experienced and appreciated. These media could present comprehensive reconstructions or imaginative projections of experience that would challenge people to examine their own conditions.

That this has not been the aim or the product of those organizations that have control over much leisure activity is readily apparent. For the most part, the situations depicted in the media are trivial, the characterizations are based on stereotypes, and the whole is concocted with reference to a standard formula: boy meets girl, boy loses girl, boy catches girl; man commits crime, police try to solve crime, criminal is punished. The entertainment goes so far in failing to challenge or develop what its creators see as a mindless audience that it frequently does not even allow them to decide how to respond. Heavy-handed mood music (scary, happy, sad) is part of the film, and television shows come equipped with laugh-tracks provided by the organization. Mass leisure gives rise to escape and diversion, and little else.[28]

There are several explanations for why mass leisure tends to be entertainment. We generally believe that advertisers, business organizations, and the mass media crowd other forms of leisure and appreciation out of the public arena by making entertainment so easily accessi-

ble. Since entertainment does not lead one to question social arrangements, it is excellent for selling products and maintaining established
institutions. An alternative explanation, popular among some social
critics, holds that the nature of mass man is basically that of a doltish
slob and that the mass entertainment is just what he wants and de-
serves.[29] This explanation provides a convenient rationalization for
those who concoct mass entertainments and has the added benefit of
snob appeal for those claiming to be intellectuals. The conservative
critic, Ernest van den Haag, states that "the mass of men dislikes and
always has disliked learning and art. It wishes to be distracted from life
rather than to have it revealed; to be comforted by traditional (possibly
happy and sentimental) tropes, rather than to be upset by new ones."[30]
Not to be outdone, the liberal critic, Arthur Schlesinger, Jr., making
an analogy to IQ tests "suggested the existence of an AQ, or aesthetic
quotient. Some few people are naturally responsive to art; the masses
are not; everyone gets exactly what he is capable of absorbing."[31] Also
in a somewhat snobbish and functionalist vein, Edward Shils finds that
mass leisure activities, which he calls "brutal culture," admirably suit
the masses.[32] We disagree with these critics and doubt that their "mass
man" exists. In mass society the burden is not on the individual who
chooses what to consume, but on the large organizations that schedule
the range of choices and the relative availability of alternatives. Blaming the mass man for the quality of leisure activity is like blaming the
incompetence of the masses for the failings of democratic institutions,
or blaming litterbugs for environmental pollution. In the following
discussion, therefore, we treat the social relations that emerge around
the use of mass leisure activities rather than whether or not "mass
man" has the ability to appreciate "high culture." The resources put
before us form the context in which we live our appreciative lives.

Figure 12.4. THE CHARACTERISTICS OF ENTERTAINMENT

1. Entertainment is standardized; it does not contain surprises.
2. Entertainment is undemanding; it does not challenge one to reflect.
3. Entertainment accepts the prevailing social context; it does not question
   established institutions.
4. Entertainment is sold as a consumer good; the quality of the object is less
   important than the audience reaction.

Prior to discussing particular examples of mass leisure, it is important to sketch out several general relations that appear in contempo-

rary appreciative activity. First there is the tendency for entertainment to be regarded as a consumer good. Hannah Arendt writes that "the commodities the entertainment industry offers are not "things"—cultural objects whose excellence is measured by their ability to withstand the life process and to become permanent appurtenances of the world . . . nor are they values which exist to be used and exchanged; they are rather consumer goods destined to be used up, as are any other consumer goods."[33] As various analysts of social class have shown, possession of goods often serves to distinguish one group as better or worse than another. As the have-nots tend to acquire what once was the sole privilege of the haves, the latter move on to new products and activities so that they can maintain their differentiation. The result is a merry-go-round of fads. As the outs learn the new dance step, the ins acquire another one. When the outs can acquire mass reproductions of the classic art masterpices, the ins begin to favor pop art, replacing a Van Gogh with a can of Campbell's tomato soup. The use of entertainment as a consumer good not only serves to distinguish social status groups, but also age groups. Traditionally adults were the trend setters, and youth borrowed songs, alcohol, cigarettes, and the like from their elders. Recently, there has been a complete reversal of this pattern, and adults are trying to consume the goods associated with youth (catching up with their children). It is now the adults who are borrowing—the rock, the dance steps, the pot.

Paralleling the development of mass entertainment as a consumer good is the transformation of the public performer into the celebrity. Whether in sports, movies, television or literature, what a person does as a performer is not as important as his personality and general image. Although he was probably a very good quarterback, Joe Namath would never have received the acclaim (or high salary) if it were not for his off-the-field antics. Richard Burton is a superb actor, but his drawing power at the box office has little to do with what he does in front of the camera. Politics, too, can be considered as entertainment; think of the media coverage of the last presidential campaign. And (with the assistance of Madison Avenue advertising firms,) politicians are being transformed for the public from people who have compiled a certain record and who espouse certain policies to celebrities with pre-packaged images.[34] In general, entertainers are frequently judged according to standards that have little or nothing to do with the entertainment they are supposedly providing.

The use of mass leisure as a consumer good to differentiate people and the replacement of the performer by the celebrity are common in many types of activities. The reason for these transformations is related to some extent to the increase of available time for leisure pursuits in mass society. This relationship is not direct, but involves the assumption that these and other changes are due to the increased control over leisure activities by firms whose profits increase as they are able to appropriate increasing amounts of people's time and money.

Figure 12.5. PERFORMER AND CELEBRITY

Performer   *Celebrity*

The quality of the   The public image is
performance is primary.   primary.

Who do you appreciate most—a performer or a celebrity?

The amount of time people have for leisure pursuits varies by age (youngest and oldest groups have relatively more time than others), occupation (generally, business executives and professionals have less time than other occupational groups), and a number of other factors, such as parenthood and commuting distance to work. Of course, there are difficulties in defining leisure time; some would define it as the remainder of the twenty-four hours that is not spent sleeping or at work, while others would also subtract the time spent on such activities as household repairing.

In any case, whatever definition is used, there is more leisure time in the contemporary world than there was in the past. It has been estimated that the increase in leisure time since 1880 for the American working male has been approximately twenty-five hours per week, most of it coming since World War II.[35] As stated previously, what fills this leisure time is to a great extent controlled by large organizations, and includes such activities as sports, television, music, movies, drugs, hobbies, shopping, and religious activities. Though religion has many functions, one of the most important in the present day is, perhaps, providing an arena for sociable activities. In 1940, 49 percent of the population of the United States belonged to religious bodies, while in 1968, 63 percent of the population belonged to such bodies.[36] Can this be accounted for merely by an increase in faith?

Sports

Although baseball may no longer be the national pastime, sport certainly ranks as one of the major leisure-time activities. There have been a number of reasons suggested to account for the relative decline of interest in baseball and the concomitant rise in enthusiasm for football. Both sports have catered to spectators primarily, rather than to participants, as have auto racing, boxing, wrestling, and, more recently, golf and tennis. Despite large numbers who turn out to view these sporting events in person, the majority of people experience them via the media. An explanation for the popularity of football, drawing upon Marshall McLuhan's idea that media often determine what content will be most popular, holds that football gained preeminence over baseball when people began to watch sporting events on television rather than listen to them on the radio. Baseball, under this interpretation, is seen as a simple sport with a clear focus which can be reported fully by a radio announcer who conveys both the necessary information and the excitement.[37] The activity on the field is "linear" in the sense that it can be verbally described in terms of single events which follow in sequence: The pitcher winds up and throws a curve to the batter who connects with the ball and sends a high pop fly into the shallow outfield where it is caught by the second baseman playing deep. In football, which is more complex and violent, twenty-two players are simultaneously performing different motions when the ball is set into motion, and a verbal recounting of the action misses a great deal. A picture is worth more than a thousand words here.

As with a number of other appreciative activities, sports differentiate groups of people. In general, sports are supposed to be the interest of males, and both the commercials (for razor blades, shaving cream, beer, cigars, hair tonic, and the like) and the concentration on strength and roughness convey a masculine atmosphere. The popular image of the spectator is that of men assembled at neighborhood taverns or at home in easy chairs with cans of beer watching the big game on television. There are some sports, however, such as wrestling, that seem to have greater appeal to women. Less obvious than this sexual distinction is the way in which various sports are enjoyed by different social strata. This especially holds true for those sports that have less than the mass appeal of football and that do not have prime-time television exposure. Polo matches and yachting races are leisure pursuits of the upper social strata, both as participants and as spectators.

Of more recent origin (and due, no doubt, to the increase in income and leisure time for members of the working class) are sports that appeal to the lower strata; these have been called "prole" sports. Prole sports seem to have evolved from existing and familiar objects in the world of work, such as automobiles, big muscles (wrestling), and so on. They place more emphasis on speed and power than do other sports.[38] Paralleling the teen-age, middle-class, Saturday-night phenomenon of cruising in cars was "the roller rink—a place where youths could meet for the exhibition of individual prowess. . . . Roller derby is the logical sporting extension and abstraction of these Saturday nights, just as stock car racing is the logical sporting extension and abstraction of Appalachian wiskey running. . . . As active (or formerly active) users of these involved artifacts, spectators can not only understand player skills, but vicariously enact their own power fantasies."[39]

One may question, however, whether or not the spectators of any sport watch it in order to appreciate the skill of the athletes. Do ice hockey fans like it better when the puck is shot into the net or when two or more players hit one another over the head with their sticks? Does the noisy exuberance of wrestling audiences increase when acts in violation of the rules are committed, despite the sham drama throughout the match? Are auto-racing spectators disappointed after witnessing a race in which there were no crashes? Tom Wolfe claims "that for every purist who comes to see the fine points of the race, such as who is going to win, there are probably five waiting for the wrecks to which stock car racing is so gloriously prone. . . . So why put up with the monotony between crashes?"[40] This monotony was eliminated with the invention of the demolition derby, the twentieth-century equivalent to gladiatorial combat. In this sport, the cars all head toward the center of the infield rather than around the track. They crash into one another and the last car that can still move is the winner.

Sports concerned with automobiles, such as stock- and sports-car racing, have increased in popularity, diffusing into the middle class from both ends of the spectrum as the importance of the automobile in everyday life has increased. Many leisure-time pursuits in the United States reflect the values of daily living, especially those of the economic sphere. Marshall McLuhan notes that ". . . games become faithful models of a culture. They incorporate the action and reaction of whole populations in a single "image."[41]

GAMES

Table games, such as poker and the popular board game of Monopoly, are examples of the generalization that games reflect the patterns of other human activities. Card playing is one of the few activities that competes with the mass media for the leisure time of great numbers of people.[42] This activity is not free from organizational control. For example, in bridge there are clubs, newspaper columns, books, and so on. Different card games, too, tend to be associated with different social strata and, as the examples of poker and contract bridge illustrate, many of the values of these different groups are reflected in the games. Poker, relying largely upon chance and aggression, reflects the fatalism and masculine ideal of lower-class males. Contract bridge, as developed by the millionaire Harold S. Vanderbilt, has obvious capitalist overtones which would appeal to members of the upper strata: "Vanderbilt's innovation was that players should bid against each other, as in a marketplace. Whoever claimed he could take the most tricks then entered into a 'contract' to either win that many or suffer penalties."[43] Bridge was later influenced by Ely Culbertson who added sexually connotative terms to the jargon, such as "vulnerability" and "going to bed with my king."[44] Bridge requires restraint, the ability to read other people's emotions, and intellectual skill. These are all qualities of the organization man and tend to make the game popular among the middle class, along with the sexy and capitalistic jargon. "Certain games are more attractive than others because games differ in the images of reality they represent to the player."[45]

Without being too facetious, one could present a case for considering sex as a game in mass society. The imagery of its jargon and the symbolism of its actions reflects concerns of power and domination ("to *take* her to bed," "to be on top"). As with bridge, there are rules, techniques, newspaper columns, books, and clubs. Many people are amateurs, and those who are professionals may be players and/or teachers. Judging by people's conversation alone, sex certainly ranks as an important leisure time entertainment. Many people are playing the game of love, with all that phrase implies about the quality of human relations.

TELEVISION

Possibly the most frequent leisure-time activity today is watching television. It is estimated that the average American sees over thirty hours a week of television programs.[46] Other figures indicate that the average home has the TV tuned in for over five hours and forty-five minutes per day.[47] Much of the information about who watches what is jealously ensconced in the safes of advertising agencies or their clients who control the content of what may be viewed on television. Their primary criterion of what should be presented is that it should appeal to as many people as possible: "Thus no programming will be shown by the networks unless aimed at the whole audience, and each network strives to gain no less than one-third of the audience."[48] This helps explain the quality of what is seen, because "in general there is a tendency toward an inverse relationship between audience size and the cultural merit of the program."[49] Although most of the programming cannot be classified as direct propaganda in favor of the capitalist economic system (the units of which pay to put the shows on), none of the fare seriously challenges general establishment values, particularly with regard to the economy, the family, nationalism, and religion. Much of television's broadcasting time can be seen as entertainment that only challenges the viewer to forget his problems and those of others. Not only do programs such as soap operas (which have an estimated 18 million viewers[50]), situation comedies, Westerns, and variety shows have this goal (perhaps implicitly), but so does much of the ubiquitous news programming. News broadcasts spend considerable time on sports information, human-interest stories and the "lighter side of the news."

Although a product of mass society, television is also a tool. Its impact furthers the masslike quality of people. Network broadcasting has done much to eliminate regional accents and, because of its wide reach, it has been able to spread various fads and fashions in speech phrases, clothing, hair styles, and life styles rapidly and effectively. As of 1970, over 98 percent of all households in the United States had at least one television set.[51] Due to its importance, more will be said about television in the chapter on communications.

RADIO

As with television, but even more so, listening to the radio is often accompanied by some other activity. The popularity of portable transistorized radios and car radios make such dual activity prevalent. The introduction of television drastically reshaped radio programming, and today there are basically two types of stations: those that play popular music with hourly news reports, and news radio stations that have items generally classified as news including editorials, cooking recipes, advice on marriage and health, and so on (a kind of talking newspaper). Not only is one's choice generally limited to these two types of stations, but within each type the various stations are frequently indistinguishable. The music stations vary somewhat in that one may be a country-and-western or a soul station, in which cases the disc jockeys will have noticable accents differing from the nationwide nonaccented majority. Many stations are network affiliated and are thereby supplied with identical musical themes as well as the same records and stock of remarks to make about them. One can drive from one end of the country to the other and, though the dial must be switched every now and then, everything sounds the same. The "Top 40" are those records with the highest sales, and, since young people are far and away the largest group of record buyers, music radio is directed at them.

Allowing for exceptions, such as Lawrence Welk's "champagne music" and, of course, jazz and classical music, music, on records, over the radio, or performed live is directed at those under thirty. Music may be a leisure activity, but it is also a big business, controlled in the United States largely by a few major record companies.[52] Popular music idols, like sport stars, are appreciated less as performers and more as celebrities. At their concerts they often cannot be heard above the din of the crowd. Although music in the past has been associated with causes, most notably the labor movement, popular music in the United States has been mainly escapist. The majority of themes deal with love, requited or not, physical or only verbal. When folk music became popular and was joined with rock in the early 1960s, there were a number of message or protest songs, such as Bob Dylan's "The Times They Are A-Changin' " and P. F. Sloan's "Eve of Destruction." Following that period, an increasingly popular theme has been drug experiences. Many of the lyrics have had multiple meanings and so the real message is appreciated only by those who have learned the code. For example, the Beatles' hit "Yellow Submarine" can be translated if one knows that "yellow jacket" is a submarine-shaped barbiturate, seconal, or a "downer" (a "downer" submerges you).[53] Is "*Lucy* in the *Sky* with *Diamonds*" referring to LSD?

DRUGS

For an unknown but seemingly increasing number of people, drugs are an important leisure-time activity, unambiguously escapist in nature and predominant among younger people, though not exclusively so. Some leisure activities involve relatively few social relations (for example, watching television or listening to records or the radio), while others, such as playing games, have a high intensity and frequency of relations. Drug activities, such as LSD trips, are on the solitary side of the continuum, except for the relations involved in learning how to use the drugs (including how to interpret their effects) and the process of obtaining them (particularly because their sale and use is illegal). Pot parties, because of the relatively mild effect of marijuana, are quite similar to the "straight" world's cocktail party with its reliance upon alcohol to loosen people up so that they may better entertain and be entertained by others. The highly emotion-charged debate over drugs frequently obscures their basic use as a means of entertainment little different from others in mass society.

The extreme controversy over drug use is as myth-ridden as the one over environmental pollution. Conservative politicians tend to make a major issue out of drug abuse because it diverts the attention of people from issues concerning the redistribution of income, the quality of the environment, alienation from work, the quality of products, and other such concerns, which business would rather play down. The conservative position makes use of many dubious claims such as the slippery-slope argument, which holds that those who smoke marijuana are somehow fated to become heroin addicts. This is similar to saying that those who drink coffee are fated to become addicted to pep pills. More important from the perspective of self-understanding, however, is the frequent claim that taking drugs distorts reality and is merely a crutch for people who do not want to face up to reality. There is no doubt, of course, that depressant drugs function to blur the sharp edges of abrasive social encounters and operate to deprive the user of motivation to meet the requirements of highly competitive and disciplined social roles. However, the "reality" that the conservatives are talking about has been socially defined, and there is no reason to assume that it is any more objective than what is experienced by the drug user. Further, if the given social situation is judged to be evil, there is a good case for escaping from role requirements. Finally, is it so clear that one is a better person for "facing up" to distressing social situations, particularly if one can do little about them? From our viewpoint, the limitation of drugs is not that they distort some reality, but that they frequently inhibit relativization and imaginatively reconceiving one's situation in concrete terms. We have no argument with those who do not seek relativization, only a conflict.

The other side of the drug debate is equally riddled by dogmas. Here, instead of the claim that reality is distorted by drugs, the argument is made that drugs give one access to a higher reality. At the limit, this position holds that authentic religious experiences are gained from taking drugs. Consciousness is supposedly expanded, and people are supposedly opened to new dimensions of awareness.[54] Those who have bad trips are in the minority and are psychologically disturbed to begin with. The drugs only bring out what is already there. This position, in all its variations, makes no less a fetish of certain experiences than the conservative position. While those in favor of established institutions always point to the worst effects of drugs, defenders of the drug culture harp on the peak experiences and sever these experiences from the rest of human events, giving them a special status of "reality." Pro-drug propaganda (mostly confined to conversation rather than publication) frequently takes on the cast of religious revivalism. It is no wonder, then, that mass religious fads like the Jesus movement and the Black Muslims often present themselves as alternatives to the drug culture and are frequently credited with curing people of addiction. People are encouraged to get high on Jesus. At least this kind of trip does not cost very much money, although its cost in the denial of critical reason is enormous.

The idea that drugs are primarily a form of entertainment is merely one perspective about drugs. Other perspectives hold that drug use is a form of deviance associated with retreat from social responsibilities, a manifestation of a pill-popping culture (a thin rationalization by those who take illegal drugs) and a symptom of one kind or another psychological maladjustment (a bludgeon of those who are against the use of drugs). The perspective that sees drugs as entertainment leaves out phenomena like extreme cases of addiction and obvious attempts at self-destruction, which other perspectives deal with better. However, the deviance perspective and the peak-experience view are equally distortive and tend to put marginal cases into central focus.

Figure 12.6. PERSPECTIVES ON DRUGS

1. Drugs distort consciousness, they are crutches for maladjusted people, and their use should be curbed. If you start on "soft" drugs, you'll eventually get addicted to "hard" drugs.
2. Drugs expand consciousness, they improve the personality, and their use should be encouraged. If you take "soft" drugs, you won't necessarily take "hard" drugs in the future.

Where do you stand in this debate and why?

OTHER ENTERTAINMENTS

Magazines (we hesitate to use the word "reading" because many are appreciated for their pictures alone) constitute another type of leisure-time activity. There are very few mass-circulation general-audience magazines, such as *Newsweek* and *TV Guide,* and most have a more specific audience. *National Review* and *Ramparts* distinguish their readers on a political basis, *Good Housekeeping* and *Playboy* on a sexual basis, and *Humpty Dumpty* and *Reader's Digest* on the basis of age. Here again, leisure pursuits are controlled by a few large organizations—those that publish multiple magazines, as well as their advertisers. According to Betty Friedan, who had worked for a woman's magazine, advertisers determined the content of the other material including the fiction pieces. Their criterion in the 1950s was to convince women to be consumer housewives, to live the feminine mystique.[55]

Unlike magazines, which as a leisure activity cater to all groups, movies have become the province of teen-agers and those in their twenties. Children and older people can find similar entertainment at home on television. In order to compete with television, movies now specialize in content that cannot be shown in homes: nudity, a variety of sexual acts, obscene language, excessive violence, and gore.

Travel as a leisure activity was once only for the wealthy, but lower transportation costs, longer holidays, and more money have made travel one of the major entertainments for the American middle class. Although it need not be so, travel, too, is escapist and far from broadening. American-style lodgings are sought out and social interaction is either with other tourists or those who cater to tourists. Places are visited to buy souvenirs, and the sights are often seen through the viewer of a camera. American travelers are helping to americanize Europe and the rest of the world. Rather than see something different, they make the different into the known.[56]

There are numerous other activities that fill up leisure time, such as the numerous hobbies people take up, from sewing through stamp and antique collecting to being amateurs at what some people do for pay as their work. There are clubs for most hobbies, often greatly influenced by the manufacturers of products used. Even shopping can be classified as a leisure-time pursuit, at least for the suburban middle class. Engaged in for hours each week by all age groups, and made possible by enclosed malls which provide all-weather protection in addition to seats, food and toilets, ambling through stores often becomes an end in itself rather than a means to appreciation.

Figure 12.7. CONTEMPORARY LEISURE ACTIVITIES

Sports	Drugs	Travel
Games	Magazines	Hobbies
Television	Movies	Shopping
Radio		

Is this list complete? If you can think of any other leisure activities write your own section on how they are performed in mass society.

EXERCISE

Make an inventory of your own leisure activities. Which activities take up the most time? Can you justify your use of leisure time?

EXERCISE

Make an inventory of your use of the news media. Which media (television, radio, newspapers, news magazines, opinion magazines, etc.) predominate? Toward what ideologies are your sources of information slanted? Do you think that you are missing out on information that you should have?

EXERCISE

Critically look at television for an evening and also look through a weekly TV program guide. Which programs are aimed at non-mass audiences? When are they broadcast? How many shows are likely to provoke people's thought, and how many are likely just to entertain? What types of shows can you think of that might be provocative and/or entertaining and that are not being aired?

SUMMARY

Why do people create and produce goods and services? Why do they make rules to order their conduct? For some people the answer merely is that human existence is an exercise in survival for its own sake. However, in practice, most people do not exist only to survive, but to appreciate the world in both its human and nonhuman aspects.

The traditional context for appreciation has been religion. However, in the modern world a process of secularization has gone on in which human activities have gained independence from religious standards and conceptions, and have developed autonomous standards. In the mass societies of today, religious institutions serve a number of functions ranging from status confirmation to resolving doubts about the role of evil in the cosmos. Religion is far from being relevant to everyone in the contemporary world, and various religious systems compete with one another and with naturalistic worldviews as possible life-styles.

In the modern world, nature tended to replace the supernatural as the context for appreciation. The boundaries of nature and culture have often been drawn sharply, disguising the fact that what is natural and what is artificial are defined by human beings through social and cultural processes. The appreciation of the natural environment tends to be distorted by conceptions of nature as a set of hostile forces to be conquered, or as a romantic ideal rather than as a part of human experience. Part of appreciating nature is appreciating the human body. A central category in appreciating the body is health, which does not have a neutral or scientific definition. In mass societies the body tends to be chopped up into cross sections, each one treated by a specialty. From beauticians to brain surgeons, the body industry alienates the human being from appreciating the life processes as a whole by drawing sharp jurisdictions and developing unintelligible jargons. Prevailing conventional wisdom holds that the sick role involves seeking expert medical help so that one can get back to the business of living quickly. Counteracting this tendency, however, is a long tradition of medical self-help.

Appreciation of products has tended, in mass societies, to narrow to entertainment. There are a multitude of mass entertainments, all of which are organizationally manipulated, and few of which challenge the audience to reconceive the human condition in novel and unfamiliar ways. Placing the burden for this situation on a doltish mass man who has a low AQ (aesthetic quotient) seems to miss the fact that organizations make pap readily available. Two tendencies can be seen in mass entertainment. First, performers become valued as celebrity images rather than as practitioners of an art or skill. Second, entertainment is devoured like a consumer good and used for status confirmation. These tendencies can be seen to operate in sports, games, and fashion. Television and the drug culture function most as escapes. Appreciation in mass society reaches its absurd reduction in the practice of shopping, where the means of procuring entertainment becomes itself an entertainment.

13
THE CONTEXT OF
APPRECIATION

In the preceding chapter we discussed the various kinds of appreciative activities that appear in mass society and are shared by its members. While not all people participate in any given appreciative activity (many are not religious, some have little or no interest in sports, and a few even refrain from watching television), only a small minority is unaffected by packaged world-views and entertainments. However, there is wide variation in the settings in which people perform appreciative activities. Appreciation is always a social activity in the sense that it involves cultural objects that have been created and produced through long chains of social relations and that have publicly available standardized usages. Appreciation, though, is frequently also social in a much more direct sense. First, people often aim their creative and coordinative activities toward specific groups of appreciators for whom these activities, in part, are performed. For example, a mother may prepare chocolate-chip cookies for her children to enjoy, or a poet may attempt to create a national literature from which his countrymen can gain enrichment. In neither of these cases is the activity (baking or poetry) directed at all human beings. Rather, it is directed at a relevant community (the family or the nation). Second, appreciative activities are often directly social because they are carried on in company with others. For example, in witnessing a live rock concert, the crowd itself is an important factor in the quality of appreciation, just as watching a television program is different when an entire family is gathered in the same room than when an isolated person sits alone. Time-honored remarks about the differences between drinking liquor alone and in company with others partially refer to this directly social aspect of appreciation. Third, appreciation is always carried on within a distinctive human context. While the object being appreciated (for example, a recording of black soul music) may be in the foreground of attention, the background of cultural objects distinctly affects appreciation. Black soul music sounds one way in the heart of the ghetto and another way in an upper-middle-class split-level house in a wealthy suburb. Thus, there are many ways in which appreciation is a social activity rather than a private one. The idea that appreciation is all a matter of taste loses some of its plausibility when one realizes how firmly embedded products and services are in social contexts.

One of the most significant ways in which appreciation is social has to do with the very standards of acceptable performances and products. How do beer drinkers learn that Schlitz, Budweiser, and Miller's are far superior products to the local (and less expensive) brew? This is partly accomplished through mammoth advertising campaigns that differentiate these products ("When you're out of Schlitz, you're out of beer"), but it is also accomplished by the docile cooperation of consumer peer groups whose members would turn up their noses if the local lager were served. Such appreciative groups convince members that they actually taste and see differences that aren't even there.[1] Those who adopt the notion that appreciation is merely a matter of taste, a private concern, are frequently upset when they are informed that their tastes are relative to the groups with which they identify and the contexts in which their appreciation is carried on. They would like to take their preferences out of context and declare that they own them, need not question them, and have no reason to change them. This is really no different from claiming ownership in one's ideas, getting upset when informed that those ideas are part of an historical tradition and claiming that the process of self-understanding invades one's right to hold whatever opinion one pleases.

Tastes have consequences, just the same as ideas, and one's tastes in appreciation and entertainment are an integral part of one's total activity. What quality of emotions and feelings is awakened when one watches a situation comedy, a detective show, a film highlighting sadism and torture? One is just as responsible for one's emotions and dispositions as for one's thoughts, creations, and decisions. One's emotional life can undergo change through exposure to new products and contexts. This is what is meant by the old term "cultivation." One does not get the idea of being cool or hip from nowhere, but liberation from such images and life-styles is most readily attained by recognizing their relativity.[2] Criticism of one's appreciative life demands some understanding of the groups in which one appreciates, of the standards of these groups, and of the cultural background to the appreciative foreground. Of course, the final aesthetic judgment is personal, but this does not mean that it is arbitrary or based on individual preference.

THE RELEVANT COMMUNITY

People tend to have one or more groups to which they refer their creative and appreciative activity.[3] Creators of all kinds refer their products and services to audiences, clients, consumers, and other such groups. Appreciators recognize common bonds with others who share similar experiences. Such groups, which serve as focal points for processes of appreciation, are termed here "communities." This use of the term community should not be confused with definitions of community stressing spatial location. All human activities and all groups have a spatial dimension, and the most important kind of space is socio-cultural space, which is not necessarily continuous and pictorial.[4] Thus, community is used here to mean a group of appreciators, whether or not they occupy the same geographical area.

In mass societies the most significant communities are massive and large-scale collectivities. While Aristotle could build up the appreciative community starting with the family as the elemental unit, working up to the neighborhood as a collection of families and finally ending up with the state, integrating an entire way of life, those examining mass society are probably better off starting with the largest units and then working down to the smaller ones.[5] This, at least, is the method that has been used by the foremost social theorists of the last century and a half, including Comte, Marx, Durkheim, and Parsons. It is a method that sheds light on certain aspects of human existence, particularly those involving large-scale organizations. It illuminates the quality of life in small groups much less, and emphasizes the adult phase of the life-cycle more than childhood. Parsons in particular has pointed to the significance of what he calls the societal community. According to him, the societal community is that phase of social activity that integrates all the other human activities into a coherent whole.[6] This is somewhat similar to the idea of appreciative community used here, although it does not incorporate the notion of the quality of appreciative experience, and it also tends to assume that the massive communities of the contemporary world successfully integrate experience into coherent wholes. Parsons tends to make the societal community equal to what is normally thought of as the nation. However, is the nation the most important appreciative community to which people relate their activities in the present day? What then is a nation? An attempt to respond to these questions is necessary to an understanding of the relevant communities in mass societies.

THE POLIS

Within the Western tradition, the prime example of the appreciative community has been the polis, or the ancient Greek city-state. Ancient Greece was composed of a number of small political-economic-appreciative units, each with its own tradition. Ernest Barker notes: ". . . these different States exhibited not merely "constitutional" differences, in the modern sense of that word, but deeper and more fundamental differences of moral aim and character. Small as was the city-state, its very size encouraged the rise of a local opinion of decency and propriety. Each city had its 'tone': each had evolved in the course of its history a code of conduct peculiar to itself."[7] The tone of the city was primarily maintained by the informal social controls of influence and appeals to obligation, and Barker remarks that these concentrated and intense controls "bore upon each individual with a weight which we can hardly imagine: where each knew his neighbour (and this is one of the conditions which Aristotle postulates for a proper city), and each was concerned about his neighbour's behaviour, it would be hard for any man to go against the tone and habit of his city's life."[8]

The importance of the polis is that it has served as a model of what an appreciative community should be throughout the centuries. The idea that a distinctive tone of life is desirable and can be maintained only through extensive and intensive face-to-face relations is still very widespread today, particularly among those who crave release from the impersonal and exploitative relations prevalent in mass society.[9] The notion that loyalty to a life-style and solidarity among individuals are ends in themselves hangs on persistently today in the face of manipulative conglomerate organizations, which use life-styles as tools for enhancing their profit, power and prestige. Through ethnic-revival movements, totalistic religious sects, and communal experiments, people attempt to return to the polis, usually without even realizing how deeply rooted in the Western tradition their aims are.[10] Yet the polis, which at its best was characterized by participation (of adult male citizens) in political decisions, moderate status differences (due to the presence of slaves), and relatively high morale, did bear upon each individual "with a weight which we can hardly imagine." This weight might not be felt as oppressive by the member of the polis because he carried it within him, but the same would not apply to the member of a mass society who has grown up in a situation characterized by widely different images of the human condition. While one escaped from the polis by being a traveler and a cosmopolitan, one escapes from the mass society by creating poor imitations of the polis.

THE NATION

The contemporary nation is almost the exact opposite of the polis. While the ancient Greeks generally took the polis for granted because they carried it with them in their very style of relating to others, the hallmark of contemporary nationalism is its strident competition with alternative appreciative communities, its use by special-interest groups as a means to gain dominance, and its pre-fabricated and manipulated character. Socrates submitted to the death sentence rather than be exiled from Athens, because he attributed his very character and the meaning of his existence to the tone of Athenian life.[11] Ardent nationalists today attempt to convince people that it is worthwhile for them to sacrifice their lives for the nation, particularly in times of war. Their appeals are freqently successful, perhaps because the nation is the most readily available focus for appreciation in mass society.

There have been a multitude of definitions of the term "nation." Some have speculated about whether common language, religion, political institutions, and technology are necessary to make a nation, or only some of these.[12] This debate is fruitless, because it assumes from the beginning that there is some standard conception of nation that might be reached after reasoned debate. All definitions of nation are weighted. Spokesmen for groups seeking greater power will often argue that a real nation must have its own territory controlled by its own government, while spokesmen for established groups will frequently argue that true nationalism is a spiritual and cultural rather than a political unity. In any case, however, the very existence of these debates indicates that the nation is a project rather than a thing.[13] It is a commitment to refer one's actions to a limited group of people, determined by some kind of historical unity and some vague conception of a common future. This unity is manufactured through the manipulation of such symbols as flags, celebrations (for example, Memorial Day, the Fourth of July, and Veteran's Day), and boasts about the superiority of the group. Nationalism is frequently used by privileged groups to bludgeon lower-standing groups into cooperation. After all, so the argument goes, we are all Americans, whether rich or poor, black or white. We are all in the same boat, so rocking it would hurt everybody. The end product of nationalism is the substitution of pride and shame for appreciation. One does not appreciate the landing of men on the moon because of its technological intricacy and grandeur, but because Americans were first on the moon and planted the Stars and Stripes there.

The nation as a unit of appreciation arose with industrialization, innovations in mass communications such as printing, and mass citizen armies. These related factors made it possible to govern large numbers of people centrally, to mobilize people to defend and invade large expanses of territory, and to bring together into common projects people who could never meet one another face to face. The national states and national groups formed in this process have provided a kind of substitute for the polis by giving people an identification with an appreciative whole (Mom, the flag, and apple pie) which would otherwise be lacking in mass society. However, despite patriotic hymns and exhortations, nationalism is no more natural than religion, and nations compete with many other possible appreciative communities for the allegiance of human beings in the contemporary world. Nationalism is an option, most favored by those social groups attempting to establish their differentiation from the working class (lower-middle-class groups) and those elite groups benefiting from restraints on free trade and the continuation of international tensions (the military, the arms industry and industries lacking competitive advantage in the international market).[14] The nation itself, as a community, exists in so far as human beings organize their activities around its maintenance and expansion.

COMPETITORS TO THE NATION

The nation, as one possible appreciative community among many, is challenged in the contemporary world by the civilization, the region, the racial-cultural whole, the class, the ethnic group and humanity in general. Some elite groups of administrators and scholars find their appreciative community in a set of cultural objects united by common ideas about the human condition, or a civilization.[15] Thus, some writers defend Western civilization, which is supposedly committed to individual rights, scientific reason, and technical progress, as a relevant appreciative community. Other elites advocate regionalism, such as the unification of Europe or a North Atlantic union, a league of Arab States, or a Pan-African community.[16] Still others, like Adolf Hitler, find the principle in a vague conception of folk and racial unity.[17] In none of these has the nation been significantly breached as a framework for appreciation. Rather, national governments have frequently used the notions of civilization, regionalism and racial-cultural unity for their own purposes (for example, Winston Churchill's idea of a unity of the English-speaking peoples, which would have given Great Britain a special relationship with the United States).[18] More significant than the preceding units are social classes and ethnic groups, which exist side by side with nations and are obvious challenges to

---

Figure 13.1. TYPES OF APPRECIATIVE COMMUNITIES

Polis:	Small community with distinctive life-style and moral code
Nation:	Large community kept together by some kind of historical unity and vague conception of the future
Civilization:	Set of cultural objects united by common ideas about the human condition
Region:	A geographical unit with well-defined historical boundaries
Racial-Cultural Whole:	A "people" with common cultural characteristics and some physical similarities
Ethnic Group:	Large community without political self-determination kept together by some kind of historical unity and vague conception of the future
Class:	An economic group with a distinctive life-style
Humanity:	All human beings, past, present, and future

With which appreciative community do you identify? Defend your identification. Try to think of other possible appreciative communities than those on the above list.

---

nationalist claims that the nation is the only satisfactory appreciative community in the contemporary world.[19]

For the founders of sociology, the favored appreciative community of sociologists has been humanity as a whole. Both Comte and Marx were humanists who saw no reason why appreciation should be arbitrarily bounded by the fact that the person lived in a particular place or grew up learning a particular language or set of habits. We concur with this judgment.

VOLUNTARY ASSOCIATIONS

The development of appreciative standards, as well as the various appreciative activities, largely take place within face-to-face groupings, such as the family, peer groups, and numerous voluntary associations. Voluntary associations are not peculiar to mass societies, but though they occur in historically documented societies as well as in the "primitive" societies studied by anthropologists, their vast proliferation and continual increase in numbers are distinctive characteristics in the contemporary situation.[20] The range of voluntary associations extends from scientific and educational groups, through religious, veteran's, athletic, hobby, trade, business and labor groups, to charitable and strictly social groups. Some examples of voluntary associations would be the American Sociological Association, the Veterans of Foreign Wars, the Knights of Columbus, the American Philatelic Society, the American Federation of Teachers, the March of Dimes, the local Chamber of Commerce, Parents Without Partners, the Freethinkers of America, MENSA, and La Leche League, to mention but a minute fraction. In 1967 it was estimated that there were 100,000 voluntary associations in the United States.[21] If voluntary associations are not restricted to nonprofit organizations, weight-watchers groups, nudist camps, and other profit-making organizations would swell the estimate considerably.

A number of ways of classifying voluntary associations have been developed,[22] but for this discussion it will suffice to place these associations on a continuum based on the degree to which their goals contain other aims than pure sociability. The ideal types of an association based purely on sociability and one based purely on performance of some external task do not exist in social life. Those organizations whose goals are the social interaction and enjoyment of members must usually devote at least some effort (money, time and the energies of members—usually officers) to their own continuation. Associations supposedly devoted to realizing some external end (for example, raising funds to support medical research for the cure of a given disease, disseminating information on a specific topic, or some other task) must allow to some extent for social participation as an end in itself for at least some members some of the time.[23] Where on the continuum a given voluntary association should be placed is a matter for observation—the decision is made after examining the particular organization. When one studies charitable associations, for example, one finds a wide variation in the percentage of contributed funds reaching the intended destination. Given the high overhead of charity balls, one questions their avowed purpose and might place the association sponsoring them far from the task end of the continuum.

Figure 13.2. TYPES OF VOLUNTARY ASSOCIATIONS

Task-oriented	*Sociability-oriented*
Political (Democratic party)	Fraternal Organizations (e.g., Elks), Women's clubs, college fraternities, and sororities
Economic (National Association of Manufacturers)	
Educational (American Sociological Association)	
Appreciative (Sierra Club)	

Task-oriented associations may become sociability oriented and vice versa.

The various voluntary associations are settings for appreciative activities (for example, bridge and square-dancing clubs) and/or set standards for appreciation (The Women's Christian Temperance Union decries the use of alcohol, the Sierra Club favors the preservation of wilderness areas, and the American League to Abolish Capital Punishment advocates standards regarding the treatment of prisoners). For the most part, specific appreciative standards are an integral part of the association, and membership participation does little to alter them. As difficult as it is to set up a voluntary association, it is often easier to initiate a new one than to change the standards of an existing organization. The numerous Protestant sects, the Veterans Against the War in Vietnam, the many women's liberation groups discussed in chapter 11, and the splinter groups of various scientific societies illustrate this point. In effect, joining an association involves adopting the whole package of standards. Due to the tendency of associations to remain controlled by small elites, one's choice among standards is effectively confined to deciding upon which organizations to join.[24] Further, the appreciative standards of any given voluntary association usually cover only a narrow range of human experience, leaving the individual to piece together the fragments of his appreciative life into a consistent whole. This allows for a certain freedom, but it is a highly personal freedom, which does not spill over into continuing social dialogue about how the whole of human activity should be organized.

Aside from the severe limitation of preventing people from participating in the development of their standards of appreciation, even the freedom to choose between organizations is often absent. Some voluntary associations, through governments granting them licensing power, businesses recognizing them as bargaining agents, or universities recognizing them as validators of status, tend to remove decisions about whether to join them from the sphere of voluntary choice. Physicians who do not join the American Medical Association may pay higher malpractice-insurance rates, those who are not members of a union may find it impossible to obtain work in a given occupation, and so forth.[25]

Just as various appreciative activities are socially differentiated, so membership in voluntary associations shows social differentiation. To the extent that such differentiation occurs, and is made explicit, the given association moves away from the task-oriented side of the continuum, because membership is no longer based first and foremost on ability to contribute to the fulfillment of a task. Thus, one would expect the associations that are closer to the sociability end of the continuum to show the greatest degree of differentiation. This seems to be the case, since there are more distinctions on the basis of sex, religion, race and social class among such "social clubs" as fraternal orders (the Loyal Order of Moose) and descent groups (Daughters of the American Revolution) than among scientific societies or conservation groups.

Different voluntary associations are concerned with one or more of the various social processes: coordination (the Democratic party), creation (the American Society of Composers, Authors and Publishers), appreciation (The Benevolent and Protective Order of Elks) and communication (American Sociological Association). Concentrating on those defined as appreciative in scope, the impulse to join is not always to participate in a given appreciative activity. Such associations are frequently used to confirm status (there are status hierarchies of fraternities on every campus that permits their existence), to serve as excuses for social interaction and to gain business opportunities (this motive is important for many who join fraternal organizations and veteran's groups). In some cases the voluntary associations replace the neighborhood as a dominant social setting. Yet another reason motivating membership in voluntary associations is to give legitimacy to an activity. For example, sociologists have recently analyzed mate-swapping clubs, showing that members reinforce one another's commitment to this activity.[26]

Particularly important in mass society is the use of voluntary associations for affirming and attaining status. In a mass society, where an individual is not known personally by most others, cues to identity are often sought by others and purposefully presented by the individual.[27] Just as the brand of automobile may reveal (though most unreliably) one's social status, association membership, and the overt indicators of it (emblematic rings, lapel pins, tie clasps, jackets, and other clothing) give others an idea of one's social identity. One may hazard a guess that the more that members display their affiliation, the more likely it is that they joined for reasons of status rather than for reasons of appreciation. Social status is even related to whether or not a person is a member of any associations: the higher one's status (education, income, occupational status, or race, for instance) the more likely it is that one is a member of one or more associations.[28] For example, of those with less than nine years of schooling, 33 percent are members of associations; of those who have completed high school, 46 percent are members, and of those who have had at least four years of college, 64 percent are members.[29]

Despite differential membership rates based on status, there has been an increase in overall associational membership over time. The same type of appreciative activity that formerly took place within a circle of friends (bowling, card playing, dancing, for example) is now increasingly taking place within a more formal circle of clubs with charters, dues and officers. This trend is also present among adolescents, where peer groups are often formally organized into fraternities, sororities, clubs, and gangs. Peer groups can be seen as the informal counterparts of those voluntary associations located at the extreme sociability end of the continuum. They are relatively small face-to-face groups, homogeneous in most status categories, especially age, race, and social class. Although most prevalent among the school aged, peer groups may be found at any age level. More and more in mass society, peer groups are located within organizations, such as factories, housing developments, and schools, rather than within the community at large. The retired old cronies who once sat and gossiped outside the courthouse now carry on their conversations within an old-age home.

Unlike many voluntary associations, the range of activity in the peer group is often broad and its standards of appreciation frequently extensive. Thus, a more well-integrated set of standards is usually available from the peer group, which is one reason why it has more influence over many individuals than the various associations. The few studies that have been done on peer groups [30] have indicated that not only are they stratified with respect to the larger society's status levels, but that the individuals composing them have differential status and power positions vis-à-vis one another. In the classic study of a lower-class-youth peer group, using the method of participant observation, William F. Whyte described a status hierarchy that was even reflected in the bowling scores.[31] The appreciative standards of a peer group are not necessarily those of established institutions. What one group may deem well dressed would be a joke in *Vogue* or *Seventeen* magazine. Peer groups also set standards for sexual conduct and other so-called moral issues, such as stealing, fighting, and drug use. Where the standards for these activities (entertainments) differ greatly from established views, status hierarchies develop where those who come closest to the group's standards are accorded the highest status.

EXERCISE

What are the appreciative standards of some of the peer groups to which you belong? How does one attain status in these peer groups? Do you agree with the standards? Do you conform to the standards? What are your reasons for agreement or disagreement, conformity or nonconformity?

For youth peer groups, and to a lesser extent for adult peer groups, there is little choice about membership. Propinquity, religion, race, and social class combine to allow for few choices among peer groups that any given person may elect to join. In his study of a midwestern high school, August Hollingshead found that the lines of social class were very rarely crossed in peer-group memberships (or in dating).[32]

EXERCISE

Devise another classification of voluntary organizations than the one presented in this book. Then take an inventory of the voluntary associations to which you belong and to which you might want to belong. Categorize them according to both classification schemes. Which types of voluntary associations are you involved in? Can you defend your choices in terms of your image of the human condition? Is your classification scheme more precise than ours? Does it alert you to features of voluntary associations which we missed?

THE FAMILY

Although there is some degree of choice about participating in an appreciative group, such as a voluntary association or peer group, a child has no choice about which family he will be born into, or even whether he will be born at all. One cannot complain too much about this restriction on freedom, because the newborn have no standards by which to judge whether or not it is worthwhile to be alive at a given time and place. In noncommunal societies the child first learns standards and techniques of appreciation in the family. This process of learning is part of the humanization, or what some sociologists call the socialization of the infant. As the child interacts with others—in school, with peers, through the media, or perhaps in church—some parental standards are challenged, others are reinforced, and new activities and standards are revealed. To the chagrin of many parents, the first standards (those of the parents) do not always prevail.[33] Some social scientists have attempted to explain this by stating that people behave in those ways for which they are rewarded, while other social scientists have claimed that people choose a set of standards that is relatively consistent.[34] Both these notions seem inadequate because they leave out the factor of voluntary choice and ignore, respectively, the fact that human beings must define what they consider to be rewards, and the evidence that people are capable of holding inconsistent standards. Parental standards of appreciation are not only eroded by contact with other groups, or through the reasoning ability of the child independent of others, but also can be weakened by the parents proclaiming one standard but acting according to another. Parents may tell a child that material possessions are unimportant yet ply him with gifts at Christmas and on birthdays, and bicker among themselves over how to keep up with the Jones's. Richard Flacks accounts for the radicalism of some students in the 1960s by claiming that these students were merely adhereing to what their liberal parents said but did not do.[35]

Although the contemporary family is the setting for much appreciative activity, the extent of such appreciation has been decreasing. Playing on fears of the disintegrating family, bowling alleys advertise: "The family that plays together stays together." Nonetheless, most bowling is not done in family groups, nor do families participate in most sports together. Viewing television is a popular family activity, but because many time slots have shows geared exclusively to one or another family member (Saturday morning cartoons for the children, Sunday afternoon sports for the men, and afternoon soap operas for the women) only a small portion of the time (prime time) can be shared by the family as a whole. The trend toward personal-size television receivers for different members of the family and the general passivity of television viewing raise questions about whether watching television is a family or a personal form of entertainment. Sex is an entertainment for the married pair, but is absolutely taboo among others in the family. Even church attendance is no longer a family affair, since different programs are frequently developed for different family members.

Although the child has no choice of family, in the United States the man or woman considering marriage does have a choice of whom to marry. The person also has a choice as to whether or not to marry at all, although the vast majority of people have increasingly chosen marriage at least once. Of those over eighteen years old, only 18.3 percent of the men and 13.5 percent of the women have never been married.[36] The American myth of mate selection, kept alive by Hollywood, is that any man and woman can fall in love and get married. Except for some ethnic pockets, marriages are not arranged by parents or a marriage broker as is and was the case elsewhere. Research indicates, however, that choice of marriage partners is highly constrained by religion, age, race, ethnic origin, and social class.[37] A prime consideration in the myth of marriage is that the couple love one another. During the Middle Ages the chivalrous knight would dread being married to the one he loved. Of course, resolving the debate about whether romantic love is a natural part of the human condition or is culturally developed and transmitted depends in part on how "love" is defined.[38] Rather than enter the debate here, suffice it to say that many agents within American society do not leave it up to human nature. As with the mythical ideal and idyl of motherhood, romantic love is extolled in movies, books, plays, songs, children's stories, television, magazine fiction, and in the newspapers. "The child . . . is told that he or she will grow up to fall in love with someone, and early attempts are made to pair the child with children of the opposite sex." Love as a prelude and basis for marriage is a notion developed in mass society. Marriage analysts have suggested "that in a rootless society, with few common bases for companionship, romantic love holds a couple together long enough to allow them to begin marriage."[39] Then the glories of motherhood (for the woman) and absorption in career (for the man) take over. The nuclear family form (husband, wife, and minor children living together with no other relatives) is, of course, adapted to high social mobility and does create bonds of dependence between the family members. There may, however, be a tension between romantic love and parental love, which heightens the tendency toward quick disappearance of the former as the married couple encounters real life.

Although the nuclear family is seen as the standard (and best) form by most Americans, in recent years alternative forms have been devised, mainly by younger people. Married couples have purposely remained childless, couples have publicly acknowledged living together without being legally married, and various types of communal living experiments have been tried. Communes have been attempted in both rural and urban settings. This form consists of a number of people who are neither related by blood nor marriage contract, or a number of married couples and their offspring, living together in one household.[40] Aside from the increased efficiency which this form allows (living expenses are cut, time is cut for food preparation, child care, and the like) it also creates an appreciative community larger than the nuclear family. The shared appreciative standards differ from one commune to the next, from drug taking or organic-food cults to bringing up children without intensely strong ties to one or two adults, and giving women the opportunity to pursue careers outside the home while still bringing up their children in a family setting. Whether these and other forms will survive as viable alternatives from which people may choose cannot yet be determined.

EXERCISE

What proportion of the families you know are complete nuclear families? Do the people in other types of families seem to suffer because they are not members of nuclear families?

Child rearing is one of the major appreciative activities of, and justifications for, the family. When the relatives of the parents lived within the household, or near by, the new mother raised her child under their guidance. The "neolocal" residence pattern of the nuclear family in the United States (where the married couple does not live near either set of relatives), the tendency to have few children closely spaced (giving children little experience in raising younger siblings), and the high value placed upon science help account for the enormous popularity of "professional" authorities on child rearing. Dr. Benjamin Spock's *The Common Sense Book of Baby and Child Care* alone sold over nine million copies from 1945 until 1959.[41] The growing interest in such appreciative activities as natural childbirth and breast feeding since the 1960s has given rise to a spate of books, newspaper articles, and voluntary associations, which also replace the personal advice of relatives. Paralleling the nature fantasies of extreme environmentalists, these movements claim that anaesthesia and bottle feeding are somehow less natural than experiencing all the pains of birth and relying on mother's milk for nutrition. In order to be natural, however, devotees of these movements attend classes, publish propaganda, watch movies, and negotiate with hospitals.

These movements correspond with the prevalent view of the original nature of children. The various editions of the U.S. Children's Bureau pamphlet, "Infant Care," echo these changing views on the nature of the child: In the early part of the twentieth century the infant was viewed as sinful and passionate, and strict discipline was deemed necessary to counteract evil and natural inclinations. This view was succeeded by one in which the child was thought to be originally innocent and had to be protected from the wickedness of the world.[42] The current view of children, consonant with the back-to-nature movements, sees the child's inclinations as natural, creative, and therefore good, and prescribes encouragement of those inclinations with the exception of gentle modification in areas like bladder control.

The pamphlets and other forms of child-care advice are aimed at women because it is the woman who is viewed as being responsible for the daily nurture of the child. The expectation was strongly held in the past, and it is still very prevalent despite about three of every ten married women with children under six years of age being in the labor force.[43] In the traditional division of labor ". . . the husband is head of his family, its main economic support, and its representative in the larger community. Women, consigned to domesticity, are mothers and homemakers."[44] Shows depicting families on television strictly adhere to this configuration, while a large proportion of actual families depart from it. Men often help with the more interesting domestic duties of child care, shopping, and cooking, and less often with cleaning. In some cases they do not merely help their wives, but assume total responsibility for the given activity. Couples are experimenting with many departures from the traditional standard; for example, the wife may pursue a career and the husband take charge of the children and house, or each partner may share the same career and the household duties. People are trying out new family arrangements, some disregarding the nuclear-family form, and others attempting to experiment within it. When a couple does marry today, its members cannot fall back upon the traditional role expectations of husband and wife with full assurance that they will be taken for granted. It is likely that they will have to work out a suitable pattern together, partially creating new alternatives and partially choosing from old ones.

EXERCISE

Analyze the standards for child rearing in one or more books on the subject. What image of the child underlies the viewpoint of the manual? What is the author's ideal of maturity? Do you agree with the author's values? If not, what is your image of the child and your ideal of maturity? Can you defend your values?

There are several interconnected reasons to account for why the familial role expectations are losing their legitimacy. Either directly or indirectly, mass society has had and continues to have an impact on the family. Since the various factors are interrelated rather than being arranged in a causal sequence, it is of little importance which one is discussed first. The industrial economy affects families through its demands for geographical mobility, particularly for those in upper status occupations. To the extent that the economy provides meaningless and boring jobs, men need to rationalize their work and frequently use their families as excuses. The emphasis placed on individuality in the economic system, including the capitalist ethic, tends to put any collectivity, such as the family, in second place to the success drive. The economy is partially responsible for various demographic trends, such as the increase in life expectancy (through more effective medical and sanitary practices) and the declining birth rate (more efficient contraceptive devices, as well as subtle influences affecting a couple's desire for a larger family, such as smaller houses, increasing costs of raising each child, economic recessions, and opportunities for women to work outside their homes). These trends, coupled with others such as the decrease in the age at which people marry and have children, present a picture in which a woman has had her last child in her mid-twenties and has, on the average, almost a half century more to live. After all her children have left home, she still has about twenty-five years in which she is no longer needed to play the role of mother. Thus, married couples hardly know one another before they have children (an estimated 25 percent of women are already pregnant at the time of marriage[45]) and then in their mid-forties find themselves alone with one another. The movement for women's equality, partially influenced by the black civil rights movement, by economic developments, and by the demographic changes noted above, also has effect on role expectations within the family. Members of the women's movement have raised serious questions about why men's activities are considered as more important than women's, and, even more fundamentally, about why activities have to be allocated on the basis of sex at all. The effect of this questioning is shown, perhaps, even more by the defensiveness of those attempting to uphold the old definitions than by the many who agree in whole or part with proposals for change.

In examining the influences that to some extent are changing the family, one should not fall into the trap of believing that at some point in time the family existed in perfect harmony with other social institutions and that everyone at some time agreed on role expectations and acted accordingly. The family has always been in a state of flux, like all other social institutions, sometimes changing faster than at other times. However, because many have endowed the family with a sacred quality and have believed that it is the lynchpin for the total civilization, for the church, for the economy, or for the national state, family role changes or supposed evidence of the decay of the family evoke visions of horror. Increases in the divorce rate, from about one divorce in twenty marriages at the turn of the twentieth century to about one in every three marriages today,[46] is taken as prima facie evidence that the family is in trouble. Yet how many unhappy families were there when the rates were lower? Further, people tend to remarry rapidly after divorce. Divorce can be understood in terms of people failing to reach a consensus on appreciative standards and activities, and the fact that they will try to find such a consensus in another marriage only seems to indicate the tenacity of the institution.

THE CONTEXT OF APPRECIATION

While people refer their activities to groups of appreciators, or communities, these communities do not exhaust the social context in which appreciation occurs. Communities are embedded in naturalcultural environments, which both shape them and are shaped by them. An understanding of what the term "naturalcultural environment" means can be grasped by considering what is meant by the term "living in the country." When a person is in the country he is certainly not confronted by nature in the raw. Rather, one sees cultivated fields, farm machinery, some tracts of undeveloped land, men wearing overalls, small courthouses and churches, barns, grain elevators, clearer sky than one sees in a city, and a host of other sights peculiar to the countryside. The total environment has a certain quality that forms an ever-present context for the appreciation of any single object composing it. One knows that one is in the country by neither natural nor cultural signs exclusively, but by a fusion of nature and culture into a single environment. From this viewpoint, there is nothing more "natural" to human beings about the countryside than there is about the city. Each simply represents a different combination of the elements of human experience into a context of life. The rats in a city tenement are just as alive as the field mice scurrying across a country road.

THE MEGALOPOLIS

Mass societies have developed a distinctive context for appreciation—the megalopolis. The megalopolis has been defined as a "continuous band of urban and suburban development, sometimes stretching for hundreds of miles."[47] Many readers of this book are probably familiar with the megalopolis because they either live in one currently or have lived in one in the past. The primary examples of the megalopolis in the United States are Bo-Wash (the Atlantic seaboard strip extending from Boston to Washington, D.C. which in 1960 contained approximately one-fifth of the total population of the United States), San-San (the Pacific seaboard strip extending from San Francisco to San Diego) and Chi-Pitts (the Great Lakes region extending from Chicago to Pittsburgh). Jean Gottmann, who has studied the megalopolis extensively, described Bo-Wash as a context for appreciation: "As one follows the main highways between Boston and Washington, D.C., one hardly loses sight of built-up areas, tightly woven residential communities, or powerful concentrations of manufacturing plants. Flying this same route one discovers, on the other hand, that behind the ribbons of densely occupied land along the principal arteries of traffic, and in between the clusters of suburbs around the old urban centers, there still remain large areas covered with woods and brush alternating with some carefully cultivated patches of farmland. These green spaces, however, when inspected at closer range, appear stuffed with a loose but immense scattering of buildings, some of them residential but some of industrial character."[48]

What is a megalopolis like as a context for appreciation? It is, in the first place, almost entirely different from the context of the city-state that was associated with the ancient Greek polis. The megalopolis is a context congruent with the contemporary nation and its imposed unity. While the Athenian or Spartan could comprehend through all of his senses the unity of his naturalcultural environment, the inhabitant of Chi-Pitts is hard-pressed to find any principle of integrity within his environment. Nobody can walk around Chi-Pitts in a single day, comfortable in the familiarity of the sights, sounds, and smells. Whatever unity Chi-Pitts has is organizationally manufactured by business and governmental conglomerates. One can perhaps take comfort in the fact that one can purchase the same gasoline in Cleveland as in Detroit or sleep in a motel run by the same chain in either city. One can be assured that the roadside burger stand will dispense nearly the same product in either city, and that the service will be pretty much the same too. Also, the post offices will generally appear the same and will sell the same stamps. Such organizationally packaged unity, often deplored by critics who deem contemporary life artificial and lacking spontaneity, is the closest equivalent that people have today to the at-homeness felt by the ancient Greek in his city-state.

Gottmann remarked that "megalopolis stands indeed at the threshold of a new way of life." This new way of life is characterized by several features that go along with aspects of mass society mentioned in previous chapters. The hallmark of the megalopolis is its heterogeneity and fragmentation. Until the end of World War II, the contexts of appreciation in modern societies were conceived of in terms of the distinction between rural and urban forms of life. Each of these forms of life was viewed as relatively homogeneous. Often the distinction was frozen into "ideal types," such as the dichotomy between folk and urban societies.[49] The model of the completely rural, or folk, society has been defined by Gist and Fava: "The communities most different from cities are folk societies—small, isolated, nonliterate, and self-sufficient—for example, tribal and village societies. In such societies, technology is simple, there is little specialization, almost all contacts are primary, and the family is paramount. These social conditions, so very different from the city and seemingly more integrated, were supposed to be especially suited to the adjustment of personality."[50]

The very opposite of the folk society was the urban society. Georg Simmel, who provided a classic description of the urban context of appreciation, described the city as a place where money provided the basis for most social relations, the intellect rather than the emotions was the most fully developed aspect of mental life, there was extensive division of labor, human relations were fragmentary, and technology was highly developed.[51] In the urban society, supposedly, individualism of all kinds held sway over traditional social bonds—for example, familial ties. Of course, the folk and urban images are ideal types that have never been fully operative anywhere in the world.

The folk society frequently functioned as a romantic dream against which the harshness of urban life was compared.[52] The urban-society image was a more negative projection that detailed frustrations associated with city living. Today, neither of them is adequate for describing the megalopolis, which does not display the homogeneity characteristic of either image. Rather, as Gottmann noted, it is a crazy-quilt of town and country, provincialism and universalism, industry and agriculture, slum and suburb, and nearly any other pair of opposites that can be used to describe mass society. There are pockets of extreme wealth and luxury (exclusive suburbs) and of grinding poverty (the various ghettos). In between these extremes there are suburbs of all varieties, as well as different kinds of neighborhoods. Part of the fragmentary character of the megalopolis is due to the ability of people who live within it to detach their small island of existence from the context in which it is embedded. In a technical sense, all who live within the megalopolis are interdependent. The potato farmer on Suffolk County, Long Island, outside New York City, depends on the city for his livelihood, while the black day laborer living in New York's Harlem depends upon the potato farmer for his sustenance. However, this fact of interdependence in the economic order does not in any way necessitate an active recognition of it in the appreciative order. In fact, in many cases the fragmentation of the megalopolis is deliberate. For example, wealthy suburbs jealously preserve their own governments so that they will be able to zone out unwanted activities and groups. Middle-class neighborhoods inside cities are jealously guarded by their inhabitants, who may appear to be more racist than the wealthy suburbanites merely because they do not have control over zoning. Mammoth corporations erect industrial parks in towns that welcome the tax monies and give the corporations free rein in land-use planning in return.

The megalopolis, like any context of appreciation, reveals in concrete terms the values guiding human activity. When one steps outside his little enclave in the megalopolis, he becomes aware that it makes substantial the values of wealth, power, and prestige. Land-use in the contemporary American megalopolis is determined by which groups have the wealth and power to appropriate the land. Farm land is eaten up by sprawling industrial parks and spacious suburbs, not because of any inexorable destiny beyond human control, but because corporations and upper-middle-class families have the money to buy the land and use it the way they wish. Blacks are confined to decaying areas of older cities, not by any accident of fate, but because other groups have the wherewithal to keep them there. Given the fact that the present economy is characterized neither by pure nor perfect competition, there is no reason to assume that current land-use patterns exhibit any kind of "rationality" whatsoever.

Viewing the megalopolis as the context for appreciation in mass society commits one to viewing the interrelations between the various life-styles contained within it. Alternative images of the context of appreciation leave out many of these interrelations. For example, some groups, such as the Urban Coalition, attempt to focus on the so-called problems of the cities. They point to the flight of the middle classes to the suburbs (depriving the cities of a tax base), the deteriorating housing, the loss of industry, the decline of population, the rising proportion of blacks, the tidal flow of commuters who earn their living in the city and then leave its problems behind when they return to the bedroom suburbs in the evening, and the skyrocketing rates of crime and narcotics use. This, however, is a strictly urban viewpoint tailored as propaganda for city administrators and their constituents. It is used to call for a redistribution of resources from the suburbs to the cities, rather than for a major change in the underlying process of allocating resources.

Thus, those who focus on the city concoct plans to draw the middle classes back through urban-renewal projects and to keep business from moving through more efficient transportation schemes and job-training programs. They hold constant the general system of interest-group competition in which wealth, power, and prestige determine who gets what. What they are concerned with is getting a greater share of the wealth through building up and capitalizing on their power and any favorable image that they might create. Of course, the image of the megalopolis has its own bias, which tends in the direction of much more comprehensive proposals for change. For example, one who views the megalopolis as a whole, focusing on its land-use, might advocate that low- and middle-income housing projects be imposed upon wealthy suburbs, or that suburban families be forced to exchange high-school-age children with poor urban families for two years of high school. We do not necessarily advocate such schemes, which probably seem barbaric, but only mention them to show that run-of-the-mill "solutions" to the problems of the cities do not exhaust all the alternatives.

Problems of the Megalopolis   It is, of course, convenient for those who live outside the older cities to think in terms of the problems of the cities. This allows them to detach themselves from the conditions inside the cities and, therefore, not to see themselves as integral parts of those conditions. Through such detachment, the suburbanite is enabled to look at the inhabitants of the cities in the same way that he might view a group of Australian aborigines. He may take either of two attitudes toward them. If he adopts a less "enlightened" attitude, he will view them as inferior and shiftless beings who deserve to live in dilapidated housing because if they had only worked hard enough they would have been able to make it out to the suburbs. The city, thus, is interpreted as a dumping ground for defective human beings. If the suburbanite adopts a more "enlightened" attitude toward the city dwellers, particularly the poor and black, he will support increased aid to the cities and perhaps even engage in projects to help save the cities. For example, middle-class students frequently feel a calling to teach in ghetto schools or become social workers in poverty-stricken areas. In their missionary zeal they lose sight of the close relations between the city and the suburbs from which they come. For them, the city is less a dumping ground than an arena in which they can demonstrate their goodwill toward others. Yet they would probably be far more effective in helping their fellow human beings if they set themselves to the task of abolishing the distinction between the city and the other islands of the megalopolis. The problem is that nobody has as yet devised a way in which this might be done.

The distortions involved in separating the city from the rest of the megalopolis can be illustrated strikingly by several statistics. The 1970 census revealed that for the first time, "the population in America's suburbs (37 percent) is greater than that in either the central cities (31 percent) or the nonmetropolitan parts of the nation."[53] Further, since World War II many of the older cities have actually been declining in population. For example, between 1950 and 1960 New York City lost

1.4 percent in population while the areas outside it gained 75 percent. Similarly, in the same period Chicago declined 1.9 percent in population while the surrounding areas gained 71.5 percent. While the city of Los Angeles registered a gain of 27.1 percent in population, the surrounding areas registered an 82.6 percent gain.[54] In the context of the megalopolis, these figures mean that the cities themselves are no longer the focal points for appreciative activity, at least in American life. They are, in a sense, satellites of the suburbs rather than the other way around. However, even this image is not wholly accurate, because the megalopolis is most like a field displaying the entire range of values in mass society.

Within the megalopolis, there is a great diversity of context, for appreciation. In a sense, it is a kind of neutral umbrella under which widely different types of activities can be performed so long as there is the wealth, power and prestige to make space and time for them. However, despite its variety, several distinctive contexts for appreciation have appeared within the megalopolis. These contexts, the suburb, the neighborhood, and the ghetto slum, will now be discussed in greater detail.

Figure 13.3. CONTEXTS OF APPRECIATION

Village Society	Urban Society	Megalopolis
Small	Large	Large
Nonliterate	High literacy	High literacy
Self-sufficient	Dependent	Dependent
Face-to-face relations	Impersonal relations	Fragmented relations
Communalism	Individualism	Fluctuating group identifications
Dominance of emotions	Dominance of intellect	Dominance of will
Homogeneity of context	Homogeneity of context	Heterogeneity of context
Small Group	Bureaucracy	Conglomerate

THE SUBURB

Suburbs have been traditionally defined by sociologists in terms of cities. Perhaps the most common definition of the suburbs has been that part of a metropolitan area (a Standard Metropolitan Statistical Area as defined by the U.S. Bureau of the Census) outside the central city. The Standard Metropolitan Statistical Area is composed of a county containing a central city of at least 50,000 inhabitants and, under certain circumstances, adjacent counties. Gist and Fava note how the concept of an SMSA is biased toward the view that the city is the typical context of contemporary appreciation: "The Standard Metropolitan Statistical Area concept is designed to delineate the limits of regular daily influence of large cities beyond physically urban territory."[55] The term suburb itself literally means "under a town." Yet, when they are combined together, the suburbs of an SMSA frequently contain more people than the central city. For example, the 1970 census showed the Chicago SMSA containing 6,978,947 people while the city of Chicago itself contained less than half that number (3,369,359).[56] Further, what is one to make of the SMSA The Bureau of the Census calls "Anaheim-Santa Ana-Garden Grove, California" or the one it calls "San Bernadino-Riverside-Ontario, California?" Each of these contains more than one million inhabitants, but where is the central city? In brief a large proportion of the middle classes has become so suburbanized that the suburbs can no longer be defined as offshoots of the city, but must instead be taken as distinctive settings for appreciation on their own.

The conventional wisdom about suburbs has interpreted them as products of a desire to return to something like the polis. For example, Robert Wood has argued: "Suburbia, defined as an ideology, a faith in communities of limited size and a belief in the conditions of intimacy, is quite real. The dominance of the old values explains more about the people and politics of the suburbs than any other interpretation."[57] Perhaps this faith, along with other factors (such as the desire to escape from black migrants to the cities), motivated people to make the trek from the cities to the suburbs in the years following World War II. However, for those who have lived in the suburbs, and especially for those who have grown up in them as they burgeoned and began to appear indistinguishable from parts of cities, this faith merely projected a myth. Limited size has little meaning when there is no space at all between one village or town and the next, and when a modest unincorporated village (West Hempstead, New York, where we both grew up) has 20,375 people. Consider with regard to the value of intimacy: there is very little difference between a white on the North Side of Chicago fearing to walk on the black South Side and a white in West Hempstead avoiding the streets of black South Hempstead so close by. If our parents expected a house in the country, they certainly did not get it, and by the time we began to reason about such things the continuity of the megalopolis was becoming clear.

Bennett Berger has noted how the suburb has been used as a compact symbol for many different ideologists. He has noted four different myths.[58] First, there is the myth that "suburbia represents the fulfillment of the American middle-class dream; it is identified with the continued possibility of upward mobility, with expanding opportunities in middle-class occupations, with rising standards of living and real incomes, and the gadgeted good life as it is represented in the full-color ads in the mass-circulation magazines." The second myth is that suburbia is simply artificial and standardized "ticky-tacky," and that it simply represents a more affluent kind of blight than the poor experience in their slums. The third myth conceives of suburbia as a microcosm of all the major trends in contemporary social life, culminating in the desire to maintain or improve social status. Finally, some critics in the Marxian tradition use "the terms 'suburb' and 'suburban' for the now embarrassingly obsolete term 'bourgeois' as a packaged rebuke to the whole tenor of American life."

None of these myths seems to capture what has appeared, at least to us, to be the focus of the quality of life in the suburbs—the denial of responsibility for what goes on in the rest of the megalopolis, the lack of recognition of the interdependence of the various parts of the megalopolis, and, to turn these others around, the desire for secure and relatively comfortable islands of appreciation in an otherwise threatening environment. Thus the suburbs have been the recipients of the mass entertainments described in the preceding chapter, the centers for increasing church membership, and the places where the hierarchy of occupational prestige is made most evident through the residential separation of status groups. A drive from the North Shore luxurious white suburb of Wilmette, Illinois, to the impoverished Southside black suburb of Robbins, Illinois, will convince one that the suburbs are neither the American dream come true nor the American nightmare of ticky-tacky incarnate.

Such a drive will also convince one that the suburbs are not exclusively the homes of organization men anxious about status nor of capitalist exploiters. Rather, the suburbs reveal the entire range of variety in the megalopolis, and show concretely the principles that guide the allocation of resources in mass societies. You can see this for yourself if you take a drive some time through the suburbs of any large SMSA. Every SMSA has its Wilmette and its Robbins, and most of the variations in between. As a suggestion, if you take such a field trip, imagine what it would be like to live in each suburb. This may allow you to relativize your situation and appreciate the variety of contexts in the megalopolis.

EXERCISE

Drive through a megalopolis, noting the changes between contexts of appreciation. Use a good road map as you travel, and mark down the class composition, as well as racial-ethnic composition, of the various suburbs and neighborhoods. Also note down areas of agricultural, industrial, commercial, and retail activity, as well as "total institutions" such as mental hospitals and prisons.

EXERCISE

Have you ever lived in a megalopolis? If so, what kind of context did you live in? What kinds of areas bordered your neighborhood? What were the most important problems in the community, who was concerned about them, and what means were used to solve them?

THE NEIGHBORHOOD

During the 1950s the suburbs were extensively analyzed by sociologists and social critics and were highlighted as emerging contexts of appreciation. During the 1960s, with the increasing intensity of racial conflicts, the emergence of city-dwelling whites as a vocal and dissatisfied political constituency, and the efforts to make the city into a focus for a complex of interest groups, the city neighborhood has become an increasingly prevalent topic for discussion. There is, of course, a romantic myth of the urban neighborhood, which emphasizes its exotic charm. A staple of pro-city propaganda is the idea that the metropolis is a network of ethnic islands whose inhabitants spend their time operating restaurants that serve delicious and off-beat food and whose streets take on the charm of old Warsaw, Naples, San Juan, Dublin, Shanghai, or any number of other places. The people in these neighborhoods supposedly have not been homogenized into the American mainstream and jealously retain enough of their old ways to be quaint but not so many that they lose their status as good Americans. It is said to be even more fun to visit these neighborhoods than to visit Indian reservations.

Pushing behind this myth, one discovers the neighborhood has become a topic of interest since the 1960s because many whites never made it to the suburbs after World War II because they did not have enough money, wanted to stay close to their jobs, did not want to leave friends or relatives, or simply enjoyed the city as a center of appreciation. As poor black migrants began to fill the cities and push out of their original residential areas, these whites became concerned with maintaining the integrity of "their" neighborhoods. This usually resulted in attempts to keep blacks from purchasing houses or renting apartments in the neighborhoods, to keep blacks from attending schools in the neighborhoods, and to make sure that the white neighborhoods got the lion's share of services from the city (for example, street paving, frequent garbage collection, ample police and fire protection, bus routes, hospitals, and a host of other benefits).

With the emergence of a black movement for equality, leading to black political pressures on city, state and national agencies, the stage was set for bitter conflicts in all areas of existence. The blacks demanded equality in the distribution of city services, while the whites fought to maintain their favored position. The battles continue unabated, and the front-line dispatches can be read daily in any city newspaper. The important thing to note about these conflicts is that their intensity stems from the fact that the whites in city neighborhoods do not have the same control over their destinies as the whites in middle-class or affluent suburbs. They are not wealthy enough to price blacks out of the market and do not control their local governments as fully as the suburbanites. Thus, they cannot afford the luxury of pretending to be in favor of equal rights while they sit comfortably in an exclusive suburb. One tactic they can use to defend their meager privileges is to romanticize their neighborhood and make it serve as a rallying point for political action and social pressures.

A field trip through the suburbs can be combined with one through the city. In driving through any large city, one will note nearly as much diversity in the neighborhoods as one would note in the various suburbs. The same values of wealth, power, and prestige guide allocation of resources in the city, and one can run the gamut between gold coast and slum in half an hour or less.[59] From this perspective, one will observe that there is a continuity between city and suburbs. Some areas of the central city are less crowded and newer than some suburbs. Some areas of the city are far more free of crime and safer in almost every respect than some suburbs. Simply crossing the boundary line of a local government does not rupture the continuity of the megalopolis as a context for appreciation. Middle-class neighborhoods are like middle-class suburbs, working-class neighborhoods are like working-class suburbs, and city slums are like suburban slums. This conclusion helps make some sense out of growing movements for neighborhood control of services within the cities. Groups, such as the blacks, which have been given inferior services to other groups, are likely candidates for urging local control. They cannot control the city government, so they hope to get a better deal for themselves by moves toward decentralization of schools, police protection, and other such services. Most often such decentralization is a sham, and effective control remains lodged in city hall. However, a tenth of a loaf is sometimes better than none. On the other hand, those groups that have a secure foothold in the city administration have no incentive to urge local control or decentralization. They are getting the lion's share already. They tend to see, though, the virtues of local control and neighborhood services (such as the legendary neighborhood school) as soon as the central administration no longer upholds their privileges. This is at the center of current debates over cross-town busing of school children for the purposes of racial integration.

THE GHETTO

During the 1960s the term ghetto became popular as a label for a third important context for appreciation within the general context of the megalopolis. In the ninth chapter we discussed the life-style of the poor blacks as a vicious circle in which inferior housing, poor health, inferior education, and limited job opportunities combined to create a nightmare that was opposite in almost every respect to the middle-class ideal. The ghetto, an area of a city from which the inhabitants cannot escape, has become a concrete symbol of this life-style. Like the suburb and the neighborhood, the ghetto is a multifaceted image that does not fully reflect the quality of life as it is experienced by the poor blacks, Spanish-speaking Americans, and other poor people. On the one hand, some people romanticize the ghetto as a particularly exotic neighborhood in which any kind of thrill can be purchased for the right price and in which the people are far more genuine and "earthy" than the members of the middle classes. On the other hand, there is the notion that the ghetto is a place where there is no cohesive community whatsoever, and all institutions such as the family are weak or in rapid decay.[60] Neither of these images is entirely accurate, and both are used for justifying various policies and attitudes toward the ghetto. The romantic myth is used by blacks who wish to demonstrate their superiority to whites, and by some whites who would counsel benign neglect toward the conditions of the ghetto. The social disorganization myth is used both by those who argue for more aid to the ghetto and those who argue against such aid, depending upon whether they view the cause of the disorganization as social injustice or the inherent "shiftlessness" of blacks. What should be realized about such debates is that they take the ghetto out of the context of the megalopolis and, thereby, make it a special problem area apart from its interrelations with the other primary contexts for appreciation. Such a tactic may be useful for short-term gains by special-interest groups, but in the long run it ignores the integral relation of the ghetto to the irresponsibility of privileged groups within the megalopolis and the general allocative principles of wealth, power, and prestige.

PLANNING

At its worst, the megalopolis shows the side of the ghetto, which is in some ways the equivalent of the total institution in the appreciative life. At its best, the megalopolis shows the side of the very affluent suburb, with its individualized architecture, green spaces, and choice of privacy or sociability. While nobody consciously planned the ghetto to turn out the way it has, many people probably had a hand in planning the design of the affluent suburb, and others consciously work to maintain and develop it through zoning manipulations and other devices. Planning the context of appreciation is a widespread activity in the megalopolis, but at present this planning is both fragmented and elitist.

Current planning is fragmented for two reasons. First, the various islands in the megalopolis have their own planning agencies, which are frequently in conflict with one another and which compete often against the planning units of business and other conglomerates. Second, planning is usually narrow-gauge in the sense that it takes account of the technical requirements of certain interest complexes (for example, auto makers, road builders, and highway users in transportation planning) and does not attempt to harmonize these requirements with other values, such as those of beauty and health.[61] Contemporary planning is also elitist, in the sense that plans for the context of appreciation are drawn up and applied without the full participation of those who will be affected by the planned activities. Planning is viewed as a specialty, or a profession, and the professional in this case serves those who can afford to pay him. Some people hope to avoid these problems by advocating comprehensive and democratic planning. However, if the foregoing analysis of the context of appreciation is correct, a precondition of such planning is activity to break down the barriers between the various islands of the megalopolis. Part of this project would be accomplished by people making the megalopolis their frame of reference rather than some other unit. The other part of the project involves measures to insure that people become responsible for their interdependence, like it or not.

SUMMARY

The appreciation of culture takes place in many varied settings. In the mass societies of today, the most significant settings are vast collectivities of human beings, particularly nations. Unlike the ancient Greek polis, where a distinctive tone of community life was maintained in the face-to-face relations of human beings, the nation is an entity manufactured by social thinkers and supported by specific groups, particularly the middle classes. While it claims to be the most important context for integrating human existence, the nation really is but one competitor for allegiance among others. Some of those others are the region, the civilization, the racial-cultural whole, and humanity.

While the nation is currently the large-scale collective setting for appreciation that has the most influence (this is because it is often backed up by the power of the state), smaller settings include voluntary associations, peer groups, and families. Formally organized voluntary associations, which can be ranged on a continuum between those that exist mainly for the sociability of their members to those that exist mainly for the attainment of some external goal, have taken over increasingly activities that were once performed by more informally organized groups (for example, the Little League organized sandlot baseball). With the rise of voluntary associations and vast creative and coordinative bureaucracies, peer groups (informal cliques of those with similar social position) have tended to appear within the interstices of organizations (for example, friendship groups at the place of work), rather than in the community at large. Supposedly there is individual choice about whether or not to join voluntary associations and peer groups. However, this choice is constrained by the special privileges conferred by and on some groups (state-backed licensing) and the presence of pre-packaged policies in most associations. Perhaps the person can choose among groups to some extent, but the price of this is fragmentation of his character. The family is highly touted as the bulwark of all social life, but in mass societies it tends to be an adjunct of other organizations—a dumping ground for the effects of business and governmental conglomerates. As an appreciative unit the family is far less cohesive than previously, and people are increasingly willing to experiment with alternative forms and to dissolve marital bonds.

While collectivities offer one group of settings for appreciation, another group of settings is found in the various naturalcultural contexts for appreciation such as urban and rural areas. The distinctive context for appreciation in mass societies is the megalopolis, which is characterized by economic interdependence and appreciative fragmentation. Such appreciative fragmentation leads to the general problem of irresponsibility towards those with whom one is bound. The suburbs, which have become the large island within the megalopolis, demonstrate this escape from responsibility by their homogeneity and by the efforts of their residents to keep them sealed off from contamination. As black migrants have flowed into the cities, residents of white neighborhoods have attempted to behave like the suburbanites, but with less success due to their limited political power. Due to the suburbanization of the megalopolis and the neighborhood defense movements, the ghetto has arisen as a residual container for those who lack the governing values of the megalopolis—wealth, power, and prestige. The contemporary megalopolis has little to hold it together besides variable commitment to nationalism, and individual and group egoisms. The problems of dilapidated housing, transportation congestion, and environmental poisoning are mere symptoms of this situation.

Communication and Inquiry

14

EDUCATION, KNOWLEDGE, AND INQUIRY

Throughout this book we have been concerned with the ways in which people understand their experience and with the effects of these understandings on the rest of human existence. There should be nothing surprising about this, since this is a textbook and, like other textbooks, its purpose is to convey the results of inquiry and also to show how inquiry is done. Thus, in the first five chapters an attempt was made to show what kind of knowledge can be gained about the human condition and how such knowledge can be attained. We did this under the assumption that it would be better to be clear about what we were trying to accomplish at the very beginning than to pretend that we were simply revealing "objective truths."

The first five chapters introduced a particular theory of what knowledge is and how it is gained, especially knowledge about the human condition. The first chapter argued that knowledge about the human condition could be most fruitfully attained by applying the process of self-understanding. This process involves clarifying one's image of the human condition, generalizing it with respect to a tradi-

379

tion, relativizing it with regard to other traditions and committing oneself to acting on the possibilities flowing from a critically examined image. The second chapter presented a brief history of social thought, in which categories were suggested that might make it easier for one to undertake the process of self-understanding. This category system, including natural law, monist, pluralist, and process theories, is only one way of classifying social thought, and is itself embedded in a theory of the human condition (the image of mass society we have developed in this book).

The third chapter described the characteristics of a human science, and suggested criteria by which scientific work about the human condition could be evaluated—factual accuracy, logical consistency, comprehensiveness, adequacy, and fruitfulness. These criteria, or standards, are adapted to the kind of human science that arises from applying the process of self-understanding to social affairs rather than the assumptions of sciences treating other aspects of experience, such as chemical reactions. Following from the description of a human science, the fourth chapter discussed the range of sociological methods that can be applied to study the human condition. Certain methods, such as the comparative-historical and the participant-observation methods, were seen as especially consistent with an adequate and fruitful human science. Finally, in the fifth chapter the scope of human science was defined by presenting a description of human action that included the components of group, cultural object, social relation, and purpose. This description of action as a conscious process extending over space and time is the view of action implied by the process of self-understanding; in this view, social thought falls into the category of "process"—an adequate and fruitful human science—and into the historical-comparative and participant-observation methods.

We are reviewing the first five chapters to contrast the approach taken to knowledge in them with the one to be taken in this chapter. In those chapters, for the most part, we considered our approach to the human sciences apart from its relations to other kinds of knowledge (or at least claims to knowledge) and apart from its relations to various social processes. However, knowing, learning, communicating, and inquiring are all human activities that are as intimately linked to other aspects of human existence as are the activities of creation, coordination and appreciation. How can one create or produce without at least some fragmentary idea of what one is doing? Even the proverbial button-pusher in an automated factory knows what a button is and has been told when to push it.

Of course, in contemporary economic activity far more is often required than mere knowledge of what a button is. The profession, which is at the pinnacle of the prestige hierarchy of work in mass society, is based on claims to specialized knowledge, usually related to scientific knowledge. The activity of coordination is similarly dependent upon knowledge. In order to follow rules consciously, break them, or devise new ones, one must know what the rules direct and be able to tell when they have been followed. Far beyond this obvious point, however, justifications of political rule have usually been based, at least in part, either on claims to some special knowledge or on the dictates of some supposedly objective morality. In current mass societies, political leaders frequently claim that their positions provide them with perspectives for making decisions, which they cannot share with anyone else. Further, they often claim to have secret information that makes their decisions rational even if these decisions appear to be irrational. To be appreciative, one must know how to use products before their experiences become available. Further, communication is an integral part of any appreciative context or setting, and appreciative standards must be known before they can be applied. In the mass societies of today, where acceptance into appreciative settings is frequently based on the ability to display one-way symbols, the human activities of knowing and communicating are particularly important. Thus, all human activities have aspects of knowing and learning to them, just as all of them are marked by coordination (through the existence of systems of roles).

The close ties between knowing and other social processes make it possible to relate kinds of knowledge to particular social relations and social groups. Drawing upon an obvious example, specialized knowledge and languages inaccessible to laymen are associated with contemporary professions. The specialized knowledge is built into the very definition of the profession, while the inaccessible language may be in part associated with maintaining high prestige and exerting control over clients. A hallmark of mass society is the evident differentiation of groups according to both the kinds and contents of knowledge they develop and communicate. The very notion of a human science presented here is effectively accessible only to those teaching and taking social science courses, and is likely to be held as a framework for viewing human existence only by a small fraction of those people (mainly dissenters from the mainstream). It is certainly not likely to be believed by those who benefit greatly from holding the notion that there is only one way of looking at the human condition, or those who believe that there is but one "objective" viewpoint from which to see social activity. This does not mean that human beings are "determined" or caused to believe certain things by forces beyond their control or understanding. Rather, simply being in certain social situations provides some options for thought and closes off others.

Along with the differentiation of knowledge and its attendant fragmentation has gone the erosion of any standard or common basis by which all can judge the truth of statements, particularly those about human activity. Some social scientists believe that there are always common standards of judgment present in what they call the common-sense world, or the world of everyday life.[1] Yet, how is one to define "common sense" in mass society? Is it what some people in the middle class learn in college from psychology and sociology courses? Is it the propaganda about human behavior disseminated by advertising agencies? Is it what is contained in the advice columns of newspapers or in manuals such as Dr. Spock's book on child care? Is it the inchoate and inconsistent opinion of some man on the street? The common sense of earlier societies has been replaced by the cacaphony of so-called branches of knowledge (some of them battering against one another) of the contemporary multiversity.

THE MULTIVERSITY

Like the megalopolis, the multiversity is a context uniting a number of diverse and often clashing activities. It is made up of innumerable political fiefdoms jealously guarding what they have, and attempting to get more. As people traverse the megalopolis going to work, to shop, to visit relatives, or to take advantage of recreational facilities, they pass across meaningless boundaries that confuse, complicate, and segment existence. Similarly, students traverse the boundaries of academic departments that wage battles with one another to obtain more money, space, students and prestige. This flux of competitive activities confuses, complicates, and veils the process of learning. Of course, it is not at all apparent that the major goal of the multiversity is the education of students, whatever its official propaganda may say. The term "multiversity" was coined by a former president of the University of California, Clark Kerr, who used his school as a prime example of the ideal type.[2] Kerr used the term to refer to the contemporary university, massive in size and interpenetrating with the major complexes of interest groups in mass society. It is helpful to conceive of the multiversity as a college that might appear in Alice's Wonderland—

everything is topsy-turvy. Traditionally, the college fostered an ivory-tower environment, in which the academic community held itself apart from other institutions and in which faculty and students who knew one another interacted around a standard curriculum and comfortable social activities. The faculty's major task was to teach, and faculty members were paid for performing this activity. In a multiversity with hundreds (sometimes thousands) of faculty members and often tens of thousands of students, face-to-face relations with all but a minute fraction of those on campus are impossible.

The mere size of the multiversity is, however, one of its least important characteristics. More important are the vast array of activities that take place under the umbrella of the multiversity. One multiversity with which we are quite familiar hosts conferences for plumbers and a variety of other nonacademic groups, owns and operates three golf courses and a hotel, sells apples to the public grown on its horticultural farms, runs a radio station, fields football and basketball teams that often draw upward of 70,000 spectators to contests, sponsors rock-and-roll and classical music concerts by nationally known artists, owns and rents out dozens of private homes, in addition to performing other activities too numerous to mention. The principle governing what is to be undertaken by the multiversity is the same as the one guiding the economic conglomerate—anything. The units of the multiversity are frequently at cross purposes with one another (the agricultural school develops new pesticides and herbicides, and the ecologists in the biology department denounce the use of these chemicals; the psychology and sociology departments vie for the right to teach the social psychology course; the language departments fight other departments to keep the language requirement for all students). Thus any particular goal for the entire multiversity would be sure to bring on even further divisive controversy. Growth is the only aim on which there seems to be agreement: "This is not to say that the university has no goals. On the contrary, the university seems dedicated to the task of building itself into a vast academic empire. . . . Many university undertakings are valuable but many others are ridiculous and even dangerous. The only quality that is common to them all is that they increase the university's size and prestige."[3] Robin Williams concurs, stating that ". . . the actual goals of university administrators are to increase the wealth, size, and public renown of their institutions."[4]

One should not get the impression that this growth is merely random. As an integral part of mass society, the multiversity's expansion is consonant with the wealth, power, and prestige of other major institutions. Specialized and technical training has supplanted the liberal-arts education, thereby providing existing bureaucracies with professional and semi-professional personnel. Even those majoring in traditional academic subjects receive training that emphasizes narrow technical competence. For example, psychology graduates can enter personnel departments in industry equipped to test and evaluate prospective and present employees, while English majors are equipped to be copy editors for publishers. When the Soviet Union's launching of the Sputnik satellite wounded American pride in 1957, science departments in the multiversity immediately swelled and produced armies of scientists and engineers. The World War II baby boom, coupled with increased industrial desire for college-trained personnel, created a demand for more college teachers. Existing graduate departments at the multiversity stepped up their "productivity" (production of degree-bearing graduates), and many undergraduate departments attempted to add a master's or a doctoral program.[5] The drive toward professionalization in many occupations has been accompanied (in fact, aided and abetted) by professional training programs set up within the multiversities. In addition to furthering the process of specialization and cultivating the professional mentality, some critics have pointed out that the multiversity encourages students to become acquiescent consumers of mass entertainments. A former Berkeley graduate student writes to the undergraduates: "The multiversity is the slickest appeal ever made for you to fortify your organization-man mentalities, for you to lead privatized lives in which it is a virtue for you to go greedily 'on the make.' "[6]

The academic departments of the multiversity reflect in miniature the context in which they are located. As in mass society in general, the hierarchy of authority is not coincident with technical competence. Indeed, members of a given department often have only the vaguest notion of the research activities of a colleague, because areas of specialization tend to be defined in terms of airtight, mutually exclusive compartments. Mirroring the different schools and departments, there are separate and jealously guarded fiefdoms within departments themselves, and factions battle with one another for space, students, monies, and prestige. Frequently the enclaves of power are supported by agencies outside the multiversity, especially through research or development grants.[7] The multiversity's fragmentation of human experience into unrelated bits through grants of departmental autonomy is intensified by the department's subdivision of its discretion into smaller specialized bits doled out to individual professors.

Teaching still is an activity within the multiversity, but it differs significantly from teaching in smaller colleges. The class size is larger: introductory lecture courses generally range from between fifty to a thousand students. And although the multiversities vie with one another to get the top people in each discipline, the published and nationally recognized professor does not do the bulk of the teaching. In many instances the academic celebrity does no teaching at all and is paid a salary to gain prestige for the institution. Clark Kerr, drawing on his experience as multiversity president, claims that the "mark of a university 'on the make' is a mad scramble for football stars and professional luminaries. The former do little studying and the latter little teaching, and so they form a neat combination of muscle and intellect."[8] Teaching is viewed as a chore to be delegated to others. The stars concentrate on their research and their consulting. They are paid for consulting, often handsomely, by governmental agencies and by various business enterprises. Those in physics can consult with NASA (National Aeronautics and Space Administration), those in chemistry and biology for drug manufacturers, those in sociology with the Bureau of the Census, those in psychology with the National Institutes of Mental Health, to list only a fraction of the examples. Consulting opportunities for those in applied fields such as education, business, and agriculture are obvious. And there is further fee-paid consultation for the luminaries in any discipline with the Educational Testing Service (making up questions for standardized examinations) or the many textbook publishers. The big-name professor may even become essentially a professional with his home office and basic retainer on the campus of the multiversity, but with his clients scattered from coast to coast.

The more grants obtained and publication credits garnered (these are the necessary credentials for consulting work) the less the teaching load. Who, then, does the teaching? As many of the readers of this book are aware, the lion's share of the teaching is done by young and inexperienced professors and increasingly by the graduate assistants. This, of course, does not mean that the teaching is of low quality or any worse than it would be if a professor was conducting the class. If one is an older academician who is unpublished there are no opportunities in the multiversity. Such people wind up at small colleges or go into business or government work related to their fields of specialization. The extent of the involvement of graduate assistants in teaching was demonstrated at a large multiversity when, during a student protest, a strike by graduate assistants effectively stopped classroom activity. The graduate teaching assistants often find it difficult to take their duties seriously since their professors view teaching as a chore or a punishment. Sometimes they are not prepared to communicate the principles of the subject they are teaching accurately, and get little or no instruction or feedback on teaching techniques. Of course, those graduate students who go on to work in the multiversity will not gain career advancement through the high quality of the teaching they do.

Figure 14.1. THE ROLE OF THE PROFESSOR

Traditional College	Multiversity
Teaching	Grant-supported research
Some independent research	Consulting to organizations
Counseling students	Service to local community
Governance of college	Specialized university committees
	Teaching

EXERCISE

Does the school which you attend fit into the multiversity pattern? If so, describe some of its different activities. If not, how does it differ from the multiversity? Make up a classification system for institutions of higher education and fit your school into it. Is the school which you attend providing you with the kind of opportunities for education which you want? If so, how is it providing these opportunities? If not, can you think of a kind of school that would give you the kind of education you want?

RESEARCH

The academic setting has traditionally been a center not only for teaching but also for the "production" of knowledge. Prior to the emergence of mass society, research was not the primary purpose of professors, but was made possible through the provision of space and equipment by the colleges (laboratory space and equipment, and libraries, for example). In addition, there frequently was an appreciative audience present, composed of colleagues and sometimes students, that was able to understand and evaluate research work. The production of knowledge in the multiversity is far more complex than it was in the college, due in part to the extreme specialization characteristic of every field of inquiry. Research is often carried on in hierarchically ordered teams but, even when it is done by a solitary scholar, equipment costs are too high to be borne by the institution. Tuitions account for a minor part of the multiversity's income.[9] Administrators of private universities turn to wealthy businessmen for additional funds, while those who run the public universities attempt to increase their budgets through lobbying politicians. Professors attempt to obtain backing for their research from public or private foundations. The grants they receive cover equipment and payment to the school for released time from teaching. The high degree of specialization also limits the possibilities for an appreciative audience, at least on the particular campus. At their best, scholarly journals and meetings sponsored by disciplinary associations serve to bring together appreciative audiences which, in narrow specializations, are scattered around the nation and the world. Thus, the multiversity does not contain a face-to-face community of scholars.

The dominant myth about research done in the natural and social sciences, as well as that done in the humanities, is that scholars are not influenced by their social and cultural context—i.e., by the demands of complexes of interest groups. Researchers frequently make the claim that the impetus or inspiration to pursue a particular line of study is either based on arbitrary personal preference or the needs of science. The latter phrase assumes a notion of science in which the advancement of knowledge exists apart from other social interests. Both the appeal to personal preference and the appeal to advancing scientific knowledge are arguments that claim independence from societal influence, particularly economic or political influence, in the choice of research problems, methods of inquiry and evaluation of the results. While most professions secure for their members the freedom to select what means should be used to solve problems in their specialty, science demands the freedom to determine both means and ends. Warren Hagstrom states: "Basic science is unlike other professions in that its practitioners not only claim autonomy in determining procedures to be used in the course of work and in evaluating the success of these procedures; they also claim the right to decide for themselves the problems they should select . . ."[10] This claim to autonomy can be criticized both as an ideal and as a reflection of fact. The ideal has already been criticized in the discussion of the professional myth in the eighth chapter. However, the ideal, even with its weaknesses, is scarcely approached in actual situations.

It was noted above that much of the research carried on in the multiversity is very expensive and is largely funded through government, business and private foundations, such as the National Science Foundation, IBM, and the Rockefeller Foundation. Some of the funds are for basic research, while other monies are for development or applied research. None of these funds are "clean," in the sense that they do not tie the researcher to some complexes of interest groups. The giant foundations, for example, represent massive concentrations of wealth gained through the capitalist system and are inclined to allocate their monies in accordance with the maintenance and expansion of existing conglomerate organizations.[11] Their directors shift back and forth between government, business, the multiversities, and the foundations, providing generalized executive talent for the organizations of mass society. The foundations themselves are conglomerates, allocating funds to widely diverse activities, emphasizing those that will add to their prestige. They advertise themselves as charitable and philanthropic institutions, but a question remains as to why philanthropy should remain a private rather than a fully public concern.

Applied research is done in the context of goals determined by the agency granting the funds, not by the researcher. The agency sets such goals as marketability (industrial grants), solution of national problems (governmental funding), or prestige (foundation grants). Frequently researchers speak of the happy coincidence through which the problems they always wanted to work on are the ones for which funds are provided. However, such good luck happens too often for such protestations to be taken seriously. Funds are made available, and people clamor for problems to be solved before scientists claim that the needs of science demand certain kinds of research. For example, in the early 1960s ecology was scarcely recognized as a legitimate field of study in most biology dpeartments. With the advent of the environmentalist movement and the consequent availability of funds, institutes for the study of the environment have sprung up at various multiversities. Of the several billion dollars of federal funds given for research to universities, slightly more than half can be classified as for applied research.[12] Further, whether or not basic and applied research can be sharply distinguished, it is not clear that research supported by basic research funds is free from social or extra-scientific influences.

THE STRUCTURE OF SCIENTIFIC ACTIVITY

One of the most widely read books concerning the sociology and history of science is Thomas Kuhn's *The Structure of Scientific Revolutions*. The major thesis of this work is that, within any scientific discipline, the scientist does not randomly address himself to any of the possible unsolved problems. Rather, the scientist works within the framework of a paradigm, defined by Kuhn as "universally recognized scientific achievements that for a time provide model problems and solutions to a community of practitioners."[13] In the physical sciences, Newtonian dynamics and Copernican astronomy are examples of paradigms. In many instances the nature of the paradigm is related, at least analogically, to the general society of the time. The Copernican paradigm, which postulated the sun as the center of the solar system, replaced the Ptolemaic paradigm, which postulated the earth as the center of the universe. This scientific revolution came at the time when Europe was beginning to realize, during the age of exploration, that it was not the center of human activity.

Kuhn concludes that the influence of the paradigm is so strong that "those unwilling or unable to accommodate their work to it must proceed in isolation or attach themselves to some other group."[14] So far as the university scientist is concerned, working outside of the dominant paradigm usually will make it impossible to obtain appointment in a department. However, if his alternative paradigm fills some need in the political or the economic sphere, and is therefore fundable, it is possible that a new department will be formed. In a sense, the founding of new departments is similar to the formation of religious sects. Thus, the paradigm limits and directs the choice of the researcher. The mechanisms of this influence are partially due to the biases of those within the scientific community who wield power, and partly to the more subtle effects of the education the scientists receive and the functions of paradigms for guiding research.

Within each branch of science there are those who have achieved eminence by having solved one of the problems set forth by the dominant paradigms and have, on the basis of their eminence, some degree of power. Not only do such people have the ability to decide whether or not to hire someone into a major department, but they also control to a great degree the possibility that others will achieve eminence. This control is exercised through so-called gatekeeper roles. One such role is editor of a scholarly journal: editors determine what ideas can get disseminated and, because publications are used for evaluation of performance in the multiversity, the scientist's whole career is at the mercy of the gatekeepers. Alfred de Grazia claims that journal editors do tend to support the currently orthodox views in their fields.[15] After an extensive empirical study, Diana Crane concurs, and attributes the shared views to common graduate training.[16] Gatekeepers are also those who serve as the consultants for the private and public foundations to pass judgment on which research proposals to fund. The paradigms for most scientific fields, including the social sciences, require rather expensive methodological techniques and equipment (survey research and computers, for example). Competing paradigms that would also require costly methodology, or even ones that do not involve high costs, suffer at the hands of the gatekeepers. Such paradigms will not be considered as legitimate by university administrators unless they are funded by grants. This prejudice is understandable when one realizes that a large portion of each grant is allocated to the university as overhead.

Aside from the tendency of scientists with power to perpetuate the paradigms under which they gained success, the professional training, graduate-school experience, and personal contacts of scientists also help to maintain the dominance of a given paradigm. Those fields with strong paradigms can be distinguished by the heavy reliance on textbooks, even for advanced graduate-level courses. Other fields, such as most parts of the social sciences, emphasize journal articles and scholarly books over texts. Kuhn notes that ". . . science textbooks refer only to that part of the work of past scientists that can easily be viewed as contributions to the statement and solution of the text's paradigm problems. Partly by selection and partly by distortion, the scientists of earlier ages are implicitly represented as having worked upon the same set of fixed problems" as those of the present paradigm.[17] The textbooks present the paradigm. This training, which Kuhn likens to religious orthodoxy, colors and directs the view of the slice of experience in which the scientist's field claims proprietary interest. In addition, the paradigm indicates problems to research that are solvable by the methods advocated by the paradigm. Thus, the results of one's research are likely to be successful, which provides an added bonus for believing in the paradigm. Some degree of success is particularly important for graduate students who earn their degrees by completing a piece of research (usually by helping a professor). Hagstrom maintains that "what the scientist has learned usually 'works,' and his technical success, regardless of any social confirmation of it, reinforces his commitments."[18]

The preceding discussion of the prevalence and influence of paradigms in science, particularly in the multiversity, serves to discredit claims by scientists of autonomy in selecting, carrying out and evaluating so-called basic research. Those doing applied research make no such claims. The extent to which "pure science" is done at all in the multiversity according to the standard that "science must not suffer itself to become the handmaiden or theology or economy or state"[19] is questionable. Toasts, such as this one reported by Merton in 1937, are now an anachronism on campus: "To pure mathematics, and may it never be of any use to anybody!"[20] The Department of Defense, for one, has found pure mathematics to be of value, and grants to do more research in it are eagerly sought by professors. It is not inaccurate to state that the basic activity of the multiversity is the production of knowledge. If one compares the much smaller allocation of funds, space and prestige to teaching as opposed to research, this claim is well supported.

STUDENT PROTEST

The relegation of teaching to at best a secondary activity in the multiversity has coincided with the recent outbreak of student protests. The overwhelming majority of protests have been concentrated in the larger universities, and the frequency and intensity of them are directly related to the number of professors who do not teach. Berkeley, Harvard, and Columbia are sites of early protests, and the example of these protests has been followed elsewhere. However, it would be as naive to attribute the protests completely to the research activities of the multiversity as it would be to attribute them to the personality traits or academic achievement of those involved.[21] The student protests are embedded in a complex web of social relations.

Many proposed explanations of the student protests of the 1960s are not convincing because they are based upon factors that were also present in earlier decades when there were few protests. Examples of such unconvincing explanations are those given by Seymour Lipset: "the need of new generations to differentiate themselves from older ones" and that students are "socially 'marginal' individuals, . . . people whose status and future are not yet established."[22] Seymour Halleck catalogues twelve hypotheses found in the literature to explain student unrest. Those opposed to student protests view them as due to permissiveness in child rearing, unwillingness of youth to assume responsibility for their own behavior, the hazards of growing up in an affluent society, or the decline of the family. Those more in favor of the protests cite as causes the Vietnam war, the deterioration of the quality of life, the hopelessness of political activity inside the system, or the carryover of a sensitivity to injustice from the civil rights movement. Still others point to the "havoc" caused by massive technological growth, to delight in performing in front of television cameras, or to increasing reliance on science rather than religion for answers to the questions of life.[23] An alternative hypothesis is that students are protesting against features of the mass society as presently constituted. For example, many protests have been directed against the "war machine" and the draft. People preparing for specialized jobs and expecting to be entertained are likely to feel that induction into the army as an unspecialized private who has no control over his work is unjust. With "progress" toward a volunteer army, the dissent has decreased and the lower positions in the military will be filled by people whose quality of life will undergo improvement in the army (poor blacks and marginal whites). All the trends in mass society are felt more acutely within the multiversity than in a small college because the former is an integral part of the most powerful complexes of interest groups while the latter may appear to be an island of independence (like a restricted suburb) because its main function is grooming and preening the elite of the future. Some of the trends centered on the multiversity are the fragmentation of knowledge into unrelated bits, the loss of appreciative communities, the treatment of people as an undifferentiated mass, and the arbitrary decisions made by elites for their own power, prestige and self-esteem.

EXERCISE

How would you explain the rise and fall of student protest movements? Give some alternative explanations and the reasons supporting them. How would you go about determining which explanations are the best?

PRIMARY AND SECONDARY EDUCATION

While the most distinctive form of schooling in mass society is the multiversity, shot through with complexes of interest groups and competing departments, the most familiar form of schooling to people in the United States is that provided by the primary and secondary schools, both public and private. In 1970 the public school systems in the United States enrolled 45,903,371 students, who were taught by 2,061,115 teachers, while Roman Catholic parochial schools alone enrolled over 4,000,000 more students, taught by nearly 200,000 teachers.[24] These figures show the extent to which schooling takes up the space and time of people in the United States, because in 1970 the total population of the United States was nearly 205,000,000 people. This means that approximately one-quarter of the population is composed of students in primary and secondary schools, not to mention those teaching them and those supplying educational materials and services. What are the functions of this vast system?

In rural societies that approach the ideal type of folk society discussed in the last chapter, school systems are not extensively developed—if they exist at all. People are taught what they are expected to know within the family and within any work groups ranging beyond the family. With the advent of the modern era, marked by industrialization, centralization of authority in bureaucracies, the confrontation of diverse appreciative groups, and scientific knowledge, people became increasingly involved in relations which demanded skills which often could not be taught to them effectively by members of their families or by small work groups. The money economy, for example, required that people be able to perform arithmetical operations (addition, subtraction, multiplication, and division) so that they could keep their accounts in order. Barter economies (based on exchange of goods) require much less abstraction. Further, arithmetical skills were needed for many types of office work and some kinds of factory work. Similarly, the increasing impersonality and bureaucratization of relations required that people learn how to understand written directions (reading), whether these directions concerned the proper ways to use a product and possible dangers involved in using it, the ways to use a tool, the orders one was to follow, or the propaganda in which one was supposed to believe. Also, people had to learn to communicate with one another at a distance if they were to be effective workers and citizens (dutiful subjects), and so the skill of writing was required. The modern school system arose to teach reading, writing and arithmetic so that people could fit into the emerging modern economy and polity.

Of course, these rather mundane functions were dressed up in an elaborate mythology which today still dominates the educational imagination of many people in the United States. Samuel Eliot Morison has defined what he considers to be the "basic principles of American education": (1) that free public and secondary schools should be available to all children; (2) that teachers should be given professional training; (3) that all children be required to attend school up to a certain age, but not necessarily the free public school, religious and other bodies having complete liberty to establish their own educational systems at their own cost."[25]

These basic principles of American education are more striking for what they leave out than for what they include. What are the grounds for believing that all children should be required to attend school? Are schools the only means by which human beings can learn certain skills, such as reading, writing, and arithmetic? Perhaps at one time they were efficient means for accomplishing such ends, but today television, radio, the newspapers, parents, and community centers might be used for such purposes. Why must teaching be made a profession? Such skills as adding, subtracting, reading, and writing have been successfully taught by amateurs. Think of all the music teachers who free-lance and teach people the system of musical notation as well as the manual skills necessary to perform. Think of the sergeants who teach military lore, the journeymen who teach apprentices their skills, the housewives who teach their daughters how to cook. Why should free public and secondary schools be available to all children? Perhaps some form of organized school system might exist to make sure that people could read a newspaper, write a letter of complaint to a corporation about a faulty product, and figure out how to fill out a short income-tax form. However, such a system would cut drastically the time spent in primary school and eliminate universal attendance in secondary schools altogether. Any special skills could be taught to people on the job.

The preceding discussion leads to the possibility that schools perform other functions besides educating people in so-called basic skills. Ivan Illich has remarked that schools are based upon the "spurious hypothesis that learning is the result of curricular teaching."[26] Perhaps they are not based on this hypothesis at all, but on a different set of assumptions that lurk beneath the prevailing mythology. First, the contemporary school is a bureaucracy in miniature, in which the students learn the kinds of behavior expected of them in the vast organizations of mass society.[27] In local school systems the basic decisions on policy are the responsibility of an elected or appointed school board (like a corporate board of directors), and the day-to-day administration is handled by a superintendent and a bevy of principals and aides (like corporate management). The teaching is done by a staff of professionals (like the specialists in industry), and their services are more or less consumed by the students (like meals are consumed in a roadside restaurant).

Since teacher and student are in a professional-client relationship, the student is expected to obey the directives of the teacher because these requirements are supposed to be for the student's own good. Those who behave in accordance with the teacher's standards are rewarded, while those who break the rules are punished. Competition between students is often encouraged, so that all will try to please the teacher rather than combining together against *her* (in 1970, 1,411,865 public school teachers were women while 649,250 were men). While they lack the unions of many of their parents, working-class and lower-class children frequently engage in the same kind of slowdown and harassment tactics used by workers to limit production and avoid excessive strain. They continually talk in class, giggle at the teacher, and generally show contempt for the lessons. They do not treat the teacher as some benevolent professional, but as a representative of management who does not have their best interests at heart at all. Most frequently, this kind of behavior is classified under the heading of discipline problem. This interpretation assumes the view that students who break the rules are deviants who must be dealt with through the methods of social control (liberals tend to favor rewards and conservatives tend to favor punishments). Perhaps, however, these unruly and apathetic students, destined for factory or other semi-skilled jobs, are simply learning the rules of the game that they will follow in later life.

The schools teach middle-class children how to be good organization men (and wives) and working-class children how to behave like workers. They teach all children how to be good nationalists. The day begins with the salute to the flag and, by the time three o'clock rolls around, the students have learned that great men make history (the founding fathers) rather than socio-cultural-personal processes, that the American economic, political, societal, and educational systems are the best in the world ("there may be some serious problems, but it's still the best system created by man"), that international affairs should be judged from the American viewpoint, and that the culmination of world history is the American commonwealth. None of this is calculated to encourage the process of self-understanding. Aside from propagating nationalism, the schools also keep children off the streets and out of their parents' hair (the baby-sitting function), keep young people out of the labor market (inflating wages) and create micro-status systems in which young people learn how to follow style trends in consumer goods and entertainments. Through athletic teams, they also generally foster some sense of community in suburbs and neighborhoods. They do not effectively teach the vast majority of people how to make simple repairs on common consumer goods (plumbing, electrical, and auto repairs), how to snuff out and criticize propaganda, how to discriminate art from entertainment, how to perform skilled jobs, and how to fight for their legal rights against administrators, officials, salesmen, and unscrupulous organizations. Instead of effectively teaching such things the schools certify people for entry into various strata of the working world through meting out grades and diplomas. Factions within them carry on a shadow-boxing debate between whether concentration should be on "quality education for an expert society" (education favoring those in the middle classes) or "education for equality" (education aimed at inducting more people into the middle classes).[28] This debate is convenient for everyone concerned because the school system remains intact whoever wins.

EXERCISE

Give an alternative list of functions for the secondary school to the one presented in this book. Which list of functions most adequately and accurately describes the activities of the school? How would you determine the functions of an organization?

"PUBLIC" INFORMATION

While educators have a vested interest in propagating the idea that learning takes place only in schools, opportunities for learning are available in great abundance to almost all members of mass society through the media of mass communications (television, radio, newspapers, magazines, books, recordings, correspondence courses, and movies). In addition, lecturers travel throughout the land, discoursing to various clubs and associations, churches dispense knowledge about the supernatural and other matters (how to resolve marital difficulties, for example), and interest groups are ever ready to dispense canned information. Of course, an enormous amount of learning takes place in face-to-face contacts among friends and members of small groups. People teach one another what they have learned elsewhere and what they have discovered themselves. It should by now be apparent that professional teachers (those who have been certified by the multiversity or one of its satellites) will never succeed in gaining a monopoly over the dispensation of knowledge. Physicians, perhaps, have some hope of persuading a small part of the middle classes that medical self-help is fraught with peril. There is no chance whatsoever that the schools will persuade anyone for very long that educational self-help is dangerous to the mind. People carry the notion of uncertified learning with them into kindergarten, which is, perhaps, why many educationists today call for organized pre-school education.

Among the most readily available sources of information and learning in mass societies are the mass media of communication. For example, in 1967, the total circulation of daily newspapers in the United States was 61,561,000, assuring that the newspaper reached even more people than the school.[29] The newspaper, which is representative of mass media, is a multifunctional educational material. According to the mythology of journalism, newspapers are supposed to keep the public informed on significant events that concern the direction of policy, and to provide an airing of alternative policies so that citizens will be able to make intelligent choices when exercising their democratic "rights." However, a perusal of nearly any daily newspaper, including the "prestige papers" such as the *New York Times* and the *Washington Post*, reveals that analysis of public policy and information on current events affecting institutions is not presented systematically. Bettors and fans buy the newspaper to learn about sports results and predictions, superstitious people gain astrological wisdom, investors learn market quotations and gossip, housewives learn recipes and social gossip, everyone learns what consumer goods are being sold and how much they cost, and what other mass media are offering (TV and radio listings, as well as listings of best sellers and "top 40" records). Interspersed between all this are "news" and "opinion" columns, often heavily slanted toward the bizarre, the violent, and the personal.

The newspapers and other mass media are conspicuous for what they leave out rather than for the disjointed multitude of things they contain. Perhaps the most important thing left out of the mass media, at least from our perspective, is any context in which to interpret the events reported. Of course, the mass media do employ a set of principles for selecting which events to include as "news" and how to report these events, but these principles are never made explicit to the readers or viewers. The framework in which news stories are written constitutes the journalist's image of the human condition. Through becoming aware of this image one will be enabled to analyze critically the "public information" directed at him day after day.

In the United States the mass media are controlled by profit-making organizations and are dependent upon advertising for much of their revenues. Further, with television and radio the controlling organizations are dependent upon the federal government for their licenses to operate, while the newspapers are partially dependent upon low postal rates for their profits. Thus, it is quite unlikely that any mass medium in the United States will either take a strong position in favor of a socialist economy or even permit serious and extended debate about the merits of noncapitalist economic systems in its pages or over its airwaves. Further, it is not likely that any mass medium will either take a strong position in favor of any political system other than "representative democracy" or even permit serious and extended debate about the merits of alternative political systems. Within the appreciative sphere, atheist pronouncements do not appear on the editorial pages or in the film clips (though religious movements may even have a page all to themselves, or Sunday-morning air time), nationalism is not questioned (though shadow-boxing may take place over how best to be patriotic), the family is praised and used as a unit of description, and the various islands of the megalopolis are torn out of their context. In the Soviet Union, arguments for capitalistic economics, representative democracy, religious belief, and suburbanization are not presented, and events are reported from the standpoint of Communist party policy. How different are the mass media in the Soviet Union from those in the United States? The differences that do appear seem to be related to the differences in the political systems of the two nations. The competitive pluralism of politics in the United States allows the media to publish or broadcast material critical of political figures holding office at a given time. However, this should not disguise the overall commitment of the mass media to upholding nearly all the myths discussed thus far in this book.

Before one even begins to read the newspaper or watch the news on TV, the context of capitalism, democratic elitism, the occupational status hierarchy, nationalism, religion, and scientific expertise has been prepared. Having pushed this context below the surface of awareness, the media proceed to report events using skin-and-bones people as the basic units of analysis rather than social processes. Some people, such as Daniel Boorstin, criticize the media for manufacturing news—staging "pseudo-events."[30] Pseudo-events are happenings that would not have taken place if the news media had not intervened and precipitated them. For example, when a senator is asked what his reaction would be if the President were to veto a certain piece of legislation that has not even been voted on yet, a pseudo-event has been created. However, criticism of the pseudo-event is founded upon the idea that somewhere there is spontaneous and "real" news, which should be discovered and then reported. Somehow the reporter is supposed to be left out of the context of the event being reported. Yet how could this occur, when the political figures who are the subjects of journalism are continuously aware of the images they are projecting through the media? If the journalists do not create the pseudo-events, the public figures will create them. Pseudo-events are like put-ons; they are encouraged by the structure of competitive relations in mass societies. They exploit personalities and are exploited by them.

EXERCISE

Watch a television newscast. What proportion of the items are, in Boorstin's terms, pseudo-events? What effect do they have? What effect could they have? If you were a reporter and given free reign, what pseudo-event would you arrange? Why?

The very basis of contemporary reporting of public affairs is commitment to the self as the unit of description. In the August 6, 1972, edition of the newspaper *Chicago Today*, a striking example of this commitment was shown. In the news columns there was a story about a child who had nearly been beaten to death by his father. One article revealed how an expert (a St. Louis County Circuit Court Judge) advocated having attorneys represent children in custody cases, while another article detailed possible misdeeds of a judge who had handled a custody case in which the beaten child was involved. In the features section there were two articles on battered children, both of which showed the personalized bias of reporting. Their titles reflect their content: "Why Would Anyone Want to Beat a Child?" and " 'I Knew I Was Capable of Killing my Son' " (the latter essay being a kind of 'true confession' of an ex-child beater). On the editorial page appeared an editorial entitled "A Bill of Rights for Children" in which it was argued that "It should be made clear that a child has a basic right to a permanent family situation, and is not to be bounced around between adoptive and natural parents merely because both claim him."[31] In all the articles in this coordinated campaign to whip up an issue, all the focus was on individuals. There were two major questions asked and answered. One was "Why Would Anyone Want to Beat a Child?" and the other was "What should be done for children who are beaten, and what should happen to their parents?" Nothing was mentioned about how the nuclear-family system might encourage the isolation and irresponsibility of parents, about how entertainment-oriented mass media might make people resent caring for children when, under other circumstances, they could be out having a good time, how the schools have failed to teach people the rudimentary principles of child care, and about how in a mass society the only power most people can exert is over their children. Instead, there were arguments in favor of "professional" representation for battered children in court and a basic right for children to a stable family life (how could such a right be enforced at present?). This is only a trifling example of how the mass media personalize public issues and take them out of their social context. Next time that you look at a newspaper or watch the TV news see how much description and explanation are phrased in terms of personalities and how much in terms of institutions and social processes. See how often present institutions are compared to alternative institutions, and how much attention is devoted to how similar situations are dealt with outside of the United States. Once you have done that you will be able to read between the lines continually, and uncover the hidden context of journalism.

PROPAGANDA MILLS

Contemporary education and journalism are forms of propaganda because they discourage relativization of the human situation by keeping their context hidden. However, teachers and journalists usually are probably not even aware of the context in which they are operating, and see themselves as "professionals," serving their clients through a commitment to the truth. They may even believe that they are encouraging independence of judgment in their clients. These observations do not hold, however, for political propagandists and commercial advertisers, whose very object is to destroy independent judgment and persuade the individual to make a commitment to support a party or personality, or to buy a product. Thus, advertisers and propagandists purposefully destroy the social context and leave the isolated self vulnerable to appeals to self-esteem and fear.[32]

The activity of persuading people to make economic and political decisions with reference to nonrational criteria is one of the most highly differentiated and bureaucratized activities in mass society. People in the United States are sometimes frightened when they learn about the incessant political propaganda supporting the ruling elites in communist countries. They believe that it would be terrible to be assailed day in and day out by appeals to work harder to realize the five-year plan or to feel enraged at the bourgeois imperialists. Such propaganda seems to be the very antithesis of freedom. However, these same people think nothing of being assailed by endless commercials for laxatives, deodorants, automobiles, floor polishes, beer, and various and sundry other products. They do not believe that they have any right to demand freedom from sales pressure. Since salesmen are everywhere—on the radio, on TV, in the newspapers and magazines, on billboards, over the telephone, on the door step, and in commercial establishments—people take them for granted as an inherent feature of the human condition. Underlying this complacency is the assumption that what goes on in one's mind most of the time is not really all that important. So what if one cannot stop a jingle advertising chewing gum from running through one's head for an entire day? Some other nonsense would, presumably, have been going through the mind instead. However, it is important to realize that the careers of many people are devoted to implanting just such jingles in the mind, and trying to envision what one's mental life would be like in the absence of advertising and propaganda.

The advertising and propaganda bureaucracies are massive and complex. DeFleur, in a description of mass media as social systems, shows how closely advertising is connected with the rest of what appears on the media. He identifies as the first phase of the communications process "research." Organizations "devoted to *research*, to measuring the preferences of media audiences, or to various forms of market research provide information to those responsible for selecting the categories of content that will be distributed to the audience."[33] This is the kind of job for which many undergraduates in psychology and sociology are prepared. The work involves determining who buys what product and why, so that the advertising message can be effective in raising sales. The second phase of the process involves selecting a "distributor" for the advertising. The propagandist must determine which kinds of programs, magazines, or what not are best adapted as vehicles and contexts for the advertising message—one would not advertise a feminine hygiene deodorant in a hunting magazine. Of course, the process goes much farther than such an obvious example, because advertisers and corporations sometimes develop TV series adapted to selling their product, or pass judgment on the kinds of articles appearing in magazines. DeFleur translates this observation into antiseptic "sociological" language which, incidentally, shows how "value-neutral" science contains its own biases: "To the audience, the research, and the distributing components, we may add the role system of the *producer* of content. This component's primary link is with the *financial backer* (or *sponsor*) component and with the distributor, from whom money is obtained and for whom various forms of entertainment content are manufactured."[34] A dyed-in-the-wool Marxist militant could not have made the point more clearly: the very content of the mass media is *manufactured* not for the audience but for the sponsor, who is presumably bankrolling the news and entertainment industry for some reason other than charity. Finally, the key integrating component of the entire mass-media social system is the advertising agency: "Linking the sponsor, distributor, producer, and research organization are the *advertising agencies.* Paid primarily by the sponsor, this component provides (in return) certain ideas and services. For the most part, it provides the distributor with advertising messages."[35] Where does the audience fit into this scheme? DeFleur remarks that the "relationship between audience and distributor seems at first to be mostly a one-way link." However, these mere appearances mask the true contribution of the audience in a mass society: the audience "does provide its *attention.* " In fact, DeFleur continues, it is "precisely the attention of the audience that the distributor is attempting to solicit": "He sells this 'commodity' (attention) directly to his financial backer or sponsor."[36] Thus, from the media's point of view they are selling part of your mind to a sponsor. We now turn to how they do it.

THE MASS MIND
_____

In order to sell products or gain supporters for political movements (or raise the status of an ethnic group, create converts for a religion, or build up the image of a voluntary association) propagandists appeal to a set of mental and emotional processes which can be conveniently called "the mass mind." The "mass mind" is not a description of how any particular human being thinks or feels throughout most of his existence, nor is it a description of some "group mind" which mysteriously governs the actions of individuals as well as their judgments and emotions. Rather, the "mass mind" describes the *image* of mental life held by propagandists. Some people may even approach conforming to this image, but this fact does not mean that they *must* continue to conform nor that the propagandists can induce them to conform. By understanding how propagandists define the mass mind, one is enabled to choose whether or not one will become an easy mark for the advertisers.

Reflections about the mass mind did not begin with propagandists and advertisers, but with social critics and thinkers. This is to be expected, because it is characteristic of propagandists and advertisers never to invent anything for themselves, but to draw upon what people have created and discovered in other contexts. Thus, in the nineteenth century, the social critic Gustave LeBon systematized the principles of the mass mind in his study of crowd behavior. According to LeBon, the crowd was the distinctive social form in mass society. People had been thrown together into cities and had lost their traditional social controls, making them vulnerable to flights of irrationality. For LeBon, the hallmark of crowds was the lack of deliberation before they took action and the lack of control during the performance of action. Crowds were subject to the sway of suggestion, because their members were incapable of critical reflection: "Any display of premeditation by crowds is in consequence out of the question. They may be animated in succession by the most contrary sentiments, but they will always be under the influence of the exciting causes of the moment. They are like leaves which a tempest whirls up and scatters in every direction and then allows to fall."[37] Crowds lack the characteristics of critical reason, particularly with regard to the suspension of judgment necessary for relativization: "The simplicity and exaggeration of the sentiments of crowds have for result that a throng knows neither doubt nor uncertainty. . . . A suspicion transforms itself as soon as announced into incontrovertible evidence."[38]

It is important to note that the characteristics of the mass mind do not appear only in concrete groups of individuals given the name of "crowds." Throughout mass society, often in the most rule-bound organizations, there is evidence of the crowd behavior identified by LeBon. Traits such as suggestibility, destructiveness, emotionality, and lack of self-control frequently appear in conglomerate organizations when the normal routine is disturbed by power struggles among administrators, demands by militant client groups, threats from other organizations, or factional struggles among competing cliques of specialists. Groups of professionals in bureaucracies may come to behave as crowds when they are cross-pressured or mobilized by authorities. This means that it is a mistake to look at crowd behavior and the mass mind as lower-class phenomena stemming from limited education and ineffective socialization. Rather, the appearance of crowds is encouraged by the power structure of mass society, which stresses top-down hierarchical authority of administrators. When this authority is questioned, those who have depended upon it to function routinely are frequently left without a focus for their activity and become open to the processes of suggestion and manipulation. Thus, crowd behavior is less a consequence of individual and cultural traits than an aspect of social organization. Further, crowd behavior may be one of the few effective means for stimulating social change in the hands of poorly organized and dispossessed social groups. It may, in fact, be a way of precipitating more coherent, responsible and participative social action.

This possible function of crowds as agents of change, however, does not eliminate the unreflective character of their behavior. Ultimately, the way to diminish crowd behavior and the mass mind is to lessen the dependence of people on hierarchical power structures and to distribute societal resources in such a way that there are no dispossessed groups. In the absence of a more egalitarian social order, it is possible for individuals to avoid being drawn into the cycle of suggestion and manipulation by applying the process of self-understanding and joining with others in strong informal organizations critical of power structures and capable of self-defense and opposition when these structures undergo their frequent and recurrent breakdowns. It is useful to distinguish between crowds that appear when there is a breakdown in authority, and crowds that are manipulated by elites for ulterior purposes. The first type is a possible agent of social change acting against elites, while the second is an attempt by elites to exploit discontent to secure their position. In either case, though, the crowd is *reactive* rather than *constructive,* since constructive social action depends upon participants acting cooperatively to realize values to which they are committed.

The most striking instances of crowds are those that gather in the same action space and time during periods of social unrest, and that engage in violent or destructive activities. However, as LeBon was careful to point out, most of the crowds in mass society exist in sociocultural space and time, their members being out of eye and ear shot of one another. When a wave of patriotic intensity sweeps through the lower-middle classes of a nation and, for example, policemen begin putting flag decals on their cruisers and wearing flag patches on their uniforms, stores begin offering free flags along with purchases of appliances, women begin wearing red, white, and blue dresses, and people begin being arrested with some frequency for showing "disrespect" for the flag, a crowd is present just as much as if a mob of people were storming a prison with the intent of freeing all the inmates. Of course, crowds which exist in socio-cultural space and time only, and not in action space and time, are vulnerable to intensive manipulation by small elites, which channel their passions into longer-term projects for gaining or maintaining advantage. For example, the owner of a department store who is concerned to increase sales may exploit patriotic fervor in order to draw people into his establishment. In some cases the elites may even be strong enough to create the very passion actuating the crowd. This may have taken place in the wave of working-class patriotism which arose in the late 1960s. The elites did not here create patriotism, nor were they personally responsible for the frustrations of many working men, but they provided symbols, rationalizations, and reinforcements to the emerging crowd. The construction workers who rampaged through downtown New York in protest against long-hairs and "peaceniks" had their arguments all ready for the television cameramen.

STIMULUS-RESPONSE

Observations on crowd behavior can be generalized into a method for getting people to do things that they might not do if they applied critical reason. This is the method of association, or what is sometimes called behaviorism or stimulus-response. The method of association is the simplest form of manipulation and also far and away the most prevalent. When using this method, the propagandist links the activity he would like people to perform with some other object they desire or fear, or with some pleasant or unpleasant experience. For example, suppose that the advertiser's plan is to have more people purchase a certain automobile. The simplest use of association would be to create billboards in which pretty girls and handsome men were clustered around the car, or in which the car appeared in a beautiful wooded glen. Here, the intent would be to have the viewer associate possession of the car with the experience of being with "beautiful" people, or with the experience of being in a beautiful environment. If successful, the advertiser will have manipulated the person looking at the billboard to buy the car because of the associations created by the advertiser. Thus, the entire principle of association in advertising is to create a context for a product, which has nothing to do with the product itself, but which will favorably dispose the person to make a purchase.

It should be evident what this means in terms of the image of mental life held by advertisers. Advertisers view human beings (including the readers of this book) as members of crowds who can be swayed into action by appeals having nothing to do with the action. How many times do you find yourself in a wooded glen with a car? Thus, association is the basic characteristic of the mass mind.

In order for association to work, the contexts in which propagandists place their products must be standardized and held constant. If people were continually rethinking their situations and reconstructing them, it would be impossible for advertisers to be sure that particular contexts would give rise to pleasant or unpleasant associations. There is nothing at all sacred about "youth" as a pleasant context. In some groups the aged are more highly esteemed than the young. However, advertisers and political propagandists have exploited the context of youth so much in selling their products and policies that a group of young people having a good time (or "seriously" working toward social betterment) has become a standardized way of eliciting a pleasant emotional climate. The readers of this book might reflect for a moment about how closely the image of youth in commercials and political propaganda accords with the directly experienced quality of their own existence. The years between eighteen and twenty-five are frequently marked by uncertainty about the future, lack of confidence in one's capacities, fear that one is going to be dragged into a meaningless life, and relative poverty. Even more poignant than the middle-aged men in rock nightclubs or the middle-aged women in hot pants are the young people who believe in the myths about themselves created by middle-aged propagandists. Youth, of course, is merely one standardized context developed and exploited by advertisers and propagandists. Others are the suburban family, the back-slapping male peer group filled with "gusto," the wise wife concerned with the good of her husband and children, and the cute little old lady filled with a youthful zest for life. How does the little old lady look to the crippled old women who have nothing to do all day but watch TV in their nursing homes? She is not on TV for their benefit, but for ours—so that we can associate the product she is selling with eternal youthfulness.

In using the method of association, advertisers and propagandists take the product out of the context in which it will actually appear when consumed and put it into a contrived context which will fill it with pleasant or unpleasant (when the propaganda is designed to prevent action or stir up hatred) associations. How many husbands will go into transports of joy upon seeing that their wives have waxed the kitchen floor with a new product? Often they will not even notice that the floor has been waxed, and if their wives gently remind them, they may feel guilty rage about neglecting to comment. Since the basic method of advertising is association and catering to (and thereby fostering) the crowd mentality, debates about "truthfulness" in advertising and propaganda do not get to the heart of the matter. Advertisers often welcome the opportunity to tell the truth about their product or candidate (so long as they can select which part of the truth to tell), but they will not so easily give up the freedom to determine the context in which that truth will appear.

EXERCISE

Look at advertisements in a magazine. To what extent do they give information about the products? To what extent do they attempt to have you associate the product with some pleasant context?

OTHER CHARACTERISTICS OF THE MASS MIND

While suggestibility and the crowd mentality are the basic characteristics of the mass mind, other mental processes are assumed and exploited by advertisers and propagandists. One of the most important is the assumption that people have some sort of drive to be consistent and some desire to be right all the time.[39] For example, it is assumed (and can to some extent be shown to be true) that a person who purchases a consumer good, particularly one with a high price tag, will attempt to screen out anything unfavorable about that product and harp on everything good about it.[40] Of course, salesmen and politicians are always ready at hand to aid people in this process of accentuating the positive and eliminating the negative (called, in the antiseptic jargon of social psychology, "resolving cognitive dissonance"). Often the process of accentuating the positive is not even undertaken consciously, but is indulged in almost by habit. It becomes a method of manipulation when established authorities and spokesmen for powerful elites begin to emit propaganda emphasizing how important it is to look at the good side of things. They treat the nation in the same way that the auto salesmen treats the new car being brought back for major repairs; both claim that people should look at the positive aspects of the situation and not tear down a basically good thing.

Of course, there is an opposite form of manipulation, indulged in by radicals and dissenters, which attempts to encourage discontent by accentuating the negative and eliminating the positive. (And, naturally, both the apologist and the radical rely upon fixed definitions of the "positive" and the "negative" to carry through their propaganda; they would go out of business quickly if people began to relativize their situations.) However, it is unlikely that they will go out of business very soon because they have been quite successful in fostering the mass mind and discouraging critical reflection—so successful, in fact, that some social psychologists believe that people "naturally" seek to live in a dream world of wishful thinking.[41]

The notion that people seek to resolve cognitive dissonance dovetails very well with the idea that people can be induced to act on the basis of pleasant or unpleasant associations. In resolving cognitive dissonance the person merely saves the propagandist the trouble of hiring pretty girls and famous athletes. Instead of being induced by a context created for him by the advertiser, the person creates his own wonderland of wooded glens and beautiful people, which then enslaves him to established commercial, political, appreciative, and educational organizations. People are continually in the process of creating their own contexts, most of which split them off from relations with others. A man, for example, may define his context as *his* family and *his* new house in the suburbs. The megalopolis evaporates for him, and the advertisers and propagandists are happy to assist in this evaporation. It is no wonder, then, that dissenters have a bad name throughout the world.

SUMMARY

The processes of knowing, learning, and communicating can be considered in two different ways. First, one can present a theory of what knowledge is and how it is gained. Second, one can relate the processes of knowing, learning, and communicating with other social processes, and show how human activity with respect to symbols is embedded in complex sets of social relations.

One important characteristic of knowledge in mass society is the progressive erosion of "common sense" as a basis for shared judgments of fact and value. In the place of common sense have come specialized knowledge and various forms of propaganda. The center for specialized knowledge in the mass society is the multiversity. The multiversity, like all the conglomerates of mass society, is guided by the aim of sheer growth in wealth, power, and prestige. It is a mirror of the fragmentation of knowledge, since it contains specialized and often conflicting departments. The faculty of the multiversity places research and consulting (sometimes euphemistically called "service") before teaching, and is closely tied in through business, governmental and foundation grants with the other conglomerates of mass society. The departments of the multiversity themselves are fragmented, though gatekeepers (eminent and powerful academicians) exert some control over the disciplines through enforcing conformity with the dominant paradigms (ways of conducting research). Student protests since the 1960s may be related to the interpenetration of complexes of interest groups with the multiversity.

Primary and secondary educational systems are satellites of the multiversity. They prepare people for the factory or the bureau not through providing skills or wisdom, but through teaching obedience, national loyalty, the professional ideal, and fashion consciousness. The systems of public information (the mass media) are similarly supports for established institutions and tend to personalize the news to such a degree that the entire context of activity remains implicit. One does not hear capitalism, representative democracy, the family, religion, professionalism, and the prestigious multiversity seriously criticized in either the public schools or the media of public information.

While the school systems and the media are implicitly propagandistic, interest groups, governments, and movements, as well as the ubiquitous advertisers, are explicitly geared to the production of propaganda. Some apologists for advertising claim that the propagandist-consumer relation is one of exchange—the propagandist gives a sales pitch and the consumer gives his attention. It is up to the reader to judge how much of a two-way relation this ends up to be. Propaganda itself fosters the image of a mass mind governed by crude association. The idea is that people will buy a product or support a program merely because an advertisement takes it out of the context in which it will actually appear and places it in a contrived and pleasing context. Until propaganda and advertising can be eliminated altogether (will this ever happen?), the best defense against them is the active encouragement of critical reason in self and others.

15

TECHNOCRACY, POLICY, AND THE FUTURE

In the nine preceding chapters, various aspects of social existence in mass society have been discussed. In this chapter the focus will shift toward discussion of the possible society of the future and its major characteristics. However, the future is a bare possibility on the margin of human existence. In one respect it is the most important dimension of time for human beings, since human existence involves imagining what future states of affairs might be and then acting to realize or avoid these imagined futures. In another respect, though, the future is the least important time dimension because human existence is filled with surprises and the best-laid plans are frequently upset with the occurrence of unexpected events. For example, hardly anyone in the 1950s would have anticipated many of the events of the 1960s. For the mind of the 1950s in the United States, if there was going to be war it would come in the form of a nuclear conflict between the United States and the Soviet Union, the tendency of youth was to prepare to be organization men, and the blacks would slowly win full equality with whites

410

through legal means. Sociologists writing in the 1950s reflected these popular beliefs and helped to foster them. Thus, the 1960s, marked by the war in Vietnam, the counter-culture of some youth, and the movement for black power (supplanting the one for civil rights), caught most people, including sociologists, unprepared. The failing of the sociologists who did not anticipate the events of the 1960s was not caused by the lack of an accurate predictive science. Rather, the sociologists, representing the popular mind, tended to be optimistic.[1] They projected into the future only those trends that fitted in with their conception of the good life—which stressed the benefits of technological development, the efficiency of bureaucratic organizations and the trend toward legal equality for all. Today many people have become pessimists, so there are sociologists representing them who predict that human beings will choke to death in their own refuse, breed so quickly that nobody will have any space in which to move around, and be poisoned by processed foods.

The swings of the pendulum between optimism and pessimism show one reason why human beings are often so inaccurate in their predictions of the future. Around their emotional tone toward existence (positive or negative) they select those features of the present that best fit their tone to project into the future. This is another way of saying that every image of the human condition has a distinctive value quality and that possibilities for the future are closely related to it. The image of the human condition promoted by sociologists in the 1950s consisted, in part, of a great celebration of American institutions.[2] Sociologists were becoming recognized as professionals and were being more and more sought after as consultants. The middle classes were in ascendency, and the topics of cocktail conversation were the suburbs and the organization man—i.e., middle-class topics. There was hope by some that a science of society would smooth the way toward progress, defined as the induction of increasing numbers of people into the middle-class life-style.[2] In the 1960s the great issues were no longer centered around the middle classes. The ghetto replaced the suburb as the most mentioned context, and the exploited, deprived, and oppressed replaced the organization man as the most analyzed personality type. Rather than discussing the dynamics of conformity, people talked about the processes of liberation. Sociologists were affected by the emergence of new issues in much the same way as were other sectors of the middle classes. They had been put in the position of reacting to events rather than shaping or anticipating them and, therefore, were apt to become less optimistic about the future, if not altogether pessimistic. In the 1950s the context of human existence had the middle classes in the foreground and other groups in the background. The professional ideal was the yardstick against which people were supposed to measure their success. In the 1960s the context had changed and many groups were disputing for the fore-ground, though the middle classes had by no means been displaced. The uncertainty, anxieties, and mixed motivations of middle-class peo-ple in the 1960s are partly reflected in current sociology and its less-than-confident vision of the future.[3]

OPTIMISM OR PESSIMISM?

The purpose of the present chapter is not to determine whether optimism or pessimism is the more reasonable attitude to take for the future. Frequently when we speak with people outside the social sciences they will say: "You're social scientists. Tell us whether there is any hope for society." We do not believe that there is any way to respond rationally to this request, even though a number of social scientists who call themselves "futurists" or "futurologists" make their living by writing and speaking on whether the future generations (if there are any) will live in a gadget-filled deodorized haven or in an impoverished stink-hole.[4]

First, whether or not one should be optimistic depends upon one's image of the human condition. Since many people have not clarified their images, much less relativized them, it is impossible even to determine if their values are consistent. Second, given a consistent set of values, the most that a social scientist can do is point out the various trends working for or against the realization of these values. It is not possible to predict which of the trends will prevail and it is even possible that the most significant trends have not yet been iden-tified and will only become known after they have had their decisive impact. Third, even a superficial inspection of the present will show that there are a number of contradictory tendencies present in the social life of mass society. There is a decided trend toward profession-alization, but there is also an increasing tendency to question the professional ideal. There is a tendency toward large-scale social plan-ning, but there is also a growing movement for equality and democrati-zation of institutions. These are only a small fraction of the many contradictions apparent in the present. Of course, one may not take these contradictions seriously and argue, instead, that the most powerful trends are consistent in one direction or the other. This will all depend, again, on one's image of the human condition as a whole.

CONSIDERING THE FUTURE

If we cannot provide the grounds for optimism or pessimism and we cannot predict the future, why should we even talk about the future at all? First, it is important to realize that the processes of cognitive dissonance tend to operate with regard to visions of the future in mass society. Ascendent social groups will tend to have optimistic visions of the future, declining groups pessimistic visions of the future, and embattled groups mixed visions.[5] The reader can see how this might apply to his own situation. It is not very difficult to determine whether or not one is optimistic. Once the determination has been made, the next step is to find the group with whose fortunes one has identified. This is not always so easy, because of the many groups competing for one's allegiance. Marx simplified the matter when he argued that people identified their fortunes with the economic class to which they belonged. However, as was pointed out in the thirteenth chapter, the nation, the ethnic group, the civilization, the region, the racial-cultural group, the family, professional groups, and even humanity are other possible frames of reference. Few people are tied to any one of these groups completely, and so there are frequently confused and mixed judgments about the future. For example, one's nation may be declining and one's social class ascending. It is also important not to confuse the group with which one might believe it moral to identify and those with which one actually identifies. In determining optimism and pessimism, the *actual* group not the *ideal* group is the significant one.

It is perhaps reasonable to state that in the mass societies of today most people take the family group (whether a present family or a possible future family) as their immediate frame of reference and the nation as their wider context. Optimism prevails when the family or nation enjoys good times, and pessimism when the opposite occurs. Robert Dahl has made this point by claiming that, at least in the United States, most people are of the type *homo civicus* rather than of the type *homo politicus.*[6] *Homo civicus* (civic man) is concerned primarily with his private life, centering around his family. *Homo politicus* (political man) has wider interests and, therefore, carries on public affairs. If one is able to determine the group with which he has identified, the next step is to see whether the fortunes of the group have colored one's view of the future. Having done this, one will likely have a much clearer vision of the human condition than previously. Also, one will be able to make a much freer choice among the various groups competing for allegiance. It is vain to believe that you can cut yourself off from attachment to all social groups. Crude self-interest usually ends up meaning support for the most powerful current groups.

The second reason to consider the future, even if one can neither predict it nor provide hope for it, is to alert people to the emerging contexts in which their choices may be framed. Perhaps there would be some comfort in believing that a professional futurologist could predict with accuracy the shape of things to come. If people held such a belief they would be relieved of having to make difficult choices in the realm of public affairs. Such denial of responsibility by masses of people is extremely distressing, but even more distressing from our viewpoint is that the main purchasers of futurology are members of elites. This merely bolsters a theme that has been repeated throughout this book: elites in mass societies have a propensity to avoid responsibility at all costs. Thus, by pointing out contexts of choice, dilemmas, contradictions, uncertainties and multiple possibilities, the study of the future may lead to an expansion of both freedom and responsibility. The values of freedom and responsibility, of course, are the ones that have guided our writing in this book, so it is only to be expected that our method for studying the future and even our vision of the future will be colored by these values.

The commitment to expanding freedom and responsibility flies in the face of much that has been written about the prospects for rationality in mass society. The past nine chapters have described an emerging context of human existence in mass societies, one that seems to discourage freedom and responsibility. Many of these developments can be summed up under the heading of "conglomerate," the characteristic context for social life today. It is in the shadow of conglomerates that people in mass society will make their choices about the shape of the future.

THE CONGLOMERATE

Conglomerates appear in all phases of life in mass society. Among the conglomerates that have been discussed in this book are the megalopolis, the multiversity, the complex, and the business conglomerate. The conglomerate can be defined as an organization that provides a container for a wide diversity of activities, some of which may be contradictory. Presiding over the conglomerate are elites of directors who exercise budgetary control over the various divisions of the organization and who attempt to maintain and expand the wealth, power, prestige, and loyalty commanded by the conglomerate at the expense of other organizations. The directors are concerned with furthering the growth of the conglomerate rather than with seeing any particular function performed. Therefore, unlike organizations of the past, there is no attempt by the leadership of the conglomerate, in so far as it has any coherent leadership, to design the organization as an effective means to a given end.

In the more traditional folk societies the dominant contexts were institutions, in which both the means and ends of activity were fixed. For example, there would be only one legitimate means to attain the end of raising children to maturity. In the more modern industrial societies, ends remained fixed, but there was greater freedom to experiment with diverse means. For example, various forms of mechanized agriculture competed with less mechanized forms. In the present mass societies, both means and ends are open. There are no completely authoritative organizations to tell the person what goals his action should serve, nor is there any readily available common-sense wisdom to tell him how to accomplish these goals. For example, in the multiversity one cannot be sure that arguing for a policy on the basis of its educational value will fall on sympathetic administrative ears. If the policy interferes with the operations of the university's hotel, for example, it is likely to be shelved. Similarly, at many multiversities the travesty of Saturday classes occurs simultaneously with pep rallies urging the students to attend the football game. In the midst of classroom activity, bull horns will be blaring invitations to entertainment and loudspeakers will be broadcasting march music.

In no conglomerate can one be certain that the announced goals of the organization have any relation to the major activities performed. In the past one could speak of the functions of an organization being usurped by other functions.[7] For example, a dying political movement might slowly come to look more like a social club than an action group. Today, however, there often are no functions to be usurped. There are merely multitudes of interest groups in each conglomerate battling for greater shares of the wealth, power, prestige and loyalty.

Conglomerates can range from formal organizations like ITT to mere containers for activity like the megalopolis. Where there is a formal organization, the directors will be legally defined; where the formal organization does not exist, any direction will come about through concerted action by those most influential in major complexes of interest groups. For example, the megalopolis demonstrates the values of wealth, power, prestige, and parochial loyalty not because any conspiracy of important members designed it that way, but because the result of interest-group competition made it that way. The conglomerate thus unites all the social processes discussed in this book —production and creation, coordination and control, consumption and appreciation, and education and communication. Within each conglomerate, all of these processes are carried on and, therefore, the walls between different functions have fallen down. Many people fear that the crumbling of the walls of separation will lead to a totalitarian society in which a tiny elite will manipulate a compliant mass. Thus they call for a return to a simpler age in which every legitimate activity had its special place and there was a place made for every legitimate activity.[8]

Besides it being nearly impossible to determine what is legitimate in mass society, there are indications that many people would refuse to return to the simple cubby-holed existence of the nineteenth century when work was work and play was play. Those who demand job satisfaction do not see any clear distinction between work and play. For many, work should also be entertaining and fun. Similarly, professors who staunchly defend islands of academic freedom in mass society miss the point that the results of their "free" research are used by other conglomerates as grist for propaganda. Where are the channels by which the professor directly communicates to the "common man?" Such islands of academic freedom seem little different from the islands of luxury in the suburbs of the megalopolis.

Perhaps the overriding feature of the emerging context of mass society is the lack of responsibility by anyone for the fate and design of the whole. Not only is responsibility not taken, it is actively shunned even by leadership groups. Directors of conglomerates, such as Clark Kerr and Richard Nixon, take credit for their successes but not for their failures. Kerr pictured himself as a storm center around which multitudes of academic and nonacademic interest groups swirled. Under such a definition, anything he could positively accomplish would be viewed as a great achievement, while any of his failures could be written off to circumstances beyond his control. The University of California, given Kerr's definition, was barely held together by a valiant administration. Similarly, American Presidents never tire of pointing out how government cannot accomplish everything. This phrase is trotted out whenever a decision has been made to turn down the requests of some group for privileges or when a policy has failed. When requests are being met or policies are succeeding, the enormous importance and effectiveness of government are noted. How many public relations directors of business conglomerates sit in suburban industrial parks thinking of reasons why business alone cannot take responsibility for the so-called problems of the cities?

The lack of responsibility for the whole can be documented in all sectors of mass society. One can begin with the work setting and the governing philosophy of work in mass society. The pinnacle of job success in mass societies is to be a professional. However, the professional ideal directly involves the narrowing of responsibility for the context in which one exists. The professional is trained to solve particular problems that appear in narrowly defined areas of experience. In many cases he has no choice as to which client he will serve and he is supposed to do his best job for every client. In mass societies, professionals increasingly work for formally organized conglomerates, which determine for them the problems they are supposed to solve and even sometimes the range of means they can use to solve them. Pharmacologists in drug companies are told to combine in a single pill a calmative and a pain reliever, and advertising men are told to sell it. It is not up to the pharmacologist to decide whether such a pill is a decent addition to human existence or to the advertiser to decide whether such a pill should be marketed.

The professional specialists within the conglomerate are cut off from the whole of human activity and left to develop their autonomy with regard to programmed goals. Not only, however, are professionals subservient to organized concentrations of power. They are also encouraged to fight among themselves for greater shares of resources. Within the conglomerate, the group that succeeds the most is the one able to marshal most effectively the various means of social control. One of the most important means of social control in a competitive system is propaganda. Thus, the organized professions are encouraged by the system of competition to inflate the importance of their specialties to the maintenance of human existence and to deflate the importance of rival professions (which means all other professions). Physicists and aeronautical engineers use scare tactics to warn people that America will certainly fall behind in its standard of life, its position in the world and its dignity unless more money is spent on visionary schemes to fly to other planets. In the meantime biologists cry that the new frontier is life, and that unless we pour more money into visionary schemes to save the environment and cure cancer once and for all there will not be anybody left to go to the moon. The social scientists add their clarion call to the debate, warning that, unless more money is spent on solving the problems of the cities, there will be no Americans left to choke on their own refuse or to live long enough to develop cancer. The irresponsibility of such propaganda should be apparent, even though some textbook writers and "educators" believe that their task with undergraduates is to persuade the students to take the viewpoint of the particular profession. They hope to send out into the world bodies and minds willing to support appeals for ever more funds.

When they look up to their superiors in power, professionals are irresponsible because they accept the goals programmed for them by elites. When they look from side to side at other professionals they are irresponsible because they attempt to inflate their own importance at the expense of others without any thought of how this will affect the entire context of human experience. However, professionals are also irresponsible even when they look down upon their clients. The professional ideal mixes two different sets of values. One is the value of specialized expertise and competence. Here the professional, like the master carpenter, is better equipped to perform certain tasks than any man on the street selected at random. The second set of values in the professional ideal centers on control and autonomy. The idea is that, because the professional has expertise, he should be allowed to make decisions on matters concerning his specialization and should only be challenged on these decisions by those who are his peers. This kind of autonomy and control has never been fully applied, and would probably be a nightmare if it were ever realized in practice. The autonomy of medical personnel is limited by the possibility of malpractice suits, while the autonomy of professors is limited by suspicious government officials, granting agencies and donors. Yet to the extent that they are able to exercise autonomy and control, professionals sometimes succeed in browbeating clients to the point at which clients will obey their directives with no further explanation. Is such autonomy and control, however, a sign of responsibility? It would appear that the opposite is true and that a professional fully responsible to his clients would try to explain to them what he is doing and why, and to provide them with a description of alternative courses of action from which they might choose. This kind of action, of course, would also involve the responsibility of clients to concern themselves with playing an active part in determining the quality of their existence.

Irresponsibility for the context of human existence is shown not only in the professional ideal, but also in the prestige hierarchies of mass society. Occupational hierarchies are based on the amount of control that people have in determining the lives of others. According to this working philosophy of inequality, the most excellent life one can lead involves doing things to other people, whether or not what is done is for their own good. Along with this control goes the desire for higher income than others and a better life-style than others (defined in terms of suburban exclusion). Thus, through making such invidious distinctions, the value of certain occupations is inflated while the value of other occupations is deflated. Yet in everyday life a plumber is often far more vital than a physician. Why, then, should the plumber's skill be valued less highly than the physician's? As long as control over others is valued for its own sake, a critical and rational assessment of the whole context of human existence will be impossible.

Irresponsibility appears, perhaps, most clearly in the political sector of existence. Here the dominant unit in mass society is the complex of interest groups. Crossing traditional boundary lines between activities, complexes such as the military-industrial complex unite groups concerned with phases of some broad sphere of human experience in efforts to gain greater wealth, power, influence and loyalty. These complexes sometimes succeed in abolishing traditional checks and balances between various functions, thereby escaping organized accountability for their deeds.

The military-industrial complex is a good example of how accountability is avoided. Members of congressional committees that are supposed to be watchdogs over defense spending desire to have military installations in their states or districts and also desire to increase the profits of munitions suppliers located in their states or districts. High profits for the munitions industry and more defense installations will aid the economy in their states or districts even if it will hurt the economy as a whole by increasing inflation and diverting resources to the military. Thus, the very people who are supposed to function as watchdogs have every interest to increase defense spending. Meanwhile, checks on munitions makers by the Department of Defense and the professional military are lessened by the fact that ex-military men serve in high positions in the defense industry. Research and development on complex weapons systems is so expensive that firms are guaranteed a profit in advance of meeting their contracts, and federal officials are anxious to hide any expensive mistakes from public view. Further, any function of independent criticism performed by the academic community is lessened by the large grants for defense research.

Finally, labor unions in the defense industry are often less concerned with battling management than with pressuring government for more defense monies. Defense contracts, after all, mean higher wages. The military-industrial complex extends into many other areas of human existence, but the preceding discussion should give some idea of its breadth and power.

Other incipient complexes, such as the one emerging around the problems of the cities, also tend to break down checks and balances. Whether or not the competition between complexes will lead to new systems of checks and balances is not clear at the moment. However, even if a balance of powers does emerge, there will still be no responsibility for the whole context of existence. The complexes will merely compete among themselves for greater shares of resources of all kinds, including the loyalties of human beings.

With the emergence of complexes and the decline of checks and balances, top leadership has become increasingly irresponsible. The idea that policies should be decided upon by elites and then sold to masses by means of propaganda and bribery (as well as judicious force, when absolutely necessary) is encouraged by the emerging structure of complexes. Since the new ways of asserting interests cut across traditional and formally defined boundaries, the public becomes confused about who is responsible for what. Scholars will appeal to their independence of judgment when they are on the payroll as consultants to the defense conglomerates. Political leaders will appeal to their restricted constitutional authority when they are daily working behind the scenes to pressure diverse groups. The very top leaders play an elaborate game of shuffling constituencies in order to gain enough independence to impose their private policy fantasies on the public.[9] Any newspaper reader can quickly become familiar with this game and its rules. It consists simply in the leader breaking promises to some groups by appealing to the needs of other groups and then reversing field. For example, aid to farmers will be cut by appealing to the needs of the consumers. Then the prices of agricultural goods will be raised by appealing to the needs of farmers. Why do leaders engage in these tactics? According to the conventional wisdom, politicians will do anything to win election. However, a deeper reason may be that leaders want to win enough independence to see some of their projects realized in real life. They are, then, perhaps seeking the control and autonomy embodied in the professional ideal and the hierarchy of occupational prestige. If this be the case, and there is reason to believe that it is then leaders are even less responsible than they would be if they were merely bending all their efforts to win reelection.[10]

EXERCISE

Find examples of leaders breaking promises to some groups by appealing to the "needs" of other groups.

Responsibility in Conglomerates

The abolition of traditional boundary lines by complexes and the consequent freeing of leaders to act out their fantasy lives in public is carried out within a set of competitive relations. The hallmark of contemporary mass societies is that the most powerful groups attempt to limit intergroup competition in every sphere of social existence. For example, business conglomerates indulge in various forms of price fixing and product differentiation to limit pure and perfect competition, political parties compete within a narrow range fixed by the rules of the game, and by the most powerful interest groups, ethnic groups compete within a context manufactured by the white Protestant majority, and ideological sects compete within a free market of ideas biased in favor of those who have the money and power to buy access to the mass media.

The myth of free competition in the various spheres of existence is one of the most effective veils covering the decline of public responsibility for the human context as a whole. Business firms pretend that the requirements of the competitive market force them to abdicate responsibility for social and political inequalities and their remediation. They plead that they must serve their stockholders first and the community as a whole only later, if at all. Meanwhile they restrict competition and attempt to gain privileges from government. Political parties continually abdicate responsibility for the human condition by blaming the opposition for failure to act. In a sense, the two parties need one another to be whipping boys for each other. It is perhaps easier for political leadership to fail in the United States than in the Soviet Union, because there is always the opposition to blame in a competitive party system. In a single-party system, scapegoats such as Jews, Trotskyites, and reds (a favorite in the old single-party American South) must be called upon for whipping-boy service.

Of course, the limitations on competition do not mean that competition between groups is abolished altogether in mass societies. The various complexes do compete with one another for resources and, even within each of the social processes, there are sometimes vicious marginal competitions between different conglomerates. For example, white ethnic groups and blacks may compete furiously for control of neighborhoods, unions may compete (sometimes violently) for the right to represent workers, businesses may engage in espionage to gain trade secrets, and political parties may smear the reputations of one anothers' candidates. The rule guiding behavior of those responsible for the various conglomerates and complexes of interest groups in mass societies is to gain ever more wealth, power, prestige, and loyalty for their organizations. Sometimes this goal involves provisional cooperation with other groups, but ultimately the system is based on competition rather than cooperation.

In other words, when cooperation is sought it is sought to increase competitive advantage in other spheres. Cooperative relations, of course, like market-splitting arrangements among business firms, may be quite durable because of the presence of still other organizations waiting in the wings to take advantage of any weakness. The ultimate appeal of the politically irresponsible is that they will be sacrificing the interests of the organization they represent if they take the wider human context into account. This rationalization reveals the ultimately competitive character of political relations in mass society.

Lack of responsibility for the entire human context is as evident in the appreciative sphere as it is in the economic and political spheres of activity. This irresponsibility is particularly evident in the systems of mass entertainments. The distinctive context of the appreciative life in mass societies is entertainment which takes the human being out of the context of his daily life and places him in a commercially contrived context. Today one can buy "total environments" in which, during leisure time, one is cut off from the rest of the megalopolis and made secure by measured doses of programmed emotional and sensory content. For those who can afford them there are panelled, sound-proofed rooms in which one can luxuriate on comfortable furniture and have one's choice of television, all-embracing stereophonic sound, picture books and magazines, or all of them at once. Incense can be burning as one puffs on marijuana cigarettes and/or gets drunk on alcoholic beverages. Of course, enough money will buy one some friends of either sex with whom one can share the environment—if other people are really all that necessary. The "total environment" described above is obviously an ideal limit in which few, if any, people spend their leisure time. However, it is the kind of thing that Aldous Huxley had in mind when he wrote his nightmare vision of *Brave New World* in which people went to the "feelies" for programmed sexual stimulation, just as they now go to the movies for programmed visual and auditory stimulation. The *Playboy* life-style for men and the *Better Homes and Gardens* life-style for women are not really all that far from

Huxley's vision. Huxley's nightmare, of course, is nothing more nor less than the dream-world of advertising men. Whether it is a beautiful dream or a nightmare depends upon one's image of the human condition, particularly upon one's notion of human purpose. If one believes that pleasure is the guiding human purpose, then the total environment of commercially contrived stimulation is indeed not only an ideal limit of a theory, but a full-fledged moral ideal.

At present there is no chance that the "total environment" will be experienced by more than a fraction of the upper middle classes. However, as people attempt to approach it and elites attempt to foster it, isolation of human beings from their whole context will increase drastically. Already there is a tendency for negative total environments to appear, which cut people off from the rest of existence and manipulate them.[12] People in mental hospitals are given tranquilizer drugs all day and left in front of television sets, old people are pushed into planned retirement villages and nursing homes, and alcoholics are sent to controlled therapy centers. Businessmen and other executives are sent on retreats where psychologists attempt to make them more sensitive, responsive to the organization, and sales conscious. Those who approach the total environment of pleasure are induced to forget those who dwell in the environment of pain, anxiety, and impotence —the total institution. The ghetto fades as the acid rock plays on.

The various total environments and approaches to them all appear within the context of the megalopolis. Given the public morality of interest-group competition, the various islands in the megalopolis are encouraged to tear themselves out of the context and to either represent themselves as special cases or as integral wholes. The ghetto is the prime example of the special case. In order to procure more funds for areas in which black people dwell, elaborate propaganda is diffused that pictures the ghetto as a negative environment. The idea is to persuade officials and their constituents that, if only enough money is spent on rebuilding and refurbishing the ghetto, this blot on the middle-class consciousness will disappear.

The opposite of pleading a special case is pleading autonomy from the rest of the human condition. Real-estate developers advertise suburbs as planned environments in which one can escape from the problems of the cities. People are made to feel lucky that they no longer have to bother with parts of the megalopolis outside their suburb, and if they are public-spirited they can always take an active part in local school-board politics or park-and-recreation development. The fate of the whole megalopolis is decided by no one in particular, and the most powerful complexes of interest groups in general. For those who are beginning the study of the social sciences, the megalopolis is the most obvious example of systematic irresponsibility for the whole in mass society. The results of the failure in public responsibility can be seen by anyone with their eyes open.

Finally, the failure of responsibility is evidenced in the multiversity and the mass media. In an important sense, the multiversity has served for us as a model of the organization of mass society because we have known it so well through our careers. The idea of conglomerates and complexes first began to dawn on us when we realized that, despite all the propaganda to the contrary, the multiversity was merely a container for a wide diversity of conflicting activities. The idea of irresponsible leadership began to become clear for us as we studied university and departmental administration from the inside. The multiversity may have a particular peculiarity of being prone to inflated rhetoric, because it functions as the organization which legitimates the other conglomerates in mass society through manipulating the myths of science and professionalism.

Figure 15.1. THE CONGLOMERATE

General Organizational Form:	An organization with multiple and often conflicting functions, which has no apparent aim but stable growth in wealth, power, influence and loyalty
Form of Exercising Power:	Complexes of similar interests cutting across the traditional boundary lines of public/private, voluntary/compulsory, profit/nonprofit, professional/managerial
Economic Form:	The multinational, multifunctional corporation
Myth:	The professional ideal and the hierarchy of occupational prestige
Political Form:	The superpower with nuclear weapons
Myth:	Elite trusteeship based on expertise in securing survival
Appreciative Form:	The megalopolis
Myth:	The suburban ideal of mass entertainment
Educational Form:	The multiversity
Myth:	Expertise in social engineering
Method of Social Control:	Manipulation of self-image to assure guilt feelings if one does not live up to the standards of the conglomerate
Standard of Social Relations:	Manipulation; the put-on

However, it is no better or worse for this than any of the other conglomerates and, if one employs the context of mass society, it should be seen neither as the nodal point for social change (the position of the New Left) nor as the last bastion of decency (the position of the old liberals and numerous academicians). The great failure of the multiversity is that it has not attempted to develop knowledge that would aid people in increasing critical awareness of their situations and that would point ways to overcoming the rampant irresponsibility in mass society. Instead of unifying perspectives, the multiversity has encouraged the fragmentation of knowledge into warring disciplines and service to existing complexes of interest groups. In protecting a vestige of academic freedom it has created a suburb of the mind.

If the multiversity is the suburb of the mind, the mass media are the slums. Here, public irresponsibility reaches its zenith with the systematic elimination of the context from the reporting of events. The mass media do not consider socialism or any other alternatives to capitalism, direct democracy or any other alternatives to democratic elitism, unified planning or any other alternatives to the megalopolis, and general education or any other alternatives to the specialism of the multiversity. In addition the media personalize events to such an extent that dominant social roles are taken for granted. For example, the disclosure that a vice-presidential candidate had spent time in a mental hospital awakened conjecture on the method of vice-presidential selection rather than discussion of whether a political system should be so personalized that it matters whether or not an official has ever been in a mental hospital. Of course, neither the multiversity nor the mass media are the "leading institutions" of mass society in the United States.[13] The leading institutions (the organizations responsible for determining values and their allocation) are still business and governmental conglomerates. However, the prime legitimation for these conglomerates is the myth of professionalism and expert knowledge. Thus, it is perhaps accurate to state that the emerging mass society is symbolized by the image of a "technocracy"—a regime of expert and technical efficiency.

TECHNOCRACY

If all political and economic roles were fully professionalized, if everyone believed in the hierarchy of occupational prestige, if elites legitimated themselves only through the myth of expert knowledge, if all competition was brought under regulation by dominant complexes, if entertainment was the only form of appreciation, if the suburban life-style was universally desired, and if all knowledge was processed by the multiversity, then a complete technocracy would exist. The distance of the present situation from such a technocracy can be judged by the degree to which the above conditions are not met in current mass societies. At the present time the top political and economic roles are not professionalized, but are occupied by people who have been favored by inheriting great wealth, winning elections and having the proper social characteristics (being white, Anglo-Saxon Protestant male with a degree from an elite college or university.)[14] However, the positions right below those occupied by this rather old-fashioned, though very persistent, elite, are held by people who claim to have professional competence. For example, during the Nixon administration, right below the President was Henry Kissinger, an ex-Harvard professor of political science. The other conditions for a complete technocracy also do not exist, but there are tendencies, which have been pointed to throughout this book, driving social life in a technocratic path. A technocracy would be a society in which wealth, power, influence, and loyalty would flow to those who made the most persuasive claims to technical expertise and professional competence. Its elite would demand autonomy in its control over human existence, because it would claim expert knowledge in the activities of government and administration.

A technocracy would probably justify its ascendancy through a myth resembling the one propounded by Davis and Moore in the functionalist explanation of inequality. Davis and Moore claimed that unequal rewards to different groups of people were inevitable in any society because the people in the positions most important to the survival of the society had to be motivated to perform their tasks effectively. This argument, which was presented and criticized in the ninth chapter, would provide a particularly good ideology for technocrats. First, it claims to be rooted in science, which would be the myth basis for any professionalized elite. Second, it leaves open the question of which functions are the most important for social survival. This would allow technocratic rulers to declare the "science" of administration the most important profession. Third, it would help relieve any guilt that members of the emerging elite might feel about their privilege, because it asserts that privilege is an inevitable feature of the human condition. Fourth, the criterion of performance—the survival of the society and its role system—would give the technocrats a framework in which to operate.

A technocracy would be a society in which all human relations would remain constant, and the only change that would occur would be increasing efficiency in molding people to pre-ordained roles. Thus, a technocracy would be inherently conservative. The reason for this is that the professional has no criterion by which to judge which ends are desirable.[15] Rule by professionals, then, would either be on the basis of the whim of those who happened to hold the top positions or on the basis of maintaining and expanding what was already present. Jean Meynaud makes the point that technocrats would not eliminate political decisions and conflicts. They would only disguise them behind the veil of "scientific management": "In other words, an examination of the foreseeable future reveals that there is no legitimate reason to assume that political relations will disappear: the important point is to ascertain who will be behind them and control them, and to whose advantage. These standard questions apply to technocratic forms of government as much as to any others."[16]

The elite of a technocracy would claim competence to rule by its expertise in determining the most efficient means to attain the public good. The public good would be defined as the maintenance of the given system of dominant roles. Thus, a technocracy might try to make sure that the family was preserved according to the middle-class ideal by requiring any wife who desired a career of her own to submit to psychiatric care until she became committed to behaving "normally." Similarly, professed atheists might be given psychiatric counseling by mental health personnel who themselves believed in God only because it was the mentally healthy thing to believe in. Experts in the mass media would devise a "media diet" for whole populations, so that individuals would not have their perspective on "reality" distorted.[17] Those who doubted the essential goodness of the nation-state might be given loyalty therapy. As is even the case now in some suburban high schools, "underachievers" would be given special counseling so that the society would have full talent utilization. These possibilities are by no means remote but are currently in existence in parts of mass society. There are many marriage counselors committed to the middle-class ideal of the wife as helpmate to the breadwinning and "protective" husband, and some judges order married couples seeking divorce to go to marriage counselors before they can receive their divorce.[18] Some psychiatrists believe that it is mentally healthy to believe in God, while the Federal Communications Commission in cooperation with the electronic media prepares a kind of media diet. Loyalty therapy may not be practiced extensively, but loyalty oaths have been required to gain certain kinds of employment. Some of the readers of this book know all too well that "underachieving" according to the standards of established institutions is in disfavor.

Some might argue that a technocracy would be a distinctive improvement over the present system, because at least jobs would be done efficiently. However, aside from the fact that professionals claiming to rule by competence might actually be quite incompetent, it is not at all clear that it would be desirable to mold people to perform existing social roles efficiently. From an outsider's viewpoint, inefficiency is very desirable when people are attempting to accomplish worthless or actually baneful ends. Another argument in favor of technocracy might be that since its principle is efficient achievement of ends, a technocratic elite would be capable of accomplishing good ends and of speeding desirable social changes. This is the argument of those who believe that if given a free hand, engineers and social scientists could solve our social problems.

Leaving aside the question of who is to decide which situations constitute social problems and in what priority order they should be "solved," the idea that engineers and scientists are capable of causing social reconstruction assumes that only ignorance stands in the way of achieving someone's utopia (usually defined in terms of full bellies, sanitary housing, freedom from certain diseases, and a "clean" environment—a utopia that might be labeled medical materialism). Of course, it is not so easy as it might seem to figure out what human beings need, particularly if one believes that there are multiple images of the human condition and that rational thought involves relativizing these images and then making responsible choices. The supporter of technocracy either has to pretend that there are no serious disagreements about a desirable future for human beings or that all the meth-

---

Figure 15.2. TECHNOCRACY

1. All political and economic roles professionalized
2. Universal agreement on the present hierarchy of occupational prestige
3. Elites legitimated through the myth of expert knowledge and supposed contribution to the survival of society
4. Competition regulated by dominant complexes
5. All organizations conglomerates
6. Entertainment the only form of appreciation
7. Suburban life-style universally desired
8. All knowledge processed by the multiversity

How far is the present American society from a technocracy?

---

ods of social control should be marshaled to make people desire the values he holds. A much more potent barrier than rational thought to the antiseptic utopia of happy and cooperative people toasting humanity with glasses of cola is the resistance of vested interests, such as military conglomerates.

COST-BENEFIT ANALYSIS

Though people in the United States do not live in a technocracy, there are many technocratic features of contemporary organizations. In addition to the familiar political refrain that "if we can send a rocket to the moon, we can solve our social problems," there is a growing tendency to make political decisions under the guise of scientific planning. The most familiar form of planning is cost-benefit analysis. Here, a problem is defined and solutions are evaluated in accordance with the benefits they are expected to procure and the resources that will have to be expended to put them into effect. In simple terms, that solution should be chosen that provides the most benefits for the least cost. There are many problems with cost-benefit analysis and related forms of planning.[19] First, they tend, like all technocratic devices, to hold the context of human existence constant and to work only on a single problem. Thus, cost-benefit analyses of housing policy do not consider the possibility of abolishing private real estate development and promotion. Second, the technical process of cost-benefit analysis cannot determine what benefits are most important—or even what a benefit is. These determinations must be made by value-commitments, not by judgments of efficiency. Third, the criteria of cost-benefit analysis are purely quantitative, and usually involve only factors that can be measured in terms of money. This means that technocratic planning is incapable of criticizing the quality of life as experienced by human beings in their everyday lives.

At present, technocratic planning is merely a way of shoring up existing elites and giving professionals greater entry into large-scale decision-making situations. During the 1960s a number of groups began making demands for increased benefits from government. Led by the blacks, disadvantaged minorities that hitherto had been relatively quiescent pointed to obvious inequalities in living conditions and demanded equality with more fortunate groups. Meanwhile the military-industrial complex was growing larger and demanding more resources for its own uses. Caught in the squeeze, middle-class taxpayers began to complain that they were the forgotten Americans, and that they deserved to enjoy life in their suburban retreats. The mobilization of new groups in the political arena and the increasing demands of established complexes and coalitions caught political leaders in a crunch. The pie was not expanding rapidly enough to satisfy everyone, yet no group seemed to be willing to trim its demands. Part of the answer to this problem was found in appeals to scientific planning and cost-benefit analysis. Planners could figure out how to divide the pie scientifically by calculating how to meet demands most efficiently. However, what demands were to be met and in what order? Politicians might pretend that planners could answer this question, but actually they were incapable of doing so. Instead, a number of different policy principles were trotted out by various interest groups and their governmental spokesmen.

One, favored mainly by conservatives and Republicans, prescribes that no group should gain any advantages at the expense of another. Therefore, improvements for disadvantaged groups can only come through increasing the size of the pie. If the pie remains the same size the disadvantaged remain where they are. A second principle, favored mainly by liberals and Democrats, urges a "reordering of priorities." Translated out of administrative language, this means that some groups should give up some of their privileges so that other groups can get a greater share of the pie. Under this principle, however, no group should be eliminated from the contest altogether. For example, the military will retain a mammoth budget, but this budget will not be as great as it once was. A third principle, favored mainly by radicals working outside the two-party system, is that income distribution is not enough. Wealth, meaning the non-taxable resources of the large corporations and the wealthy individuals, should be distributed to the people. The "people" in this case would be represented by a populist (anti-big business) or outright socialist government. The point here is not that any one of these proposals is superior to its competitors, but that any of them could be applied with equal ease by technocratic planners. Under the Nixon administration the game plan has been to apply the rule that no group should gain any advantages at the expense of another. This principle, which may superficially sound fair, is actually very conservative because it assumes that any privileges which have already been gained are justified. Thus, the appeal by politicians caught in a crunch to "cost-benefit" analysis conceals the value-commitments involved in policy making. A pure technocracy would be no more immune to so-called "political" considerations.

EXERCISE

Listen to or read a debate on policies to resolve a social problem. Which standards of public policy (liberal, conservative, radical) are implied in the various proposed solutions? Can you generate and justify any other standards of public policy?

Not only are technocratic tendencies evident in planning procedures, but they are also present in appeals for a "fourth branch of government" and a National Council of Social Advisers. The fourth branch of government, which has awakened controversy in recent years, would "(a) collect all the data necessary to continually track the state of the nation; (b) define potential problems suggested by the information; (c) develop alternative plans to cope with the problems; and (d) evaluate ongoing projects in terms of real time and advise the people accordingly."[20] The Council of Social Advisers would be an agency composed of three members appointed by the President who as a result of "training, experience, and attainments" would be "exceptionally qualified" to appraise policies and suggest new ones.[21] It is likely that if the United States moves towards the model of a pure technocracy it will do so through the addition of agencies such as the fourth branch of government or the Council of Social Advisers. These agencies would not at first disturb the traditional channels of decision making, but would merely be adjuncts to the federal administration, building up its power at the expense of other conglomerates. Whatever administration was in power could use such agencies to give scientific legitimation to its policies. However, in time the politicians could become captives of the technocrats and simply accept the policies that they had provided. This prospect might seem frightening, but we are by no means sure that it would be any worse than the present.

The foregoing discussion should not be viewed as a condemnation of planning and a celebration of spontaneity and private enterprise. The problem of technocracy is not that it embodies planning, which is merely one aspect of human reason, but that it puts planning in the hands of an elite of specialists. This involves a serious mistake about human existence. Planning the context of the human condition is not a technical specialty that can be professionalized but an activity involving choices among competing images of society. All human beings are enfolded in a public situation and related to various social groups. They are always giving their support to some future or another, whether or not they are aware of this. Putting it bluntly, technocracy only means that people surrender their choices to elites which will act to maintain the system as is, or will change it in accordance with the wishes of the most powerful complexes of interest groups. For those who expect to hold high positions in the technocracy, pure or adulterated by tradition, these arguments will fall on deaf ears. Others will know what to expect if present tendencies continue.

SELF-ESTEEM

For those concerned with resisting the development toward a technocracy (and they may be in a decided minority) it is important to understand the principal means of social control employed in contemporary mass societies and the ways in which liberation from this control is possible. All established and emergent social orders in the past have used all the means of social control to maintain and extend their dominance. Force has been a staple of human affairs, as has bribery, fraud and the manipulation of procedures. However, by far the most effective and economical means of social control is guilt and related modes of programmed self-regulation. In earlier agricultural societies guilt was fostered by belief in the immortal soul. People were led to believe that if they did not obey social rules they were sinners. Their guilt could only be removed by confession, repentance and good works. Added to the control mechanism of guilt was the reward and punishment system of the afterlife. If one sinned by violating the social norms one might suffer eternal damnation in hell (the Western variety) or return to earth as a lower form of life (the Eastern variety). On the other hand, if one was obedient, heaven or release from pain was in the cards. With the secularization of modern life the control mechanism of guilt and the expectation of an afterlife were weakened. Certainly these controls still exist in the mass societies of today, but they are no longer as certain in their operation as they probably once were. Further, while some psychiatrists may consider belief in God to be part of a normal and healthy personality, religious appeals are somewhat incongruous with the scientific mythology of the technocracy. Finally, the "soul" itself has fallen into disuse as a way of characterizing the human individual, except perhaps by astronauts and devotees of the Jesus movement.

With the erosion of the soul, new guilt-producing mechanisms have arisen to cement conformity. These center around the new idol of mass society: the self. While most of the readers of this book may not be sure whether or not they have souls, they are certainly convinced that they have selves. After all, is it not a self that is reading the book? The answer to this question is not at all as certain as it may seem. William James once set about seriously to find his "self" and the results were quite embarrassing. After a thorough search James became convinced that the self was merely a feeling between the nose and the throat centered on the vocal chords. Yet he was not satisfied with this conclusion as the final answer, so he developed the idea, which is basic to the first five chapters of this book, that the self is merely a phase in the flow of human experience. In fact, James identified three different selves centered on three distinct experiences. He defined the "material self" as everything that a person calls his own, including physical body and significant property. Thus, he extended the self beyond the skin. The second self was the "social self," defined as the ideas that other people have about a person. Here James extended the individual person into the experience of others, making the individual a phase of social processes. Finally, James defined a third self, the "spiritual self," which functioned as an ideal judge of activity. This spiritual self could be a conception of God or a set of moral principles. In any case, it provided a cultural dimension to the person which freed him from dependence on present feelings and social relations.[22]

While James is often quoted as a founding father of social psychology, his investigations fell short of identifying the self that most people today believe that they have,—the self manipulated by psychiatrists, journalists, advertisers, public school teachers, and all other bureaucratized and professionalized mind workers. The fourth self James did not discover was the self of "self-esteem." The notion of self-esteem is embedded in the works of contemporary psychologists. Those who follow Freud speak of the need for ego strength; those who follow the so-called humanists speak of the need for self-esteem as a prelude to self-actualization; the symbolic interactionists state that mental health requires a positive self-image; and the neo-Freudians discourse on the importance of a strong identity for a full life.[23] The notion of self-esteem is so firmly fixed in the mass mind that it is difficult even to define it. Just as the fish is the last one to know he is enslaved by water, the member of mass society is the last one to know that he is enslaved by self-esteem.

Appeals to self-esteem are a staple of relations in mass society. According to popular mythology, every woman knows that it is not wise to bruise the ego of a man she wants to catch. Rather, she concentrates on building up the ego. What does this term "ego," synonymous with self-esteem, mean? The "self of self-esteem" may be defined as that image of the self that the person holds as an accurate representation of the self. Thus, the fourth self is an image, just like the images that make up the social self. However, it is not an image of the person held by others, but an image of the person held by that person. In mass societies the quickest way to a person's heart, pocketbook or compliance is through building up his fourth self. Conversely, the quickest way to damage a person is to depreciate his fourth self. People tend to treat their self-esteem like a stock market investment. They watch its rise and fall day by day, and feel elated or depressed accordingly. They are continuously on the lookout for signs of impending doom or success. This is why they are so concerned with the opinions of others. They are primarily concerned with the state of their social self as an indicator of how they should view their fourth self. Further, people continually propagandize themselves about their fourth selves. They tell themselves how good they are, how failures really are not failures at all, and how successes reflect so well on them. At extremes they spend free moments polishing up their fourth selves and contemplating them with joy. Often they engage in relations with others merely to demonstrate their fourth selves in action—to themselves. The put-on, a characteristic relation in mass society, depends on the inflation of the fourth self in both parties. The victim is so preoccupied with his fourth self that he does not realize that it is all a game until too late. The exploiter is manipulating the victim to show himself how cool he is. After all, the exploiter is not craving submission or appreciation from a contemptible victim.

Figure 15.3. THE FOUR SELVES

1. The Material Self:	Everything a person calls his own, including physical body and significant property
2. The Social Self:	The ideas that other people have about a person
3. The Spiritual Self:	The person's moral principles and projects
4. The Self of Self-Esteem:	The image of the person held by that person

---

The self of self-esteem is the greatest barrier of all to carrying on the process of self-understanding. It tends to freeze or clot conscious life into a perpetual recycling process in which satisfaction is gained not through creativity, participation, appreciation, inquiry, love, and self-development, but through talking to oneself. It is interesting to note that those who grew up before the emergence of the conglomerate often view talking to oneself with suspicion—as vaguely sinful or unhealthy. However, the quickest way to gain ego-strength or a positive self-image is to propagandize oneself. Witness the way black people in the United States built up their self-esteem by telling themselves that black is beautiful. This is merely an example of collective self-esteem. George Herbert Mead went so far as to define the human essence as the ability to talk to oneself.[24] The fourth self is perhaps the most sacred object in mass society. Yet it is truly no more than an idol that functions to induce conformity to emerging institutions in place of the soul.

WAYS THAT SELF-ESTEEM CAN FUNCTION

How does the self of self-esteem function as a social control device in mass societies? The answer to this question will become evident upon determining where this image comes from. The basic components of the fourth self are, of course, James' three selves. The self-image is a compound of selected features of the material self (most importantly an image of the body), selected features of the social self (in most cases the more favorable judgments and images of the person expressed by others) and selected moral idealizations from the culture (perhaps some of the views of the human essence present in religious traditions). However, in mass societies there is frequently a fourth component in this compound—images of standardized selves fabricated by the mind workers. Such images began to appear at the very beginning of the secularization process when philosophers such as Hobbes and Machiavelli abandoned traditional religious definitions of the human essence for so-called scientific definitions of human nature. Some of these images were discussed and criticized in the second chapter (where schools of social thought were discussed) and in the first chapter where the barriers to self-understanding were detailed. Up until the twentieth century the most important image of the human being challenging religious interpretations was that of "economic man," motivated by greed for profits. In the twentieth century, however, the self industry has reached its fullest development with the emergence of conglomerates. The image of economic man is still fostered today by business conglomerates, particularly in the training of salesmen. However, many jobs in conglomerates demand a dampening of profit motivation and a shift of competitive motivations toward technical achievement according to bureaucratic standards, compliance with orders from superiors and cooperation with teams of specialists. Along with this development has come a host of new packaged self-images ranging from those marketed by human-relations technicians and industrial psychologists to those sold by various branches of psychiatry. What has happened in mass society is the disappearance of theological or philosophical views of the self from preeminent positions in the culture, and the ascendancy of purported scientifically developed images. Of course, farmers, workers and clerical personnel can still get along with the religiously based self-images, and there are thousands of clergymen to promote them. High-level professionals, particularly academicians, have the security to cultivate philosophically based self-images, and there are existentialists, phenomenologists and other high-class mind workers to market them. Older ideological images, such as the Marxist one glorifying the producer and the racist or nationalist ones glorifying particular "group minds" persist among dispossessed classes and declining middle classes respectively. However, for the rising professionalized and semi-professionalized middle classes there are the "scientific" images of psychiatry and related mental fields.

Many readers of this book hold self-images that were originally fabricated by some group of mind workers, such as the images of the well-adjusted personality, the well-rounded man, the high achiever, the self-actualizing individual, the authentic personality, the playboy, or the corporation wife. The professional ideal is merely one of the most tenacious of these fabricated images—the one that will be held by the members of any emerging technocracy. Thus, in mass society self-images are packaged and marketed for specific groups within the conglomerate social structure. Mind workers, promoting the most diverse and contradictory images, coexist in relative peace because they are directing their efforts at different groups. Of course, the various mind workers fight jurisdictional disputes as they compete for control of human experience. However, as time goes on it is likely that the competition will settle down, just like the competition between business and other conglomerates has abated. When and if that happens you will know that the technocracy has solidified and the older elites have passed from the scene.

At present, there is a severe contradiction in the system of packaged self-images. Each group of mind workers claims that its image is universally valid for all human beings. Since all cannot be correct, one who recognizes this absurd situation gains a degree of freedom. However, particularly if one is preparing for a profession, there is every reason not to recognize the absurdity because the packaged self-image can be exceedingly useful for gaining success. One who makes the image of professional achievement the basis of his self-esteem is well fitted for bureaucratic competition. Day by day as he pursues his career he will check to see whether or not he has worked hard enough, whether or not he has made any slips that will hinder his promotion, whether or not he has projected the proper image to others. Such exceeding self-concern will cut him off from relations with others, except for competitive relations with rivals and supportive relations with a small circle of friends or family, and will sever him from the total context of human existence. In free moments he will ceaselessly polish up his professional image so that he will be able to drive himself to even further achievements and success. His aim will be success as defined by whatever conglomerate he is in, and the conglomerate will foster his self-image. If you want to be a technocrat you will adopt this self-image, fit yourself for competition and take enormous pride in any accomplishments you make in your narrow area of specialization. Of course, you should not count on success, because there will be many like you.

If you do not want to be a technocrat, what should you do? Exponents of the counter-culture have marketed their own self-image based on pleasure and doing your own thing. This tends to be merely a prescription for self-isolation and irresponsibility. Others would attempt to diffuse philosophically based self-images more widely. We would suggest that you go one step further and question whether self-esteem is so important after all. Even if you shed the fourth self, you will still have three others.

SUMMARY

The hallmark of mass society is systematic irresponsibility for the entire human context. The irresponsibility is fostered by the dominant organizational form in mass society—the conglomerate—which is a container for diverse and often contradictory activities principled to sheer growth in wealth, power, influence and the command of loyalty. The conglomerate is manifested in every phase of social existence in mass society. Business conglomerates, complexes of interest groups, the megalopolis and the multiversity all show features of the conglomerate form. The summation of tendencies of change in mass society is the technocracy. In a technocracy rule would be by professionals who would mold people efficiently to the performance of pre-ordained social roles. The technocracy and the conglomerate are consistent with one another because the professional elite, legitimized on the basis of expertise in means, could conceivably sanction any activity furthering its own perpetuation.

The motivational principle that would be emphasized by a technocracy and which is quite evident in contemporary life would be technical achievement within bureaucratic confines. In order to achieve in a competitive system, people usually develop overweening self-esteem which isolates them from others and from their context and which is encouraged by the conglomerates. Mind workers, marketing packaged selves, are ever ready to serve the conglomerates and those who want to make it up the organizational ladder.

NOTES

Chapter 1. THE HUMAN CONDITION

1. Bertrand Russell, *Has Man a Future?* (Baltimore: Penguin Books, 1961), p. 127.

2. See also Jean-Paul Sartre, *Being and Nothingness* (New York: Philosophical Library, 1956); Sartre, *Nausea* (New York: New Directions,1964).

3. E. H. Carr, *The New Society* (New York: St. Martin's Press, 1960).

4. Joe McGinniss, *The Selling of the President, 1968* (New York: Trident Press, 1969).

5. The relations between social science and despair are discussed by theorists of mass society. See William Barrett, *What is Existentialism?* (New York: Grove Press, 1964); E. H. Carr, *What is History?* (New York: Knopf, 1961); José Ortega y Gasset, *The Revolt of the Masses* (New York: New American Library, 1950); Karl Jaspers, *Man in the Modern Age* (Garden City, N.Y.: Doubleday, n.d.).

6. Talcott Parsons has described this "deflationary cycle" in social relations. See Talcott Parsons, *Politics and Social Structure* (New York: Free Press, 1969).

7. Henry W. Malcolm, "The Crisis in Morality: Human vs. Institutional," *New University Thought* 5 (Special Issue, 1966–67): 92.

8. Bertrand Russell has distinguished between knowledge by acquaintance and knowledge by description. See Bertrand Russell, *The Problems of Philosophy* (London: Oxford University Press, 1957), pp. 46–59.

9. The belief that money is the most important factor in human existence is reflected in the best seller list. For example, see Adam Smith, *The Money Game* (New York: Random House, 1968).

10. David Riesman with Nathan Glazer and Reuel Denney, *The Lonely Crowd* (New Haven: Yale University Press, 1961). For experiments on conformity see Solomon E. Asch, "Effects of Group Pressure upon the Modification and Distortion of Judgments," in *Groups, Leadership and Men,* ed. H. Guetzkow (Pittsburgh: Carnegie Press, 1951), pp. 177–90.

11. The idea that there are elites of wealth and power in contemporary societies is long-standing, but not undisputed, in sociology. The history of this view can be found in James H. Meisel, *The Myth of the Ruling Class* (Ann Arbor: University of Michigan Press, 1962); Renzo Sereno, *The Rulers* (New York: Frederick A. Praeger, 1962).

12. R. D. Laing, *The Politics of Experience* (New York: Ballantine Books, 1967); Philip Rieff, *The Triumph of the Therapeutic* (New York: Harper & Row, 1966).

13. This attitude has been called "vulgar pragmatism." See Abraham Kaplan, *American Ethics and Public Policy* (New York: Oxford University Press, 1963).

14. Howard Ross Smith, *Democracy and the Public Interest* (Athens: University of Georgia Press, 1960).

15. Elijah Jordan described this phenomenon as the "sale situation." See his *Business be Damned* (New York: H. Schuman, 1952).

16. McGinniss, *The Selling of the President.*

17. The unity of thought and action is a central principle of many schools of twentieth-century thought, for example, Marxism, pragmatism, and existential phenomenology. See Joan Huber Rytina and Charles P. Loomis, "Marxist Dialectic and Pragmatism: Power as Knowledge," *American Sociological Review* 35 (April 1970): 308–18.

18. Jules Henry has described the implicit philosophy of advertising. See his *Culture Against Man* (New York: Random House, 1963).

19. Riesman et al., *The Lonely Crowd;* Jay M. Jackson and Herbert D. Saltzstein, "The Effect of Person-Group Relationships on Conformity Processes," *Journal of Abnormal and Social Psychology* 57 (1958): 17–24.

20. McGinniss, *The Selling of the President.*

21. The judgment that basic beliefs about the human condition affect others besides the individual people who hold them is rooted in an existentialist perspective on the human condition. See Michael A. and Deena Weinstein, "Sartre and the Humanist Tradition in Sociology," in *Sartre: A Collection of Critical Essays,* ed. Mary Warnock (Garden City, N.Y.: Doubleday, 1971), pp. 357–86.

22. Georges Sorel, *Reflections on Violence* (Glencoe, Ill.: Free Press, 1950); Seymour M. Lipset, *Political Man* (Garden City, N.Y.: Doubleday, 1963).

23. Some social thinkers believe that personal growth is a middle-class luxury or illusion. See Frantz Fanon, *The Wretched of the Earth* (New York: Grove Press, 1965); Michael Novak, "Politicizing the Lower Middle," *Commonweal* 40 (6 June 1969): 343.

24. Regis Debray, *Revolution in the Revolution?* (New York: Monthly Review Press, 1967).

25. Arthur Bentley developed the concept of "clotting." See his *Relativity in Man and Society* (New York: G. P. Putnam's Sons, 1926).

26. The origins of the idea that the self is property have been discussed by C. B. Macpherson in his *The Political Theory of Possessive Individualism* (Oxford: Clarendon Press, 1962).

27. Sigmund Freud, *A General Introduction to Psychoanalysis* (Garden City, N.Y.: Doubleday, 1953); Abraham H. Maslow, *Motivation and Personality* (New York: Harper & Row, 1954).

28. Augustine, *The City of God* (New York: Hafner, 1948), IV: 4.

29. Michael A. Weinstein, "New Ways and Old to Talk About Politics," *Review of Politics* 35 (January 1973): 41–60.

30. The social relativity of the idea that human beings are inherently greedy is shown by E. T. Hiller, *The Nature and Basis of Social Order* (New Haven: College and University Press, 1966); Radhakamal Mukerjee, *The Philosophy of Social Science* (London: Macmillan, 1960).

31. William H. Whyte, Jr., *The Organization Man* (Garden City, N.Y.: Doubleday, 1957).

32. John Kenneth Galbraith has presented a defense of committees in his *The New Industrial State* (Boston: Houghton Mifflin, 1971).

33. Whyte, *The Organization Man.*

34. C. Wright Mills, *The Sociological Imagination* (New York: Grove Press, 1958).

35. Uniqueness of the self is a prominent theme in American thought. See Josiah Royce, *The World and the Individual,* vol. 2 (New York: Dover Books, 1959).

36. The defense of tradition has been undertaken by many twentieth-century conservatives. See Russell Kirk, *The Conservative Mind* (Chicago: Henry Regnery, 1954); Robert A. Nisbet, *Community and Power* (New York: Oxford University Press, 1962).

37. Ortega y Gasset, *The Revolt of the Masses.*

38. The systematic analysis of world-views and their social relativity has been undertaken by F. S. C. Northrop, *The Meeting of East and West* (New York: Macmillan, 1946); Stephen C. Pepper, *World Hypotheses* (Los Angeles: University of California Press, 1957); Pitirim Sorokin, *Sociological Theories of Today* (New York: Harper & Row, 1966).

39. The analysis of the relations between beliefs about the human condition and social groupings is called the sociology of knowledge. See Peter L. Berger and Thomas Luckmann, *The Social Construction of Reality* (Garden City, N.Y.: Doubleday, 1966); Burkart Holzner, *Reality Construction in Society* (Cambridge, Mass.: Schenckman, 1968); Karl Mannheim, *Essays on the Sociology of Knowledge* (London: Routledge & Kegan Paul, 1952); Robert K. Merton, *Social Theory and Social Structure* (Glencoe, Ill.: Free Press, 1949).

40. Karl Marx and Friedrich Engels, *The Communist Manifesto* (New York: Appleton-Century-Crofts, 1955), pp. 29–30.

41. This situation has been called mental "entropy" by Gunter Remmling. See his *Road to Suspicion* (New York: Appleton-Century-Crofts, 1967).

42. Gyorgy Lukacs, *History and Class Consciousness* (Cambridge, Mass.: MIT Press 1971).

43. For a critique of this view, see Robert Boguslaw, *The New Utopians* (Englewood Cliffs, N.J.: Prentice-Hall, 1963).

44. This phenomenon has been referred to as "pseudo-gemeinschaft" by Fritz Pappenheim. See his *The Alienation of Modern Man* (New York: Monthly Review Press, 1959), p. 68.

45. Stokely Carmichael and Charles V. Hamilton, *Black Power* (New York: Random House, 1967); Eldridge Cleaver, *Soul on Ice* (New York: McGraw-Hill, 1968).

46. R. D. Laing, *Self and Others* (New York: Pantheon Books, 1969).

47. W. I. Thomas identified the "self-fulfilling prophecy." See his *On Social Organization and Social Personality* (Chicago: University of Chicago Press, 1966).

48. The idea that the human condition is trivial may be referred to as "vulgar existentialism," similar to Kaplan's "vulgar pragmatism." For a serious interpretation of the "absurd," see Albert Camus, *The Myth of Sisyphus and Other Essays* (New York: Knopf, 1955).

49. Such indecision when confronted with multiple possibilities is another vulgarization of contemporary philosophy. In this case, the philosophical school of phenomenology uses the bracketing of commitment to aid in the analysis of conscious experience, not to hinder action. Human beings cannot live in the "realm of essence" though they may experience multiple perspectives.

50. Justus Buchler has referred to the "spoliation of the possible" involved in any human action. See his *Toward a General Theory of Human Judgment* (New York: Columbia University Press, 1951).

Chapter 2. A BRIEF GUIDE TO SOCIAL THOUGHT

1. For some "maps" of social thought, see Don Martindale, *The Nature and Types of Sociological Theory* (Boston: Houghton Mifflin, 1960); Nicholas S. Timasheff, *Sociological Theory* (New York: Random House, 1957).

2. The idea was suggested in a personal letter to one of the authors from Professor Haring, dated January 24, 1971.

3. Peter M. Blau, *Exchange and Power in Social Life* (New York: Wiley, 1967).

4. John Courtney Murray, *We Hold These Truths* (Garden City, N.J.: Doubleday, 1964), p. 310.

5. Ibid.

6. Ibid., p. 311.

7. Ibid.

8. Sidney Hook, *Political Power and Personal Freedom* (New York: Collier Books, 1962), p. 73.

9. Erich Fromm, "Man for Himself," in *Philosophy for a Time of Crisis*, ed. Adrienne Koch (New York: E. P. Dutton, 1959), pp. 166–67.

10. Mary Elizabeth Walsh and Paul Hanly Furfey, *Social Problems and Social Action* (Englewood Cliffs, N.J.: Prentice-Hall, 1958), p. 4.

11. Ibid., p. 11.

12. Ibid., p. 4.

13. Karl Marx and Friedrich Engels, *The Communist Manifesto* (New York: Appleton-Century-Crofts, Inc., 1955), p. 9.

14. Ibid., p. 22.
15. Ibid., p. 27.
16. Ibid., p. 28.
17. Simone de Beauvoir, *The Second Sex* (New York: Knopf, 1952); Kate Millett, *Sexual Politics* (New York: Avon, 1970).
18. See Talcott Parsons' *Social System* (Glencoe, Ill.: Free Press, 1951) for such a division into sectors.
19. Talcott Parsons, *The Structure of Social Action* (Glencoe, Ill.: Free Press, 1949).
20. Herbert Marcuse, *Reason and Revolution* (Boston: Beacon Press, 1960), p. vii.
21. See the list of suggested readings at the end of this chapter for some major works of these schools of thought.
22. George Santayana, *Dominations and Powers* (New York: Charles Scribner's Sons, 1953). See the excellent discussion of liberty in the first several chapters.

Chapter 3. SOCIOLOGY AND SCIENCE

1. The view of human science presented in this chapter is not the only one. Many sociologists believe that the human sciences should follow the model of the natural sciences and seek to explain social activity in terms of invariant or statistical relations between events. Our viewpoint is that human science should describe intentions, purposes, and analogies, as well as finding correlations and causal laws.
2. Science fiction has relied heavily on this interpretation. See Karel Capek, *R.U.R.* (Garden City, N.Y.: Doubleday, 1923); Capek, *War With the Newts* (New York: G. P. Putnam's Sons, 1937); Mary Shelley, *Frankenstein* (New York: Dutton, 1963).
3. The legal theorist Jerome Frank presented the grounds for "fact skepticism" in the legal process. See his *Courts on Trial* (Princeton: Princeton University Press, 1949). See also Wilfrid E. Rumble, *American Legal Realism* (Ithaca: Cornell University Press, 1968).
4. An extended discussion of the ways in which facts are relative to images of the human context is found in Pitirim Sorokin, *Social and Cultural Dynamics*, 4 vols. (New York: American Book, 1937–41).
5. Robin George Collingwood, *The Idea of History* (Oxford: Clarendon Press, 1946).
6. Thomas S. Kuhn, *The Structure of Scientific Revolutions* (Chicago: University of Chicago Press, 1962).
7. Example of this perspective are Floyd Hunter, *Community Power Structure* (Chapel Hill: University of North Carolina Press, 1968); C. Wright Mills, *The Power Elite* (New York: Oxford University Press, 1956).
8. An example of this perspective is David Easton, *A Systems Analysis of Political Life* (New York: Wiley, 1965).
9. This perspective is developed by Jean-Paul Sartre in his *Search for a Method* (New York: Random House, 1968).
10. Alvin W. Gouldner, *The Coming Crisis of Western Sociology* (New York: Basic Books, 1970).
11. Sartre, *Search for a Method.*

12. This is the way in which William James saw original experience.

13. George Herbert Mead, *Mind, Self and Society* (Chicago: University of Chicago Press, 1947).

14. Gordon W. Allport, *The Nature of Prejudice* (Garden City, N.Y.: Doubleday, 1958).

15. This attitude, which is quite popular, was expressed in the eighteenth century by Edmund Burke in his *Reflections on the Revolution in France* (London: Dent, 1960).

16. This question is phrased in terms of "applied science"—What is the most effective way of realizing a goal? A similar question can be asked from a pure science perspective—What are the effects of an institution on other social relations? For example—Do day-care centers weaken family ties?

17. All public issues are debated within wider frameworks about the nature of human affairs. For example, the "energy crisis" and "environmental pollution" carry judgments about the actual and possible relations of human beings to nature.

18. Susanne Langer, *Philosophy in a New Key* (New York: New American Library, 1964).

19. This procedure is called "operationalization"—the effort to define terms by repeatable physical operations. See Abraham Kaplan, *The Conduct of Inquiry* (San Francisco: Chandler, 1964), pp. 39–42.

20. Henry Pratt Fairchild, ed., *Dictionary of Sociology* (Ames: Littlefield, Adams & Co., 1955), p. 336.

21. The idea that the process of naming is itself creative of human experience and meaning is emphasized by John Dewey and Arthur F. Bentley in their *Knowing and the Known* (Boston: Beacon Press, 1949).

22. The ways in which definitions of violence can be shifted can be grasped by considering two contrasting discussions of the terms. See Newton Garver, "What Violence Is," *Nation* 206 (24 June 1968): 820; Robert E. Fitch, "The Uses of Violence," *Christian Century* 85 (17 April 1968): 483.

23. The uses of "word magic" are catalogued and analyzed in the discipline of general semantics. See Alfred Korzybski, *Science and Sanity* (New York: International Non-Aristotelian Library Publishing, 1941); S. I. Hayakawa, *Language in Thought and Action* (New York: Harcourt Brace Jovanovich, 1972).

24. For the corruption of language and its possible consequences, see George Orwell, *1984* (New York: New American Library, 1961).

25. Arnold Rose has emphasized the importance of contradiction in revealing "covert culture"—the judgments underlying rhetoric. See his "Varieties of Sociological Imagination," *American Sociological Review* 34 (October 1969): 625.

26. On middle-class snobbery, see Andrew M. Greeley, *Why Can't They Be Like Us?* (New York: Dutton, 1971).

27. For proponents of the natural science view, see George C. Homans, *The Nature of Social Science* (New York: Harcourt Brace Jovanovich, 1967); Hans L. Zetterberg, *On Theory and Verification in Sociology* (Totowa: Bedminster Press, 1965).

28. John Stuart Mill, *Utilitarianism* (Indianapolis: Bobbs-Merrill, 1971).

29. The notion that insight is the final test of judgments about the human condition appears in the works of many twentieth-century sociologists. Georges Gurvitch speaks of "direct integration into wholes in *Traité de Sociologie*

(Paris: Presses Universitaires de France, 1958–60). Similarly, Paul Hanly Furfey discusses an "integrative sociology" based on insight in *The Scope and Method of Sociology* (New York: Harper, 1953).

30. The extension of self-understanding is one of the goals of our public morality. For a similar statement, see Thomas Landon Thorson, *The Logic of Democracy* (New York: Holt, Rinehart & Winston, 1962).

31. The social movement Technocracy bases its propaganda on the theme that people do not have a choice about whether or not government by experts will come about, but that they do have a chance to aid in the arrival of such a government. People, thus, have a chance not a choice.

Chapter 4. METHOD WITHOUT MADNESS

1. William Ernest Hocking, "Marcel and the Ground Issues of Metaphysics," *Philosophy and Phenomenological Research* 14 (June 1954): 465.

2. Abraham Kaplan, *The Conduct of Inquiry* (San Francisco: Chandler, 1964), p. 28.

3. Alfred de Grazia, ed., *The Velikovsky Affair* (New Hyde Park, N.Y.: University Books, 1966).

4. Thomas S. Kuhn, *The Structure of Scientific Revolutions* (Chicago: University of Chicago Press, 1962).

5. For some of the debates which have characterized the history of sociology, see Roscoe C. and Gisela J. Hinkle, *The Development of Modern Sociology* (Garden City, N.Y.: Doubleday, 1954).

6. George A. Lundberg, *Can Science Save Us?* (New York: David McKay, 1961.

7. Richard LaPiere, "Attitudes vs. Actions," *Social Forces* 13 (March 1934): 230–7.

8. Eugene J. Webb et al., *Unobtrusive Measures: Nonreactive Research in the Social Sciences* (Chicago: Rand McNally, 1966).

9. A related phenomenon, in which people change their behavior simply because they know that they are being studied, is called the "Hawthorn effect." See Leon Festinger and Daniel Katz, *Research Methods in the Behavioral Sciences* (New York: Holt, Rinehart & Winston, 1953), p. 101.

10. Don D. Smith, "Levels of Political Information in the American Public" (Paper presented at the annual meetings of the Southern Sociological Society, Atlanta, Georgia, 1968).

11. Floyd Hunter, *Community Power Structure* (Chapel Hill: University of North Carolina Press, 1953).

12. E. H. Carr, *The New Society* (New York: St. Martin's Press, 1960), p. 13.

13. Durkheim used many other methods besides the historical method. For example, he used the demographic method in his study of suicide.

14. For examples of ideal types, see Hans Gerth and C. Wright Mills, eds., *From Max Weber* (New York: Oxford University Press, 1946).

15. Hannah Arendt, *The Origins of Totalitarianism* (New York: Meridian Books, 1958).

16. Ferdinand Toennies, *Community and Society* (East Lansing: Michigan State University Press, 1957).

17. Emile Durkheim, *The Division of Labor in Society* (Glencoe, Ill.: Free Press, 1947).

18. Emile Durkheim, *Suicide* (Glencoe, Ill.: Free Press, 1951).

19. For a discussion of the various explanations of political violence, see H. L. Nieburg, *Political Violence* (New York: St. Martin's Press, 1969).

20. Erving Goffman, *Asylums* (Garden City, N.Y.: Doubleday, 1961).

21. Elliot Liebow, *Tally's Corner* (Boston: Little, Brown, 1967).

22. Webb et al., *Unobtrusive Measures*. See particularly the section "Contrived Observation: Hidden Hardware and Control," pp. 142–70.

23. Bronislaw Malinowski, *Argonauts of the Western Pacific* (New York: Dutton, 1961), p. 18. Malinowski developed the technique of participant observation.

24. For example, see William F. Whyte, *Street Corner Society: The Social Structure of an Italian Slum* (Chicago: University of Chicago Press, 1955).

25. For examples of nonparticipant observation, see Peter M. Blau, *The Dynamics of Bureaucracy* (Chicago: University of Chicago Press, 1963).

26. See the special issue "On Language and Conduct," *Sociological Focus* 3 (Winter 1969–70), particularly the articles by Irwin Deutscher, Aaron V. Cicourel, and R. Bruce Anderson.

27. Martin Trow, "Small Businessmen, Political Tolerance and Support for McCarthy," *American Journal of Sociology* 64 (1958): 270–81.

28. Pitirim Sorokin, *Fads and Foibles in Modern Sociology and Related Sciences* (Chicago: Henry Regnery, 1956).

29. Stanley Milgram, "Behavioral Study of Obedience," *Journal of Abnormal and Social Psychology* 67 (1963): 371–78.

30. Harold Leavitt, "Some Effects of Certain Communication Patterns on Group Performance," *Journal of Abnormal and Social Psychology* 46 (1951): 38–50.

31. Fritz J. Roethlisberger and William J. Dickson, *Management and the Worker* (Cambridge, Mass.: Harvard University Press, 1943).

32. Harold Guetzkow, ed., *Simulation in Social Science* (Englewood Cliffs, N.J.: Prentice-Hall, 1962).

Chapter 5. HUMAN ACTION

1. Restrictive empiricism began with the eighteenth-century Scottish philosopher David Hume who rejected the idea that people could be intuitive about self-evident truths. For Hume, what is known is what is sensed. In the nineteenth century Auguste Comte argued that science could only be based on associations between observed events, not on "causes" (which could not be sensed). In the twentieth century logical positivists and behaviorists have carried on the tradition of restrictive empiricism, altering it to include standards of logical consistency which are not sensed.

2. The idea that only "publicly observable" experiences are open to scientific investigation has been held by many social thinkers. Logical positivists speak of verifying hypotheses through sense experience ("the verification principle"). Pragmatists speak of reducing concepts to physical operations ("operationalization"). Some phenomenologists speak of socially constructed shared experience as the basis of science ("intersubjectivity").

3. Recently, a new discipline, "the sociology of sociology," has grown up to study the social context of sociological research. See Larry T. Reynolds and Janice M. Reynolds, eds., *The Sociology of Sociology* (New York: David McKay, 1970).

4. The revolt against restrictive empiricism began at the turn of the twentieth century when William James coined the term "radical empiricism" to name the critical description of all human experience. At the same time the European movement of "phenomenology" led by Edmund Husserl widened the definition of experience in a way similar to James. Sociologists who have adopted an expansive definition of experience to guide their work include Georges Gurvitch ("hyper-empiricism"), Maurice Hauriou ("hyper-positivism") and Pitirim Sorokin ("integral epistemology").

5. Michael A. Weinstein, "New Ways and Old to Talk About Politics," *Review of Politics* 35 (January 1973): 41–60.

6. Joseph Kockelmans, ed., *Phenomenology* (Garden City, N.Y.: Doubleday, 1967). See especially part 3, "Phenomenology and the Sciences of Man," pp. 411–555.

7. David Easton, *The Political System* (New York: Alfred A. Knopf, 1953).

8. Georges Gurvitch, *Dialectique et Sociologie* (Paris: Flammarion, 1962), 8. Translation was done by the authors.

9. Ibid., p. 7.

10. The dialogic view of the self is taken by "symbolic interactionists" in sociology. See Jerome G. Manis and Bernard N. Meltzer, eds., *Symbolic Interaction* (Boston: Allyn & Bacon, 1967).

11. Henri Bergson made the intuition of time the basis of his philosophy. See his *Creative Evolution* (New York: Modern Library, 1944).

12. For the changing notions of the proper scope of sociology, see Don Martindale, *The Nature and Types of Sociological Theory* (Boston: Houghton Mifflin, 1960).

13. Auguste Comte held the view that sociology was the master science.

14. Among others, the British sociologist Morris Ginsberg held that sociologists should investigate the relations among different areas of human existence.

15. The view that sociology takes what is left after the other social sciences have made their choices of subject matter is sometimes called the garbage-can theory.

16. The problem-solving or pragmatic view of sociology is exemplified in John Dewey's *The Public and its Problems* (New York: Henry Holt, 1927).

17. Martindale, *The Nature and Types of Sociological Theory.*

18. Ibid., pp. 17–19.

19. Ernst Cassirer, *An Essay on Man* (New Haven: Yale University Press, 1944).

20. Peter L. Berger and Thomas Luckmann, *The Social Construction of Reality* (Garden City, N.Y.: Doubleday, 1966).

21. The belief that one's culture puts one at the center of human affairs is called "ethnocentrism." See William Graham Sumner, *Folkways* (New York: New American Library, 1960), pp. 27–30. "Ethnocentrism is the technical name for this view of things in which one's own group is the center of everything and all others are scaled and rated with reference to it" (pp. 27–28).

22. Discussions of individualism are found in: John Dewey, *Individualism Old and New* (New York: G. P. Putnam's Sons, 1962); William Ernest Hocking, *The Lasting Elements of Individualism* (New Haven: Yale University Press, 1937); David L. Miller, *Individualism* (Austin: University of Texas Press, 1967); David Riesman, *Individualism Reconsidered* (Glencoe, Ill.: Free Press, 1954).

23. Arthur F. Bentley, *Behavior, Knowledge, Fact* (Bloomington, Ind.: Principia Press, 1935). We thank Dr. Randall E. Triplett for sharing with us the results of his analysis of Bentley's treatment of the category of space in social science.

24. Kurt Lewin, *Field Theory and Social Science* (New York: Harper, 1951).

25. A.L. Kroeber, *Anthropology* (New York: Harcourt Brace Jovanovich, 1963). Kroeber coined the term "superorganic" to refer to culture.

26. This position is "phenomenological" in that intention is made an integral part of the action to be described. The opposing position, "behaviorism," studies only public observable "behavior," leaving intention out of its accounts of action.

27. MacQuilkin De Grange, *The Nature and Elements of Sociology* (New Haven: Yale University Press, 1953).

28. The use of social and biographical "background data" in survey research illustrates the importance of action-time to sociologists.

29. An overview of the humanistic movement in sociology can be found in John F. Glass and John R. Staude, eds., *Humanistic Society* (Pacific Palisades, Calif.: Goodyear Publishing, 1972).

30. The notion of the self as an achievement is developed by Justus Buchler in his *Toward a General Theory of Human Judgment* (New York: Columbia University Press, 1951).

31. Florian Znaniecki, *The Cultural Sciences: Their Origin and Development* (Urbana: University of Illinois Press, 1952), p. 212.

Chapter 6. HUMAN RELATIONS IN A MASS SOCIETY

1. For an account of the origins of the French Revolution, see Georges Lefebvre, *Coming of the French Revolution* (New York: Vintage Books, 1957).

2. Jean-Paul Sartre, *Search for a Method* (New York: Vintage Books, 1963), p. 7.

3. There are many variants of Marxism in contemporary thought. For a sampling of revisions of Marx's thought, see Eric Fromm, ed., *Socialist Humanism* (Garden City, N.Y.: Doubleday, 1966). For a view on the barriers to revolution, see Herbert Marcuse, *One-Dimensional Man* (Boston: Beacon Press, 1966).

4. The image of interest-group society goes back to the founding of the American republic. Contemporary pluralists draw upon the *Federalist Papers*, which were written to persuade people to vote for the American constitution (Alexander Hamilton, John Jay, and James Madison, *The Federalist Papers* [New York: Washington Square Press, 1964]). See particularly Federalist X by Madison on the dangers of faction. In the nineteenth century Senator John C. Calhoun from South Carolina defended slavery from the standpoint of pluralism (*A Disquisition on Government* [Indianapolis: Bobbs-Merrill, 1953]). In the twentieth century the image of interest group society became a part of social science; see Arthur F. Bentley, *The Process of Government* (Cambridge, Mass.: Belknap Press of Harvard University, 1967); David Truman, *The Governmental Process* (New York: Knopf, 1951).

5. For an account of dilemmas in social life, see Peter M. Blau, *Exchange and Power in Social Life* (New York: Wiley, 1967). For the effects of cross-cutting interests, see Seymour M. Lipset, *Political Man* (Garden City, N.Y.: Doubleday, 1959).

6. Michael A. Weinstein, "Life and Politics as Plural: James and Bentley on the Twentieth Century Problem," *Journal of Value Inquiry* 5 (Winter 1971): 282–91.

7. Criticisms of the image of interest-group society can be found in Peter Bachrach, *Theory of Democratic Elitism* (Boston: Little, Brown, 1967); Richard F. Hamilton, *Class and Politics in the United States* (New York: Wiley, 1972).

8. Among the most important social thinkers who have written about mass society are Hannah Arendt, E. H. Carr, Erich Fromm, Ortega y Gasset, William Ernest Hocking, Karl Jaspers, Emil Lederer, and Gabriel Marcel.

9. For accounts of elite theory, see James H. Meisel, *The Myth of the Ruling Class* (Ann Arbor: University of Michigan Press, 1962); Renzo Sereno, *The Rulers* (New York: Frederick A. Praeger, 1962).

10. Philosophies of resistance are found in Albert Camus, *Resistance, Rebellion and Death* (New York: Knopf, 1960); Karl Jaspers, *Man in the Modern Age* (Garden City, N.Y.: Doubleday, 1957).

11. According to Michael Novak the ethnic awakening occurred as a reaction to elites distributing greater resources to racial minorities. See Novak's "White Ethnic," *Harper's Magazine* 243 (September 1971): 44.

12. Critical synthesis of world cultures has been advocated by Lewis Mumford, *The Condition of Man* (New York: Harcourt Brace Jovanovich, 1944); F. S. C. Northrop, *The Meeting of East and West* (New York: Collier Books, 1966); W. Warren Wagar, *The City of Man* (Baltimore: Penguin Books, 1967).

13. George Simpson, ed., *Emile Durkheim on the Division of Labor in Society* (New York: Macmillan, 1933).

14. Harold Lasswell identified the most important social development of the twentieth century as the "skill revolution"—the emergence of technicians to positions of economic and political power—see his *Politics: Who Gets What, When, How* (Cleveland: World, 1958).

15. Ferdinand Toennies, *Community and Society* (East Lansing: Michigan State University Press, 1957).

16. Henry Sumner Maine, *Ancient Law* (New York: Holt, 1864). For a commentary on Maine and similar thinkers, see Benjamin Lippincott, *Victorian Critics of Democracy* (New York: Octagon Books, 1964).

17. Robert Redfield distinguished between folk and urban societies. See his *Peasant Society and Culture* (Chicago: University of Chicago Press 1956). Howard Becker distinguished between sacred and secular societies. See Howard Becker and Harry Elmer Barnes, *Social Thought from Lore to Science* (Washington: Harren Press, 1952).

18. Fritz Pappenheim, *The Alienation of Modern Man* (New York: Monthly Review Press, 1959).

19. Joe McGinniss, *The Selling of the President 1968* (New York: Trident Press, 1969).

20. For discussions of atomization, see Robert A. Nisbet, *Community and Power* (New York: Oxford University Press, 1962); José Ortega y Gasset, *The Revolt of the Masses* (New York: New American Library, 1950); David Riesman et al., *The Lonely Crowd* (New Haven: Yale University Press, 1961).

21. Robert Sommer, *Expertland* (Garden City, N.Y.: Doubleday, 1963).

22. "Divorce Statistics Analysis, "United States 1963," *Public Health Service Publication*, No. 1000, Series 21, No. 13, pp. 6–39.

23. James Curtis, "Voluntary Association Joining: A Cross-National

Comparative Note," *American Sociological Review* 36 (October 1971): 872–80.

24. Robert Michels, *Political Parties* (New York: Collier Books, 1962).

25. Seymour M. Lipset et al., *Union Democracy* (Glencoe, Ill.: Free Press, 1956).

26. Curtis, *"Voluntary Association Joining,"* p. 874.

27. The relations between various media of communication and the quality of experience have been traced by Marshall McLuhan in his *Understanding Media* (New York: New American Library, 1971).

28. Ibid.

29. The concept of mass culture has been defined and analyzed by Dwight MacDonald in his *Against the American Grain* (New York: Random House, 1962).

30. Stereotyping has been discussed by Walter Lippmann in his *Public Opinion* (New York: Macmillan, 1922).

31. Robert Cirino, *Don't Blame the People* (Los Angeles: Diversity Press, 1971), p. 2.

32. Destructive "games" in human relations have been described by Eric Berne in his *Games People Play* (New York: Grove Press, 1964).

33. The problems of discovering a "real self" in a mass society are described by William Barrett in his *What Is Existentialism?* (New York: Grove Press, 1964).

34. Irving J. Rein, *Rudy's Red Wagon* (Glenview: Scott, Foresman, 1972), p. 9.

35. "Anomie" was described by Emile Durkheim in his *Suicide: A Study in Sociology* (New York: Free Press, 1951).

36. Riesman, *The Lonely Crowd*, p. 21.

37. William H. Whyte, Jr., *The Organization Man* (Garden City, N.Y.: Doubleday, 1957).

Chapter 7. THE CULTURE OF MASS SOCIETY

1. Clyde Kluckhohn and Alfred L. Kroeber have reviewed the various definitions of culture in the social sciences. See their *Culture* (New York: Vintage Books, 1952).

2. A technological interpretation of history has been given by V. Gordon Childe, *Man Makes Himself* (New York: New American Library, 1951).

3. Kluckhohn and Kroeber, *Culture*.

4. Such an engineer's approach is illustrated by R. Buckminster Fuller's *Utopia or Oblivion: The Prospects for Humanity* (New York: Bantam Books, 1969).

5. Elijah Jordan, *The Good Life* (Chicago: University of Chicago Press, 1952).

6. Representative of this school of thought is Leslie A. White, "The Symbol: The Origin and Basis of Human Behavior," in *Readings in Anthropology*, ed. Jesse D. Jennings and E. Adamson Hoebel (New York: McGraw-Hill, 1966), p. 288.

7. The differences between nineteenth- and twentieth-century thought can be summed up in the contrast between two thinkers: Karl Marx and George Herbert Mead. For Marx, the human being was basically a producer, a laboring animal who created and used tools. For Mead, the human being was basically a communicator, a symbolizing animal capable of retaining and transferring meanings beyond particular situations.

8. An example of this view is found in Philip S. Haring, *Political Morality* (Cambridge, Mass.: Schenkman, 1970).

9. This statement essentially constitutes a definition of sociology. The focus of sociology, from our perspective, is human relations rather than cultural objects or personal projects. The phases of human action, however, are so highly interrelated that only for the purposes of abstraction can any one phase of action be separated from the others.

10. William Graham Sumner called this coherence a "strain of consistency." See his *Folkways* (New York: New American Library, 1960), p. 21.

11. Erich Fromm, *Marx's Concept of Man* (New York: Frederick Ungar, 1961).

12. Charles H. Percy, "Quality of Work in America," *Chicago Tribune,* 20 April 1973, p. 14. Empirical studies of alienation are discussed in Michael Aiken and Jerald Hage, "Organizational Alienation: A Comparative Analysis," *American Sociological Review* (August 1966): 497–507.

13. This fear is discussed in Erich Fromm, *The Revolution of Hope: Toward a Humanized Technology* (New York: Harper & Row, 1968).

14. The theses of multiple and single invention are discussed in Melville J. Herskovitz, "The Processes of Cultural Change," in *The Science of Man in the World Crisis,* ed. Ralph Linton (New York: Columbia University Press, 1945), pp. 143–70; Julian H. Steward, "Cultural Causality and Law: A Trial Formulation of the Development of Early Civilizations," *American Anthropologist* 51 (January–March 1949): 1–27.

15. Guy E. Swanson, *Social Change* (Glenview: Scott, Foresman, 1971), p. 27.

16. John Kenneth Galbraith, *The New Industrial State* (Boston: Houghton Mifflin, 1967).

17. Examples of the "organizational society" interpretation are Robert Presthus, *The Organizational Society* (New York: Vintage Books, 1962); Kenneth E. Boulding, *The Organizational Revolution* (Chicago: Quadrangle Books, 1968).

18. H. H. Gerth and C. Wright Mills, eds., *From Max Weber* (New York: Oxford University Press, 1958).

19. Peter M. Blau, *The Dynamics of Bureaucracy* (Chicago: University of Chicago Press, 1963).

20. Jerry Jacobs, " 'Symbolic Bureaucracy': A Case Study of a Social Welfare Agency," *Social Forces* 47 (June 1969): 413–21.

21. We employ a special use of "conglomerate" here. A conglomerate will be defined as any organization that performs a diversity of often conflicting tasks and, therefore, which cannot be assigned any specific purpose. Since conglomerates cannot be assigned specific purposes, their performance can be evaluated only in terms of sheer growth in wealth, power, influence and command of loyalty. In our perspective, the conglomerate is the characteristic form of organization in mass society. Its only end is the accumulation of means.

22. Theodore Lowi, *The End of Liberalism* (New York: W. W. Norton, 1969); C. Wright Mills, *The Power Elite* (New York: Oxford University Press, 1959). Mills remarks: ". . . if events come out well, talk as though you had decided. For then men had moral choices and the power to make them and are, of course, responsible. If events come out badly, boldly say that you didn't have the real choice, and are, of course, not accountable: they, the others, had

the choice and they are responsible. You can get away with this even though you have at your command half the world's forces and God knows how many bombs and bombers. For you are, in fact, an unimportant item in the historical fate of your times; and moral responsibility is an illusion, although it is of great use if handled in a really alert public relations manner" (pp. 25–36).

23. Nicholas S. Timasheff, "What is 'Sociology of Law'?" *American Journal of Sociology* 43 (1937): 225–35.

24. Harold Lasswell, *Politics: Who Gets What, When, How* (Cleveland: World 1958).

25. Kingsley Davis and Wilbert E. Moore, "Some Principles of Stratification," *American Sociological Review* 10 (April 1945): 242–48.

26. John Kenneth Galbraith, *The Affluent Society* (Boston: Houghton Mifflin, 1969).

27. Winston White, *Beyond Conformity* (New York: Free Press, 1961).

28. Jacques Ellul, in A. H. Teich, ed., *Technology and Man's Future* (New York: St. Martin's Press, 1972). Ellul comments: "Technique is essentially independent of the human being who finds himself naked and disarmed before it. Modern man divines that there is only one reasonable way out: to submit and take what profit he can from what technique otherwise so richly bestows upon him. If he is of a mind to oppose it, he finds himself really alone" (p. 97).

29. Gerald E. Myers, "Self and Body Image," in *Phenomenology in America,* ed. James M. Edie (Chicago: Quadrangle Books, 1967), pp. 147–60.

30. The put-on is analyzed by Jacob Brackman in his "Onward and Upward with the Arts," *New Yorker,* 24 June 1970, p. 34.

31. Roy Ald, *The Youth Communes* (New York: Tower Publications, 1970).

32. Herbert Marcuse has called the phenomenon of mindless consumerism "repressive desublimation." He remarks: "The people recognize themselves in their commodities; they find their soul in their automobile, hi-fi set, split level home, kitchen equipment. The very mechanism which ties the individual to his society has changed and social control is anchored in the new needs which it has produced" (in Teich, ed., *Technology and Man's Future,* p. 79).

33. Michael Harrington, *The Other America* (Baltimore: Penguin Books, 1962).

34. Robert Boguslaw, *The New Utopians* (Englewood Cliffs, N.J.: Prentice-Hall, 1965).

35. Thomas S. Kuhn, *The Structure of Scientific Revolutions* (Chicago: University of Chicago Press, 1962). Kuhn remarks: "When in the development of a natural science, an individual or group first produces a synthesis able to attract most of the next generation's practitioners, the older schools gradually disappear. In part their disappearance is caused by their member's conversion to the new paradigm. But there are always some men who cling to one or another of the older views, and they are simply read out of the profession, which thereafter ignores their work" (p. 18).

36. Walter B. Simon, "Social Classes, Multilingualism and Social Change" (manuscript, 1972).

37. Gary Allen, "More Subversion than Meets the Ear," in *The Sounds of Change,* ed. R. Serge Denisoff and Richard A. Peterson (Chicago: Rand McNally, 1972), pp. 151–66.

38. Pitirim Sorokin, *Fads and Foibles in Modern Sociology* (Chicago: Henry Regnery, 1956), p. 104.

Chapter 8. THE QUALITY OF WORK IN MODERN LIFE

1. Sebastian de Grazia, *Of Time, Work, and Leisure* (Garden City, N.Y.: Doubleday, 1964), p. 35.

2. W. H. D. Rouse, trans., *Great Dialogues of Plato* (New York: New American Library, 1956).

3. Aristotle, *The Politics*, trans. T. A. Sinclair (Baltimore: Penguin Books, 1962).

4. Two different perspectives on the Catholic position are illustrated by Fulton J. Sheen, *God and Intelligence in Modern Philosophy* (Garden City, N.Y.: Doubleday, 1958); and Henri de Lubac, *Teilhard de Chardin: The Man and His Meaning* (New York: New American Library, 1967).

5. de Grazia, *Of Time*, p. 41.

6. Don Martindale, *Institutions, Organizations and Mass Society* (Boston: Houghton Mifflin, 1966), p. 211.

7. For a critique of the applicability of the Protestant Ethic to contemporary conditions, see Charles A. Reich, *The Greening of America* (New York: Random House, 1970).

8. Jules Henry, *Culture Against Man* (New York: Vintage Books, 1963), p. 13.

9. John Dewey, *Reconstruction in Philosophy* (New York: New American Library, 1950), p. 144.

10. Irving Tallman and Ramona Morgner, "Life-Style Differences Among Urban and Suburban Blue-Collar Families," *Social Forces* 48 (March 1970): 334–48.

11. Some of the definitions of professions are found in William Goode, "Community Within a Community: The Professions," *American Sociological Review* 22 (April 1957): 194; Everett C. Hughes, *Men and Their Work* (Glencoe, Ill.: Free Press, 1953), pp. 78–87; Geoffrey Millerson, *The Qualifying Associations* (London: Routledge & Kegan Paul, 1964), p. 10.

12. Everett C. Hughes, "The Humble and the Proud: The Comparative Study of Occupations," *Sociological Quarterly* 11 (Spring 1970): 147–56.

13. Ibid., p. 154.

14. Ronald M. Pavalko, *Sociology of Occupations and Professions* (Itasca: F. E. Peacock, 1971), p. 21.

15. Goode, *"Community,"* pp. 194–200.

16. Charles F. Sloane, "Police Professionalization," *Journal of Criminal Law, Criminology and Police Science* 45 (May–June 1954): 77–83; George H. Brerton, "The Importance of Training and Education in the Professionalization of Law Enforcement," *Journal of Criminal Law, Criminology and Police Science* 52 (May 1961): 111–21; Robert Bain, "The Process of Professionalization: Life Insurance Selling" (Ph.D. dissertation, University of Chicago, 1959); Norman K. Denzin and Curtis J. Mettlin, "Incomplete Professionalization: The Case of Pharmacy," *Social Forces* 46 (March 1968): 375–81; Elliott A. Krause, "Structured Strain in a Marginal Profession: Rehabilitation Counseling," *Journal of Health and Human Behavior* 7 (Spring 1965): 55–62; Marie R. Haug and Marvin B. Sussman, "Professional Autonomy and the Revolt of the Client," *Social*

Problems 17 (Fall 1969); Marvin B. Sussman and Marie R. Haug, "From Student to Practitioner: Professionalization and Deprofessionalization in Rehabilitation Counseling," *Working Paper* #7 (Cleveland: Case Western Reserve University, 1970); William Goode, "The Librarian: From Occupation to Profession?" *Library Quarterly* 31 (October 1961): 306–18.

17. C. Wright Mills, *The Power Elite* (New York: Oxford University Press, 1956).

18. Radhakamal Mukerjee, *The Social Structure of Values* (London: Macmillan, n.d.).

19. Radhakamal Mukerjee, *The Philosophy of Social Science* (London: Macmillan, 1960).

20. Karl Marx, "Alienated Labor," in *Man Alone: Alienation in Modern Society*, ed. Eric and Mary Josephson (New York: Dell, 1962), pp. 93–105.

21. Robert Blauner, *Alienation and Freedom: The Factory Worker and His Industry* (Chicago: University of Chicago Press, 1964).

22. For Herbert A. Simon the only significant motivation for workers is earning a livelihood. See Herbert A. Simon, *Administrative Behavior* (New York: Macmillan, 1957).

23. Ely Chinoy, *Automobile Workers and the American Dream* (New York: Doubleday, 1955).

24. Fred H. Blum, *Toward a Democratic Work Process* (New York: Harper, 1953).

25. Nancy Morse and Robert Weiss, "The Function and Meaning of Work and the Job," *American Sociological Review* 20 (April 1955): 191–98.

26. H. H. Gerth and C. Wright Mills, eds., *From Max Weber: Essays in Sociology* (New York: Oxford University Press, 1946), p. 50.

27. C. Wright Mills, *White Collar* (New York: Oxford University Press, 1951), p. 227.

28. For the nineteenth-century background to twentieth-century thought, see Michael A. Weinstein, *Philosophy, Theory and Method in Contemporary Political Thought* (Glenview: Scott, Foresman, 1971).

29. John Horton, "The Dehumanization of Anomie and Alienation: A Problem in the Ideology of Sociology," in *Humanistic Society: Today's Challenge to Sociology*, ed. John F. Glass and John R. Staude (Pacific Palisades: Goodyear, 1972), p. 141.

30. The problems of transition from pre-revolutionary to post-revolutionary society have been discussed by Paul M. Sweezy in his "The Transition to Socialism," *Monthly Review* 23 (May 1971): 1–16.

31. This perspective on human activity is frequently called by the revealing term "human engineering."

32. Horton, in Glass and Staude, *Humanistic Society.*

33. Peter Bachrach, *The Theory of Democratic Elitism: A Critique* (Boston: Little, Brown, 1967).

34. For a brief history of the human-relations approach from a critical perspective, see William H. Whyte, Jr., *The Organization Man* (Garden City, N.Y.: Doubleday, 1957), pp. 36–51.

35. Charles B. Spaulding, *An Introduction to Industrial Sociology* (San Francisco: Chandler, 1961).

36. Ibid.

37. F. J. Roethlisberger and William J. Dickson, *Management and the Worker* (Cambridge, Mass.: Harvard University Press, 1947).

38. Marx's thesis was questioned by those who thought that *control* of organizational resources is more important than *ownership* of the means of production in determining alienative conditions. See, for example, Gaetano Mosca, *The Ruling Class* (New York: McGraw-Hill, 1939); Robert Michels, *Political Parties* (New York: Collier Books, 1962).

39. Bachrach, *The Theory of Democratic Elitism*, p. 105.

40. Spaulding, *An Introduction to Industrial Sociology*, p. 224.

41. The concept of "countervailing powers" and their role in expanding freedom is developed by John Kenneth Galbraith in his *American Capitalism: The Concept of Countervailing Power* (Boston: Houghton Mifflin, 1956).

42. Philip Taft, "A Labor Historian Views Changes in the Trade Union Movement," *Monthly Labor Review* 92 (September 1969): 8–11.

43. George A. Miller, "Professionals in Bureaucracy: Alienation Among Industrial Scientists and Engineers," *American Sociological Review* 32 (October 1967): 755–68; Barney Glaser, "The Local-Cosmopolitan Scientist," *American Journal of Sociology* 69 (November 1963): 246–60; Proshanta K. Nandi, "Career and Life Organization of Professionals: A Study of Contrasts Between College and University Professors" (Ph.D. dissertation, University of Minnesota, 1968); Alvin W. Gouldner, "Cosmopolitans and Locals: Toward an Analysis of Latent Social Roles," *Administrative Sciences Quarterly* 2 (December 1957): 281–306 and *Administrative Sciences Quarterly* 2 (March 1958): 444–80.

44. Peter M. Blau and W. Richard Scott, *Formal Organizations* (San Francisco: Chandler, 1962).

45. Peter M. Blau, *The Dynamics of Bureaucracy* (Chicago: University of Chicago Press, 1963).

46. The term "impression management" was coined by Victor Thompson in his *Modern Organization* (New York: Knopf, 1961). Also see Erving Goffman, *Asylums* (Garden City, N.Y.: Doubleday, 1961).

47. Frantz Fanon, *The Wretched of the Earth* (New York: Grove Press, 1965).

Chapter 9. INEQUALITY AND ITS DIMENSIONS

1. Kingsley Davis, *The Population of India and Pakistan* (Princeton: Princeton University Press, 1951).

2. Georges Gurvitch has noted the complexity of the estates system. See his *Traité de Sociologie* (Paris: Presses Universitaires de France, 1958).

3. C.B. Macpherson has traced the origins of this defense in his *The Political Theory of Possessive Individualism* (Oxford: Clarendon Press, 1962).

4. Richard Hofstadter, *Social Darwinism in American Thought* (New York: George Braziller, 1959).

5. Arthur Jensen, "How Much can we Boost IQ and Scholastic Achievement?" *Harvard Educational Review* 39 (Winter 1969): 1–123. In order to understand the complexity of Jensen's position one must refer to the debate over whether special efforts should be made by schools to try to bring low-achieving groups up to the levels of higher-achieving groups. Jensen's supporters would tend to argue that commitment of resources to such "compensatory education" would not be productive.

6. Lionel Tiger, *Men in Groups* (New York: Random House, 1969).

7. Talcott Parsons, "Analytical Approach to the Theory of Social Stratification," *American Journal of Sociology* 45 (1940): 841–62.

8. Kingsley Davis and Wilbert E. Moore, "Some Principles of Stratification," *American Sociological Review* 10 (April 1945): 242–49.

9. Ibid., p. 243.

10. Melvin M. Tumin, "Some Principles of Stratification: A Critical Analysis," *American Sociological Review* 18 (August 1953): 387–94; George A. Huaco, "A Logical Analysis of the Davis-Moore Theory of Stratification," *American Sociological Review* 28 (October 1963): 801–4; Curt Tausky, "Parsons on Stratification: An Analysis and Critique," *Sociological Quarterly* 6 (Spring 1965): 128–38.

11. Walter Buckley, "Social Stratification and Social Differentiation," *American Sociological Review* 23 (August 1958): 369–75.

12. José Ortega y Gasset, *The Revolt of the Masses* (New York: New American Library, 1950).

13. This does not exclude the existence of widespread myths such as the "Horatio Alger" idea that through hard work and good luck one can rise from rags to riches. These myths, however, are not officially embodied in all public policies, and are actively disputed by many political leaders.

14. Ortega, *The Revolt of the Masses.*

15. E. H. Carr, *The New Society* (New York: St. Martin's Press, 1960).

16. W. Lloyd Warner and Paul S. Lunt, *The Social Life of a Modern Community* (New Haven: Yale University Press, 1941); Allison Davis, Burleigh B. Gardner, and Mary R. Gardner, *Deep South: A Social Anthropological Study of Caste and Class* (Chicago: University of Chicago Press, 1941); W. Lloyd Warner et al., *Democracy in Jonesville* (New York: Harper, 1949); August B. Hollingshead, *Elmstown's Youth* (New York: Wiley, 1949).

17. National Opinion Research Center, "Jobs and Occupations: A Popular Evaluation," in *Class, Status and Power,* ed. Reinhard Bendix and Seymour Martin Lipset (Glencoe, Ill.: Free Press, 1953), pp. 411–26.

18. Ibid., p. 412.

19. Peter M. Blau, "Occupational Bias and Mobility," *American Sociological Review* 22 (August 1957): 392–99; Joel E. Gerstl and Lois K. Cohen, "Dissensus, Situs and Egocentrism in Occupational Ranking," *British Journal of Sociology* 15 (September 1964): 254–61.

20. Robert W. Hodge et al., "Occupational Prestige in the United States, 1925–63," *American Journal of Sociology* 70 (November 1964): 286–302.

21. Alex Inkeles and Peter H. Rossi, "National Comparisons of Occupational Prestige," *American Journal of Sociology* 61 (January 1956): 329–39.

22. David Riesman et al., *The Lonely Crowd* (New Haven: Yale University Press, 1961).

23. Ideologies are sets of ideas about human existence that have social functions beyond the clarification of experience. Some of the functions of ideologies are to organize diverse and conflicting experiences into managable wholes (simplification), to justify the demands of particular groups engaged in conflict, to promote solidarity within groups, and to spur human beings to act decisively in crises.

24. Vernon K. Dibble, "Occupations and Ideologies," *American Journal of Sociology* 68 (September 1962): 229–41.

25. Howard S. Becker, "The Professional Dance Musician and his Audience," *American Journal of Sociology* 57 (September 1951): 136–44.

26. Sanford Dornbusch, "The Military Academy as an Assimilating Institution," *Social Forces* 33 (May 1955): 316–21.

27. See, for example, Robert K. Merton, George C. Reader, and Patricia L. Kendall, eds., *The Student Physician* (Cambridge, Mass.: Harvard University Press, 1957).

28. Ronald M. Pavalko, *Sociology of Occupations and Professions* (Itasca: F. E. Peacock, 1971), p. 155.

29. Robin M. Williams, Jr., *American Society* (New York: Alfred A. Knopf, 1960).

30. Pavalko, *Sociology of Occupations and Professions.*

31. Ibid., p. 158.

32. Laurence F. Peter and Raymond Hull, *The Peter Principle* (New York: William Morrow, 1969).

33. Max Weber, "Class, Status, Party," in *From Max Weber: Essays in Sociology*, ed. H.H. Gerth and C. Wright Mills (New York: Oxford University Press, 1946), pp. 180–95.

34. Ibid., p. 193.

35. Ibid., p. 194.

36. Kaare Svalastoga, *Social Differentiation* (New York: David McKay, 1965), p. 63.

37. Gerhard Lenski, "Social Participation and Status Crystallization," *American Sociological Review* 21 (August 1956): 458–64.

38. W. L. Warner, Marchia Meeker, and Kenneth Eells, *Social Class in America* (Chicago: Science Research Associates, 1949).

39. Robert Lynd and Helen Lynd, *Middletown* (New York: Harcourt Brace Jovanovich, 1929).

40. John F. Cuber and William F. Kenkel, *Social Stratification in the United States* (New York: Appleton-Century-Crofts, 1954), p. 25.

41. T. H. Marshall, "Changes in Social Stratification in the Twentieth Century," *Transactions of the Third World Congress of Sociology* 3 (1956): 1–17.

42. J. A. Kahl, *The American Class Structure* (New York: Holt, Rinehart & Winston, 1957), p. 186.

43. E. Digby Baltzell, *The Protestant Establishment* (New York: Vintage Books, 1964).

44. Thorstein Veblen, *The Theory of the Leisure Class* (New York: New American Library, 1953).

45. J. M. Beshers, *Urban Social Structure* (New York: Free Press, 1962).

46. Herman Miller, "Statistics and Reality," *The New Leader* 47 (30 March 1964): 15.

47. *Statistical Abstracts of the United States* (1969), p. 323.

48. James B. Conant, *Slums and Suburbs* (New York: McGraw-Hill, 1961), pp. 2–3.

49. Patricia Sexton, *Education and Income* (New York: Compass Books, 1964).

50. Svalastoga, *Social Differentiation*, p. 84.

51. Elizabeth Waldman, "Educational Attainment of Workers," *Monthly Labor Review* (February 1969): 18.

52. National Urban League, *Education and Race* (New York: National Urban League, 1966), p. 16.

53. "The New Feminism," *Ladies Home Journal*, August 1970, p. 64.

54. Rebecca Kirtland, "Biased Counseling Contributes to Decline of Professional Women," *Lafayette Journal and Courier*, 8 January 1970, p. B4.

55. *The Spokeswoman* 2 (1 September 1971): 2.

56. James S. Coleman, "Equal Schools or Equal Students?" *The Public Interest* 1 (Summer 1966): 70–75.

57. William H. Sewell, "Inequality of Opportunity for Higher Education," *American Sociological Review* 36 (October 1971): 793–809.

58. Peter M. Blau and Otis Dudley Duncan, *The American Occupational Structure* (New York: Wiley, 1967).

59. Peter Y. de Jong, Milton J. Brawer, and Stanley S. Robin, "Patterns of Female Intergenerational Occupational Mobility," *American Sociological Review* 36 (December 1971): 1033–42.

60. Michael Young, *The Rise of the Meritocracy* (Baltimore: Penguin Books, 1958).

61. Svalastoga, *Social Differentiation*, p. 136.

Chapter 10. POLITICS AND SOCIAL CONTROL

1. Max Rheinstein, ed., *Max Weber on Law in Economy and Society* (New York: Simon and Schuster, 1967), p. 9.

2. Aristotle's defense of slavery based on natural superiority and inferiority has become famous. See Aristotle, *The Politics*, trans. T. A. Sinclair (Baltimore: Penguin Books, 1962).

3. The idea that an elite of the wise should rule has been a part of Western social thought ever since Plato wrote the *Republic*. Plato's ideal rulers were "philosopher-kings" who were able to comprehend the whole of human activity and then assign people to their "proper" social functions. The elitisms of the nineteenth and twentieth centuries have not been based on philosophical wisdom but on claims to scientific knowledge of the causes of human activity. Such elites of scientific planners have been proposed by Auguste Comte, Lester Frank Ward, George Santayana, and B. F. Skinner.

4. For an overview of the functions of ideology and a history of thought on this phenomenon, see Willard A. Mullins, "On the Concept of Ideology in Political Science," *American Political Science Review* 66 (June 1972): 498–510.

5. Gaetano Mosca, *The Ruling Class* (New York: McGraw-Hill, 1939).

6. Arthur F. Bentley, *Relativity in Man and Society* (New York: G. P. Putnam's Sons, 1926), pp. 196–97; H. H. Gerth and C. Wright Mills, eds., *From Max Weber* (New York: Oxford University Press, 1958), p. 94.

7. Howard R. Smith, *Democracy and the Public Interest* (Athens: University of Georgia Press, 1960). Smith first noticed this phenomenon with regard to the appeals of industrial trade associations for higher tariffs and lower quotas against foreign competitors.

8. Georges Sorel, *Reflections on Violence* (New York: Peter Smith, 1941).

9. Richard M. Merelman, "The Development of Political Ideology: A Framework for the Analysis of Political Socialization," *American Political Science Review* 63 (September 1969): 750–67.

10. Samuel Stouffer, *Communism, Conformity and Civil Liberties* (Gloucester: Peter Smith, 1963).

11. Don D. Smith, "Levels of Political Information in the American Public" (Paper presented at the annual meetings of the Southern Sociological Society, Atlanta, Georgia, 1968).

12. Murray Edelman, *The Symbolic Uses of Politics* (Urbana: University of Illinois Press, 1964).

13. Ibid.

14. Kimball Young, "Comments on the Nature of 'Public' and 'Public Opinion'," in *Public Opinion and Propaganda*, ed. Daniel Katz et al. (New York: Holt, Rinehart & Winston, 1954), p. 64.

15. Edelman, *The Symbolic Uses of Politics*.

16. W. E. Binkley and M. C. Moos, "The Multi-Group Nature of the State," in Katz, *Public Opinion*, p. 26.

17. Robert A. Dahl, *Who Governs?* (New Haven: Yale University Press, 1961) pp. 223–27.

18. For a defense of participation, see Peter Bachrach, *The Theory of Democratic Elitism* (Boston: Little Brown, 1967).

19. Lester W. Milbrath, *Political Participation* (Chicago: Rand McNally, 1965).

20. Elihu Katz and Paul F. Lazarsfeld, *Personal Influence* (New York: Free Press, 1964).

21. Talcott Parsons, *Politics and Social Structure* (New York: Free Press, 1969).

22. Bachrach, *The Theory of Democratic Elitism*.

23. Floyd Hunter, *Community Power Structure* (Chapel Hill: University of North Carolina Press, 1953).

24. Dahl, *Who Governs?*

25. C. Wright Mills, *The Power Elite* (New York: Oxford University Press, 1959). Mills remarks: "The top of American society is increasingly unified and often seems willfully coordinated: at the top there has emerged an elite of power. The middle levels are a set of stalemated balancing forces: the middle does not link the bottom with the top. The bottom of this society is a politically fragmented and even as a passive fact, increasingly powerless (mass)" (p. 324).

26. Suzanne Keller, *Beyond the Ruling Class: Strategic Elites in Modern Society* (New York: Random House, 1963).

27. Bachrach, *The Theory of Democratic Elitism*.

28. For discussions of the military-industrial complex, see Fred J. Cook, *The Warfare State* (New York: Macmillan, 1962); John M. Swomley, Jr., *The Military Establishment* (Boston: Beacon Press, 1964).

29. Ehrlich called the practices underlying codified law the "living law." See E. Ehrlich, *Fundamental Principles of the Sociology of Law* (Cambridge, Mass.: Harvard University Press, 1936).

30. William A. Westley, "The Escalation of Violence Through Legitimation," *Annals of the American Academy of Political and Social Science* 36 (March 1968): 120–26.

31. Discussions of the concept of role are found in Raymond G. Hunt, "Role and Role Conflict," in *Current Perspectives in Social Psychology*, ed. Edwin P. Hollander and Raymond G. Hunt (New York: Oxford University Press, 1971), pp. 279–85; Ralph Linton, *The Cultural Background of Personality* (New York: Appleton-Century-Crofts, 1945), pp. 75–82.

32. The origins of law in informal rule systems ("folkways" and "mores") was described by William Graham Sumner in his *Folkways* (New York: New American Library, 1960).

33. The limiting point of perfect socialization has been described by Talcott Parsons in his *Social System* (New York: Free Press, 1951).

34. Talcott Parsons, "Some Reflections on the Place of Force in the Social

Process," in *Internal War: Problems and Approaches*, ed. Harry Eckstein (New York: Free Press, 1964).

35. Behaviorists, such as B. F. Skinner, do seem to hold that rewards and punishments exhaust the methods of social control.

36. Robert Nisbet, *The Social Bond: An Introduction to the Study of Society* (New York: Knopf, 1970), p. 292.

37. Gresham M. Sykes, *Social Problems in America* (Glenview: Scott, Foresman 1971), p. 9.

38. See, for example, Robert A. Dentler and Kai T. Erikson, "The Functions of Deviance in Groups," *Social Problems* 7 (Fall 1959): 98–107.

39. *The Challenge of Crime in a Free Society* (Washington: U.S. Government Printing Office, 1967), pp. 8–9; Daniel Bell, "What Crime Wave?" *Fortune*, January 1955, pp. 96–99, 154–56; Fred J. Murphey et al., "The Incidence of Hidden Delinquency," *American Journal of Orthopsychiatry* 16 (1946): 686–96.

40. United States Bureau of the Census, *Statistical Abstract of the United States: 1970* (Washington, D.C.: 1970), p. 141.

41. Ibid.

42. See, for example, Donald J. Black, "Production of Crime Rates," *American Sociological Review* 35 (August 1970): 733–48.

43. See Marshall B. Clinard and Richard Quinney, *Criminal Behavior Systems: A Typology* (New York: Holt, Rinehart & Winston, 1967), pp. 1–18, for a summary of many different systems of classifying crime.

44. George B. Vold, "The Organization of Criminals for Profit and Power," in Clinard and Quinney, *Criminal Behavior Systems*, p. 396.

45. Ibid., p. 402.

46. Frederic Homer, *Guns and Garlic: Myths and Realities of Organized Crime* (West Lafayette: Purdue University Studies, 1974).

47. Paul D. Rheingold, "The MER/29 Story—An Instance of Successful Mass Disaster Legislation," *California Law Review* 56 (January 1968): 116–18.

48. For further discussion of political crime, see Clinard and Quinney, *Criminal Behavior Systems*.

49. Emile Durkheim, *Suicide* (Glencoe, Ill.: Free Press, 1951).

50. United States Bureau of the Census, *Statistical Abstract*, p. 147.

51. Ibid.

52. Ibid.

53. E. Bittner, "The Police on Skid-Row: A Study of Peace Keeping," *American Sociological Review* 32 (October 1967): 699–715.

54. Black, "Production of Crime Rates," p. 740.

55. Ibid., p. 746.

56. Arthur Niederhoffer, *Behind the Shield: The Police in Urban Society* (Garden City, N. Y.: Doubleday, 1967).

57. Glen Elsasser, "High Court to Rule on Cairo Bias Suit," *Chicago Tribune*, 3 April 1973, Section 1A, p. 11. "The Cairo plaintiffs charged in a civil rights suit that the state's attorney recommended longer sentences and higher bonds for blacks than for whites and refused to initiate criminal proceedings against whites for assaults on blacks."

58. Erving Goffman, *Asylums: Essays on the Social Situation of Mental Patients and Other Inmates* (Garden City, N.Y.: Doubleday, 1961).

59. Gresham M. Sykes, *The Society of Captives: A Study of a Maximum Security Prison* (Princeton: Princeton University Press, 1958), p. 52.

60. United States Bureau of the Census, *Statistical Abstract*, p. 159.

Chapter 11. PATTERNS OF INTERGROUP RELATIONS

1. For a discussion of the origins of revolutions, see C. Crane Brinton, *The Anatomy of Revolution* (New York: Prentice-Hall, 1952).

2. Benjamin Disraeli, *Sybil, or, The Two Nations* (London: Oxford University Press, 1925).

3. For example, see Stokely Carmichael and Charles V. Hamilton, *Black Power* (New York: Random House, 1967).

4. David Easton, *The Political System* (New York: Knopf, 1953).

5. Talcott Parsons, *The Social System* (Glencoe, Ill.: Free Press, 1951).

6. The idea that the existence of groups depends upon the allegiance given to them is found in the works of Friedrich Baerwald. See his "A Sociological View of Depersonalization," *Thought* 21 (Spring 1956): 55–78; "Humanism and Social Ambivalence," *Thought* 42 (Winter 1967): 543–60.

7. Talcott Parsons, "On the Concept of Value-Commitments," *Sociological Inquiry*, 38 (Spring, 1968), pp. 135–60.

8. For a discussion of unequal exchanges, see Peter M. Blau, *Exchange and Power in Social Life* (New York: Wiley, 1967).

9. H.L. Nieburg, *Political Violence* (New York: St. Martin's Press, 1969).

10. For a discussion of mutuality, see E.T. Hiller, *Social Relations and Structures* (New York: Harper, 1945).

11. Herbert A. Simon, *Administrative Behavior* (New York: Macmillan, 1960).

12. For a contemporary defense of capitalism, see Milton Friedman, *Capitalism and Freedom* (Chicago: University of Chicago Press, 1962).

13. John Kenneth Galbraith, *The New Industrial State* (Boston: Houghton Mifflin, 1967).

14. Arnold W. Green, *Sociology: An Analysis of Life in Modern Society* (New York: McGraw-Hill, 1964), p. 349.

15. Ibid.

16. Edward F. Cox et al., *The Nader Report on the Federal Trade Commission* (New York: Richard W. Baron, 1969).

17. The system of interest group domination of policy has been called "interest group liberalism" by Theodore Lowi in his *The End of Liberalism* (New York: W. W. Norton, 1969). Lowi describes the system as such: "It may be called liberalism because it expects to use government in a positive and expansive role . . . it posits strong faith that what is good for government is good for the society. It is 'interest-group liberalism' because it sees as both necessary and good that the policy agenda and the public interest be defined in terms of the organized interests in society" (p. 71).

18. Austin Ranney, *The Doctrine of Responsible Party Government* (Urbana: University of Illinois Press, 1962).

19. Frank J. Sorauf, *Party Politics in America* (Boston: Little, Brown, 1968).

20. William H. Riker, *The Theory of Political Coalitions* (New Haven: Yale University Press, 1962).

21. H. L. Nieburg, *Political Violence.*

22. Lewis A. Coser, *Continuities in the Study of Social Conflict* (New York: Free Press, 1967); Anthony Oberschall, "The Los Angeles Riot of August, 1965," *Social Problems* 15 (1968): 322–41.

23. For a discussion of the importance of "conceivable change" in liberation, see Laud Humphreys, *Out of the Closets: The Sociology of Homosexual Liberation* (Englewood Cliffs, N.J.: Prentice-Hall, 1972), pp. 86–90.

24. Nieburg, *Political Violence.*

25. E. H. Carr, *The Twenty Year's Crisis* (New York: St. Martin's Press, 1961).

26. Fred J. Cook, *The Warfare State* (New York: Macmillan, 1962).

27. Milton M. Gordon, *Assimilation in American Life: The Role of Race, Religion, and National Origins* (New York: Oxford University Press, 1964).

28. Stewart G. Cole and Mildred W. Cole, *Minorities and the American Promise* (New York: Harper, 1954), chap. 6.

29. Ruby J. R. Kennedy, "Single or Triple Melting Pot? Intermarriage Trends in New Haven, 1870–1940," *American Journal of Sociology* 49 (January 1944): 331–39.

30. E. Digby Baltzell, *The Protestant Establishment* (New York: Random House, 1964).

31. Emory S. Bogardus, *Social Distance* (Yellow Springs: Antioch Press, 1959).

32. Pierre L. Van den Berghe, *South Africa, A Study in Conflict* (Middletown: Wesleyan University Press, 1963).

33. Gordon, *Assimilation in American Life,* pp. 146–47.

34. This tendency to deemphasize qualitative judgments appears in the writings of Michael Novak. See his "White Ethnic," *Harper's Magazine* 243 (September 1971).

35. See Table 337 of *Statistical Abstract of the United States: 1970* (Washington, D.C.: U.S. Government Printing Office, 1970), pp. 227–28, for the proportion of men and women in various job categories. See Table 543 (p. 360) for numbers of women in the 91st Congress. In this Congress there were 524 males and 11 females.

36. John Gagnon and William Simon, "Is a Women's Revolution Really Possible? No," *McCall's,* October 1969, pp. 76 ff.

37. Kate Millett, *Sexual Politics* (Garden City, N.Y.: Doubleday, 1970); Betty Friedan, *The Feminine Mystique* (New York: Dell, 1963).

38. Robin Morgan, ed., *Sisterhood Is Powerful* (New York: Vintage Books, 1970). This collection has a great deal of information on the various organizations in the women's movement.

39. Valerie Solanis, *SCUM Manifesto,* n.d.

40. *WEAL* membership invitation announcement, 1969.

41. The most famous of these publications are Simone de Beauvoir's *Second Sex* (the classic of the pre-movement era), Betty Friedan's *The Feminine Mystique,* Caroline Bird's *Born Female,* and Kate Millett's *Sexual Politics.* Newsletters include *Off Our Backs* and *Spokeswoman.*

42. Carol Kleiman, "And the Man from NEVER," *Chicago Tribune,* 15 February 1970, p. 7.

43. Theodore Roszak, *The Making of a Counter Culture* (Garden City, N.Y.: Doubleday, 1969).

44. See Jules Henry's powerful description in his chapter on human obso-
lenscence in *Culture Against Man* (New York: Random House, 1963).
45. For descriptions of the scientific ideology, see Robert K. Merton,
Social Theory and Social Structure (New York: Free Press, 1957), pp.
537–49; Michael Polanyi, *Science, Faith and Society* (Chicago: University of Chicago Press, 1964).
46. Thomas S. Kuhn, *The Structure of Scientific Revolutions* (Chicago: University of Chicago Press, 1962).
47. This position is advocated by Heinz Eulau in *Behavioralism in Political Science* (New York: Atherton Press, 1969).
48. John Stuart Mill, "On Liberty," in *The Essential Works of John Stuart Mill*, ed. Max Lerner (New York: Bantam Books, 1961).
49. Eric Hoffer, *The True Believer* (New York: New American Library, 1962). Hoffer comments: "To be in possession of an absolute truth is to have a net of familiarity spread over the whole of eternity. There are no surprises and no unknowns. All questions have already been answered, all decisions made, all eventualities foreseen. The true believer is without wonder and hesitation. 'Who knows Jesus knows the reason of all things' " (p. 80).

Chapter 12. APPRECIATION OF THE HUMAN CONDITION

1. Jane Jacobs, *The Death and Life of Great American Cities* (New York: Random House, 1961); Lewis Mumford, *The City in History* (New York: Harcourt Brace Jovanovich, 1961).
2. It is possible to argue that sociology itself was a product of industriali-
zation. Certainly, the founders of the discipline, Saint-Simon, Comte, and Marx, were concerned with the problems created by the emergence of new social groups forming around the industrial process. For Saint-Simon and Comte the new significant group was the managerial and technical elite, while for Marx it was the propertyless workers. For all three thinkers, the dominant actors in history were *collective actors:* classes and other groups. Without such a notion of collective actors sociology would probably not have appeared as a distinct discipline.
3. For an example of the work of the consumer movement, see Edward F. Cox et al., *The Nader Report on the Federal Trade Commission* (New York: Richard W. Baron, 1969).
4. Howard Becker, "Sacred and Secular Societies Considered with Ref-
erence to Folk-State and Similar Classifications," *Social Forces* 28 (May 1950): 361–76.
5. Peter Berger, *The Noise of Solemn Assemblies* (New York: Doubleday, 1961). Berger remarks: "Our religious spokesmen tell us that America is secular—and they are right once more, if they mean that the religious institution exists in the society as a segregated enclave, surrounded by actions that have little if any relationship to religious motives."
6. Georges Gurvitch has noted the importance of the Promethean con-
ception of the human condition in the modern era. See his *Déterminismes Sociaux et Liberté Humaine* (Paris: Presses Universitaires de France, 1955).
7. R. H. Tawney, *Religion and the Rise of Capitalism* (New York: Harcourt Brace Jovanovich, 1926).
8. Becker, "Sacred and Secular Societies."

9. Talcott Parsons, *Politics and Social Structure* (New York: Free Press, 1969), pp. 439–72. See also Andrew M. Greeley, *The Denominational Society* (Glenview: Scott, Foresman, 1972). Greeley observes: "Religious functionaries usually representing all three of the major faiths are proudly exhibited at major and even not so major public and private functions. Churches, church property, and church schools are generally tax exempt. Clergymen need not serve in the armed forces. Professed atheists or agnostics are at a distinct disadvantage in seeking public office" (p. 157).

10. Dan Golenpaul Associates, *Information Please Almanac*, 1965 (New York: Simon & Schuster, 1964), pp. 544–46.

11. For a discussion of the "problem of evil," see Josiah Royce, *The World and the Individual*, series 2 (New York: Dover Publications, 1959).

12. "Myth" is used here not to refer to something factually incorrect which should be scorned and repudiated, but to an imaginative characterization of significant aspects of human existence.

13. Bernard Lazerwitz, "Religion and Social Structure in the United States, in *Religion, Culture, and Society*, ed. Louis Schneider (New York: Wiley, 1964), p. 428.

14. Barbara W. Hargrove, *Reformation of the Holy: A Sociology of Religion* (Philadelphia: F.A. Davis, 1971).

15. See the discussion of natural law in the second chapter.

16. Hugo G. Nutini, "The Ideological Bases of Levi-Strauss's Structuralism," *American Anthropologist* 73 (June 1971): 542.

17. Lewis Mumford, *The Condition of Man* (New York: Harcourt Brace Jovanovich, 1944).

18. The idealization of nature is a prominent theme of nineteenth-century romanticism. See Jerry Combee and Martin Plax, "Rousseau's Noble Savage and European Self-Consciousness," *Modern Age* 17 (Spring 1973): 173–82.

19. For the history of American attitudes towards nature, see Henry Nash Smith, *Virgin Land* (New York: Vintage Books, 1962).

20. We are indebted to Mr. Arthur Kroker of McMaster University for his penetrating ideas on images of nature in Western thought.

21. Erving Goffman, *Stigma* (Englewood Cliffs, N.J.: Prentice-Hall, 1963).

22. H. Jack Geiger, "The New Doctor," in *The New Professionals*, ed. Ronald Gross and Paul Osterman (New York: Simon & Schuster, 1972), p. 102.

23. William A. Glaser, *Social Settings and Medical Organization: A Cross-National Survey of the Hospital* (New York: Atherton Press, 1970).

24. Talcott Parsons, *The Social System* (Glencoe, Ill.: Free Press, 1951).

25. David L. Larson and Elmer A. Spreitzer, "Intrinsic and Extrinsic Meanings of Work as Related to Disability Inclination: Another Look at the Sick Role Concept," *Sociological Focus* 4 (Summer 1971): 88.

26. Gene G. Kassebaum and Barbara O. Bauman, "Dimensions of the Sick Role in Chronic Illness," *Journal of Health and Human Behavior* 6 (Spring 1965): 18.

27. The American Contract Bridge League alone has about 165,000 members. Hugh Gardner, "Bureaucracy at the Bridge Table," in *Side-Saddle on the Golden Calf*, ed. George H. Lewis (Pacific Palisades, Calif.: Goodyear Publishing, 1972).

28. Dwight MacDonald, *Against the American Grain* (New York: Random House, 1962).

29. José Ortega y Gasset, *The Revolt of the Masses* (New York: New American Library, 1951).

30. Ernest van den Haag, "A Dissent from the Consensual Society," in *Mass Culture Revisited*, ed. Bernard Rosenberg and David Manning White (New York: Van Nostrand Reinhold, 1971), p. 91.

31. Bernard Rosenberg, "Mass Culture Revisited," in Rosenberg and White, *Mass Culture Revisited*, pp. 3–21.

32. Edward Shils, "Mass Society and its Culture," in Rosenberg and White, *Mass Culture Revisited*, pp. 61–84.

33. Hannah Arendt, "Society and Culture," in Rosenberg and White, *Mass Culture Revisited*, pp. 96–97.

34. Joe McGinniss, *The Selling of the President 1968* (New York: Trident Press, 1969).

35. Arthur B. Shostak, *Blue Collar Life* (New York: Random House, 1967), p. 187.

36. U.S. Department of Commerce, *Statistical Abstract of the United States 1970* (Washington, D.C.: U.S. Government Printing Office, 1970), p. 42.

37. Marshall McLuhan, *Understanding Media* (New York: McGraw-Hill, 1966), pp. 211–12.

38. George H. Lewis, "Prole Sport: The Case of Roller Derby," in Lewis, *Side-Saddle on the Golden Calf*, p. 43.

39. Ibid., p. 45.

40. Tom Wolfe, "Clean Fun at Riverhead," in Lewis, *Side-Saddle on the Golden Calf*, p. 38.

41. McLuhan, *Understanding Media*, p. 208.

42. The U.S. Playing Card Association estimates that over 35 million Americans play bridge. Jack Olsen, *The Mad World of Bridge* (New York: Holt, Rinehart & Winston, 1960), p. 237.

43. Hugh Gardner, "Bureaucracy at the Bridge Table," in Lewis, *Side-Saddle on the Golden Calf*, p. 139.

44. Ibid., p. 141.

45. Ibid., p. 152.

46. Rosenberg and White, *Mass Culture Revisited*, p. 247.

47. Nicholas Johnson, "Television and Violence: Perspectives and Proposals," in Rosenberg and White, *Mass Culture Revisited*, pp. 169–95.

48. Ibid., p. 173.

49. Gerhart D. Wiebe, "The Social Effects of Broadcasting," in Rosenberg and White, *Mass Culture Revisited*, p. 155.

50. Nicholas Johnson, "Television and Violence: Perspectives and Proposals," in Rosenberg and White, *Mass Culture Revisited*, p. 177.

51. U.S. Department of Commerce, *Statistical Abstract of the United States 1970*, p. 687.

52. See Michael Lyndon, "Rock for Sale," in Lewis, *Side-Saddle on the Golden Calf*, pp. 313–21.

53. Gary Allen, "More Subversion than Meets the Ear," in *Sounds of Social Change*, ed. R. Serge Denisoff and Richard A. Peterson (Chicago: Rand McNally, 1972), p. 159.

54. Tom Wolfe, *The Electric Kool-Aid Acid Test* (New York: Farrar, Straus, & Giroux, 1968).

55. Betty Friedan, *The Feminine Mystique* (New York: Dell, 1965).

56. Daniel J. Boorstin, *The Image: A Guide to Pseudo-Events in America* (New York: Atheneum, 1961).

Chapter 13. THE CONTEXT OF APPRECIATION

1. Solomon E. Asch, *Social Psychology* (Englewood Cliffs, N.J.: Prentice-Hall, 1952).

2. Theodore Roszak, *The Making of A Counter Culture* (Garden City, N.Y.: Doubleday, 1969).

3. Talcott Parsons has called the reference for creative and appreciative activity the "societal community." See his *Politics and Social Structure* (New York: Free Press, 1969).

4. Roland Warren, *The Community in America* (Chicago: Rand McNally, 1963), p. 9.

5. Aristotle, *Politics*, trans. T. A. Sinclair (Baltimore: Penguin Books, 1962).

6. Parsons, *Politics and Social Structure*, p. 2.

7. Ernest Barker, *The Political Thought of Plato and Aristotle* (New York: Dover Publications, 1959), p. 5.

8. Ibid.

9. For alternative models of community, see Paul and Percival Goodman, *Communitas* (Chicago: University of Chicago Press, 1947).

10. Robert A. Nisbet, *The Quest for Community: A Study in the Ethics of Order and Freedom* (New York: Oxford University Press, 1953).

11. Plato, "The Apology" and "The Crito," in W. H. D. Rouse, ed., *Great Dialogues of Plato* (New York: New American Library, 1956).

12. For the history of nationalism and of its meanings, see Elie Kedourie, *Nationalism* (New York: Frederick A. Praeger, 1960); Hans Kohn, ed., *Nationalism: Its Meaning and History* (New York: D. Van Nostrand, 1965).

13. J.-T. Delos, *La Nation I: Sociologie de la Nation* (Montreal: Editions de l'Arbre, 1944).

14. For a discussion of the class basis of nationalism, see Pierre Elliott Trudeau, *Federalism and the French Canadians* (Toronto: Macmillan of Canada, 1968).

15. Arnold J. Toynbee, *Civilization on Trial* (New York: Oxford University Press, 1948).

16. For example, see Clarence K. Streit's appeal for North Atlantic union in his *Union Now* (New York: Harper, 1940).

17. Adolf Hitler, *Mein Kampf* (New York: Reynal & Hitchcock, 1941).

18. Winston Churchill, *A History of the English-Speaking Peoples*, 4 vols. (New York: Dodd, Mead, 1956–58).

19. Georges Gurvitch, *Vocation Actuelle de la Sociologie* (Paris: Presses Universitaires de France, 1950). Gurvitch has described social classes and ethnic groups as settings for appreciation.

20. M. G. Smith, "On Segmentary Lineage Systems," *Journal of the Royal Anthropological Institute of Great Britain and Ireland* (1956): 39–79.

21. Arnold M. Rose, *The Power Structure* (New York: Oxford University Press 1967), p. 218.

22. For example, see Charles R. Warriner and Jane Emery Prather, "Four

Types of Voluntary Associations," *Sociological Inquiry* (Spring 1965): 138–48.

23. R. F. Bales and P. Slater, "Role Differentiation," in *Family, Socialization and Interaction Process*, ed. T. Parsons and R. F. Bales et al. (Glencoe, Ill.: Free Press, 1955).

24. Joseph R. Gusfield, "The Problem of Generations in an Organizational Structure," *Social Forces* 35 (May 1957): 323–30.

25. Robert H. Salisbury, "An Exchange Theory of Interest Groups," *Midwest Journal of Political Science* 13 (February 1969): 1–32.

26. For example, a session on the Sociology of Mate-Swapping was held at the 36th Annual Meeting of the Midwest Sociological Society in April 1972.

27. For conspicuous consumption and status maintenance, see, respectively, Thorstein Veblen, *The Theory of the Leisure Class*, and Erving Goffman, *The Presentation of Self in Everyday Life*.

28. Herbert H. Hyman and Charles R. Wright, "Trends in Voluntary Association Memberships of American Adults: Replication Based on Secondary Analysis of National Sample Surveys," *American Sociological Review* 36 (April 1971): 191–206.

29. Ibid., p. 198.

30. There is little census data on them and their lack of formal organization makes them more difficult to identify and study than economic organizations or voluntary associations.

31. William F. Whyte, *Street Corner Society* (Chicago: University of Chicago Press, 1955).

32. August B. Hollingshead, *Elmtown's Youth* (New York: Wiley, 1949).

33. For a discussion of role conflict, see Raymond G. Hunt, "Role and Role Conflict," in *Current Perspectives in Social Psychology*, ed. Edwin P. Hollander and Raymond G. Hunt (New York: Oxford University Press, 1971), pp. 279–85.

34. Behaviorists are associated with the rewards interpretation, while cognitive psychologists are associated with the consistency perspective. These debates go back to the nineteenth century. At that time materialist philosophers stressed the importance of pleasure and pain in human existence while idealist philosophers emphasized the significance of coherence and harmony.

35. See Richard Flacks, "Who Protests: The Social Bases of the Student Movement," in *Protest!*, ed. Julian Foster and Durward Long (New York: William Morrow, 1970), p. 141. Flacks notes: "Activist students greatly resembled their parents in their intellectualism and their skepticism about conventional middle-class values. They were clearly attempting to fulfill their parents' expectations concerning personal autonomy and humanitarianism. They shared, and indeed were more explicit about, their parents' criticisms of themselves for failing to lead lives which were fully consistent with their values."

36. U.S. Department of Commerce, *Statistical Abstract of the United States 1970* (Washington, D.C.: U.S. Government Printing Office, 1970), p. 32.

37. August B. Hollingshead, "Cultural Factors in the Selection of Marriage Mates," *American Sociological Review* 15 (1950): 619–27.

38. José Ortega y Gasset, *On Love* (Cleveland: World, 1957).

39. William J. Goode, "The Theoretical Importance of Love," *American Sociological Review* 24 (1959): 39.

40. Roy Ald, *The Youth Communes* (New York: Tower Publications, 1970).

41. Orville G. Brim, Jr., *Education for Child Rearing* (New York: Russell Sage, 1959), p. 342.

42. Martha Wolfenstein, "Trends in Infant Care," *American Journal of Orthopsychiatry* 23 (1953): 120–30.

43. U.S. Department of Commerce, *Statistical Abstract*, 223.

44. John Sirjamaki, "Culture Configurations in the American Family," *American Journal of Sociology* 53 (1948): 464–70.

45. William J. Goode, *The Family* (Englewood Cliffs, N.J.: Prentice-Hall, 1964), p. 27.

46. Luman H. Long, ed., *The World Almanac and Book of Facts: 1972* (New York: Newspaper Enterprise Association, 1971), p. 87.

47. Noel P. Gist and Sylvia Fleis Fava, *Urban Society* (New York: Thomas Y. Crowell, 1964), p. 74.

48. Jean Gottmann, *Megalopolis* (New York: Twentieth Century Fund, 1961), p. 25.

49. Robert Redfield, "The Folk Society," *American Journal of Sociology* 52 (January 1947): 293–308.

50. Gist and Fava, *Urban Society*, pp. 441–42.

51. Georg Simmel, "The Metropolis and Mental Life," in *The Sociology of Georg Simmel*, trans. and ed. Kurt H. Wolff (Glencoe, Ill.: Free Press, 1950), pp. 409–24.

52. Morton and Lucia White, *The Intellectual Versus the City* (New York: New American Library, 1962).

53. Long, ed., *The World Almanac*, p. 145.

54. Gist and Fava, *Urban Society*, p. 74.

55. Ibid., p. 43.

56. Long, ed., *The World Almanac*, pp. 154, 166.

57. Robert Wood, *Suburbia—Its People and Their Politics* (Boston: Houghton Mifflin, 1958), pp. 18–19.

58. Bennett Berger, *Working-Class Suburb* (Berkeley: University of California Press, 1960), pp. 99–100.

59. Alvin Boskoff, *The Sociology of Urban Regions* (New York: Appleton-Century-Crofts, 1962). See especially "Ecological Organization: Understanding the Socio-Geographic Differentiation of Urban Communities," pp. 97–115.

60. Elliot Liebow, *Tally's Corner* (Boston: Little Brown, 1967).

61. Lewis Mumford, *The City in History* (New York: Harcourt Brace Jovanovich, 1961). Mumford notes: "The form of the metropolis, then, is its formlessness, even as its aim is its own aimless expansion. Those who work within the ideological limits of this regime have only a quantitative conception of improvement: they seek to make its buildings higher, its streets broader, its parking lots more ample" (p. 544).

Chapter 14. EDUCATION, KNOWLEDGE, AND INQUIRY

1. Peter L. Berger and Thomas Luckmann, *The Social Construction of Reality* (Garden City, N.Y.: Doubleday, 1967). Berger and Luckmann comment: "Common sense contains innumerable pre- and quasi-scientific interpretations about everyday reality which it takes for granted. If we are to describe the reality of common sense, we must refer to these interpretations" (p. 20).

2. Clark Kerr, "Selections from The Uses of the University," in *The Berkeley Student Revolt: Facts and Interpretations*, ed. Seymour Martin Lipset and Sheldon S. Wolin (Garden City, N.Y.: Doubleday, 1965).

3. Richard Fallenbaum, "University Abdicates Social Responsibility," in Lipset and Wolin, *The Berkeley Student Revolt*, p. 64.

4. Robin M. Williams, Jr., *American Society* (New York: Alfred A. Knopf, 1960), pp. 318–19.

5. Kenneth D. Roose and Charles J. Anderson, *A Rating of Graduate Programs* (Washington, D.C.: American Council on Education, 1970), pp. 5–8.

6. Bradford Cleaveland, "A Letter to Undergraduates," in Lipset and Wolin, *The Berkeley Student Revolt*, p. 49.

7. James Ridgeway, *The Closed Corporation* (New York: Random House, 1968).

8. Clark Kerr, "Selections from *The Uses of the University,*" in Lipset and Wolin, *The Berkeley Student Revolt*, p. 49.

9. Robert H. Connery, ed., *The Corporation and the Campus, Proceedings of the Academy of Political Science* 30 (1970): 92. Student tuition and fees account for 18% of the university's income, federal government support 24%, state and local government support 25%, private gifts and grants 8%, income from auxiliary enterprises 12%, other income (e.g., loans 11%, and endowment earnings 2%).

10. Warren O. Hagstrom, *The Scientific Community* (New York: Basic Books, 1965), p. 108.

11. For a critique of the role of the foundations in American life, see Rene A. Wormser, *Foundations: Their Power and Influence* (New York: Devin-Adair, 1958).

12. U.S. Department of Commerce, *Statistical Abstract of the United States* (Washington, D.C.: U.S. Government Printing Office, 1970), p. 136.

13. Thomas S. Kuhn, *The Structure of Scientific Revolutions* (Chicago: University of Chicago Press, 1962), p. x.

14. Ibid., p. 19.

15. Alfred de Grazia, "The Scientific Reception System and Dr. Velikovsky," *American Behavioral Scientist* 7 (1963): 38–56. De Grazia points out: "The principal elements of the reception system are doctrines and an operational formula with typical tactics of acceptances and rejections. . . . And a set of tactics is employed to admit or reject offerings determined to have succeeded or failed according to the formula. For instance, a journal will return a manuscript with a polite note of refusal or fit an article meeting its criteria into its publishing schedule" (p. 45).

16. Diana Crane, "The Gatekeepers of Science: Some Factors Affecting the Selection of Articles for Scientific Journals," *American Sociologist* 2 (November 1967): 195–201.

17. Kuhn, *The Structure of Scientific Revolutions*, p. 137.

18. Hagstrom, *The Scientific Community*, p. 11.

19. Robert K. Merton, "Science and the Social Order," in *Social Theory and Social Structure* (New York: Free Press, 1957), p. 543.

20. Ibid.

21. Leonard L. Baird, "Who Protests: A Study of Student Activists," in *Protest!*, ed. Julian Foster and Durward Long (New York: William Morrow, 1970), pp. 123–33.

22. Seymour Martin Lipset, "University Student Politics," in Lipset and Wolin, *The Berkeley Student Revolt,* pp. 4–5.

23. Seymour L. Halleck, "Hypotheses of Student Unrest," in Foster and Long, *Protest!,* pp. 105–22.

24. Luman H. Long, ed., *The World Almanac and Book of Facts: 1972* (New York: Newspaper Enterprise Association, 1971), pp. 331, 404.

25. Samuel Eliot Morison, *The Oxford History of the American People* (New York: Oxford University Press, 1965), p. 291.

26. Ivan Illich, "The Institutional Spectrum," in *The Political Experience,* ed. Michael A. Weinstein (New York: St. Martin's Press, 1972), p. 85.

27. Jonathan Kozol, *Death at an Early Age* (Boston: Houghton Mifflin, 1967).

28. Melvin L. DeFleur et al., *Sociology: Man in Society* (Glenview: Scott, Foresman, 1971), p. 567.

29. Melvin L. DeFleur, *Theories of Mass Communication* (New York: David McKay, 1970), p. 20.

30. Daniel Boorstin, *The Image* (New York: Harper, 1961).

31. *Chicago Today,* 6 August 1972, p. 26.

32. Jules Henry, *Culture Against Man* (New York: Random House, 1963).

33. DeFleur, *Theories of Mass Communication,* p. 165.

34. Ibid., p. 167.

35. Ibid.

36. Ibid.

37. Gustave LeBon, *The Crowd* (New York: Viking, 1960), p. 37.

38. Ibid.

39. Leon Festinger, *A Theory of Cognitive Dissonance* (New York: Harper & Row, 1957).

40. Ibid.

41. Leon Festinger and J. Merrill Carlsmith, "Cognitive Consequences of Forced Compliance," *Journal of Abnormal and Social Psychology* 58 (1959): 203–10.

Chapter 15. TECHNOCRACY, POLICY, AND THE FUTURE

1. Seymour M. Lipset, *Political Man* (Garden City, N.Y.: Doubleday, 1960).

2. See C. Wright Mills, *The Sociological Imagination* (New York: Grove Press, 1961) for a critique of the "great celebration" and S. M. Lipset, *Political Man.*

3. For a review of the class basis of much contemporary sociology, see Hugo O. Engelmann, "Review of *The Coming Crisis of Western Sociology,*" *International Review of Sociology* 1 (September 1971): 1–9.

4. For example, see Herman Kahn, *Thinking About the Unthinkable* (New York: Avon Books, 1971).

5. E. H. Carr, *The New Society* (New York: St. Martin's Press, 1956).

6. Robert Dahl, *Who Governs?* (New Haven: Yale University Press, 1961). Dahl comments: "Because the acquiescence of homo civicus is always a necessary condition for rulership, and to gain his consent is often economical, in all political systems homo politicus deliberately employs some resources to influence the choices of homo civicus. Political man invariably seeks to influence

civic man directly, but even in the democratic systems civic man only occasionally seeks to influence political man directly" (p. 225).

7. For an example of this view, see Peter M. Blau and W. Richard Scott, *Formal Organizations* (San Francisco: Chandler Publishing, 1962).

8. Talcott Parsons, *Politics and Social Structure* (New York: Free Press, 1969). Parsons calls this attitude "deflation."

9. Richard E. Neustadt, *Presidential Power* (New York: New American Library, 1964).

10. Michael A. Weinstein, "Politics and Moral Consciousness," *Midwest Journal of Political Science* 14 (May 1970): 183–215.

11. Aldous Huxley, *Brave New World* (New York: Harper, 1946).

12. Aldous Huxley, *Brave New World Revisited* (New York: Harper & Row, 1958).

13. The term "leading institutions" was coined by James K. Feibleman in his *Institutions of Society* (London: George Allen and Unwin, 1956), pp. 228–29.

14. G. William Domhoff, *Who Rules America?* (Englewood Cliffs, N.J.: Prentice-Hall, 1967).

15. Jean Meynaud, "from *Technocracy,*" in *The Political Experience,* ed. Michael A. Weinstein (New York: St. Martin's Press, 1972).

16. Ibid., p. 238.

17. Marshall McLuhan, *Understanding Media* (New York: New American Library, 1964). McLuhan suggests media diets.

18. For the ways in which "therapy" is used to impose oppressive role-definitions on women, see Phyllis Chesler, *Women and Madness* (Garden City, N.Y.: Doubleday, 1972).

19. See Yehezkel Dror, *Public Policymaking Reexamined* (Scranton: Chandler Publishing, 1968) for an overview of models of public policymaking.

20. John Lear, "Public Policy and the Study of Man," *Saturday Review,* 7 September 1968, p. 60.

21. The Council of Social Advisers appears in the Full Opportunity and Social Accounting bill sponsored by Senator Walter Mondale of Minnesota in 1968.

22. William James, *Principles of Psychology* (New York: Holt, 1890), chap. 10.

23. For summaries of these ideas, see Morton Deutsch and Robert M. Krauss, *Theories in Social Psychology* (New York: Basic Books, 1965); Gardner Lindzey and Elliot Aronson, eds., *The Handbook of Social Psychology,* vol. 1 (Reading, Mass.: Addison-Wesley, 1968).

24. For a discussion of Mead's ideas, see Jerome G. Manis and Bernard N. Meltzer, eds., *Symbolic Interaction* (Boston: Allyn & Bacon, 1967).

INDEX

473

ABOUT THE AUTHORS

DEENA WEINSTEIN

Deena Weinstein is associate professor of sociology at De Paul University in Chicago, Illinois. From 1971 to 1974 she was assistant professor of sociology at De Paul, and prior to that was assistant professor of sociology at Radford College in Radford, Virginia (1967–68). Born in Brooklyn, New York, in 1943, Dr. Weinstein spent her high school years in the suburb of West Hempstead, New York, where she learned firsthand about mass society. She received her B.S. degree in biology from Queens College of the City University of New York in 1964 and her M.A. degree in anthropology from Case Western Reserve University in Cleveland, Ohio, in 1967. Dr. Weinstein received her Ph.D. in sociology from Purdue University in West Lafayette, Indiana, in 1971, presenting a dissertation on the functions of social science associations, parts of which have been published.

Dr. Weinstein's research interests are in sociological theory, occupations and professions, the sociology of knowledge, and organizations. Her published works include studies of dialectical and existential methodologies in the works of Blau, Ginsberg, and Sartre; an analysis of the changing functions of professional organizations; and two books, *Roles of Man* and *Clash of Perspectives*. She has presented numerous papers on her research and continues to work on her overriding project of providing a concrete criticism of contemporary institutions from an existentialist perspective.

MICHAEL A. WEINSTEIN

Michael A. Weinstein has been professor of political science at Purdue University since 1972. From 1970 to 1972 he was associate professor, and from 1968 to 1970 assistant professor, of political science at Purdue. Prior to that he was assistant professor of political science at Virginia Polytechnic Institute in Blacksburg, Virginia (1967–68). Born in Brooklyn, New York, in 1942, Dr. Weinstein also spent his high school years in West Hempstead, New York, where he developed his interest in social criticism. He received his B.A. degree in political science from New York University in 1964 and his M.A. and Ph.D. degrees from Case Western Reserve University, in political science, in 1965 and 1967 respectively. His dissertation was about the idea of freedom in the thought of George Santayana.

Dr. Weinstein's research interests are in general sociological theory, the role of politics in social life, and the relations between philosophy and the social sciences. His published works include numerous studies of twentieth-century social thinkers, particularly the books *Philosophy, Theory and Method in Contemporary Political Thought* and *Systematic Political Theory*. He has written numerous papers and lectured on his work, and has directed his studies toward determining the effects of contemporary organizations on the struggle for human freedom.

Deena and Michael Weinstein have worked together on many projects. They share a common interest in pointing out the dangers to human freedom in contemporary life, unmasking myths, and encouraging social criticism. Believing that social science is a cooperative as well as a personal endeavor, it is difficult for them to determine where the work of one ends and the contribution of the other begins. Believing that social science is intrinsically evaluative, they direct their joint efforts in research and action toward encouraging freedom in all human contexts.